Managing Information Assurance in Financial Services

H. R. Rao
University at Buffalo, State University of New York, USA

Manish Gupta
M&T Bank, USA

Shambhu J. Upadhyaya
University at Buffalo, State University of New York, USA

IGI PUBLISHING
Hershey • New York

Acquisition Editor:	Kristin Klinger
Senior Managing Editor:	Jennifer Neidig
Managing Editor:	Sara Reed
Assistant Managing Editor:	Sharon Berger
Development Editor:	Kristin Roth
Copy Editor:	Heidi Hormel
Typesetter:	Michael Brehm
Cover Design:	Lisa Tosheff
Printed at:	Yurchak Printing Inc.

Published in the United States of America by
IGI Publishing (an imprint of IGI Global)
701 E. Chocolate Avenue
Hershey PA 17033
Tel: 717-533-8845
Fax: 717-533-8661
E-mail: cust@igi-pub.com
Web site: http://www.igi-pub.com

and in the United Kingdom by
IGI Publishing (an imprint of IGI Global)
3 Henrietta Street
Covent Garden
London WC2E 8LU
Tel: 44 20 7240 0856
Fax: 44 20 7379 0609
Web site: http://www.eurospanonline.com

Library of Congress Cataloging-in-Publication Data

Managing information assurance in financial services / H. R. Rao, Manish Gupta, and Shambhu J. Upadhyaya, editors.
p. cm.
Summary: “This book provides high-quality research papers and industrial practice articles about information security in the financial service industry. It provides insight into current information security measures, including: technology, processes, and compliance from some of the leading researchers and practitioners in the field”--Provided by publisher.
Includes bibliographical references and index.
ISBN 978-1-59904-171-1 (hardcover) -- ISBN 978-1-59904-173-5 (ebook)
1. Financial services industry--Security measures. 2. Financial institutions--Security measures. 3. Data protection. 4. Computer security. I. Rao, H. R. (H. Raghav) II. Gupta, Manish. III. Upadhyaya, Shambhu.
HG104.M36 2007
332.1068'4--dc22

2006039661

British Cataloguing in Publication Data
A Cataloguing in Publication record for this book is available from the British Library.

All work contributed to this book is new, previously-unpublished material. The views expressed in this book are those of the authors, but not necessarily of the publisher.

Managing Information Assurance in Financial Services

Table of Contents

Foreword

In an era when virtually all the tools of our daily lives are connected to and reliant upon computer networks, a cyber attack could knock out electricity, drinking water and sewage systems, assembly lines, communications and, of course, our financial institutions—to name just a few.

We must improve our ability to respond to these threats. And our response must go beyond immediate defensive measures.

We need to conduct the research and development (R&D) necessary to make computers and networks much harder to break into and much less subject to damage when they are violated. That requires a focused, well-funded R&D effort in cyber security—something I championed as chairman of the House Committee on Science.

My legislation, the Cyber Security Research and Development Act was signed into law by President Bush in 2002. It authorized $903 million in new federal funding for R&D in this critical area. Under the bill, the National Science Foundation created new cyber security research centers, individual investigator grants, and fellowships.

The result has been new research—conducted at leading-edge universities, like the State University of New York at Buffalo—that is producing innovative and creative approaches to computer security, drawing more researchers into the field and to developing a cadre of students, who will become the next generation of cyber security researchers and protectors of our information networks.

That is why I am so pleased and honored that Professor Upadhyaya asked me to provide the foreword to this text. Looking at these chapters, authored by top experts from academia, industry, and international partners, I feel like the cyber security legislation we drafted in the science committee four years ago is having some real impact on real problems in 2006. This is good news by any measure.

U.S. Rep. Sherwood Boehlert (R-NY)

Chairman, House Committee on Science (2001-2006)

October 11, 2006

The Hon. Sherwood Boehlert was chairman of the U.S. House of Representatives' Committee on Science (2001-2006). He was first elected to represent Central New York in the House of Representatives (1982). Recognized as the leading Republican environmentalist in the House, Boehlert has made a name for himself as a champion of federal investment in science and technology.

Boehlert received a bachelor's degree from Utica College (1961). Before serving as Oneida County Executive (1979-83), he was manager of public relations at Wyandotte Chemical (1961-64) and served two years in the U.S. Army (1956-58). Boehlert also served as chief of staff for two Congressmen, Alexander Pirnie (1964-72) and Donald Mitchell (1973-79).

Preface

While advances in information technology and adoption of Internet as a services delivery channel have enabled financial services institutions to provide more convenient financial services, they also have diversified and complicated the nature of risks. Financial services institutions are actively utilizing the Internet to operate and provide financial services to consumers, to businesses and to other service institutions. Advances in Internet technology also have provided a new and different business and risk environment than traditional direct-contact "brick and mortar" models. Financial services firms have to adopt information technology developments for their benefits and competitive advantages and to remain viable and competitive in the business environment. At the same time, risks and challenges to developing and maintaining a secure and safe computing environment have never held such high stakes. This book provides high-quality research, industry and practice articles in the area of information assurance in the financial services industry. The main focus of the book is to provide overview of issues involved in managing information assurance in financial services through insights into current information security measures—technology, processes, and compliance—being researched on or deployed in financial services institutions. The book hosts topics on management and strategy; technologies and countermeasures; and issues and trends. The chapters in this timely and important book are a compilation of topics on how to manage information assurance in financial services and provide a comprehensive understanding of the issues involved. The authors of the chapters are leading researchers and practitioners in the field. Their research and insights manifested in the chapters are highly relevant to the overall objectives of the book.

Organization of the Book

The 14 chapters of the book are organized into three sections based on following broad themes:

- Management and Strategy
- Technologies and Countermeasures
- Trends and Issues

The section "Management and Strategy" covers topics such as determination of return on information security investments; in-depth review of principles and strategies of risk management in banking; strategies for developing information assurance alignment with key business objectives; overview of information security issues; and empirical investigation of trends in banking and risk management strategies. The section "Technologies and Countermeasures" include chapters on security usability in the electronic banking arena and managing authentication and identity access in financial services organizations. The chapters in the last section "Trends and Issues" discuss social and human issues of information security, such as phishing and pharming, identity theft and fraud intelligence, access control mechanisms and regulatory compliance issues. A brief description of each of the chapters follows.

Chapter I, *Analyzing Risks to Determine a New Return on Security Investment: Optimizing Security in an Escalating Threat Environment* expands upon standard methods of calculating the return on security investment (ROSI) in several ways. First, it accounts for the dynamic nature of threats, vulnerabilities, and defenses as they apply to the finance sector. Second, it takes a more holistic view of security investments by using a portfolio method. Dr. Warren Axelrod of The United States Trust Company (N.A.) discusses the protection of information assets from two different perspectives. One is the hierarchical view of security measures, such as avoidance, deterrence, and prevention. The other is defense in depth, wherein various security tools and processes, such as firewalls, identity and access management, and intrusion detection and prevention products, are combined for greater overall protection. The reader will gain a deeper understanding of the factors that affect the risks and returns of investments in security measures, tools, and processes and will find that using the portfolio approach leads to more cost-effective security.

Banks play an important role in the financial system contributing to efficient and well-functioning transfers of capital and risk between those in excess (savers) and those in need (borrowers) of money. Traditionally, financial risks, like interest rate, foreign exchange, and credit risks, have been the most important and typical ones for banking operations. However, lately the risk environment of banks has changed considerably. In Chapter II, *Risk Management in Banking: A Review of Principles and Strategies*, Dr. Göran Bergendahl and Dr. Ted Lindblom, both of University of Gothenburg, Sweden, stress the vital importance for the single bank to have a more sophisticated and well-structured approach to risk management than it had 15 years ago. The chapter's main focus is on how banking objectives, such as profitability and growth, should govern risk management and how these objectives are made operational in the management of those assets and liabilities exposed to changes in market prices and in customer repayments of loans.

Chapter III, *Developing Information Assurance Alignment in Financial Services*, is based on research work in eight financial services organizations (four international financial services organizations, two national retail banks and two multinational banks). The chapter focuses on information assurance strategy in financial services and discusses two important questions: How can senior executives align information assurance strategy with corporate strategy?, and what factors influence decisions regarding information assurance strategy? Dr. Jean-Noel Ezingeard, Dr. Elspeth McFadzean, and Dr. David Birchall of Henley Management College, UK, explain why information assurance strategy needs to be aligned with corporate strategy, and why boards of directors in financial services need to take a strong interest in the development of their organization's IA strategy. The chapter highlights three key drivers: risk assessment and/or risk reports—including legal requirements, such as Sarbanes-Oxley and Basel II; protection of shareholder value; cost and the need to keep IA costs under control while delivering a suitable level of protection for the organization's information. The chapter also explains how requirements of various stakeholders can be reconciled when they are in conflict.

The banking sector is identified as a critical infrastructure by the federal government. Dr. Kevin Streff of Dakota State University (USA) in Chapter IV, *Information Security in Banking*, provides an overview of information security in the banking sector; outlines the information and technology common to most banks; explains the information security law and regulation banks must comply with; and explores the information security controls necessary to protect the banking infrastructure in the United States. The chapter reviews what banks need to do to protect the confidentiality, integrity, and availability of information, including the presentation of an information security program design that community banks should use as a framework for information protection.

Chapter V, *Security Risk Management Strategy of Financial Services Institutions*, develops a novel security risk management strategy of financial services institutes. Dr. Guoling Lao and Dr. Liping Wang of Shanghai University of Finance and Economics, China, present the systematic and cybernetics theory as the instruction; regards the risk analysis process; the management strategy implementation; and the monitor and audit as an organic security management system. The strategy presented in the chapter is an auto-adapted open system to defeat various safe threats dynamically. By comparing management of electronic-commerce (e-commerce) security risk with that of traditional financial risk, the chapter suggests accurate security risk measurement in the way of quantitative analysis and further integration of the e-commerce security risk with traditional financial risks. This article attempts to make improvement on the basis of existing research and studies and provide a proper security risk management strategy for financial services institutes engaged in e-commerce.

In electronic banking (e-banking), user authentication with mobile phones and special-purpose cryptographic tokens is a promising alternative to conventional approaches, such as digital signatures on a personal computer (PC). Special-purpose tokens that do not have external connections avoid viruses transmitted via the Internet. Moreover, phones and tokens are mobile. Chapter VI, *New Technologies in E-Banking: Convenient and Trustworthy?*, assesses the potential of new technologies for user authentication (verification of the user's identity) on the basis of a practical test and an analysis of trust. Dr. Niels Jørgensen of Roskilde University, Denmark, conducts a practical test comprised of a password generator, mobile phones with SMS, WAP, and 3G, and (conventional) PC-based authentication using digital signatures—all as used by a Danish electronic bank. The test indicates that in some ways the hardware-based technologies are indeed easier to use. Also, the trust analysis indicates that the secrecy of the new approaches may be a weakness, since there is no publicly available analysis of their security. The chapter suggests that secrecy of the hardware-based technologies may be justified by the need to prevent various attacks, such as physically opening a password generator to determine its secret key, and that a prerequisite for consumer trust may be the introduction of security evaluation methods that do not disclose the secret parts of the technologies to the public and are conducted by public authorities or independent third parties.

Authentication is a prime challenge for banks today as end users' digital identities are being compromised through increasingly sophisticated means. Chapter VII, *Stronger Authentication: Responding to the Crisis of Confidence*, provides a timely review of the authentication concept and key authentication technologies, namely password tokens, biometrics, smart cards, smart tokens, and out-of-band authentication. Dr. Alvin Y.C. Yeo, SIM University, Singapore, proposes an integrative model that frames three key considerations in choosing an authentication solution—cyber threat types, regulatory requirements, and business considerations. . The chapter begins with a review of the authentication concept and key authentication technologies. Next, the author proposes his integrative model and explores the implications for financial institutions. Finally, the chapter concludes with pragmatic suggestions by proposing a set of evaluation criteria for choosing authentication solutions and key legal considerations.

When designing and implementing a system that handles sensitive or valuable information, there can be few discussions that do not include some reference to ensuring adequate security. At a strategic level, there will be high-level requirements for security that will safeguard the system, which must ultimately translate to practical solutions and physical implementations. Chapter VIII, *Smart Cards for Security and Assurance*, focuses on the technical implementation of security requirements and, in particular, the use of smart cards as trusted security tokens. In this chapter, Dr. Konstantinos Markantonakis, Dr. Keith Mayes, and Dr. Fred Piper of Smart Card Centre, all of the University of London examine the significance of tamper resistance by exploring the different hardware and software platforms in relation to smart card attacks. They also highlight certain issues around the deployment of smart card technology in the financial industry.

After years of neglect, identity and access management (IAM) is now strongly ensconced in the modern information technology enterprise. Businesses are driven by the desire for greater business ecosystem and process efficiency, automatic regulatory compliance, and, frankly, the deep-seated aversion to negative press resulting from identity theft and other information asset intrusions. In Chapter IX, *Unified Identities in Complex Financial Organizations*, Peter Orondo of Acclaim Consulting Group Inc., USA, makes the case for a unified approach to managing identities in a complex enterprise in the financial services sector. He discusses the framework for evolving unified policies and processes and prescribes optimal organizational governance to implement them. He also discusses the relationship with regulatory compliance and other critical information enterprise functions and includes nonprescriptive, strategic positions that progressive organizations may take to streamline enterprise identity and access management.

In Chapter X, *Identity Management and Access*, Nick Pullman of Citigroup, USA, and Dr. Kevin Streff of Dakota State University, USA, discuss the role of identity and access management in the financial services industry. Identity and access management is a very broad concept that has far reaching rewards or consequences within an organization. This chapter provides a survey of the topics within identity and access management so that managers and security administrators of financial institutions can gain an understanding of the issues and possible solutions. The chapter discusses the core concepts of identity and access management, how they can fit into an enterprise solution, and how the individual concepts within identity and access management work together. Finally, the authors discuss the future trends of identity and access management. After reading this chapter, readers should be able to understand (1) the identity lifecycle and how to manage it; (2) understand the proliferation of identities and how to consolidate them; (3) the core concepts behind IAM, including single sign on, access control, authentication, authorization, identity integration, provisioning, and password management; and (4) how to implement an IAM solution from both a technical and managerial perspective.

Phishing and pharming continue to plague many financial institutions and e-commerce Web sites. Sophisticated criminals now have turned to a new activity, "rat-ing," where criminals can watch everything the user is typing from other parts of the globe. Various countries also have passed identity fraud legislations, but the global nature of cybercrime raises difficult legislative problems of jurisdiction as criminals use offshore servers and Internet sites to avoid domestic regulations. In Chapter XI, *Swallowing the Bait, Hook, Line and Sinker: Phishing, Pharming, and now Rat-ing!*, Dr. Sylvia Kierkegaard of IAITL, Denmark, analyzes some of the national and international initiatives that have been enacted by the European Union and the United States, specifically in the area of curtailing phishing activities and its variants. The chapter discusses the American and European initiatives to combat fraud in cyberspace. It discusses the salient provisions of the U.S. Anti-Phishing Act as well as a handful of identity theft bills that are pending in the U.S. Congress. The chapter analyzes whether the proposed legislations will actually deter cybercrime. The author suggests that with so many technology issues, the problems of phishing, pharming, and rat-ing are not things that can be solved by legislation only but also require technology and security awareness.

In Chapter XII, *The Evolution of Fraud Intelligence*, David Porter of Detica Corporation, UK, discusses the latest innovations in fraud detection, with a particular focus on insider fraud and organized fraud. The author argues that as fraud continues to grow at an alarming rate across the financial services sector. This constant evolution in fraudster behavior means that financial institutions need to keep their technology-based countermeasures constantly updated, particularly given the increasing involvement of organized crime. In addition to upgrading their current operational detection systems, this chapter aims to encourage organizations to improve on current levels of data and information assurance in order to ensure the generation of high quality intelligence on the enemy and to adopt a structured framework for better understanding and description of exactly what we mean by "intelligence."

Increasingly, enterprises are offering online financial services. Often, access to such financial services is based on mutually agreed upon subscriptions. In subscription-based financial services information assurance occurs as an ancillary to subscriptions; the control terms embedded in subscriptions are formalized by control policies and enforced by generic access control mechanisms. In Chapter XIII, *Managing Information Assurance in Subscription-based Financial Services*, Dr. Victoria Ungureanu of Rutgers University, USA, reviews the main access control mechanisms that can be used to govern subscription-based financial services. The overall performance of these mechanisms is analyzed with respect to several important features of subscription-based financial services. Namely, the chapter analyzes the impact of the following features: (1) the number of clients/subscriptions potentially can be large; (2) the number and types of subscriptions offered by a provider varies in time; (3) subscription terms may change; and (4) subscriptions terms may contain may take into account mutable information. Furthermore, the chapter presents in detail one mechanism that achieves good performance.

The U.S. Sarbanes-Oxley Act (SOA) introduced significant changes to financial practice and corporate governance regulation, including stringent new rules designed to protect investors by improving the accuracy and reliability of corporate disclosures. Briefly speaking, it requires management to submit a report containing an assessment of the effectiveness of the internal control structure and a description of material weaknesses in such internal controls and of any material noncompliance. Such mandatory regulations can have broader ramifications on firm profitability, market structure, and social welfare, many of which were unintended when policy makers first formulated this act. Moreover, the tight coupling between compliance activities, information disclosure, and information technology investments can have implications for infromation technology governance because of the potential to change relationships between technology investments and business. Dr. Anindya Ghose of New York University in Chapter XIV, *Information Disclosure and Regulatory Compliance: Economic Issues and Analysis*, provides intuitive insights into the trade offs involved for firms in disclosure of such information and lays the ground for some research questions that would be of interest to academics, industry executives, and policy makers, alike.

The professionals, managers, and researchers working in information technology or information security in financial services industries would benefit from the chapters. The authors are from both industry and academia and present a complete array of very relevant and insightful chapters for a wide range of audiences. Due to the depth and breadth of coverage of topics in information assurance, auditors and lawyers from financial services institutions also will find this book a very helpful resource. Given the relative absence of relevant and quality books in the area of information assurance in financial services, this volume provides immense scholarly value to the information technology discipline, in general, and even more to information security, in particular, for financial services institutions.

Section I

Management and Strategy

Chapter I

Analyzing Risks to Determine a New Return on Security Investment: Optimizing Security in an Escalating Threat Environment

Warren Axelrod, United States Trust Company, N.A.

Abstract

This chapter expands upon standard methods of calculating the return on security investment (ROSI) in several ways. First, it accounts for the dynamic nature of threats, vulnerabilities, and defenses as they apply to the finance sector. Second, it takes a more holistic view of security investments using a portfolio method. The protection of information assets can be viewed in two ways. One is the hierarchical view of security measures, such as avoidance, deterrence, and prevention. The other is defense in depth, wherein various security tools and processes, such as firewalls, identity and access management, and intrusion detection and prevention products, are combined for greater overall protection. The reader will gain a deeper understanding of the factors that affect the risks and returns of investments in security measures, tools, and processes and will find that using the portfolio approach leads to more cost-effective security.

Background

The year 2005 became known as the year of the privacy breach, although the first half of 2006 is shaping up to be its equal or worse based upon the breaches reported. Security breaches involving personal information are announced in the press almost daily, and there are Web sites that track these incidents. Some of the more noteworthy recent incidents involving lost or stolen personal data are described in Appendix A.

The direct costs to individuals and companies from such breaches have increased by orders of magnitude during the past couple of years. This has in large part been due to recent laws and regulations that impose financial burdens and damage to reputation as a result of mandated or strongly suggested actions, such as customer notification, provision of credit monitoring, and the like.

In addition, regulators have begun to levy substantial fines and are requiring costly remediation and long-term auditing of those found not to protect customer data adequately. A number of U.S. examples, including Petco, ChoicePoint, CardSystems, and DSW Shoes, can be found on the Web site of the Federal Trade Commission (FTC) at www.ftc.gov. Resulting costs to companies are frequently orders of magnitude greater than what it would have cost to avoid or prevent these incidents in the first place.

The chapter covers the following topics:

- A brief history
- Nature and scope of breaches
- Security and privacy options
- In-depth defense strategy
- ROSI by category and in aggregate

A Brief History

In the late 20th century, the determination of how much to spend on security was mainly based on highly subjective analyses. First, statistics relating to the number of threats and successful attacks, cost of remediation, and costs of successful attacks (by viruses, worms, hacks, etc.) were collected and tallied up. The out-of-pocket costs thus estimated were further subjected to a risk analysis, where some "guestimates" of the chances of particular events occurring and the related level were used to determine expected loss. The *2005 Tenth Annual CSI/FBI Computer Crime and Security Survey* stated that the 639 respondents to the survey, who were able to provide estimates of incurred losses, suffered losses of $130 million in total, with the loss per respondent dropping 61% from 2004 (Computer Security Institute/Federal Bureau of Investigation, 2005). Analysts used that estimated loss as a basis for deciding how much should be spent on security measures. A positive return was achieved if the cost of security implementations was assessed to be less than the expected losses, which the security measures were to prevent.

While it was recognized that there were other risks and losses that might be affected by not having adequate security measures, it was mostly possible to justify some reasonable level of security expenditures from avoidance of viruses and hack attacks alone. Intangible costs, such as those relating to loss of reputation from the publicity surrounding a breach were seldom, if ever, identified and quantified, explicitly. However, it is no longer possible to ignore the indirect and intangible costs, since they dominate so many situations these days.

Highly Regulated Environment

Over the past several years, there has been a proliferation of laws and regulations advocating, and often mandating, tighter and more costly security processes for financial institutions. Recent laws in the United States, such as the Gramm-Leach-Bliley Act (GLBA), which is officially known as The Financial Services Modernization Act of 1999, and California Senate Bill 1386, focus on restricting access to and consequent misuse of customers' personal information. These laws have been followed by regulations, such as the Federal Reserve Bank's Regulation P for banking institutions and Securities and Exchange Commission (SEC) Regulation S-P for securities firms, and guidance papers created by groups of regulatory bodies. The recent rash of reported incidents of theft and loss of customer information (excerpted in Appendix A) has generated a further flurry of legislative initiatives at the federal and state levels, with attempts by Congress to supersede the proliferation of inconsistent, and sometimes contradictory, state laws. It is not clear how this will all shake out.

While the Sarbanes-Oxley Act of 2002 (SOX) did not appear to specifically address security, it has been generally recognized that there are implicit security-related requirements in the act. Examples of these include the controlling of access to certain information and restricting the ability of those with authorized access to modify the financial records of the company. SOX also addresses maintenance of the integrity of such data and its availability to authorized users when needed. The focus of such controls is on financial data rather than personal information. Nevertheless, the ability to control access to and use and modification of data is common to both GLBA and SOX so that, indirectly, compliance with SOX implies a measure of compliance with GLBA. While the argument might seem to be somewhat convoluted, I have seen a number of cases where such transference has in fact occurred.

Regulators, such as the SEC, also have focused their attention on how sensitive information should be erased and media containing such data destroyed. More recently, there have been a number of reports from government agencies, such as the Federal Financial Institutions Examination Council (2005), on identity theft and how it might be attenuated.

For affected organizations, this veritable flood of legislative and regulatory interest in the protection of personal information has raised the stakes considerably. It also provides organizations with the necessary justification for adding security controls and resources, whether or not a comprehensive cost-benefit analysis would favor such implementation. Particular measures, which might be favored by lawmakers and regulators, might result in the suboptimization of spending on security from the general data protection perspective. In fact, many of the proposed measures are aimed at solving what are arguably relatively small components of the overall problem. Be that as it may, such laws and regulations are intended to resolve certain high-profile issues, such as identity theft and fraud, and place responsibility squarely on the shoulders of senior executives of affected companies. This latter aspect is probably the most important of all because without the enforced commitment of senior management, many critical security investments would not be approved.

Nature and Scope of Breaches

The population of compromised organizations includes such major firms as Bank of America, CitiFinancial, Ameritrade, LexisNexis, ChoicePoint, Time Warner, CardSystems Solutions, Marriott, and the Veterans Administration (VA). The CitiFinancial loss of tapes opened up 3.9 million personal records to possible abuse, and the CardSystems Solutions hack exposed personal information of 40 million members of MasterCard, Visa, American Express, and Discover to potential fraud. A laptop stolen from the home of a VA employee reportedly contained the personal information of some 28.6 million veterans and others. ChoicePoint has been fined $15 million by the Federal Trade Commission, in addition to other costs incurred. CardSystems lost significant customer business and was quickly bought out in its weakened state.

Ironically, in many cases, the data might not have actually been misused or otherwise compromised, particularly if devices or media items, such as laptops, magnetic or optical disks, or magnetic tapes, were lost or mislaid rather than stolen or purposely attacked and successfully invaded. For example, the above-mentioned VA laptop was subsequently recovered and a forensics analysis of the machine indicated that the data had not in fact been compromised. However the VA had already incurred significant costs and been subjected to severe embarrassment and criticism prior to the retrieval of the laptop and accompanying storage device. Also, if equipment is stolen for its intrinsic value rather than the data contained in its internal media (such as hard disks in laptops or flash memory in handheld devices), it is less likely that the data will be compromised. Nevertheless, costs of customer and public notification and remedial actions can be huge regardless of whether the misappropriated information was misused or not.

As of June 2006, some 32 states in the United States had passed breach notification and response laws. Some states require action on the basis of loss alone, regardless of what may have actually happened to the data. More lenient federal laws have not yet been enacted. As a result, many financial firms are taking a conservative approach by notifying customers and providing mitigation services to customers whenever devices or media are unaccounted for. In an excellent article by Smedinghoff (2005), he advises how companies should respond in regard to their disclosing security breaches to those who might be affected.

In its widely-quoted report *Lost Customer Information: What Does a Breach Cost Companies?* the Ponemon Insititute (2006) analyzed the results of a survey of 14 companies that had experienced data breaches. The Ponemon Institute found that the estimated total cost, which included direct and indirect costs as well as estimates of lost revenue, ranged from about $500,000 to $52.2 million, with an average cost per user in the $140 range. In one example, the cost per lost record was estimated at about $2,800, with by far the largest cost components being those relating to existing customers moving to other firms and potential customers deciding against doing business with any firm reporting a security breach.

Mimoso (2006) presents an excellent discourse on the aftermath of such incidents as they have affected security professionals. Five security managers, from such well-known organizations as LexisNexis, University of California at Berkeley, Georgia Technology Authority, ChoicePoint, and CardSystems, were asked about what they did differently after experiencing publicly announced incidents. Interestingly, even though the title of the article suggests survival, 40% of the original security professionals at these organizations had already been replaced. It is also of some concern that the remedies proposed in most cases only avoid the organization falling victim to the same threat as previously, rather than anticipating new threats and guarding against them also, as required for U.S. financial firms under GLBA.

While the above discussion references U.S. laws, there are many privacy laws on the books of a number of other countries. Here are a number of examples:

- Privacy Act of 1993 (New Zealand)
- Hong Kong Personal Data Ordinance of 1995
- Personal Data Protection Directive of 1998 (European Union)
- UK Data Protection Act of 1998
- Personal Information Protection and Electronic Documents Act of 2000 (PIPEDA) – (Canada)
- Privacy Amendment Act of 2000 (Australia)

Each has its own definitions, provisions, disclosure, and reporting requirements, and the like, so that multinational companies must allow for these laws and consequent regulations as they transact business across the globe.

It may be many years before there is a noticeable easing in the rate of increase of reporting such security breaches. After all, it is generally held that many incidents are not even reported to law enforcement and others. It is likely that the ratio of reported incidents to actual incidents will increase over time. This phenomenon will likely result in a continuing increase in reporting, as we are seeing in 2006, even if the absolute number of events were to go down.

As a consequence of this increased exposure, proposals to spend on security, which were previously rejected by management as not having a sufficiently high return on security investment (ROSI), may now show an excellent ROSI—or, perhaps more accurately, return on privacy investment (ROPI).

However, before going much further, we should define "security" and "privacy," especially as there is so much confusion and misuse of these terms.

Security is a condition that results from the establishment and maintenance of protective measures that ensure a state of inviolability from hostile acts or influences. The most widely used definition of computer security is <u>c</u>onfidentiality + <u>i</u>ntegrity + <u>a</u>vailability (CIA).

Though the above CIA model has been generally accepted by security professionals, there are some, including this writer, who believe that the definition is inadequate because of its emphasis on protection. As a result of this focus, there are several important measures not being sufficiently addressed explicitly, such as deterrence, avoidance, awareness, and enforcement. I will write more on this later.

Privacy is, in a general sense, the interest that individuals have in sustaining a "personal space," free from interference by other persons and organizations. This definition and several other related ones can be found at Richard Clarke's (2005) Web site at www.anu.edu.au/Roger.Clarke/DV/intro.html. More specific to our discussion is "information privacy," which is defined as the interest that individuals have in controlling, or at least significantly influencing, the handling of data about themselves.

While privacy can be affected and enforced predominantly through security measures, it also should be noted that there are many aspects of security that are not aimed specifically at privacy.

Security and Privacy as Insurance

Spending on information technology (IT) security and privacy is similar to buying insurance. You can spend large amounts of money to buy security products and/or insurance premiums, but, if you are fortunate, you may never "collect" on either. You may choose to self-insure and possibly be hit by a catastrophic loss. You also may skimp on security and suffer major successful breaches and consequent losses. What it comes down to is the subjective estimates of the probability of a loss and what the corresponding magnitude might be; and what you are willing to pay to prevent and to recoup were such an event to take place.

Security measures today are heavily biased towards the prevention of incidents and limiting damage that might be caused by them. Insurance, on the other hand, is about survivability and compensation for losses. In fact, there is a trade off among prevention, protection, and survivability, since companies generally can elect to spend varying amounts on each aspect in order to maintain a desired level of physical, electronic, and financial protection.

In this chapter, we will take some well-established assessment models to demonstrate the impact of increasing risk and higher potential costs in the light of recent events, even though such models are often questioned in security and privacy circles. Recent events have pointed to areas of vulnerability not previously considered important. Current legislation and regulations have resulted in a much more painful and costly revelation process. Consequently both the *risks*, in terms of expectation of events happening, and the *losses*, in terms of the costs resulting from notification, remediation, and loss of reputation have all increased significantly.

Costs of Security Breaches

When a security breach is experienced, there are a number of costs incurred almost immediately and others that extend over time. Some, such as the cost of mailing notification letters, are tangible and easy to measure, while others, such as the loss of potential business, are intangible and can only be roughly estimated.

If a breach is internal and does not involve business partners or customers either directly or indirectly, it is likely that the costs, which can be tied to the breach, will be limited to those related to:

- Researching the root cause of the breach and its extent
- Ending further damage
- Repairing any damage done
- Restoring activities back to normal
- Coming up with means of avoiding recurrence in the future

Costs are likely to be limited to the time and effort needed to perform the above tasks. They can usually be readily calculated for both internal and external staff. The opportunity costs of diverting these workers to addressing the breach, resolving related issues, and not having services available need to be included also, even though they are much more difficult to determine.

If the breach extends beyond the boundaries of the organization, then a whole series of other costs and losses are incurred. This particularly applies when sensitive customer information is disclosed, stolen, or lost. In a June 2005 report, *Governing for Enterprise Security,* Allen (2005) of the Software Engineering Institute at Carnegie Mellon University, lists the following enterprise security objectives:

- Achieving and preserving trust
- Maintaining stakeholder value
- Demonstrating ethical and socially conscious behavior
- Maintaining compliance with new and expanding laws and regulations
- Ensuring that use and handling of data complies with the enterprise's information security and privacy practices
- Offering and fulfilling business transactions

Incidents, which might be detrimental to one or more of the above objectives, will undoubtedly lead to considerable measurable and intangible costs and losses. Those who were responsible for evaluating and instituting (or *not* instituting) the security measures in the first place will likely not have accounted for these factors.

Validity of Risk-Return Assessments

Assessing risks and returns on investment are well-established techniques for project prioritization and capital budgeting. However, some (including me) have raised questions as to whether such methods are fully applicable to security investments. The argument is that since security risk depends on many uncontrollable and unknown circumstances, in addition to which the vast majority of security incidents may never be reported, then estimates as the probabilities of events and losses relating to them are so inaccurate as to invalidate the process. In place of such risk assessments, Parker (2005) recommends that one substitute such methods as safeguard and application benchmarking.

Parker (2005) describes a series of losses, which may be incurred when incidents are publicly revealed, including:

- Efforts and resources applied to assisting in the investigation for law enforcers and legal counsel (these will likely include time of internal staff, costs of consultants and outside counsel, and computer-related and administrative expenses)
- Civil and, possibly, criminal litigation costs as a result of infringing laws and/or regulations, including the loss of time and attention of key staff who must testify
- The replacement of staff who may have left voluntarily or involuntarily, and the costs related to the termination of such staff and the hiring of new staff
- Damage to the victim organization's public image and reputation, including the costs of public relations and other communications, the loss of current and prospective customer business, and the efforts to explain the incident to management, customers, business partners, and shareholders
- Possible increases in insurance premiums, increases in deductibles, and reductions of coverage
- Loss of customer trust, market initiative, and competitive position and strength
- Losses from copy-cat attacks as previously unknown vulnerabilities might be exposed to a broad audience, including potential evil doers
- Costs related to shoring up the vulnerabilities by increasing security posture through acquisition of products and services and possibly outsourcing (or insourcing—depending on the nature of the incident) of security or operational functions and services

Axelrod (2004, p. 64) notes that with risk assessments, "... some costs might be hidden or excluded altogether, either unintentionally or through the analysts' ignorance or inexperience." However, the author points out a potentially more sinister aspect, whereby an analyst might purposely distort the information to favor a particular outcome. This is easily done, as estimates of the less tangible items can be highly subjective.

The Risk-Return Relationship

Let us now examine the relationship between security and privacy risks and the returns that might be expected from investment in security measures.

Risk analysis provides management with estimates of the expected losses from anticipated events. Expected loss, which is the magnitude of a loss multiplied by the probability that the loss will be incurred, is a potential cost to the organization. Conversely, the avoidance of a loss is considered a benefit or saving. In evaluating the benefit of a particular investment in security tools or services, we are looking at loss reduction and risk mitigation resulting from security measures as a benefit, in addition to any direct cost savings, such as from staff reduction, which might apply.

It should be recognized that the reduction in losses achieved by particular security measures will likely change over time as new threats appear, new vulnerabilities are discovered, and experience is gained through handling actual incidents. In addition costs of acquiring and implementing security measures will change over time because of competition in the marketplace, obsolescence of existing products and services, and the creation of new tools and capabilities.

Assuming that one is able to derive risk-based estimates of the benefits of security measures, and the costs of such measures are available, then one of a number of evaluation methods can be derived (Axelrod, 2006), as described below. Also, Harris (2006) provides an excellent summary of risk management and methodologies and frameworks.

Cost-benefit analysis (CBA). The measure used here is the benefits-to-cost ratio and is simply the benefits divided by the cost. If the result is greater than one, then it is a favorable investment, as opposed to an unfavorable ratio of less than one. For example, if the benefit derived from a security measure costing $100,000 is $125,000, then the benefit-to-cost ratio is 1.25. The extent to which the ratio must be above unity for an investment to be seen as worthwhile is a somewhat subjective management decision. It is interesting to note that some researchers have considered (incorrectly in my view) the cost-benefit ratio to be the same as return on investment (ROI).

ROI. This is really the "rate" of return on investment and is the ratio of the net benefits (total benefits minus total cost) to total cost. Using the same example as above, the net benefits are $25,000, so that the ROI is 25% or 0.25, being the $25,000 divided by the total cost of $100,000. It should be noted that the ROI is always the benefit-to-cost ratio less one.

Neither the CBA or ROI methods account for the time value of money, whereby a dollar obtained some time hence is worth less than today's dollar, because today's dollar can be invested and earn interest to yield an amount greater than a dollar at some future time. These methods also do not take into account the relative size of the investments, which is often required because of limitations in capital available for investing. Therefore, it is not too helpful to know that a particular costly investment yields a higher return, if the budget does not allow for the expenditure.

There are two methods that do take into account the time value of money, those being net present value (NPV) and internal rate of return (IRR). NPV is essentially the value of the net benefits of an investment expressed in today's dollars. As before, a positive NPV is usually required for an investment to be accepted, but how high it needs to be is again a subjective management view. The IRR is the interest rate that will make the NPV zero. This rate is then compared to a "hurdle rate." If it exceeds the hurdle rate, the investment is acceptable, though it might be rejected on other grounds, such as the size or the relative priority of the investment.

NPV and IRR also have their deficiencies. For one, they assume a constant interest rate over time, which clearly is not the case. A more detailed explanation of the limitations of the various approaches appears in an article by Gordon and Loeb (2002).

It is interesting to note that the CSI/FBI survey report (2005, p. 2), mentioned earlier, states that "[a] significant number of organizations perform some form of economic evaluation of their security expenditures." They report that of those performing such evaluations, 38% use ROI, 19% use IRR, and 18% use NPV.

For the purposes of this chapter, we shall use the CBA method, even though it is limited, because it simplifies the discussion. However, I suggest that you look into the NPV and IRR methods, if you have not done so already, as they are more accurate and representative than CBA or ROI, despite the limitations of the former.

Security and Privacy Options

We now look at two major approaches available for implementing privacy and security. One approach is the so-called defense-in-depth structure, where a number of layers of protective tools are applied. This will be examined subsequently.

A more holistic approach views security as a hierarchy of measures such as deterrence, avoidance, prevention, protection, detection, response, restoration, or cure, and reconstruction, or any combination of these.

In Figure 1, we show how this hierarchy works. But again, we need to first define our terms.

A "threat" is an intentional or unintentional act which, if successful, might result in damage to, misuse of, or destruction of assets (in our case, information assets).

A "vulnerability" is a weakness or exposure, which if exploited by a threat, could result in a damaging incident.

Therefore a security or privacy "incident" or "breach" occurs when threat meets vulnerability and is successful in taking advantage of the "chink in the armor" to compromise the system, network, application and/or data.

Figure 1. Defending against threats

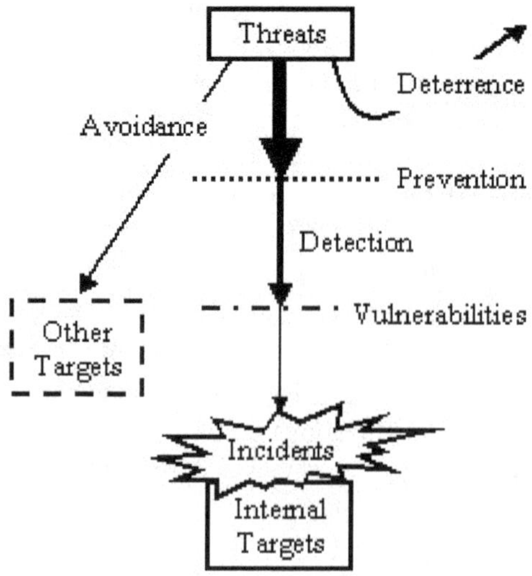

Consequently, as we see in Figure 1, going from top to bottom, threats might be diverted initially through avoidance and/or deterrence measures. With avoidance, the existence of a network, system, application, and/or data is not presented to a potential hacker or someone who might have otherwise inadvertently done damage. Deterrence should discourage a person contemplating doing something bad from acting adversely or encourage those with no evil intentions to be more careful.

Remaining threats are subjected to screening or prevention measures. To the extent that these measures are effective, there may still be some threats that get through the defenses. While not preventing an incident, monitoring or detection tools can help determine which threats are getting through for forensics purposes and to update the screening products so as to trap subsequent threats of the same kind.

Given that the threat is still active, vulnerabilities still have to be present for an incident to happen. Patching, upgrading and deactivation of offending features can go a long way to protect against threats.

We will now consider each of these categories in turn.

Avoidance

Avoidance is the first line of defense. The basic principle of avoidance is the "need to know." If it is not required that someone have access to certain functions and data, particularly personal information describing customers and employees, then such access should not be given to them. If particular server services are not required or specific ports are not needed, then those services and ports should be shut down.

It is specifically in the need-to-know area that GLBA and related laws and regulations kick in. Implementation of methods to affect this, such as restricting access or the blocking, disguising, or encrypting of data, is often complex, expensive, and time consuming, particularly for older systems, which were built for ease of use and access and not with the expectation of having to comply with such legal and regulatory restrictions. Also, recent publicity has highlighted the risks from the use and transportation of physical media, such as magnetic tapes, optical disks, and paper. Mitigation of this latter risk is generally thought to be achievable by converting to secure electronic transmissions of encrypted data, rather than encrypting and password protecting the data on the electrical, magnetic, optical, or other media, to avoid the risks of physical transportation. An indication of the importance of this area to financial institutions is the recent report by BITS (2006), the technical arm of the Financial Services Roundtable, entitled *BITS Key Considerations for Securing Data in Storage and Transport: Securing Physical Media in Storage, Transport, and for Data Erasure and Destruction.*

Deterrence

Deterrence—or what you do if avoidance and protection measures are inadequate, infeasible, or not cost-effective—usually involves specifying a detailed policy to interested parties, such as employees, consultants, and business partners, and delineating the consequences of not following it. As perhaps the most underrated of all security and privacy measures, it is generally accomplished through awareness programs and enforcement procedures. It is often the least expensive of measures to implement, but its benefits are also among the most difficult to quantify. How do you know, for example, how many individuals might have been dissuaded from performing nefarious acts because persons were caught and publicly punished? Spending on deterrence includes creating security and privacy policy and standards, making anyone who might have the potential of doing harm (either intentionally or accidentally) aware of these, and otherwise enforcing them. The deterrent aspect of a security awareness program is to inform potential perpetrators of the painful actions that will likely be taken against them, were they to fail to comply with or actively evade the policy. Similarly those without evil intentions will likely take additional steps to ensure that they will comply with policy.

Another critical aspect of deterrence is for management to be seen to take the promised actions when someone contravenes policy. Such highly visible actions will give pause to those contemplating infringement. It is noteworthy that the U.S. Internal Revenue Service almost always publicizes high-profile tax evasion cases as a deterrent just prior to when most are about to prepare and submit their tax returns.

The downside of deterrence is loss of credibility and potential legal consequences, if the suggested remedial actions are not taken.

Prevention

The basic security rule of prevention is "defense in depth." Standard processes for preventing the unauthorized access to and misuse of information carried within computer systems and over networks include defensive technologies, such as routers, firewalls, intrusion detection and prevention systems, antivirus software, Spam filtering, Web site blocking, vulnerability patching, and the like.

Some of the benefits of these preventative measures can be estimated, although one cannot know with any precision what the cost impact of an intrusion might have been had it not been deflected. The direct cost of a virus or worm can be expressed in terms of staff resources required to determine the cause, to evaluate the extent of the damage caused by the infection, and to clean (or rebuild) the systems. Other costs, such as lost productivity, are much harder to measure, although the annual CSI/FBI survey (2005) attempts to do so.

Data Protection

Trends in legislation and regulation appear to be moving towards a universal requirement for encrypting electronically held personal data when created, at rest, and in motion, as a means of protecting the data against unauthorized access and use.

Encryption is not a panacea in that tools are readily available to criminals for decrypting data. It is well known that there are effective "cracking" programs used for decrypting password files. The same concept is readily extended to personal data. Encryption is also costly in resources, time lags, and administration. Nevertheless, the commonly held view of lawmakers and regulators, often under the advisement of vendors, is that you are "off the hook" in terms of having to publicize a breach and/or notify customers if the compromised information is encrypted.

Detection

The most obvious tool in this category is the so-called intrusion detection system (IDS), which is currently morphing up the "food chain" to the intrusion prevention system (IPS). The concept here is that it is better to respond immediately and block an intrusion than to report it after the fact. IPS should more accurately be called an intrusion response system (IRS). An IPS does not actually "prevent" an attempted intrusion, rather it detects an attack and respond by blocking or diverting it, thereby avoiding damage. The danger with an IPS is that "good traffic" will often be blocked along with the bad. This is the opposite of IDS where the greatest is concern is a flood of "false positives," which increase the risk of missing real intrusions.

However, the area of detection, which comprises monitoring, analyzing, and reporting, is becoming increasingly sophisticated. It is beginning to offer the detection of anomalous behavior and suspicious traffic emanating from both authorized and unauthorized individuals and systems, often insiders and trusted systems, which are thought to comprise the vast majority of security breaches—most of which very likely go undetected.

It is interesting to note here that very many security breaches are not detected directly. Most often the consequent fraud is what alerts companies to the fact that a breach might have occurred. For example, the recently announced CardSystems Solutions breach was first noticed when fraudulent activity took place on accounts that had the common feature that they were processed by CardSystems. It was only after the fact, when CardSystems brought in a third party to perform a forensics analysis, that a malicious program, which had been inserted into the processing company's systems to harvest credit card data, was discovered. This common occurrence of not detecting the malware when it is first introduced, calls into question the efficacy of detection systems.

The current art of detection systems has greatest value in after-the-fact forensics analysis, where the systems record and report activities that can be readily searched through once the analysts know what they are looking for.

IDS is somewhat controversial, with the Gartner Group essentially stating in 2004 that IDS was dead and that IPS was taking over. However, given the difficulties in implementing IPS products, it is likely that the market for IDS with IPS features will continue in the marketplace for some time to come.

IDS is quite expensive to implement and use—especially in terms of trying to aggregate, correlate and analyze the huge quantities of data thrown off by these systems—and might be of questionable value relative to other approaches. However, IDS has become a security standard, much as firewalls were in the late 1990s.

Response and Recovery

Protective measures are designed to prevent bad things from happening to a company's computer and network environments. However, one can argue that funding for preventative measures should be balanced against funding for responding to actual events, since it is not possible to avoid all bad events. Such survivability spending includes costs of resiliency and recoverability.

While the scope of the incident response process generally extends throughout an organization, the security incident response component can be considered to be a real security expense. Security incident response is triggered whenever a significant security incident occurs. One can consider a security event to be the result of a failure of the deterrence, avoidance, prevention, and protection measures since if the latter had been fully effective, the event would not have occurred. Thus, in a very real sense, additional funds and effort expended on the incident prevention measures will likely result in a reduction in the frequency and extent of required response exercises.

As noted above, IPS products really can be considered to be in the response space, since they automatically react to a detected potential incident. The concept here is that an automated IPS can respond much more quickly and accurately than a human responder and, thereby, contain an incident before it becomes more extensive. The downside of such systems is that they might misinterpret an event and react to it in a way that diminishes the value of the environment that it is trying to protect. It should be noted that this is a long-standing problem of detection and prevention programs. Missile detection systems have been known to mistake a flock of flying geese for incoming missiles, for example. Such an error could result in unfounded retaliatory actions that would have a devastating impact in the case of nuclear missiles.

Restoration

Restorative or curative measures include on-site fall back, disaster recovery, and business continuity efforts aimed at bringing back an acceptable level of operation in the light of a compromise or destruction of the primary capabilities and facilities. This is not the re-establishment of the former primary facility, which we will call "reconstruction" and comment on in the next section.

The money and effort spent on redundant backup facilities is usually determined by the resilience and strength of the primary facility and the criticality of the functions operating in the facility. Moitre and Konda (2000) call this "survivability," and they indicate that survivability can be traded off against protective security and resiliency measures. That is to say, if the critical functions operate in a "military strength" primary facility, with hardened perimeter, back-up power, communications, and so on, the likelihood of having to roll over to a back-up facility is reduced. Therefore it can be argued that one might reduce expenditures on the back-up facility, possibly by using a shared service, since the likelihood of invoking the back-up is small.

However, in the United States, the financial services sector is subject to resiliency requirements mandated by its regulators. Consequently, the back-up and recovery requirements are strongly advised, if not compulsory in many cases.

Reconstruction

Often restored facilities are not permanent, as they may not have the infrastructure, location, facilities, and so on required of a permanent facility. Therefore there is frequently a final step, namely, bringing everything back to the way it was prior to the incident. This means rebuilding facilities, replacing equipment, and so forth. Information security is involved here as it would be in any set-up situation, and there are consequent costs of installing and testing the necessary security components.

Defense-in-Depth Strategy

It is well recognized that any single product does not provide the protection needed in today's complex environment. Consequently, security products and services are usually layered within and across the system and network infrastructure of an organization in order to protect against different threats and to catch attacks that have been able to penetrate other layers.

There are a variety of products, such as network and application firewalls, IDS, IPS, antivirus and antispam software and services, e-mail and message traffic content scanners, Web site blockers, encryption, and identity and access management products. Some of the newer products embody artificial intelligence or behavioral capabilities, which avoid the need for human intervention in many situations.

Firewalls

Firewalls can block traffic of certain descriptions and from specific sources and not permit access to certain ports and services. Application-based firewalls look at the specific nature of the traffic as it pertains to particular applications and block unsubstantiated traffic. Firewalls differ from routers in that they produce logs that can be analyzed after the fact to determine inappropriate activity.

Use of firewalls is practically universal. It is a minimum requirement, certainly in protecting what falls within the perimeter from nefarious activities. They also are used on internal networks to section off parts of the infrastructure. The management of firewalls has become commonplace and is usually controlled from within the network engineering group.

As they have reached commodity status, firewalls are seldom subjected to ROI analysis. They are a basic requirement and as such must be installed at critical nodes of the infrastructure. To the extent that some firewalls might be considered discretionary, particularly those on the internal network, they might be subjected to analysis.

IDSs

IDSs do not block traffic. Instead, they monitor the traffic as it flows across the network or on the host computer or endpoint (personal computer) and report against previously determined profiles or signatures. They are also after-the-fact devices in that they do not take any action but can be used for forensic analysis. From time to time, an IDS might pick up the early stages of an attack, where the attacker is reconnoitering prior to invasion. Usually some form of data aggregation and correlation "engine" is needed to identify and draw attention to such suspicious behavior. If the curious activities are detected, then action, such as blocking traffic emanating from a particular source, can be taken proactively.

There have been heated discussions in the industry, with the Gartner Group at the fore, about whether or not IDSs are passé. Gartner is looking to IPSs as the proactive technology to supercede IDSs. In fact rhere is room for both devices and manufacturers are coming up with hybrids, which encompass both technologies. IDSs only monitor, so there is a risk that they will either miss something or detect malevolent activities when it is too late to do much about them. On the other hand, IPSs can cause problems if they misinterpret good traffic for bad and block it, and it is the risk of screening out valuable transactions that has concerned a number of potential buyers.

Other Areas

All that can really be stated with certainty is that technologies are evolving and that what may have been valid just a short time earlier may no longer pertain. This is particularly true when a new type of threat or incident is observed. For example, prior to the highly publicized losses of computer tapes, there was little to justify more secure and expensive handling methods. Once financial firms learned of several incidents and the ensuing adverse publicity and costly responses, they quickly upgraded their own handling and transportation procedures.

ROSI by Category and in Aggregate

Each category of security tools or procedures should have a demonstrable value if used in isolation. Categories of security tools and procedures include firewalls, IDSs, IPSs, correlation engines, antivirus, identity and access management (IAM), awareness/training, and incident response. The value of any of these tools is difficult to measure, if indeed it can be measured, because no organization implements just a single method or tool. Therefore any analysis will be contaminated with the effects of the interaction of the tools.

For the sake of example, let us assume that the specific value of an individual method can be measured, as can the variance or variability of that value around some mean value. As an example, we might identify a threat for examination as "the proliferation of computer worms and viruses." The means of mitigating this risk might include the deployment of antivirus software and an aggressive awareness program.

In general, an awareness program is among the least costly of avoidance methods. It is simply a matter of advising e-mail system users not to open "suspicious" e-mails, particularly any attachments thereto, and not to click on any links incorporated into the e-mail. This can certainly assist in avoiding the most blatant of viruses. However many viruses and worms will infect systems without anyone having to do anything. It is here that the antivirus software comes into play. It scans for known viruses and blocks threatening attachments. It does not block viruses of hitherto unknown form (or "signature"), which is where its weakness lies. However, it is possible that a well-defined awareness program can lead to behavior that from time to time will avoid a virus that the antivirus software has been unable to detect.

Awareness or notification (warnings) may be less effective than antivirus software for known viruses, since the former is more prone to human error. Also the range of effectiveness is likely to be much broader for awareness. Antivirus software, in this case, not only has a greater return, but it is less variable in its effectiveness. Since both methods work in a similar manner in that they work well if the threat is known from prior experience, then they can be considered positively correlated. That is to say, their combined impact is some aggregation of both approaches.

There might be cases where the combined impact of two or more tools is less than the sum of the components or even less than one or both of the components. That is to say, by adding one tool or process, the effectiveness or the benefit of the other tool or process may be reduced, possibly by more than the benefit of using the second tool. It is difficult to come up with good examples, but one example might be the use of firewalls and the addition of a correlation and notification engine, where the notification engine might have a negative effect, if it produces so many false positives that an actual event is camouflaged and ignored, but management has the sense that greater control has been invoked. This would not be a condemnation of the tool itself, but more of the way in which it has been set up.

Optimizing the Security Portfolio: Or, How Much Security is Enough?

Given that one might be able to evaluate individual security technologies and tools, one against the other, the question arises as to what is the ideal combination of tools, practices, and procedures that will provide the optimum level of security. Would that the answer were as simple as the question?

In the above section, we looked at comparing one tool against another. In the portfolio approach, we determine the optimal combination of tools and practices that lead to the highest level of security for a given expenditure.

As an example, let us assume that we have $1 million to spend on protective measures, such as firewalls, IDS, IPS, and encryption as well as awareness training. We also assume that, for a given expenditure on a particular technology, we know what the benefit is. This is shown in Table 1.

This means that, for example, if $100,000 is spent on firewalls, then the estimated benefit will be $200,000. However, once the expenditure reaches $300,000, there is no incremental benefit for additional investment in firewalls. And even at $300,000, it is a break-even proposition, suggesting that there may be better places to put the company's money. These relationships are similar for other tools and technologies. However, for IPS in this example, there is very little benefit (i.e., $50,000) to spending $100,000, but an expenditure of $200,000 yields a $300,000 benefit. This is meant to illustrate a case where the benefits do not kick in until a critical mass is in place. In Table 2 we look at the benefit-to-cost ratios for each of the cases in Table 1.

If we were to just take the maximum benefit-cost ratio for each tool category (indicated with an asterisk), we could decide that the expenditures should be as in Table 3.

Thus an expenditure of $1 million, distributed across the various tools as shown, would yield $1.9 million in benefits, which is an ROSI rate of 90%. If we had an additional $100,000 to spend, the benefit-to-cost ratio would be increased slightly to 1.909, as shown in Table 4.

However, this might not be the overall best selection from a benefit-to cost perspective. For example, if the additional $100,000 were to be spent on IPS and $100,000 less were spent on IDS, the benefit-to-cost ratio would increase to 1.950 for the same $1 million cost, as in Table 5.

Please note that the absolute and relative numbers here are fictitious and meant only to illustrate the argument. Also note that there are computational methods, such as linear programming, that calculate the optimum combination of expenditures on security tools subject to constraints on costs. The particular method used depends on the nature of the cost and benefit equations, whether the equations are linear or not, how the variables might change over time, the measurability and predictability of costs and benefits, and so on. In this chapter we have adopted a simpler approach for the purposes of clear exposition.

Now we look at the impact of a change in laws or regulations that requires notification of customers if personal information is lost and was not encrypted. In the example in Table 6, the value of encryption has suddenly jumped because having personal data encrypted might avoid having to go public with a breach. An additional investment in encryption could yield so much more in benefits that it ups the average benefit-to-cost ratio considerably.

This demonstrates that, rather than optimizing for each individual tool, additional value might be squeezed out from an equivalent expenditure by adjusting expenditures on specific tools. As shown above, the incremental value per dollar spent on various tools will differ. It makes economic sense to apply the funds to those areas yielding the highest return but only to the extent that the incremental value remains highest and greater than the incremental cost.

Table 1. Benefits derived from various security measures and different expenditure levels

Expenditures >	$100,000	$200,000	$300,000	$400,000	$500,000
Firewalls	$200,000	$300,000	$300,000	$300,000	$300,000
IDS	$100,000	$250,000	$360,000	$360,000	$360,000
IPS	$50,000	$300,000	$600,000	$800,000	$800,000
Awareness	$400,000	$450,000	$450,000	$500,000	$500,000
Encryption	$50,000	$250,000	$450,000	$450,000	$450,000

Table 2. Benefit-to-cost ratios for various security measures and expenditure levels

Expenditures >	$100,000	$200,000	$300,000	$400,000	$500,000
Firewalls	2.0*	1.5	1.0	0.75	0.6
IDS	1.0	1.25*	1.2	1.2	1.2
IPS	0.5	1.5	2.0*	2.0	1.6
Awareness	4.0*	2.25	1.5	1.25	1.0
Encryption	0.5	1.25	1.5*	1.13	0.9

Table 3. Expenditures and benefits for highest benefit-to-cost ratios

Tool	Benefit-to-cost ratio	Corresponding expenditure	Corresponding benefit
Firewalls	2.0	$100,000	$200,000
IDS	1.25	$200,000	$250,000
IPS	2.0	$300,000	$600,000
Awareness	4.0	$100,000	$400,000
Encryption	1.5	$300,000	$450,000
Total	1.90 Average	$1,000,000	$1,900,000

Table 4. Expenditures and benefits for highest benefit-to-cost ratios with increased expenditures

Tool	Benefit-to-cost ratio	Corresponding expenditure	Corresponding benefit
Firewalls	2.0	$100,000	$200,000
IDS	1.25	$200,000	$250,000
IPS	2.0	$400,000	$800,000
Awareness	4.0	$100,000	$400,000
Encryption	1.5	$300,000	$450,000
Total	1.909 Average	$1,100,000	$2,100,000

Table 5. Expenditures and benefits for highest benefit-to-cost ratios with different mix

Tool	Benefit-to-cost ratio	Corresponding expenditure	Corresponding benefit
Firewalls	2.0	$100,000	$200,000
IDS	1.0	$100,000	$100,000
IPS	2.0	$400,000	$800,000
Awareness	4.0	$100,000	$400,000
Encryption	1.5	$300,000	$450,000
Total	1.95 Average	$1,000,000	$1,950,000

Table 6. Expenditures and benefits for highest benefit-to-cost ratios with different mix

Tool	Benefit-to-cost ratio	Corresponding expenditure	Corresponding benefit
Firewalls	2.0	$100,000	$200,000
IDS	1.25	$200,000	$250,000
IPS	2.0	$400,000	$600,000
Awareness	4.0	$100,000	$400,000
Encryption	3.0	$400,000	$1,200,000
Total	2.208	$1,200,000	$2,650,000

Trade Off Against Survivability

Another point to add is that, in many circumstances, it might be worthwhile to invest in recovery and restoration, or survivability, rather than put that same money into data protection. Table 7 shows an example of increasing total expenditures by $500,000 over and above the example in Table 6. Nevertheless the total benefit-to-cost ratio rises to more than three.

The results of restricting the budget to that which was originally suggested to be spent on information security by reducing spending on security by $500,000, which is the estimated cost of response improvements, are shown in Table 8.

Again we have a situation where, if the activities with the higher cost-to-benefit ratios are substituted for those with lower ratios, the overall ratio will increase substantially.

Table 7. Comparison of benefits and expenditures

Tool	Benefit-to-cost ratio	Corresponding expenditure	Corresponding benefit
Security	2.2	$1,200,000	$2,650,000
Response	5.0	$500,000	$2,500,000
Total	3.029	$1,700,000	$5,150,000

Table 8. Comparison of benefits and expenditures with different mix

Tool	Benefit-to-cost ratio	Corresponding expenditure	Corresponding benefit
Security	2.45	$700,000	$1,715,000
Response	5.0	$500,000	$2,500,000
Total	3.51	$1,200,000	$4,215,000

Enforcement Pays

Enforcement not only pays, but it is crucial to the success of any security program.

While security tools might avoid and prevent adverse security incidents, they are valueless if they are not properly implemented and managed. Also, if employees, consultants, vendors, and others are not aware of the preventative and protective measures or if they have not been adequately trained in their use, then all may be for naught. The ideal security measures are those that do not require any actions to be taken by unknowledgeable individuals, apart from those that are forced by the systems.

However, if certain security-related decisions cannot be completely avoided, then one might have to resort to deterrent measures. These may require awareness, training, and signoff by individuals, accompanied by a warning that, in the event of noncompliance, certain disciplinary measures will be taken. That is why awareness and training can have such a high return, since the success of the program depends on them.

The Dynamics of Deterrence

The risk equation is rapidly changing based on two major trends:

1. The increased privacy legislation and regulations making for higher penalties and costs were a breach of personal information to take place
2. The greater culpability within organizations whereby the board of directors and executive management are increasingly becoming personally exposed to civil and criminal charges

As a result, the deterrence factor is increasing rapidly, However, there are major problems in regard to compliance.

The rate of change of the rules makes it difficult, if not impossible in some cases, to introduce appropriate and acceptable measures to comply with the laws and regulations within a reasonable timeframe. This leaves organizations exposed during the implementation phases to the extent that the mitigation projects extend beyond deadlines for compliance.

The need to comply with laws and regulations will sometimes divert valuable resources to relatively low-risk endeavors at the expense of not dealing with much higher risk issues. At the same time, projects to protect personal information, highly demanding of the same resources, are put on the back burner, often with damaging repercussions.

Summary and Conclusion

This chapter reviewed the basis for decisions on how much to spend on new and/or enhanced security measures. Largely, even if organizations are quite successful in determining returns at the technical level, risk factors and returns, which include less tangible costs and not readily measured benefits, make for results that are often much more difficult to measure and interpret.

While the examples shown in this chapter are somewhat simplistic, they are provided for illustrative purposes. The reader should make the mental transition from these examples to more sophisticated techniques, which they can either apply themselves or engage the services of an expert.

Overall, the security professional must constantly keep abreast of the latest laws and regulations and what they mean to the organization. This chapter promotes the idea of examining the risks related to security and argues in favor of the rational selection of products and services that provide the most cost-effective mitigation.

References

Allen, J. (2005). *Governing for enterprise security* (Tech. note CMU/SEI-2005-TN-023). Pittsburgh, PA: Carnegie Mellon University/Software Engineering Institute. Retrieved June 28, 2006, from http://www.cert.org/archive/pdf/05tn023.pdf

Axelrod, C. W. (2004). *Outsourcing information security*. Boston: Artech House Publishers.

Axelrod, C. W. (2006). Cybersecurity and the critical infrastructure. *Information Systems Control Journal*, (3), 24-28.

BITS. (2006). *BITS Key considerations for securing data in storage and transport: Securing physical media in storage, transport, and for data erasure and destruction*. Washington, DC: Financial Services Roundtable/BITS. Retrieved June 28, 2006, from http://www.bitsinfo.org/downloads/Publications%20Page/bitsdatatrans.pdf

Clarke, R. (2005). *Introduction to dataveillance and information privacy, and definitions of terms*. Retrieved June 28, 2006, from http://www.anu.edu.au/people/Roger.Clarke/DV/Intro.html

Computer Security Institute/Federal Bureau of Investigation. (2005). *The tenth annual CSI/FBI computer crime and security survey.* Retrieved June 28, 2006, from www.gocsi.com

Federal Financial Institutions Examination Council. (2005). *Authentication in an Internet banking environment*. Retrieved June 28, 2006, from http://www.ffiec.gov/pdf/authentication_guidance.pdf

Gordon, L. A., & Loeb, M. L. (2002). Return on information security investments: Myths vs. realities. *Strategic Finance,* 26-31.

Harris, S. (2006). Alphabet soup. *Information Security, 9*(4), 48-54.

Mimoso, M. S. (2006). Security survivor all-stars. *Information Security, 9*(4), 25-36.

Moitra, S. D., & Konda, S. L. (2000). *The survivability of network systems: An empirical analysis.* (Tech. Report CMU/SEI-2000-TN-021). Pittsburgh, PA: Carnegie Mellon University/Software Engineering Institute. Retrieved June 28, 2006, from http://www.cert.org/archive/pdf/00tr021.pdf

Parker, D. (2005). Learning from our enemies. *The ISSA Journal,* 20-25.

Ponemon Institute. (2005). *Lost customer information: What does a breach cost companies?* Retrieved June 28, 2006, from http://www.pgp.com/library/ponemon_reg_direct.html

Smedinghoff, T. (2005). The new law of information security: What companies need to do now. *The Computer & Internet Lawyer, 22*(11), 9-25.

Appendix A: Recent Security Breaches Involving Sensitive Information

Prior to February 2005, there were occasional notices of security breaches involving the potential compromise of sensitive data, particularly personal customer information, hitting the press. In the past several months, there has been a veritable flood of announcements. It appears that the frequency of major events has increased from one or two every couple of months to weekly occurrences, such as:

- On Feb. 15, 2005, it was reported that persons falsified their identities to gain access to ChoicePoint's applications and obtain personal information on 145,000 individuals.
- On Feb. 25, 2005, Bank of America, 205, DSW Shoes revealed that 100,000 customer accounts had been hacked. That number was then increased by 1.3 million accounts as was revealed on April 18, 2005.
- On March 10, 2005, it was announced that hackers had broken into databases held by LexisNexis and obtained personal information of some 32,000 individuals. A month later, on March 12, 2005, they revealed that an additional 280,000 accounts had been compromised.
- On May 2, 2005, Time Warner made public that computer tapes lost in transit to an Iron Mountain facility, contained personal information from 600,000 current and former employees.
- On June 6, 2005, CitiFinancial announced that UPS had lost computer tapes in transit containing personal information of some 3.9 million loan customers.
- On June 16, 2005, MasterCard announced that data from as many as 40 million accounts, including its own customers and those of Visa, American Express, and Discover, had been jeopardized by a breach at CardSystems Solutions.

- Georgia Technology Authority announced on March 30, 2006 that 573,000 state pensioners had had their bank-account details compromised by a hacker exploiting a security flaw.
- On May 19, 2006, the American Institute of Certified Public Accountants (AICPA) reported that an unencrypted hard drive containing the personal information of some 330,000 members had been lost in transit.
- The Department of Veterans Affairs announced on May 22, 2006, that an employee's laptop and computer storage device, containing personal information about 28.6 million veterans, had been stolen.
- On May 30, 2006, Texas Guaranteed Student Loan Corp. let it be known that they had been notified by subcontractor Hummingbird that equipment, which contained personal information of 1.3 million Texas Guaranteed borrowers, had been lost by an employee.
- Ernst & Young disclosed on June 1, 2006, that a laptop, which contained personal information of 243,000 customers of Hotels.com, had been stolen from an employee.
- The Internal Revenue Service (IRS) disclosed on June 5, 2006, that a laptop has been lost in transit and it contained personal information of 291 employees and job applicants.
- On June 14, 2006, American Insurance Group (AIG) announced that a server, which had been stolen on March 31, 2006, contained personal information, including medical records, of 930,000 customers.
- The Federal Trade Commission (FTC) announced on June 22, 2006, that two laptops had been stolen, containing personal and financial data of 110 persons.

The Privacy Rights Clearinghouse maintains a list of data breaches reported since the ChoicePoint incident, which was reported on Feb. 15, 2005. The list is available at www.privacyrights.org/ar/ChronDataBreaches.htm. As of June 27, 2006, the list includes more than 200 incidents accounting for some 88.4 million persons in the United States exposed to potential identity theft. In a number of cases, the extent of the exposure was reported as "unknown," "thousands," "a significant number," and the like, so that the actual number of persons exposed could be much higher. For example, there were two reports from March 2, 2006, alone, that were not included in the total but together may have accounted for the compromise of 3.3 million identities.

Appendix B: Return on Cyber Security Investment (ROCSI) as it Relates to Return on Critical Infrastructure Protection Investment (ROCIPI)

Critical infrastructure protection is the stepchild of security. That is because no one appears to be willing to take on the responsibility and costs entailed. Every enterprise is dependent, to a lesser or greater extent, on the broad-based infrastructure, particularly the critical infrastructure sectors of the nation and the world. The critical infrastructure includes such sectors as energy, IT, telecommunications, financial services, and transportation.

Is it that there is just not an adequate ROCSI for the public and/or the private sectors to invest in protection for the common good? Or is it that everyone understands that there will be a huge return, but no one is willing to put in the effort and funds? If there is a real need (as I think many recognize, at least intellectually), then it will take legislation and regulations to make it happen. In that way, legislators and regulators tilt the balance of the ROI equation, making it so painful not to comply, in terms of cost and other deterrents, that the investment will be made (no matter what).

An early attempt at this was Presidential Decision Directive No. 63 (PDD-63), which dealt with the protection of the nation's critical infrastructure. Issued in May 1998, PDD-63 required that the government and private industry do what was considered necessary to protect the critical infrastructure from attack or other events by May 2003. Unfortunately PDD-63 was a casualty of the change in administration and has not to date been fully replaced. Consequently, little has been achieved beyond the initial flurry of effort in response to PDD-63, when information sharing and analysis centers (ISACs) were formed for sectors such as finance, IT, and energy.

Recently there has been some attention paid to establishing a cyber-security research and development program (R&D), although funding for such R&D remains an issue. Other initiatives proposed by PDD-63, such as assessing the vulnerabilities of the critical infrastructure and embarking upon an awareness program, have been given little attention. A more extensive treatment of this topic can be found in Axelrod (2006).

As with other endeavors that require huge amounts of funding, securing the nation's critical infrastructure will need major government and private sector commitments and strong, determined leadership. It also requires sufficient incentives and/or threats of punitive action to "persuade" the private sector to play its part in shoring up the 80% or so of the infrastructure that they are deemed to own. The perceived ROCSI has to be shifted to a level that will result in ameliorative action being taken.

Chapter II

Risk Management in Banking: A Review of Principles and Strategies

Göran Bergendahl, University of Gothenburg, Sweden
Ted Lindblom, University of Gothenburg, Sweden

Abstract

Banks play an important role in the financial system contributing to efficient and well-functioning transfers of capital and risk between those in excess (savers) and those in need (borrowers) of money. Traditionally, financial risks, like interest rate, foreign exchange and credit risks, have been the most important and typical ones for banking operations. However, lately the risk environment of banks has changed considerably. In this study we are stressing the vital importance for the single bank to have a much more sophisticated and well-structured approach to risk management than it had 15 years ago. Our main focus is on how banking objectives such as profitability and growth should govern risk management, and how these objectives are made operational into the management of those assets and liabilities exposed to changes in market prices and in customer repayments of loans.

Introduction

Only a decade ago the banking industry in Scandinavia was recovering from the massive credit losses that many major and market-leading banks experienced during the bank crises in the early 1990s. Those credit losses were more or less an inevitable outcome of the deregulation of the financial markets in the 1980s. The banks had entered into a largely biased and uncritical over lending to real estate investment companies. Real estate prices were rocketing, indirectly giving the banks an opportunity for rapid growth and an increased market share on commercial lending. However, that lending was associated with a very high exposure to market risks and credit risks. When market prices on real estate property fell drastically and the "bubble" did burst, the banks' interest rate margins and initial (accounting) profitability were unsatisfactory in relation to the additional risk they had taken (Lindblom, 1993). In many cases they did not have enough equity capital to absorb the losses, let alone an adequate amount of qualified capital to comply with the capital adequacy requirements stipulated by the Basel Accord of 1988. As a consequence of the poor risk management of the banks some of them were acquired by other banks or even nationalized (particularly in Norway), whereas other and mainly larger banks were either rescued by government bailouts or by receiving new equity capital from their owners (e.g., SEB in Sweden).

Today there appears to be a similar battle for market share on household mortgage loans, particularly in Sweden. House prices are booming and households' demand for new mortgage loans is increasing rapidly. After a period of historically low inflation, interest rates are extremely low at the moment with variable mortgage loan rates lower than 3%. Fixed loan rates are only marginally higher. However, banks are not only competing with low interest rates. Starting with the state-owned mortgage bank, SBAB, many banks have begun to offer low interest rate mortgage loans to household customers up to as much as 95% of the estimated market value of their residential property. Compared to the traditional level of 75%, this means that the collateral security margin is now five times lower for these mortgage loans. Some analysts are warning for a new bubble, especially after the Swedish Central Bank lowered its repo rate by 50 basis points to 1.5% in the summer of 2005 (Riksbanken, 2005). Financial analysts as well as the executive board of the Central Bank do not seem to be equally concerned, claiming that the lending of banks is more wide-spread and diversified this time. Moreover, they argue that most household customers would be likely to be quite reluctant to leave their home in the case of increasing interest rates. They would rather try to manage higher mortgage rates by cutting consumption and purchasing costs, in general. The more or less nonexistent customer response on the recent turn to a small upward trend of market interest rates and the repo rate (currently back to 2%) seems to lend support to this latter view. Albeit lately the executive board of the Central Bank appears to have become slightly more concerned about the high indebtedness of households. Deputy Governor Irma Rosenberg expressed the following view in March 2006 when giving an introductory speech at the Swedish Sawmill Managers Association's annual general meeting in Stockholm:

If this development continues, we Executive Board members believe there is a risk that a situation could build up where a sudden slow down in house prices later on would cause households to perceive their debt burden as overly high and to rapidly increase their saving. (Riksbanken, 2006)

Although there might be no urgent danger today for the banking industry or the financial system as such, the situation for certain single banks seems more ambiguous. When a bank increases its low-interest rate mortgage lending to households by requiring less collateral security margins, its credit risk exposure gets higher and more pronounced. Clearly this has implications for the future profitability and growth of the bank, but it also raises questions about the ability of individual banks to accurately assess credit risks and, more importantly, how well modern banks identify and manage risks, in general. The latter is being emphasized more and more by regulatory agencies as the business environment of banks has changed radically in the past 10 years due to increasing globalization of financial markets and far-reaching innovation and development of financial products/instruments. "Within an individual bank, the new banking environment and increased market volatility have necessitated an integrated approach to asset-liability and risk management techniques" (Van Greuning, 2003, p. 3).

In this chapter we stress the vital importance for a single bank to have a much more sophisticated and well-structured approach to risk management than it had 15 years ago (cf. Gardener, 1987; Bergendahl, 1989). Our main focus is now on:

1. How banking objectives such as profitability and growth will govern risk management
2. How these objectives are made operational in the management of those assets and liabilities exposed to changes in market prices—particularly foreign exchange and interest rates—and in customer repayments of loans

Just as the Basel II Accord, the new Basel Accord for international convergence of capital measurement and capital standards, we also consider how banks (should) manage operational risks.

Background: The Nature of Banking Risks

Risk may be defined as: "uncertain future events that could influence the achievement of an organisation's strategic, operational and financial objectives" (Cooper, 2000, p. 15). Like most organizations a bank is exposed to various kinds of risks in its daily operations. These risks can be classified into three main groups: financial, operational, and environmental. Traditionally, financial risks have been the most important and typical ones for banking operations. They concern the risks for rapid changes in interest rates, foreign exchange rates, and customer credit repayments. Therefore, an appropriate management of financial risks has been essential for the profitability and the growth of banks. To accomplish this may not be a trivial task, though. "Financial risks are also subject to complex interdependencies that may significantly increase a bank's overall risk profile" (Van Greuning, 2003, p. 3). In addition, the management of operational risks, like the risk of losses due to inefficient internal processes, failures, and/or fraud, is becoming more evident and crucial for the financial performance of banks. The modern bank is offering a wide range of complex financial products and services that must be properly priced and processed on demand. Aparicio and Keskiner (2004) assert that "the new dimensions of volume, automation and speed at which banks operate today are giving rise to an increased possibility of failure of these operations" (p. 15). Moreover, environmental risks are becoming more evident to banks along with intensifying competition, increasing internationalization, and changing legislation and regulation. As these risks to a large extent cannot be controlled by the individual bank, they set the agenda for the management of other risks. In this respect the Basel II Accord deserves special attention as its proposed implementation at the end of 2007 (BIS, 2004) is putting pressure on banks to look over and develop internal procedures for managing not only financial risks but also operational risks. As Cooper (2000) notes risk management in banking has evolved to become "an integral part of generating sustainable growth in shareholder value" (p. 15).

In general Scandinavian banks fulfill the three key functions of a financial system. It means a) that they facilitate an efficient redistribution between savings and consumption/investments; b) that they contribute to a risk reduction as well as a risk allocation between their different types of customers; and c) that they develop and maintain a well functioning, and from a societal perspective, efficient payment system. The financial and operational risks generated by these operations may then be estimated in terms of short-term and long-term exposures. This is evident when a traditional bank is acting as an intermediary between depositors and borrowers by utilizing scale and scope economies with regard to searching costs, monitoring costs, and the management of risks. Normally, depositors demand high liquidity and low (preferably zero) risk on generally small savings amounts, whereas a borrower is mostly in need of a larger sum of money for a longer time period, in order to make an investment in a "risky" project. In order to meet these conflicting preferences, the bank has to take positions exposing itself to short-term as well as long-term risks. One may say that the bank is acting as an asset transformer (cf. Desmukh, Greenbaum, & Kanatas, 1983). It is transforming asset risk (low risk savings into high risk investments ("credit risk")), asset maturity (short-term savings into long-term investments ("liquidity risk"and("interest rate risk")), and asset volume (attract a large number of low amount savings and allocate to a smaller number of large investment loans ("operational risk")).

In principle a bank's exposure to different kinds of risks may be related either to the product markets or to the capital markets. This is displayed in Table 1 in which different kinds of

Table 1. Risk exposures of banks in terms of product and capital market risks

Product market risks	Capital market risks
• Credit	• Interest rate
• Strategic	• Liquidity
• Regulatory	• Currency
• Operating	• Settlement
• Commodity	• Basis
• Human resources	
• Legal	
• Product	

banking risks have been categorized as examples of either product market risk or capital market risk.

Product market risks concern mainly operating revenues and expenses and are attributed accordingly to the profit and loss statement of the bank. However, it should neither be a question of only considering the financial performance for the current year nor only accounting measures. "All too often, focusing on earnings creates a situation in which the long-term value of a firm is sacrificed in an effort to maximize short-term interest income" (Black, Brown, & Moloney, 2003, p. 32). The time horizon must be extended in order to capture the long-term exposure to risk. Clearly, the annual profits of a mortgage loan to a household customer, for example, remains nothing until the loan is fully refunded. As accounting measures are based to a large extent on historical performances, it is also important to consider the present value of expected future cash flows to reflect how the risk position taken by the bank will affect its economic (market) value. This goes for capital market risks, too.

Capital market risks concern borrowing and lending activities related to the balance sheet of the bank as well as its trading and various commitments in the form of off-balance sheet activities. Together these on- and off-balance sheet activities will affect the true asset and liability positions taken by the bank, which are disclosed if market values are used. That generates implications for its asset and liability management (ALM) activities. "Traditional ALM methods have typically over-emphasized short-term gains, based on static, partial views of the balance sheet that fail to account for the risks associated with future changes in market value" (Black et al., 2003, p. 32).

General Purposes for Risk Management in Banking

Risk management is a dynamic process. The rapid progress in technology is constantly affecting existing internal processes and systems. Business units and divisions are frequently reorganized, merged, acquired, and/or sold. In particular, the ever-changing financial environment is dynamic, as well. New financial products and services are developed, offered, and executed to new and old customers in a never-ceasing stream. Moreover, as is put forward by for example, Pyle (1997), banking operations are subjected to a changing regulation in form of new capital adequacy requirements. "Banks and similar institutions need to meet forthcoming regulatory requirements for risk measurement and capital" (Pyle, 1997, p. 2). However, he has been careful to acknowledge the importance of satisfying managers' need for adequate internal risk measures for allocating capital to the most risk-rewarding business operations from a bank perspective.

Thus, risk management in banking concerns the principles and procedures for discovering, estimating, and evaluating the bank's exposures to product and capital market risks and for controlling and managing those exposures properly in accordance with internal and external demands. This is repeatedly stressed by financial analysts. "Given the central role of market and credit risk in its core business, a financial institution's success requires that it be able to identify, assess, monitor and manage these risks in a sound and sophisticated way" (Rowe, Jovic & Reeves, 2004, p. 15).

Seen from a corporate governance perspective, risk management in banking should encourage and facilitate decisions and activities in the bank that create shareholder value. Considering the regulatory framework for banking operations, a bank's risk management activities ought to be founded upon two general purposes:

1. To assist management and employees to operate efficiently in a risky environment
2. To keep the operations of the bank in compliance with government regulations

The first general purpose concerns which principles and procedures should be implemented from a financial business perspective. Procedures are very much a question of "best practice," that is, implementing adequate techniques, tools, and organizational solutions to support business decisions in accordance with the principles adopted by the bank. Hence, the principles that would be most beneficial for the financial performance of the bank in terms of sustainable growth and profitability in a risky environment should govern the implementation of appropriate procedures. As risk is generally two-sided (with the exception of some operational risks), having both an upside and a downside, it is essential to balance continuously the trade off between risk and return. This may be regarded as an overall financial objective for the bank to accomplish an efficient approach to risk management. Other important financial principles for risk management are related to the skill of obtaining good ratings, protecting the business from being seriously hit by unfavourable events, minimizing risk exposures, assigning equity capital, absorbing unexpected losses, improving and rationalizing internal processes, and complying with regulatory requirements. That leads us to the second general purpose for risk management.

The second general purpose concerns how to comply with government regulations in the best way. This purpose has always been an evident and most natural condition for the (risk) management of banks. The regulatory framework is very much an integrative part of banking. This fact has been further accentuated in the comprehensive work that for a number of years was conducted by the Basel Committee on Banking Supervision, in order to revise and develop the current international regulatory standards governing the capital adequacy of banks. Such standards are important for the maintaining of a "fair" competition between banks, in general, and among internationally operating banks, in particular. However, these standards are also vital for the overall efficiency and robustness of the financial system and for many single bank stakeholders as these standards affect the risk exposure and solvency of targeted institutions. The outcome of the committee's work (the Basel II Accord) may be seen as a major step forward to making international regulatory capital requirements more in accordance with "economic capital," that is, the true amount of capital required to absorb unexpected losses due to risk exposures. However, the new accord implies a tighter and more detailed supervision with far-reaching (cost) implications for the risk management procedures adopted by banks (cf. Herring, 2005). It includes a number of novel innovations that will be discussed in some more detail later in this chapter.

Procedures Leading to an Efficient Management of Banking Risks

As for businesses, in general, banks must take on risks in order to achieve returns. That also forms the basis for the leading principle of efficient banking: to optimize the trade off between returns and risks. Then, a set of procedures may be used to balance risk and return, like gap management, duration analysis, and value at risk. Unfortunately, there is no single leading procedure for managing all kinds of banking risks as the nature of these risks may differ substantially depending on the type of business transaction. The bank "must choose tools and techniques appropriate for particular risk elements" (Cooper, 2000, p. 18). At the same time, it is important to realize that a specific risk is seldom fully independent of other risks. Rather, there are interdependencies that may either increase or decrease an aggregate risk exposure of the bank. That is obvious when it comes to the financial risk management. However, relationships also may exist between operational risks and financial risks, which is indicated by the classification in Table 1 into product market and capital market risks. This calls for an integrated risk analysis procedure at different organizational levels or business lines where such relationships among individual risks might arise. The existence and importance of these relations may be discovered and analyzed, either by using simulation and regression models, emphasizing "expected losses," or through scenario-based methods like "stress-testing" models that concern effects and severity of "unexpected losses."

When examining risk management procedures in U.S. banks, Drzik (2005) arrived to the conclusion that over the past 15 years these banks have significantly strengthened their ability to measure and quantify financial risks. They have made large investments in order to adopt new methods and procedures to improve their approach to credit risk management, in particular, but also to the management of market and interest rate risks. "Most banks introduced portfolio management disciplines, as they increasingly recognized the risk impact of geographic and industry concentrations and began to move away from the traditional 'buy and hold' approach to credit origination and ownership" (Drzik, 2005, p. 27). Despite these improvements, the author is careful to emphasize that there are still several major challenges left for the banks to take on in the risk management area:

- A first challenge concerns the assessment of operational risks. Unlike financial risks, these risks are generally "unknown" to banks in terms of frequencies, loss probabilities, and the severity of losses. High priority therefore should be given to the development of risk measurement techniques that solve this problem.
- A second challenge is to (further) integrate the risk management into the bank strategy. Modern risk management should not be a 'passive' device supporting only decision makers, but rather it should lead and guide business decisions in order to achieve the best possible risk-return trade off for each business transaction.
- A third important challenge is to make the bank's risk profile more transparent to external stakeholders as this has implications for market evaluations of the bank as well as for its credit ratings. Hence, in order to attract potential investors, banks ought to be proactive instead of reactive, passively awaiting new statutes and acts imposed by regulators and legislators as a response to, for example, "scandals" like the Enron debacle.

- A fourth challenge is directed towards banks' internal governance of human resources. The "mantra" and leading principle of (financial) risk management to always focus on risk-return trade offs for business transactions should permeate through the employees in the organization. For this reason, the author proposes changes in the way banks are managing and rewarding human resources. "Making risk management a strong participant in setting compensation policy and levels will be a controversial, but probably necessary step toward creating the much-desired organization-wide 'risk culture'" (Drzik, 2005, p. 36).

Clearly, risk management of a bank will never work properly—regardless of the degree of sophistication—without a thorough implementation into all levels of the organization. It is essential that risk management procedures and related activities are well organized and structured. Modern risk management is not a one person job for some chief credit officer (CCO) at the middle management level. It concerns the top management and the lower levels, too. Based on his experience as group general manager for risk management at ANZ (a major banking group in Australia and New Zealand), Kupper (1999) emphasizes the importance of implementing a consistent risk culture into all levels of the organization. Such a risk culture includes communication of risk management principles, development and maintenance of core risk management expertise at different business areas, as well as procedures for controlling and monitoring the adherence to leading principles. "Risk management is a business responsibility and should not be delegated entirely to a support function" (Kupper, 1999, p. 33). Today, this is realized by many banks appointing a chief risk officer (CRO) with responsibility and accountability for a much extended operation area. "CROs are typically responsible for virtually all types of risks that banks face, are frequently key participants in their institutions' strategic planning process, and often report directly to the president, chief executive officer (CEO), or even the board" (Drzik, 2005, p. 27).

In Table 2 we have distinguished six central steps to an efficient risk management approach for banks.

To define principles that should govern the implementation of procedures and the decisions to be taken in a risky environment is essential for a successful approach to risk management in banking. It requires that these principles are clearly communicated to the key decision makers in central business lines and at different organizational levels of the bank. Evidently, this also allows for making decisions in accordance with the "second challenge" stated by Drzik (2005): "to maximize the trade-off between risk and return for each business transaction".

Table 2. Steps to efficient risk management in banking

1.	Decide and declare overall goals in terms of risk and return.	(Define principles))
2.	Detect and distinguish exposures to risk in business lines.	(Identify risks)
3.	Explore and estimate financial consequences of exposures.	(Assess risks)
4.	Determine adequate measures and establish accountability.	(Manage risks)
5.	Control development of exposures and financial performance.	(Monitor risks)
6.	Review and examine consistency of principles and procedures.	(Evaluate risk management)

As has already been pointed out, the leading principle from a shareholder perspective is to set an objective in terms of a desired trade off between risk and return. This desire, of course, must be reachable within the existing regulatory framework. However, there are banks that emphasize other goals. Certain banks put a priority to an objective of growth. Usually, they do so by expanding the volumes of customer credits. An obvious problem with this approach is that such an expansion often results in the bank finding itself obtaining riskier and riskier customers. Many commercial banks have consequently failed when adopting such an objective. Those are banks that seldom have any risk management strategy.

Other banks stress profitability together with a low risk strategy ahead of growth. For them, customer deposits may be given a much higher priority than customer credits. Here we often find smaller savings banks, which remain small (but less risky). Having no shareholders, they operate in the interest of their major stakeholders, such as depositors. These banks are putting special attention to their "service efficiency" (Bergendahl & Lindblom, 2003). Their leading principle for risk management is often simply to avoid huge exposures to risk.

In addition to these examples of objectives used in practice, there is also empirical evidence of banks that are successful in having both a high growth and a high profitability. Nordea appears to be such an example. Its approach to risk management will be demonstrated below.

To identify risks is the next key step towards an efficient risk management framework. It is important to be aware of and constantly detect significant risks assumed—the earlier such risks are discovered and identified the better the opportunities are for taking adequate actions. This kind of information may give input to a more accurate pricing of products and services but will also give a most valuable insight into what kind of events that might seriously damage the financial performance of the bank.

At this step the basic procedure is twofold:

1. Define a set of possible future contingencies, in terms of "states." Such a state or scenario is a possible history of the economy over a given period.
2 Use a decision-tree technique to identify exposures to risk that thereafter may be assessed in the third key step to efficient risk management.

This kind of analysis is often "reactive." It may be initiated by a large financial engagement of the bank, like a huge credit to a commercial customer, a substantial portfolio of credits in some region or specific industry, or a significant trading position on the financial market. However, in line with the experiences given by Dedman and Robert-Tissot (2001), a previous loss area also may be a "trigger" to undertake an analysis, particularly when it comes to the identifying of operational risks. According to these authors, "the same basic causes tend to recur time and again" (Dedman & Robert-Tissot, 2001). They, therefore, recommend an extended review of previous losses and claims, not only within the bank itself, but also within per banks. With this kind of a more "proactive" approach, vulnerable areas with exposure to risk may be identified at the outset of each business transaction.

To assess risks accurately is a science by itself. The quantitative measurement of risks is the heart of risk management. Today there exists a bulk of sophisticated statistical models to estimate and to measure risk exposures and their corresponding economic consequences for banks. In modern risk management, such models are generally forward looking, aiming at capturing the volatility or variation of a target variable like profits, market value, credit losses, and so forth. Bessis (2002) groups quantitative indicators into three categories:

1. Sensitivity to changes in movements of market parameters (e.g., duration gap analysis)
2. Volatility of target or other random variables (captures the "magnitude" of variations around the average or expected value and is a basis for various statistical models when risk is "two-sided," e.g., credit portfolio analysis)
3. Down-side risk measures to capture the adverse deviations only (e.g,. a value-at-risk analysis)

Credit risks and interest rate risks seldom follow each other. Consequently, banks may not rely upon the same instruments to measure the corresponding exposures. Rating models and scoring models are mainly used to explore and measure the exposure to credit risks, while value-at-risk (VaR) and duration gap analysis are used for determining interest rate risks.

For purpose of illustration, let us consider an example of a fictitious and simple bank with the amount of assets and liabilities displayed in Table 3.

The bank's duration on equity is obviously 21 years ((400·4+400·2–400·0–300·1)/100). If the market rate changes from 5% to 6%, the loss on equity will become: 21/(1+0.05) percent or approximately $20 billion. Such a bank is extremely vulnerable to an increase in the market rate. Furthermore, if simultaneously the credit losses rise to a level of 5% or 0.05*400 = 20bn USD, such a bank must operate with extremely high margins to survive. It is forced to balance high risks with high returns. Very few banks (if any) are successful with such "balancing acts."

As declared by Kupper (1999), traditional methods of assessing risks may sometimes fail due to "unexpected" exceptional moves and changes in markets or risk relationships. Under such adverse conditions, the conventional wisdom is no longer valid. "To develop an understanding of what might happen under extreme circumstances, banks need to adopt a stress-testing regime that systematically analyses the impact of different scenarios on their earnings" (Kupper, 1999, p. 28).

To manage risk concerns measures and actions taken by the decision makers to ensure that the identified and assessed exposures to risk are implemented accurately, that is, in accordance with the principles adopted by the bank. However, in this case, these risks are associated with very high sensitivity or volatility in returns; limits may be set on the level

Table 3. An example of a duration gap analysis

		Amount (bn USD)	Duration (yrs)
Assets	Bonds	400	4
	Customer credits	400	2
Liabilities	Customer deposits	400	0
	Fixed-rate deposits	300	1
Equity		100	

of the bank's exposure to the risks in order to avoid severe losses. The bank may then either add a constraint, stipulating a maximum exposure to a particular risk or specify a specific objective that aims at minimizing its exposure to the risk, given a certain acceptable return. This is evident in a case of a down-side risk, which is typical for many types of operational risks. As was accentuated by Drzik (2005), the management of operational risks may be far from easy due to the lack of reliable statistics. Taking up his "first challenge" to design more appropriate procedures for managing operational risks, important questions to be answered are then:

1. Shall the bank avoid exposures when both the probability of loss and the severity of loss are high?
2. Shall the bank engage itself in loss prevention and loss reduction actions?
3. Shall the bank insure risks when the chance of loss is low, but the severity is high?

A special focus also may be set on the managing of certain financial risks, such as foreign risks associated with exchange rate changes or unexpected interventions by a foreign government. A certain concern must then be devoted to risk financing arrangements and practices (especially insurance solutions), which vary throughout the world. These actions mainly should be associated with instruments that are available for risk reduction, such as swaps, options, futures, and forwards.

At this step, accountability must be established. The allocation of responsibility is indeed essential for the quality of decisions made and, thus, the accuracy of measures taken to manage risks. Decision makers confronting an exposure to risk should be given adequate tools and incentives to take decisive actions. Kupper (1999) prudentially puts forward the following statement: "individual lines of business are best placed to manage the risk of their activities" (p. 31).

To monitor risks thoroughly and (almost) continuously, of course, is vital for how well risk exposures are being managed in the bank. This step includes the examining of the actual performance of decision makers that are responsible for risk exposures being dealt with in accordance with stipulated objectives. Thus, it is a more or less continuously running ex-post examination of the extent to which the adopted principles and procedures governing the exposure to risks are efficient and adhered to, making corrections or adjustments of both the measures applied and the objectives adopted by decision makers. Considering the "fourth challenge" emphasized by Drzik (2005), the performance of "accountable" decision makers should be examined rather frequently as an important part of the bank's compensation policy.

To evaluate risk management is the final central step towards obtaining consistency between the general principles and the procedures adopted by the bank. This kind of overall re-evaluation is important as it gives valuable feedback to management with strategic implications. Particular emphasis should be put on the following issues and questions:

1. **Efficiency:** Does the current risk management approach give accurate incentives for obtaining an appropriate balance between loss prevention, risk assumption, insurance and hedging?
2. **Safety and environmental:** Follow up regulations and contractual warranties and provisions. Is there any conflict of interest vis-à-vis the current regulatory framework?
3. **Follow up:** Control that the risk management principles and procedures chosen are implemented accurately.

This review and examination has to be conducted regularly (preferably on an annual basis) on the initiative of the board of the bank. In line with the "the third challenge" expressed by Drzik (2005), there is, of course, an opportunity for bank management to act proactively by utilizing this evaluation to disclose and visualize the risk profile of the bank to its external stakeholders.

Implications of the New Basel Accord for Risk Management in Banking

The Basel II Accord rests on three fundaments, referred to as "pillars" (BIS, 2004). The first pillar defines criteria and approaches for determining minimum capital requirements in internationally operating banks with regard to three types of risks—credit, market, and operational. The second pillar specifies a supervisory review process for ensuring the quality of individual banks' approaches to assessing risk and establishing capital needs accordingly. Finally, the third pillar introduces market discipline to reinforce regulatory capital standards and review processes by setting out a number of requirements on banks to publicly disclosure central quantitative, as well as qualitative features of the risk management principles and procedures the bank applies. It thus seems as if banks will be more or less forced to take on the "third challenge" highlighted by Dzrik (2005).

This new regulatory framework is an extensive revision of the current Basel Accord (including an amendment concerning market risk). It is revised almost beyond recognition. Both the supervisory review process pillar and the market discipline pillar are new interesting inventions, making the opinions of external regulators and market forces more important for the safety and stability of financial systems as well as for the risk management principles and procedures adopted by banks. This puts pressure on individual banks to develop risk management procedures, to educate personnel, and to recruit new qualified staff members. Regulators must have access to very skilled analysts, too. This may give rise to a potential problem as the most skilled analysts will be very attractive recruiting targets for large banks.

Table 4 presents a comparison between the current Basel Accord and the new accord in terms of fundamental differences.

Table 4. Fundamental differences between Basel I and Basel II accords

Basel I Accord	Basel II Accord
Focus on a single risk measure (stipulated by the regulator)	Emphasis on the supervisory review process and market discipline: banks may use their own internal methodologies
One-size-fits all: only one approach for determining regulatory capital required	Flexibility: several approaches available => incentives for better risk management
Broad brush structure	Increased risk sensitivity

Source: Based on Bessis (2002).

The first pillar in the new accord is sharing some of the features of the current accord, albeit very few. The definitions of qualified capital in Tier I and II as well as the risk-weighted capital ratio coefficient of 8% are still left, but the way to determine and to calculate risk weights has been radically changed. Whereas the old accord assigns uniform risk weights on credits related to the type of institution concerned, the modified "standardized approach" proposed by the new accord is far more fine tuned when it comes to risk classification. Instead of institution type, it focuses on public credit ratings, aiming at assessing the underlying risk more accurately. However, the new accord does not only propose this standardized approach for assessing credit risk. A bank may qualify for using one of two proposed "internal ratings-based approaches," that is, either the "foundation" or the "advanced" approach. The former approach lets the bank use its own input figures for the probability of default of lenders, whereas the latter one leaves more of the risk assessment to the bank itself. The incentive for banks to try to qualify for a more sophisticated approach is that the more advanced approach in use, involving internal databases and models, the lower the regulatory capital requirements relative to banks using a less advanced approach. In order to qualify for using a more advanced method, however, the bank must fulfil a number of requirements under the second pillar, including the conducting of stress-testing analyses and risk-adjusted performance measurements for different business activities (Rowe et al., 2004).

Regardless of the approach chosen, the new accord should lead to a much better correspondence between regulatory capital and economic capital than today (Caruna, 2005). The use of the advanced internal ratings-based approach, of course, should work best in this respect. This might be an attractive incentive for larger banks to choose t and, at the same time, strengthen their approach to risk management. In that respect the new accord is also good for the financial system. It is no secret that differences between the regulatory capital and economic capital opens up the door for arbitrage activities commonly referred to as "regulatory capital arbitrage" (Calem & LaCour-Little, 2004; Jones, 2000; Rowe et al., 2004) Under the current regulatory regime (Basel I Accord), many banks seem to routinely use securitization and other financial "innovations" in order to reduce the capital needed to comply with regulatory requirements without taking on any additional risk exposure of significance. Aparicio and Keskiner (2004) give an example of one such innovation: "The Accord had loopholes as well—since it did not require any regulatory capital for credit agreements with a term of less than one year, several institutions initiated the '364-day facility' under which the banks committed to lending for only 364 days, with the facility being continuously rolled over" (p. 5).

Although the implementation of the Basel II Accord will substantially reduce opportunities for regulatory capital arbitrage, the creativity within banks to "get round" regulatory requirements should never be underestimated. The new accord will not completely close the gap between regulatory and economic capital. This is, of course, obvious in the case of a bank that chooses or is obliged to use the "standardized" approach, which is not fine tuned enough. Even if it uses the alternative "internal ratings-based" approach differences might arise because of the impact of geographic diversification on the portfolio's credit risk (Calem & LaCour-Little, 2004). The fact that the new accord also requires that banks set aside regulatory capital to account for operational risk may give rise to discrepancies as such risks are difficult to measure in practice. Just as for the assessment of credit risks, the accord proposes simpler "external-based" as well as more sophisticated "internal-based" approaches to determine how much capital to set aside. The simpler approaches set the focus on either the aggregated operational risk exposure of the bank in terms of a fixed percentage (based on statistical analysis of all banks) of its total gross income (the "basic indicator approach") or the operational risk exposures of eight prespecified business lines of the bank (the "standardized approach"). In accordance with its predefined risk profile, each business line is charged a "risk weighted" percentage of its gross income, summing up to a total charge for the operational risk of the whole bank. Evidently, the accuracy of the operational risk charge will depend on how much or how little the bank differentiates itself from an "average" bank. In this respect, the charges on banks that qualify for using an internal-based approach (i.e., the "advanced measurement approach") should be in more accordance with the true risk profile of the bank in regards to operational risk exposure.

While some researchers and analysts seem to accept the extension of regulatory capital to account for operational risk (e.g., Rowe et al., 2004), others strongly question it (e.g., Herring, 2002): "It is by no means clear that capital regulation is the most efficient means of achieving a reduction in the exposure of institutions operational risk" (Herring, 2002, p. 7). In times of recession in the general economy, Herring (2005) argues that Basel II in fact might worsen the situation by amplifying banks tendency to act procyclically. The opposite is likely to occur in a recovery.

Hudson (2003) goes even further by raising the question whether the Basel II Accord as such will mean the end of risk management. He stresses that banks will have to spend a lot of time in order to comply with the detailed requirements stipulated by the accord. He foresees a lot of efforts and resources needed for interpreting regulatory requirements, for implementing adequate procedures, and for providing public information. "There will be little time left over for innovation and creative development. A more risk-sensitive accord was what we wanted. Now that we have it, will it be worth the cost?" (Hudson, 2003, p. 35).

Risk Management in Nordea: A Brief Case Study

Above we have stressed that the main purposes for risk management in banks are: a) to assist management and employees to operate efficiently in a risky environment, and b) to keep these operations in compliance with government regulations. We will now investigate how a large Nordic banking group—Nordea—manages these risks.

Nordea is the outcome of a series of bank mergers in the Nordic countries. In 1997, the Finnish bank Merita merged with the Swedish bank Nordbanken and took the name of MeritaNordbanken. That formation also contained banks in three Baltic countries as well as a bank in Russia (the International Moscow Bank). In March 2000 there was a new merger between MeritaNordbanken and the Danish bank Unidanmark/Unibank. The outcome was a conglomerate called Nordic Baltic Holding (NBH).

In October 2000, NBH acquired the Norwegian bank Christiania Bank og Kreditkasse. As a consequence, NBH changed its name to Nordea, an abbreviation of "Nordic countries" and "new ideas." The new ideas were identified in terms of financial solutions that were t better for the customer, better than the competitors', and better than before. They would also be delivered at a lower cost and with a higher quality than before.

Later on Nordea acquired the Swedish payment organization Postgirot Bank as well as the Baltic and Polish banks LG Petro, Kredyt Bank, and Sampo Polska.

In 2002, Nordea arranged a "Capital Markets Day" to synchronize all its newly merged activities. At that occasion Nordea's CEO Lars G. Nordström announced four key messages for success. They were (1) to improve quality and reduce volatility of earnings, (2) to improve capital efficiency, (3) to maintain a stable credit quality, and (4) to improve cost-efficiency. Furthermore, he identified the following three key variables:

- Focus, that is to concentrate on the strength of the bank
- Speed, that is to be quick and flexible in operation and always adjust to market conditions
- Performance, that is to continuously improve the business operations of the bank

The risk management of the Nordea group will now be described and analyzed in detail by using the six steps to an efficient risk management approach presented in Table 2. Nordea has specified them as follows:

1. **Define purposes:** A main objective for Nordea is "to create value for shareholders, measured by a total shareholder return." As a consequence, Nordea "aims at an overall balanced risk-taking in order to enhance shareholder value." Economic profit is the interpretation and measure for such a value creation. That leads to a focus on income, costs, and risk. Economic capital is a measure of the amount of capital required. The less risk, the less need for economic capital. Accordingly, Nordea will focus on the economic capital needed for credit risk, market risk, life insurance risk, operational risk, and business risk (Nordea 2005). Steps to be taken are (Nordea, 2002):
    a. Development of existing credit scoring and rating models
    b. Price according to risk
    c. Further reduction of economic capital and noncore assets
    d. Maintain the capital ratio targets (Tier 1 ratio >6.5%)
2. **Identify risks:** Nordea's main focus is on credit risk, market risk (capital and product related), and operational risk. The credit risk originates from "various forms of

lending but also from guarantees and documentary credits" (Nordea, 2005, p. 21). It includes country risk and settlement risk, that is, the risk of losing the principal of a financial instrument. The market risk comes from movements in market variables, such as interest rates, foreign exchange rates, equity prices, and commodity prices. The operational risk is the risk of losses resulting from inadequate or failed internal processes, people, or systems.

3. **Assess risks:** Nordea focuses on rating and scoring in order to measure credit risks. Rating models are used for corporate customers and bank counterparts, while scoring models are applied to households and small customers. Three inputs are used to assess the "expected loss (EL)," namely the "probability of default (PD),", the "loss given default (LGD)," and the "exposure at default (EAD)," where EL = PD x LGD x EAD (Nordea, 2005). The credit risk exposure is then measured as the sum of the current exposure and the potential future exposure (Nordea 2005). Nordea determines the economic capital for credit risk with capital factors based on PD and LGD. At the end of 2004, the total credit risk exposure (after close-out netting) was estimated to a current exposure of 4.864 million EUR and a potential future exposure of 18.631 million EUR (Nordea, 2005).

   For Nordea, the market risks are given as the risk of losses in market value as a result of movements in interest rates, foreign exchange rates, equity prices, and commodity prices. The main exposures come from the investment portfolios. However, Nordea has observed that there is no single risk measure that captures all market risks. Consequently, Nordea applies VaR-models, stress testing, scenario simulation, basis point values, net open positions, and option key figures (Nordea, 2005).

4. **Manage risks:** Nordea uses risk mitigation techniques like close-out netting arrangements or agreements that give Nordea the option to terminate contracts at specific time periods. "The basic principle is that market risks are eliminated by matching assets, liabilities and off-balance-sheet items" (Nordea, 2005, p. 27). The board of directors has set the maximum level of risk on investment portfolios to the investment earnings of one quarter's normalized earnings. The board itself decides on limits for the market risks and the liquidity risks. The Asset and Liability Management Committee (ALCO) decides on financial operations and financial risks, including structural interest income risks (SIIR). The Risk Committee monitors the development of risk on an aggregate level.

   Operational risks are managed through a solid internal control and quality management. An annual report on the quality on internal control is delivered to the board (Nordea, 2005).

5. **Monitor risks:** The board's Executive Credit Committees (corporate and retail) are set to monitor the credit portfolio, including the major exposures from industry and major customers. Nordea has established an internal validation process in order to prove that the rating models, procedures, and systems are in accordance with the Basel II requirements.

6. **Evaluate risk management:** The new Basel accord has been set up to improve risk sensitivity. Nordea's economic capital (EC) framework is aligned with Basel II requirements and has resulted in the following re-evaluation of the program (Nordea, 2005):
    - Continuous work with the validation of rating and scoring models and the parameters PD, LGD, and EAD
    - Define the requirements for the future internal and external reporting as well as the future need for IT infrastructure

Summing up, the Nordea Group seems to follow in a powerful way the above listed steps for efficient risk management. For credit risks, Nordea is moving towards Basel's internal rating based approach (IRB) beginning in2007-08 and onwards. Substantial efforts and resources will be used "to close the gaps between the Group's EC framework and the anticipated IRB requirements of Basel II" (Nordea, 2005, p. 33). It seems evident that at Nordea profitability is given a larger weight than growth. On the other hand, the bank has been successful in emphasizing a high profitability, which has provided a basis for a large growth as well.

Conclusion

Today banks are facing many new challenges within the area of risk management. A common approach is that risk management in banking should encourage and facilitate (shareholder) value creating decisions and activities in all business lines. However, the risk environment of banks has changed dramatically in the past decade due to increasing globalization of financial markets and far-reaching innovation and development of financial products/instruments. Regulatory capital standards are being changed beyond recognition and with much tougher requirements for banks' approach to risk assessment. The new Basel accord emphasizes internal procedures to assess risks in the bank, regular supervisory reviews, and market discipline. Moreover, the new regulatory regime requires that banks set aside capital to capture unexpected losses due to their operational risk exposure. All these changes have implications for the future profitability and growth of banks. A bank's risk management is now a strategic issue at the top-management level.

In this chapter, we have stressed the importance for banks to adopt a sophisticated and well-structured approach to risk management, in order to operate more efficiently in the new risky environment. Such an approach involves both the procedures to discover and to estimate the extent of the bank's risk exposures and the principles for controlling and managing them properly. For risk management, we have distinguished two main purposes:

1. To assist management and employees to operate efficiently in a risky environment
2. To keep the operations of the bank in compliance with government regulations

The main and leading principle should be to optimize the trade off between risk and return, but the bank also must comply with new regulatory requirements. Then, a set of procedures may be used to balance risk and return in different banking operations. We have outlined the following six central steps to an efficient risk management in banking:

1. Define principles
2. Identify risks
3. Assess risks
4. Manage risks
5. Monitor risks
6. Evaluate risk management

We have demonstrated how to conduct in practice an analysis of a bank's risk management. We have shown that by using those steps on Nordea—a very successful commercial bank in Scandinavia, which has in the last five years had both high profitability and growth.

References

Aparicio, J., & Keskiner, E. (2004, May). *A review of operational risk quantitative methodologies within the BASEL-II framework* (Working Paper). France: Accenture Technology Labs.

Bergendahl, G. (1989). The management of assets and liabilities in banks. *Revue de la Banque*, 6.

Bergendahl, G., & Lindblom, T. (2003, September) *Evaluating the performance of Swedish savings banks according to service efficiency*. Paper presented at the European Association of University Teachers of Banking of Finance, Dublin, Ireland.[*To be published in European Journal of Operational Research.*]

Bessis, J. (2002). *Risk management in banking* (2nd ed.). Chichester, UK: Wiley.

BIS. (2004, June). *International convergence of capital measurement and capital standards: A revised framework*. Basel Committee on Bank Supervision, Bank for International Settlements.

Black, R., Brown, K., & Moloney, J. (2003). Asset and liability management: What dies the future have in store? *Balance Sheet, 11*(2), 32-38.

Calem, P., & LaCour-Little, M. (2004). Risk-based capital requirements for mortgage loans. *Journal of Banking and Finance, 28*(3), 647-672.

Caruna, J. (2005). Implementation of Basel II. *Financial Markets, Institutions and Instruments, 14*(5), 253-265.

Cooper, C. (2000). How good are banks at managing business risk? *Balance Sheet, 8*(1), 15-19.

Dedman, R., & Robert-Tissot, S. (2001). Risk management: Where banks fail. *Balance Sheet*, *9*(2), 16-19.

Desmukh, S. D., Greenbaum, S. I., & Kanatas, G. (1983). Interest rate uncertainty and the financial intermediary's choice of exposure. *Journal of Finance*, *38*(1), 141-147.

Drzik, J. (2005). New directions in risk management. *Journal of Financial Econometrics*, *3*(1), 26-36.

Gardener, E. P. M. (1987). *Interest rate risks and banks*. Bangor, UK: University College of North Wales.

Herring, R. (2002). *The Basel 2 approach to bank operational risk: Regulation on the wrong track*. (Working Paper). Philadelphia: The Wharton School, University of Pennsylvania.

Herring, R. (2005). Implementing Basel II: Is the game worth the candle? *Financial Markets, Institutions & Instruments*, *14*(5), 267-287.

Hudson, R. (2003). Dealing with Basel II: Basel II—The end of risk management? *Balance Sheet*, *1*(4), 32-35.

Jones, D. (2000). Emerging problems with the Basel Capital Accord: Regulatory capital arbitrage and related issues. *Journal of Banking and Finance*, *24*(1/2), 35-58.

Kupper, E. F. (1999). Risk management in banking. In *Risk and Capital Management Proceedings* (pp. 21-39). Australian Prudential Regulation Authority. Retrieved from http://www.apra.gov.au/RePEc/Home.cfm

Lindblom, T. (1993). Credit losses in Nordic banks. In J. Revell (Ed.), *The changing face of European banks and securities markets* (pp. 174-190). UK: Macmillan.

Nordea. (2002, November 18). *Capital markets day*. Stockholm.

Nordea. (2005). *Annual report*. Stockholm.

Pyle, D. H. (1997, May). *Bank risk management: Theory*. Paper presented at the Conference on Risk Management and Regulation in Banking, Jerusalem, Israel.

Riksbanken. (2005). *Separate minutes of the executive board meeting, No. 11*. Stockholm: Sveriges Riksbank.

Riksbanken. (2006). *Rosenberg: Some questions regarding current monetary policy* (Press Release).

Rowe, D., Jovic, D., & Reeves, R. (2004). The continuing saga—Basel II developments: Bank capital management in the light of Basel II—how to manage capital in financial institutions. *Balance Sheet*, *12*(3), 15-21.

Van Greuning, H. (2003). *Analyzing and managing banking risk: A framework for assessing corporate governance and financial risk*. Herndon, VA: World Bank Publications.

Chapter III

Developing Information Assurance Alignment in Financial Services

Jean-Noël Ezingeard, Kingston University London, UK

Elspeth McFadzean, Henley Management College, UK

David Birchall, Henley Management College, UK

Abstract

A number of recent high-profile organizational failures have been compounded by the inadequacy of the data, information, and intelligence available to decision makers at key moments. In several other cases, the interpretation and communication of information to key stakeholders later was seen to have been distorted, if not downright dishonest. Whilst executives are being required to pay more attention to aspects of information assurance (IA) and security, few understand how to ensure its proper management and how to develop an IA strategy.

Introduction

This chapter is based on research work in eight financial services organizations (four international financial services organizations, two national retail banks, and two multinational banks).

The first section explains why information assurance strategy needs to be aligned with corporate strategy. The arguments developed center on the risks of misalignment.

The second section explains why boards of directors in financial services need to take a strong interest in the development of their organization's IA strategy. It highlights three key drivers: risk assessment and/or risk reports—including legal requirements, such as Sarbanes-Oxley and Basel II, protection of shareholder value, and cost—and the need to keep IA costs under control whilst delivering a suitable level of protection for the organization's information. It also covers barriers to involvement of the board of directors, such as lack of familiarity with technical issues and general lack of awareness and understanding.

An important aspect of ensuring that an IA strategy meets the aims and objectives of the business is the need to understand the requirements of the stakeholders. In the financial services industry, these requirements are significant. This section presents a model of both external stakeholder requirements and internal stakeholder requirements.

The section concludes by explaining how these requirements can be reconciled when they are in conflict.

The last section presents five IA trade offs that need to be resolved during the IA strategy development process, once the stakeholder requirements are understood. Each trade off is illustrated with examples from financial services.

Developing an information assurance (IA) strategy is fraught with difficulties. One of the toughest challenges faced by organizations in financial services is to ensure a good level of alignment between their IA efforts and their business strategy. Whilst most financial services organizations recognize the importance of protecting their information assets, this is not always being matched by an increased strategic approach to IA. In many organizations, there is a lack of alignment between IA policies and corporate strategy (Deloitte Touche Tohmatsu, 2003).

This stems from three reasons. Firstly, it is difficult to ensure adequate communication among all the functions of the business involved with developing the IA efforts and those in charge of the overall strategic direction of the organization. Business strategists and IA specialists lack a common understanding, resulting in limited dialogue and inadequate definitions of what constitutes successful performance for IA issues (Birchall, Ezingeard, &McFadzean, 2003). Secondly, whilst most business strategies are concerned with growth, innovation, and enterprise, most IA strategies are concerned with ensuring that processes and procedures are followed and that risks are managed. They are, therefore, often associated with rigidity and seen to conflict with business objectives. Thirdly, even if the IA strategy is developed in a way that ensures its alignment with business strategy, communicating the IA strategy is a difficult exercise.

This chapter is built on research work we undertook in eight financial services organizations based in Europe (four international financial services organizations, two national retail banks, and two multinational banks). The chapter focuses on IA strategy in financial services and discusses three questions:

- How can senior executives align IA strategy with corporate strategy?
- What are the dilemmas that need to be resolved during the alignment process?
- What factors influence their decisions regarding IA strategy?

Background

The Importance of Alignment

The lack of alignment between many operational IA interventions and business strategy is of increasing concern to IA experts. In particular, the lack of alignment between business strategy and IA technology is seen as one of the biggest causes of IA project failure (Deloitte, 2005). Too often IA projects are seen by nonspecialists as not responding to a business need, or as not sufficiently driven by a strategic imperative. This is compounded by the lack of involvement of the IA function in many business initiatives. For instance, a recent survey showed that fewer than half of organizations involved their information security function in major strategic initiatives, such as service enhancement or product launch (Ernst & Young, 2005).

The idea has its origins in the concept of strategic fit, popularized by Peters in the 1980s, who argued that success was driven by congruence among seven elements—strategy, structure, systems, style, staff, shared values, and skills—(Peters & Waterman, 1982). The idea is linked to Miller's view that it is how the "whole" is organized that leads to success (Miller, 1981)—a school of thinking later called the configuration school (Miller, 1987). There is reasonable consensus amongst business strategy specialists that strategic alignment leads to superior performance.

In the field of information systems (ISs), there are many studies that confirm that alignment is important to business success (Bergeron, Raymond, & Rivard, 2004) and information technology (IT) success (Sabherwal & Kirs, 1994). For instance, Chan, Huff, Barclay, and Copeland(1997) show that alignment of IS strategy and business strategy is a component of business performance. The same research also reported that alignment between IS strategy and business strategy is a better indicator of business performance, than IS strategic orientation itself—implying that "best practice" applied indiscriminately to business needs does not automatically lead to beneficial results. Other studies have illustrated that lack of alignment could result in significant (and costly) IS failures (Sauer, Dampney, & Southon, 1997).

Alignment Challenges

In discussing alignment in financial services organizations in Europe, we came across five alignment challenges (illustrated in Box 1). The first two challenges are linked with communication: engaging the board and silos. Communication is essential in order to achieve a shared understanding of IA requirements among the managers in charge of designing and implementing IA, those in charge of other business functions, and those in charge of corporate governance in the organization. Two other challenges are concerned with tensions caused by external requirements (auditing in one case and IA standards in the other). Many external stakeholders will propose fairly normative requirements for the IA practices of financial organizations. Such requirements may actually conflict with the strategic objectives of the business, and the tension will need to be resolved. The fifth challenge is concerned with values and culture that can at times also conflict with IA requirements.

How Can We Achieve Better Alignment?

The Three Pillars of the Alignment Process

Strategic fit is primarily about identifying the elements that need to be aligned. Moreover, it is about understanding how this alignment should be achieved. This led strategy gurus to define fit as *process* (how to achieve fit) and *content* (what fit looks like) (Venkatraman & Camillus, 1984). More specifically, when looking at process, two further aspects need to be considered (Reich & Benbasat, 2000). Firstly, the strategic planning process itself needs to be considered (in the case of IA this would be how the IA strategy is put together, and how it influences business strategy). Secondly, social relationships in the organization need to be examined. In practice, this means that there are three essential pillars:

- **The involvement of the board:** This includes in approving the IA strategy and how the authority for areas, such as risk and resource management, conflict resolution, and responsibility for IA is shared throughout the organization. The Board of directors must support both the plan for IA and its alignment to corporate strategy. Lack of support can increase uncertainty and ambiguity regarding the organization's strategic goals.
- **A shared understanding of external stakeholders' requirements:** Too often, and particularly so in financial services, IA strategies are driven by external pressures, such as Sarbanes-Oxley (ITGI, 2003; Economist, 2004) or the Capital Requirements Directive. Whilst it is vital that organizations in financial services should be compliant with the regulations that apply to them, our research shows that good practice also can be found in areas other than the traditional sources. Therefore, a mechanism needs to be in place to capture the views of a wide range of groups both inside and outside the organization.
- **Overcoming internal tensions:** Alignment is based on strategic fit and functional integration. Thus, relationships within the organization and communication among

Box 1. Five Cases of alignment challenge (First published in Birchall, Ezingeard, McFadzean, Howlin, & Yoxall, 2004)

Alignment challenge 1: Engaging the board

Bank 1, one of the largest in the UK, has a large retail presence as well as many other business units and subsidiaries. It is governed using a federal philosophy, with each business unit operating largely autonomously. According to one of its IA specialists, the bank's board is only "waking up" to the IA challenge and needs to identify the right questions to ask. This is a significant challenge, since many of the bank's business units pursue very different commercial strategies. In its desire to maintain the federal philosophy, the board has traditionally relied on exception reporting in dealing with IA matters—waiting to be alerted to unsatisfactory IS issues through the bank's control committee structure. This challenge is compounded by the perception, at the board level, that IA reporting had been too technically oriented in the past. Ensuring that IA goes beyond exception reporting will require the board's full engagement as, at first sight, it might require more central control, which is against the stated business strategy.

Alignment challenge 2: Silos

Bank 2 operates mainly in the UK, where it has a large High Street presence. Because of its history, the bank has a tradition of working in silos with different sections of the business looking after different products, almost independently. Information and knowledge have not traditionally been shared between these silos. The bank now has a strategy of moving away from silos to create "one" organization—but some managers feel IA gets in the way. Information security concerns are quoted as an excuse not to share information across the existing silos.

Alignment challenge 3: Meeting audit requirements

Bank 3 is one of the largest retail banks in Germany. As a cornerstone of its strategy, the bank has outsourced most of its information systems functions. As a result, a large part of IA is carried out through the annual internal control audits, rather than by the internal IT function. This policy was put in place to ensure that sufficient controls were kept internally, while IT was being outsourced. The audit reports regularly question the bank's outsourcing strategy from an IA point of view. They are often critical of the IA risks taken by outsourcing IT. Outsourcing, therefore, has become a significant IA alignment challenge for the bank, with the outsourcing strategy going against internal IA recommendations.

Alignment challenge 4: External influences

Bank 5 is one of the largest European banks, with a significant retail and investment banking presence across Europe and the rest of the world. On one side, the IA function at the bank has developed policies and procedures based on industry standard best practices. Aligning these policies and procedures with business strategy is not formally looked at. Here, IA is not necessarily in conflict with business strategy, but there is a risk that it might become so. Industry standard IA best practices may not be appropriate for the bank, its business strategy, and organizational ethos.

Alignment challenge 5: Values and culture

Bank 4 is a medium-sized retail bank, which operates only in the UK where it is a niche player. Its business strategy places strong emphasis on empowering its staff to deliver the highest levels of customer service. In the words of its CEO, the bank is "driven by values, not procedures." Directors have reflected hard on how the strategic importance placed on empowerment could be maintained, while still maintaining good levels of IA. They have opted for an IA strategy that stresses that IA is not about top-down control and procedures. Ensuring alignment between IA strategy and business strategy leaves the bank no choice—it needs to ensure that its employees feel empowered on IA matters, also.

different areas and levels are important in enabling alignment. Managers in three areas (internal control, ISs, and asset management) must develop mutually supportive, shared goals and an understanding of the business as a whole.

These three elements are discussed below.

The Necessity for Board Involvement

Our research clearly shows that boards of directors in financial services need to take a strong interest in the development of their organization's IA strategy. There are three drivers for this: compliance, protection of shareholder value, and cost.

Compliance issues—including legal requirements such as Sarbanes-Oxley and the *Basel II* Accord (implemented in Europe under the Capital Requirements Directive)—are weighing strongly on the minds of boards of directors. Such requirements make it a board responsibility to ensure that the risk management processes of the organization are compliant. Risk can only be managed through adequate provision of risk management information and the management of information security-related risk itself (often treated under operational risk in most financial services regulations). This, in turn, makes it necessary for boards to pay particular attention to how IA is handled.

Our research in financial services organizations in Europe suggests that compliance is an area where board involvement with IA strategy development, implementation, or monitoring does take place. This is, in fact, the most common area of influence, where because of its responsibilities for the management of risk and its reporting to shareholders, the board requests appropriate information from those responsible for risk at lower levels in the organization. It is also because of this responsibility for the overseeing of the risk management processes that many boards in the organizations we interviewed involved themselves in approving policies and procedures for IA. Board support was sought for IA policies (such as the guidelines for acceptable use of computers) because it gave these issues greater authority.

The second driver for board involvement is the protection of shareholder value. As the market capitalization of most companies now far exceeds their book asset value, the board has a responsibility to protect intangible assets, such as brand value and intellectual capital. There is also a decreasing tolerance by customers for publicized security breaches (DTI, 2004; Treanor, 2000). Hence, Dutta and McCrohan (2002) strongly suggest information security concerns should rise to the highest levels of the organization. If customers migrate because of the inconvenience or the risk of failing computer systems, stability, and reliability become competitive drivers, particularly in the light of growing consumer concern for information privacy (Culnan & Armstrong, 1999; Swartz, 2003; Tweney, 1998).

In addition, research has shown that there is a strong correlation between companies that admit to breaches occurring within their confidential ISs and a reduction in their stock market price (Campbell, Gordon, Loeb, & Zhou, 2003; Ettredge & Richardson, 2003). Thus, IA must become a concern from a board perspective (NACD, 2001; Von Solms, 2001). Our own research in Europe found that the protection of shareholder value was an influence on IA practice in some of the organizations interviewed but by no means all. Our interpretation of this lack of realization regarding the link between shareholder value and IA is that the potential for IA to deliver competitive advantage has not yet been included on the agenda of those responsible for the overall strategic direction.

Last, but not least, the need to keep IA costs under control, whilst delivering a suitable level of protection for the organization's information, is an important factor for boards to take into account. As the board oversees capital expenditure, it will, either directly or indirectly, influence IA strategy and practice. This can be by providing hurdled rates of return that have to be passed by all project proposals—including IA projects—or taking an interest in the ROI equation for IA investments. In the words of one of our interviewees discussing his board's attitude to IA investments:

They want hard and fast measures; they want to know what contributes to the bottom line ... if you can't prove that it's going to result in growth and revenue, or a big profit ... then of course they're not interested.

Although few in number, these three levels of influence clearly represent an opportunity for aligning business objectives and IA objectives, since it is the board that has an overall view of the organization's strategy and direction. However, our interviewees also cited two weaknesses regarding board engagement with IA.

- **Lack of familiarity with technical issues:** While IA discussions may be restricted at board level because of perceptions of its technicality, most interviewees agreed that IA is not just a technical issue but is still perceived as such by many boards. Some interviewees in an IA function used terms like "I am trying" to describe their efforts to convince board members to take a greater interest in IA issues and their attempts to convince them that IA was not a technical matter. Breaking this barrier down at the board level was seen by one interviewee (responsible for IA in a multinational bank) as key to achieving alignment. In her words:

  You have to talk more of the business security aspect and align it with [IA] policies and directives.

- **General lack of awareness and understanding:** This was a recurrent theme in interviews. There is a recognized danger that board members will fail to see the importance of IA in the organization. As boards have significant influence over implementation success and, by definition, a good understanding of the strategic direction of the organization, they can be the first point at which alignment is achieved or fails.

Board-level engagement clearly should be limited to the strategic issues, but by focusing on the three levels of engagement, greater alignment between business strategy and IA strategy should result.

A Shared Understanding of External Stakeholders' Requirements

The need to understand the requirements of external stakeholders is an important aspect of ensuring that an IA strategy meets the aims and objectives of the business. In the financial services industry, these requirements are significant not only because of heavy national and transnational regulations but also because financial services organizations are constantly in the public eye. Concerns such as the security of customers' financial assets or the risk of fraudulent activity can stir tremendous media hype. The table below identifies 10 key stakeholders that were deemed to be significant by respondents in our research, as well as some specific issues linked with these stakeholders.

Table 1. Understanding the influence of external stakeholders on IA policy development

Stakeholder	Requirements	Issues
IA certification bodies and other professional associations	IA bodies are the main initiators of best practice guidelines, methodologies, and certification.	Whilst most guidelines are compatible with each other, the cost of compliance to voluntary frameworks and standards can be prohibitive because of the large number of requirements.
External auditors	External auditors play a significant role in approving risk management frameworks in most financial organizations around the world. Their requirements are often for demonstrable compliance.	The auditors' advice sometimes can conflict significantly with existing practice within the organization. In the case of compliance with Sarbanes-Oxley, for instance, auditors can work from normative checklists that impose requirements that would be unnecessary, if a holistic assessment was conducted.
Shareholders	Shareholders increasingly pay attention to risk management systems in their assessment of an organization in which they invest. Their requirements are for trustworthy statements of risk exposure, but also cost effective assurance mechanisms.	Our research has shown that analysts rarely focus on how risk statements are produced.
Government agencies	Many regulatory frameworks originate from government or transnational agencies (such as, ENISA in Europe). The requirements imposed by these agencies are either advisory or mandatory.	Advisory requirements are not always subject to the same scrutiny and consultation processes as for mandatory ones during their inception. The distinction between advisory and mandatory requirements is not always made explicit by IA professionals and advisors.
Consultants	Consultants are often used for advice on IA policies and linked processes. In doing so, they can be the source of complex recommendations.	Consultants' recommendations can reinforce barriers and silo thinking, as they are often engaged for specific projects.

continued on following page

Table 1. Continued

Hard/software suppliers	IT suppliers are the main providers of the tools that organizations implement as part of their IA efforts. They are also the main originators of vulnerabilities in the systems.	Technical choices made by a third-party supplier of IT products can have a significant and long-term impact on the customer's IA practice. Such choices are not always made explicit to the customer and are only brought to light if the right questions are asked during the due diligence phase of the procurement decision.
Customers	Customers are the main assessors of the success of IA strategies. Ultimately, they refuse or withdraw their custom if they feel that their private information or assets are at risk. Furthermore, customers are also one of the main sources of information security risk.	Few financial services organizations have found a way to survey customer's appetite for risk. Most financial services organizations are still struggling to improve the security of customer-facing systems.
Suppliers	Suppliers can represent a significant source of IA risk, particularly if they handle customer information. The ability of suppliers to demonstrate certain levels of IA compliance can be critical to accreditation or audit requirements. Some financial services organizations have withdrawn from outsourcing arrangements because the supplier could not demonstrate a sufficient level of protection.	Robust due diligence and adequate documentation may not be sufficient to allay public fears. The public relations aspect of most purchasing relationships needs to investigated and managed.
Trade unions	Trade unions will be concerned about the impact of IA policies on their members. Therefore, they will need to be consulted during an IA policy development phase.	They also can use IA as an argument to fight other decisions. For instance, one of the UK's largest banks (Lloyds TSB) was threatened with legal action in 2005 by one of its staff unions over the transfer of jobs to off-shore centers in India on the grounds that the move breached EU Data Protection legislation.
Insurers	Insurers will want to ensure that the risks they are underwriting are managed.	Only rarely have insurers reduced insurance premiums when an organization demonstrated superior risk management processes.

Our research suggests that external stakeholders are important for the development of an IA strategy. Firstly through the influence they indirectly exert on the development of corporate IT and IA strategies. Understanding this influence, therefore, is key to understanding alignment requirements. In particular, external stakeholders can influence *risk awareness*. In particular, customers' or auditors' requirements are usually taken very seriously and can cause rapid change in IA policies. These requirements can be used very successfully by IA professionals to get the agreement of senior management to fund an IA initiative. They also

Box 2. Case study: How customers influence IA practice (First published in Birchall et al., 2004)

A large bank incorporates customer desires strongly into IA decisions for its Internet banking services. By recognizing that customers want simple and uncomplicated systems, the decision was to use browser-based software from the outset, requiring no separate downloads. The head of IA understands that ease-of-use is a prime driver for Internet customers and that requiring them to use dedicated software would be a barrier to use, reducing business effectiveness. It worked because of the recognition that customers already trust the bank with their personal and financial information. By leveraging that trust relationship to reassure customers that the bank would not take inappropriate risks with Internet systems, customers accepted the system as secure without requiring additional visible trappings of security.

can prompt senior management to ask probing questions of their IA experts. Conversely, some stakeholders may help "soften" risk perceptions by insisting on a trading relationship that is not hindered by cumbersome security measures (see the case study on customer influence).

The second sphere of influence of external stakeholders is that of *best practice*. As explained in Table 1, external stakeholders may insist that the organization follows best practice, or at least exert a strong influence. We found evidence of influence from stakeholders in the supply chain as well as the more traditional influencer of best practice adoption, such as regulators. As pointed out in Table 1, there can be issues with this influence in so far as IA best practice should always be determined by careful analysis, rather than by just following best practice as purported elsewhere. In any case, in circumstances where an organization is fiercely independent about the way it decides to implement IA, it may not be dramatically influenced by "best practice,", but external stakeholders may provide useful networking opportunities with peers and training or research organizations. These, in turn, may help develop new knowledge and skills.

Overcoming Internal Tensions

In many organizations in financial services, IA is first and foremost an internal control issue. For these organizations IA is a (key) part of risk management—typically reporting to the board's audit subcommittee. Here the objective of IA is to ensure that management information is available and can be trusted. This view is becoming increasingly important in many organizations, pushed by legislative and regulatory drivers, such as section 404 of the Sarbanes-Oxley Act or those of the Basel II Accord.

Internal control is, however, not the only way of looking at IA. Whilst most financial services organizations will have large teams of experts working on internal control projects from an IA angle, other teams in the same organization are also likely to implement IA projects in other functions. Hence, ISs, in particular, are the function where the locus of IA projects may well reside. Many IA projects are then seen as essentially technical, linked with information security rather than assurance. The chief information officer would normally be accountable for such projects, reporting to the board through the ISs, rather than the internal control line. The emphasis of such projects is to protect the ISs of the organization, thereby maintaining business continuity and the trust of business partners.

A third way of looking at IA that emerged as important during our research is that of asset management. In some organizations, IA projects are undertaken in the broader context of threat management. Such projects would normally be undertaken on behalf of a wider "security" function that would also encompass physical security. A key objective of such projects would be to maintain the security of all of the organization's assets, including proprietary knowledge and information.

Considering IA as essentially an internal control matter, an ISs matter, or an asset management matter does not appear to influence the success of IA efforts. On the other hand, we have seen evidence of tensions between the different functions of the organization in so far as they all can be accountable for part of the IA efforts. Firstly, this can mean that no one is actually accountable for the totality of the IA policy of the organization—in particular at board level, since all three areas typically report through different executive lines. Secondly, it can mean that the organization may "re-invent the wheel" constantly.

Three simple rules of engagement can help reduce these internal tensions:

- Acknowledging the strategic importance of IA decisions, by ensuring either that the board is involved in vetting such decisions or that IA practitioners are involved in strategic decision making
- Better communication among the functions involved with IA and the rest of the business, as well as providing a broad communication of IA goals throughout the organization. As pointed out by one of our interviewees, "Good IA is the art of communication"
- Clear mechanisms to ensure that the business impact of IA decisions is checked, at either the project or policy level

Examples of how this can be achieved in practice vary, but in our research we have come across interesting illustrations of how this can be done simply. For instance, in one of the banks we studied a security forum was implemented. The bank, a multinational bank with headquarters in central Europe, runs this as a series of exchanges, where different parts of the business can swap ideas with IA staff. This has been beneficial for the participants as the following case study shows. Through the bank's forum, alignment is maintained because the forum facilitates communication. At the same time, control is used to ensure alignment. By ensuring that the IA function scrutinizes all IT projects at a detailed level, the bank leaves no room for basic technical flaws that could have a negative security impact.

Box 3. Case study: The security forum

Cross-functional representation is a key objective of the bank's security subcommittee. The subcommittee—or security forum—brings together senior business managers from all major business support functions, such as logistics, IT, and legal, to discuss IA. It is more than just a "talking shop" and is in charge of checking the business case for IA initiatives, ensuring that IA projects are aligned with business objectives (at least operationally). Detailed technical scrutiny of all project proposals ensures alignment of projects with the bank's IA strategy. The bank has a team of purely technical experts in charge of assessing elements of the risk in all new IT initiatives.

The Dilemmas of Alignment

We have so far described why achieving alignment between IA and business strategy is difficult in financial services. We have argued that, by involving the board, understanding external stakeholder requirements, and finding mechanisms to overcome internal tensions, it is possible to create an environment that is conducive to aligning IA and business strategy. The last question that remains to answer is: what are the actual dilemmas of alignment?

In order to resolve some of the tensions that will have been brought to light through board involvement and a clear understanding of stakeholder requirements, key strategic choices will need to be made. One way of looking at these choices is through an understanding of the dilemmas that have to be resolved. Resolution can come from either favoring one pole of the dilemma to the detriment of another or making a compromise. Another possibility is to try and move away from the tension altogether by reframing the problem. There are essentially five such dilemmas, summarized in Table 2.

Managers with accountability for internal control, ISs, and asset management must be able to define coping strategies for each of these trade offs aligned with the strategic aims of their organizations. These coping strategies, however, will be dependent on risk appetite and the strategic direction of their company. Subsequently, coping strategies are likely to vary greatly from one financial services organization to another but are typically formulated in response to the need to manage a dilemma. For example, firms involved in a low-risk environment that use innovative market strategies will require systems that will encourage creativity. IA for them is likely to be synonymous with the need to maintain a blanket level of compliance. Thus the dichotomy of high procedural control versus creativity is not very strong.

Table 2. The five dilemmas of IA alignment

Dilemma	Explanation
Procedural control—Creativity	IA relies on strict checks, balances, and procedures that can often be seen as stifling creativity. Creative solutions are also often necessary to deal with complex IA problems.
Top-down control—Trust	Strict top-down control may need to be exerted in order to maintain a strong IA environment. However, this can send out a message to the employees about a lack of trustworthiness that could cause tensions between the two groups.
Exposure—Ease of doing business	Financial services organizations rely on electronic trading and electronic exchanges of information. In order for these to be facilitated (for instance, in e-banking), it is sometimes necessary to include simple security measures that are easy to use by customers. However, this also can be disadvantageous to the company as it could decrease security overall.
Insourcing—Outsourcing	Outsourced processes are an integral part of most financial services organizations. The control of outsourcing arrangements (including those for the provision of IA services) is an area that most IA auditors feel uncomfortable with.
Reputation—Expenditure	There is a dilemma between reputation (that can be affected by poor IA) and the expenditure necessary to achieve a comprehensive set of IA goals.

On the other hand, organizations that are very aggressive in their market and are involved in high-risk environments require high security, stringent risk management systems, as well as processes that encourage creativity. Consequently, they must find a coping strategy that will fulfil both ends of this trade off: sharing information and encouraging creativity versus high procedural control. One such coping strategy could be the use of IA skunk groups that operate alongside other project groups but keep a "low profile."

References

Bergeron, F., Raymond, L., & Rivard, S. (2004). Ideal patterns of strategic alignment and business performance. *Information & Management, 41*, 1003-1020.

Birchall, D., Ezingeard, J.-N., & McFadzean, E. S. (2003). *Information security: Setting the boardroom agenda.* London: GRIST Ltd.

Birchall, D., Ezingeard, J.-N., McFadzean, E., Howlin, N., & Yoxall, D. (2004). *Information assurance: Strategic alignment and competitive advantage.* London: GRIST.

Broadbent, M., & Weill, P. (1993). Improving business and information strategy alignment: Learning from the banking industry. *IBM Systems Journal, 32*, 162.

Campbell, K., Gordon, L. A., Loeb, M. P., & Zhou, L. (2003). The economic cost of publicly announced information security breaches: Empirical evidence from the stock market. *Journal of Computer Security, 11*, 431-448.

Chan, Y. E., Huff, S. L., Barclay, D. W., & Copeland, D. G. (1997). Business strategic orientation, information systems strategic orientation, and strategic alignment. *Information Systems Research, 8*, 125-150.

Culnan, M. J., & Armstrong, P. K. (1999). Information privacy concerns, procedural fairness, and impersonal trust: An empirical investigation. *Organisation Science, 10*, 104-115.

Deloitte. (2005). *2005 global security survey.* Deloitte Touche Tohmatsu.

Deloitte Touche Tohmatsu. (2003). *Global security survey.* Deloitte Touche Tohmatsu.

DTI. (2004). *Information security breaches survey*. DTI and PriceWaterhouseCoopers.

Dutta, A., & McCrohan, K. (2002). Management's role in information security in a cyber economy. *California Management Review, 45*, 67-87.

Economist. (2004, March 6). File that—The Sarbanes-Oxley act is causing a quantum leap in the storage industry. *The Economist, 370*(8385), 72.

Ernst & Young. (2005). *Global information security survey 2005.* Ernst & Young LLP.

Ettredge, M., & Richardson, V. J. (2003). Information transfer among Internet firms: The case of hacker attacks. *Journal of Information Systems, 17*, 71-82.

ITGI. (2003). *IT control objectives for Sarbanes-Oxley.* Rolling Meadows, IL: IT Governance Institute.

Miller, D. (1981). Toward a new contingency approach: The search for organisational Gestalts. *Journal of Management Studies, 18*, 1-26.

Miller, D. (1987). The genesis of configuration. *Academy of Management Review, 12,* 686-701.

National Association of Corporate Directors (NACD). (2001). *Information security oversight: Essential board practices.* Washington: National Association of Corporate Directors.

Peters, T. J., & Waterman, R. H. (1982). *In search of excellence: Lessons from America's best run companies.* New York: Harper and Row.

Reich, B. H., & Benbasat, I. (2000). Factors that influence the social dimension of alignment between business and information technology objectives. *MIS Quarterly, 24,* 81-113.

Saberherwal, R., & Kirs, P. (1994). The alignment between organisational critical success factors and information technology capability in academic institutions. *Decision Sciences, 25,* 301-330.

Sauer, C., Dampney, C. N. G., & Southon, G. (1997). Fit, failure, and the house of horrors: Toward a configurational theory of IS project failure. *Eighteenth International Conference on Information Systems.*

Swartz, N. (2003). The cost of Sarbanes-Oxley. *Information Management Journal, 37,* 8.

Treanor, J. (2000, August 1). Security fear shuts online bank. *The Guardian.*

Tweney, D. (1998). The consumer battle over online information privacy has just begun. *InfoWorld, 20,* 66.

Venkatraman, N., & Camillus, J. C. (1984). Exploring the concept of "fit' in strategic management. *Academy of Management Review, 9,* 513-525.

Von Solms, B. (2001). Corporate governance and information security. *Computers & Security, 20,* 215-218.

Chapter IV

Information Security in Banking

Kevin Streff, Dakota State University, USA

Abstract

The banking sector is identified as a critical infrastructure by the federal government. In this chapter, the author provides an overview of information security in the banking sector, outlines the information and technology common to most banks, explains the information security law and regulation banks must comply with, and explores the information security controls necessary to protect the banking infrastructure in the United States.

Introduction

The events of Sept. 11, 2001, have brought into focus several security issues that make the United States vulnerable to a host of attacks. In the United States, more than 85% of the critical infrastructure and assets are not owned by the federal government but rather by the private sector (Chabrow, 2002a, b; Garten, 2002; U.S. Department of Homeland Security, 2002; Verton, 2003). Presidential Decision Directive No. 63 (1998) identifies eight key sectors that are extremely vulnerable to attack, including telecommunications, electrical power systems, gas and oil storage and transportation, banking and finance, water supply systems, transportation, emergency services, and continuity of government.

Banking is one of these critical infrastructures. The international banking system is a complex network of interconnected banks and regional and national clearinghouses. The U.S. payment system is the largest in the world, where millions of transactions that are valued in the trillions of dollars are settled every day. For example, in 2003 Fedwire processed 123 million transactions valued at more than $436 trillion (Tucker, 1978). Fedwire is a real-time gross settlement system operated exclusively by the Federal Reserve System and allows a depository institution to transfer funds from its Federal Reserve account to a Federal Reserve account of another bank (Tommaso, 2003).

What if the banking infrastructure of the United States were made unavailable for a week by hackers or terrorists? What social and economic ramifications would occur? This chapter outlines the information and technology common to most banks, addresses the security law and regulation banks must comply with, and discusses information security controls necessary to protect the banking infrastructure in the United States.

Information in Banking

Banks store, process, and transact a variety of information to meet the various stakeholders. This section outlines the value of this information and highlights three types of information that are widely used in banks and in particular need to be kept available, confidential, and accurate.

The Value of Information

What was once stored in the vault of a bank was considered the most valuable asset a bank could have. Why else would an entity build a room with cement walls, a steel door, and an alarm system to alert the owner if anyone had tampered with it? But, what if the most important asset a bank has today cannot be locked in a vault, but rather is electrical impulses, ones and zeros, that fly across copper wires from computer to computer? What if the most valuable asset to the bank is the information stored on its computers and network? Customers are providing more than just their financial assets to be safely held by a bank. More importantly, this information is now becoming a liability to the bank, which needs to have controls in place to alleviate its associated risk. What information is stored on bank systems and how is it used? How do banks balance the need for convenience with the need to secure the information of the bank?

Customer Information

Customer information is most often considered the data with the most liability surrounding it and is the most popular type of information discussed. This information has been a hot topic for government, here and abroad. Customer information covers a wide variety of data that is collected about an individual. It can include common items, such a first and last name, mailing address, and phone number, to information that is much more sensitive, such as Social Security numbers, account numbers, and credit card numbers. Customer information is the most popular type of information stored at the bank and is the focus of much discussion and legislation. Customer information is not only a concern for financial institutions. From the year 2000 to 2002, identity theft complaints to the Federal Trade Commission from retail stores in the United States have increased fivefold, from 31,117 in 2000 to 161,819 in 2002 (U.S. Department of Justice, 2003). Customer information is used in a variety of ways throughout a bank. Fraudsters need this information to conduct identity fraud or theft.

Bank Information

Another form of information that is used within a bank is bank information. This type of information is generally classified as information used internally by the bank for operations. Examples of this type of information include: bank meeting minutes, memos, procedures, policy, guidelines, forms, vendor contracts, system configurations, and examination or audit information. This information is considered sensitive and must be protected. This information is considered confidential because it may contain information that either would give the bank's competitors an advantage, allow the bank to be vulnerable to attack, or cause damage to the bank's reputation. Further, this information can often be used to gain access to customer and financial information.

Financial Information

Financial information is another vital classification of bank information. Financial information encompasses account amounts, savings, deposit and loan values, ratios, call reports, and financial statements. This type of information can become combined with either customer information or bank information to raise its importance to the organization.

Technology in Banking

Banks use a variety of technologies, depending upon the businesses in which they are engaged. This said, most banks have a core banking system, a funds-transfer system, a network, and an ATM system. Banks have many more systems that support its business, however, these systems store, process, and transact the most important and sensitive information at the bank.

Core Banking Systems

A core banking system is one of the most crucial systems in a bank. The core banking system's main functionality is to maintain a record and process transactions that are taking place on the bank's accounts. Most are a modularized system that can complete a variety of activities, such as processing transactions directly at the teller line, generating loan documents, and managing the bank's payroll. These systems also can provide a variety of other services, from integrating with check imaging, to providing information for Internet banking. This type of system takes a variety of forms from being purely Windows-based to running on a variety of other operating systems, such as UNIX or IBM's AIX. The system either can be hosted in house or be outsourced to a large provider or bank. If hosted off site, the bank usually employs a dedicated line to the vendor to facilitate access to the core banking system. The system is typically accessed via dummy terminals over a serial network, via terminal emulation software or a native Windows client. These systems usually handle a variety of tasks and the functionality is modularized to enable additional services that are provided by the vendor. This also facilitates banks automating portions of their operations and not others. The system will accept all types of transactions that take place in the bank, either automatically or manually. For example, if a customer deposits a check into an account via a teller the transaction is processed and either put into the system by the bookkeeping department or directly by the teller at the counter. If the teller directly enters the transaction, this is an extension of the core banking software or another product called the deposit platform. A loan origination platform may be used to generate and track loan files for the loan department. Lastly, the core banking system's core functionality is the bookkeeping process. This allows the entering and proofing of transactions and the generation of financial information about the bank and its accounts. Most of the security controls in a bank will be wrapped around the core banking system as it contains a wealth of information that falls into all three of the information areas described previously.

Internet Banking

Internet banking is quickly becoming an essential service for any size bank. Internet banking services vary, but basic access to account information is the core functionality. Additional functions include providing access to check imaging, viewing credit card accounts, transferring money to other accounts, and even accepting online applications for new accounts or loans. Only larger operations will host an Internet banking system internally; others outsource the hosting to a vendor. A dedicated line or VPN is used to transmit account information on a schedule, in batches, or near real-time basis to the Internet banking provider. Internet banking has raised major concerns when it comes to information security. This is due to the bank using a service that stores information on almost every customer and, in some cases, allows customers to modify their accounts, which, if not managed appropriately, greatly increases the risk to the bank. Not only do customers have access to bank account information but so do millions of other people on the Internet.

Automated Clearinghouse and Electronic Funds Transfer Systems

Electronic funds transfer (EFT) is defined as the transfer of funds between two parties, without the physical exchange of monies. These can be individuals or institutions (Federal Financial Institutions Examination Council (FFIEC)). To manage these transfers software, such as FedLine, a system developed by the Federal Reserve, is employed to manage and secure the transactions. In general, these systems facilitate the electronic transfer of funds for banks and their customers. The main functionality is the ability to send wire transfers between two people or institutions. Wire transfers are direct transfers of funds and offer very little protection for the parties participating in the transaction. When a transfer is initiated, the funds are directly transferred into the receiving account and there is no recourse to reverse the transaction. This is why fraud often is initiated using wire transfers.

Another function the software provides is the reception of automated clearing house (ACH) files, which are transferred to the core banking system for processing. ACH is a funds transfer method that contains instructions to directly debit or credit a deposit account, such as a checking or savings account. Traditionally used to receive direct deposit paychecks, it is now used for bill payments, corporate payments, and government payments, such as tax returns. ACH is created in two ways, either via electronic check conversion or Internet-originated/telephone initiated payments. Electronic check conversion occurs when a retailer converts the magnetic ink character recognition (MICR) information from a check to an electronic transaction at the point of sale or at a lock-box location (FFIEC, 2004a). MICR is the series of numbers located at the bottom of a check. These numbers consist of a Federal Reserve region number, a bank's routing number, the specific account number, and the individual check serial number. As of 2002, the electronic payments network (EPN) handles approximately 30% of all ACH traffic, while the remaining amount is handled by the Federal Reserve (FFIEC, 2004).

In the past, products such as FedLine have been PC-based and used modems to send and receive transactions with the funds transfer provider, either the Federal Reserve or a third party. Recently, the Federal Reserve released FedLine Advantage, a Web-based application for pulling ACH files from the Federal Reserve and completing wire transfers over the Internet.

ATM and Debit Card Networks

The automated teller machine (ATM) has been around since the early 1960's and began as a cash dispensing machine. England's Barclay's Bank, for example, installed the first cash dispenser in 1967. The machine used paper vouchers issued by the bank, rather than the magnetic strip that everyone has come to expect on credit and ATM cards. In 1968, Don Wetzel envisioned the idea of the modern ATM, while waiting in line at a Dallas bank. In 1969, Wetzel's employer, Docutel, installed the first modern ATM in Long Island, NY. This machine was only used to dispense cash and recorded the transactions on a tape using MICR encoding. Today's ATM and credit card networks span the nation and transactions appear to seamlessly flow from the point of sale or ATM to the proper bank holding the card holder's account. This is actually enabled though the use of ATM networks. An ATM network is a collection of ATM machines, communication lines, and communication equipment used to interconnect ATM's. ATM and point-of-sale machines use either a phone line or dedicated network connection to communicate with their processor (Hayashi, Sullivan, & Stuart, 2003).

In the early years of ATMs, networks were only owned by larger institutions, but in the mid-1970s shared networks emerged as smaller banks joined together to offer their ATM services across more geographically dispersed areas. As the machines and communication lines have advanced, the functionality of ATMs has increased from just allowing cash withdrawal to real-time account balances, accepting of deposits, transferring between accounts, and even purchasing stamps. Along with the growth of ATM's was the installation of point-of-sale terminals that allow customers to directly pay for purchases using their debit card. Two types of debit card transactions can be done. Online debit occurs when a card holder verifies their personal identification number (PIN). Offline debit occurs when a card holder signs a physical receipt to prove his or her identity. ATM networks are tied together by switches. Just as in the computer world, ATM switches route traffic from one provider or bank to another. ATM and debit transactions either are handled by the bank or are outsourced to a third party service provider. (Hayashi et. al., 2003)

Networks

Networking technology is the heart of almost any IT operation. Networks allow a variety of systems to interconnect and share resources. A variety of local area networks, wide area networks, firewalls, intrusion detection systems, switches, and dedicated lines are used to move information between systems, branches, organizations, and communities. A local area network (LAN) is a network that is located and provides communications between hosts in one physical location. LANs vary drastically from institution to institution. Some consist of a few workstations and an Internet connection, while others contain multiple segregated networks with servers and work stations. A wide area network (WAN) provides communications between multiple geographically dispersed locations. These are often used to connect multiple LANs together. Two technologies typically used to connect different locations are frame-relay and dedicated lines. A frame-relay line is a shared switched network that can be used to connect multiple sites. Frame-relay lines are best used when not a great deal of constant communications will occur. A dedicated line is a solid connection that is only used to transmit data between the two endpoints. Usually quite expensive, they are best used when a constant level of communications is occurring between two sites.

Firewalls are now a necessity on most networks. This equipment controls the flow of information to and from one network to another. Another device that is often used on medium to large networks is an intrusion detection system (IDS). These systems are used to monitor internal and external traffic to determine, if the network is under attack.

Trends in Bank Security

Many issues and trends are affecting the bank environment. Some of the key issues include: technology integration, outsourcing, and multifactor authentication. Each is explained in further detail.

Technology Integration

Technology has changed the way that many of us complete a variety of tasks. From the way we communicate to how we shop for Christmas presents have all been greatly affected by technology. Banking is no exception. Information technologies not only automate the bank's back-room operations but are now becoming a necessary tool for reaching current and prospective clients. The systems discussed previously are just a few of the ways technology is being integrated into the banking industry. Originally, technology was limited to the core banking system and the associated dummy terminals, printers, and proofing machines. Until recently, many smaller community banks did not have the need for a network and Internet connectivity let alone firewalls, VPNs, dedicated lines, or intrusion detection systems (IDS). Technology now enables banks to market to a wider array of customers and also retain customers as they grow or relocate.

Outsourcing

As the requirements for technology and its management have increased, small- to medium-sized institutions have come to rely heavily on outsourcing to provide services and to keep them affordable and manageable. A variety of bank functions can be outsourced. Most often, items such as electronic banking (e-banking), IDS, network management, and credit card services are outsourced. Many of these services are critical to the operation of the bank and must be handled with great care. Outsourcing is defined as any function that is not performed by the bank itself, but rather by a contracted third party. Great rewards come with outsourcing certain functions in the bank, such as lowered operating and personnel costs, quick development and implementation, instant access to talent, and the need to not do extensive training. These great rewards are offset by the risk involved. The threat of information disclosure, reliability, and errors all detract from the benefits. What is crucial about outsourcing is that the same assurances that a bank gives about internally provided services still ring true for systems or services that are outsourced. Customer information is to remain confidential regardless of whether it is stored on a local system or in a vendor's data center. Even though a bank may outsource a function of its business, it is still its responsibility to maintain the confidentiality, integrity, and availability of the information and service.

There are a variety of ways that a bank can mitigate some of the risks that are inherent with outsourcing. The most important of these is due diligence. Performing due diligence on vendors during the selection process is the first step in ensuring a good, reliable relationship between the bank and a vendor. Due diligence is the process of scrutinizing a vendor to assess the quality of their products or services. The Federal Financial Institutions Examination Council (FFIEC) recommends several items about a vendor be checked when performing due diligence. The items are listed below:

- Existence and corporate history;
- Qualifications, backgrounds, and reputations of the company's principals, including criminal background checks where appropriate;
- Other companies using similar services from the provider that may be contacted for reference;
- Financial status, including reviews of audited financial statements;
- Strategy and reputation;
- Service delivery capability, status, and effectiveness;
- Technology and systems architecture;
- Internal controls environment, security history, and audit coverage;
- Legal and regulatory compliance, including any complaints, litigation, or regulatory actions;
- Reliance on and success in dealing with third-party service providers;
- Insurance coverage; and
- Ability to meet disaster recovery and business continuity requirements. (FFIEC, 2004)

One the most important parts of dealing with a third party is having a solid contract in place. A contract is a legally binding document that spells out the expectations of the parties in the agreement. Solid contracts are the first line of mitigation in outsourcing and the first place to consult if a problem with a vendor arises. The contract should clearly outline the expectations of data privacy, levels of services, and legal recourse if the conditions of the contract are not completed. At a minimum, the contract should outline the following: start and term, conditions and right to cancel, the ownership of data, timely return of data in a machine-readable format, costs of transition, limitations as appropriate, dispute resolution, and confidentiality of the bank's data (FFIEC, 2004). Another type of contract that is often used in outsourced scenarios is a service level agreement (SLA). SLA is a legal contract that lays out the bank's quality of service expectations from the vendor. SLAs may be used for bandwidth, response times, or up-time expectations.

Banks also will use financial and security audits or reports to assess the condition of a vendor. The most recognizable of these reports is a statement of auditing standards (SAS). This document signifies that provider has had an independent review completed of its internal controls over information technology. There are two types of SAS 70 audits that are conducted. A type I audit lists the controls that the service organization has put in place as of a specific date. A type II report takes this process one step further by evaluating the effectiveness of the controls over a six-month period. The SAS 70 is the standard audit used by vendors to allow a bank and its auditors to assess the level of controls and their effectiveness without testing them itself (Coolige, 2006) Another form of mitigating outsourced risk is through insurance. Insurance can be used when other controls cannot fully mitigate the risk associated with a specific type of outsourcing.

Two Factor Authentication

The ineffectiveness of using just user names and passwords has been brought to light in recent years though the exploitation of systems that relied on only one-factor authentication. A factor is an item that is used to identify oneself to a system. Factors are either something you know, such as a password, something you are, such as your finger print, or something you have, such as a key chain or USB token. Multifactor authentication occurs whenever a system requires two or more types of identification to gain access. This is especially important in Internet banking and has been a focus for examiners. This also was brought to light by a lawsuit against Bank of America in late 2005 by a business owner. The business owner had his computer compromised by a piece of software called a key logger. The software recorded the owner's key strokes on his computer and captured his online banking user name and password. The thief then proceeded to transfer more than $90,000 to an account outside the United States (Smith, 2005). Some argue that it was the bank's responsibility to not allow the large transaction, but others believe it was the business owner's responsibility to maintain his computer to protect his information. No matter who is at fault, it raises the concern that more needs to be done in determining who someone is online.

A variety of vendors are currently working on solutions to secure e-banking systems. These range from tokens and one-time passwords to biometrics. Tokens are something that you have, be it a USB token, smart cards, or a key chain token. A USB token is a device that contains a small microprocessor and is plugged into the machine that will be used to access secure information. Once the system recognizes the token, the user is prompted for his or her password. Once the password and token are verified, the user is allowed access to the system. A smart card is similar to a USB token as it also contains a microprocessor but is in the form of a card about the size of a credit card. These devices require a device to read them attached to the machine. Once the card is inserted, the system verifies the card and prompts the user for the card's PIN. Once both have been verified, the user is allowed access. A key chain token, or password generating token, can be used to provide a second factor to authentication by presenting a random password each time the user attempts to access a system. This means the user does not have to remember a password, and the same password is never used twice. Biometrics is an area that has received a large amount of attention recently. Biometrics is using a part of who you are as a factor for authentication. A variety of characteristics are used including fingers, facial recognition, retina scanning, iris scanning, voice recognition, and keyboard dynamics. Each has its benefits and downfalls. The major issues with biometrics are the reliability of the technology and the cost to implement a biometric solution.

Bank Security Laws

Banking is a highly regulated industry. Information security regulation requires banks to protect the confidentiality, integrity, and availability of customer information. Several of the important laws that require information security protection are highlighted next.

Bank Secrecy Act

The Bank Secrecy Act (BSA) was passed by the U.S. Congress in 1970. The BSA was passed to help government agencies detect and prevent money laundering. It required financial institutions to keep records of large transactions (exceeding $10,000) and report suspicious activity to the Internal Revenue Service (IRS).

Gramm-Leach-Bliley Act

Passed by Congress in 1999, the Gramm-Leach-Bliley Financial Services Modernization Act, allowed commercial and investment banks to consolidate. Prior to the Gramm-Leach-Bliley Act, the Glass-Steagall Act prohibited a bank from offering commercial banking, investing, and insurance.

Sarbanes-Oxley Act

In 2002 Congress passed the Sarbanes-Oxley Act (SOX). It was passed in response to many corporate and accounting scandals. This act places responsibility of ensuring that proper auditing and security controls are in place and being performed on the management of a company or corporation.. This law holds the CEOs and CFOs lawfully accountable for violations of security laws.

Information Security Issues in Banking

Protecting the confidentiality, integrity, and availability of customer, bank, and financial information has been problematic for banks. This section describes several of the key issues banks are facing to protect valuable information.

Technology-Enabled Cyber Crimes

Technology-enabled cyber crimes are easy to commit. The definition of cyber crime is criminal activity in which computers or networks are a tool, a target, or a place of criminal activity. There are many activities that fall under cyber crime, including the peer-to-peer downloading of copyrighted material, unauthorized access to a computer system, deploying malicious code on a computer or network, and denial of service attacks on a network. However, the principle crime that endangers the banking world is having someone gain unauthorized access to a bank's network (Dittrich & Himma, 2006).

Imagine that one day while going through the mail a person comes across a letter from his or her bank and open it thinking it is just a statement. To that person's surprise it is not a statement, but a letter from the bank saying that they have been a victim of a cyber crime. An incident occurred over several months in late 2003 and early 2004. A security breach was a theft of a database at BJ's Wholesale Club Inc., which resulted in thousands of credit and debit cards being compromised. The best method to combat these threats is to educate people on the types of cyber crime and how to protect themselves (Fisher, 2004).

Identity Fraud

Identity fraud occurs when a person uses another person's personal data in some way that involves fraud or deception, typically for economic gain. The person or people who commit identity fraud in a short amount of time cause damage to the victim's reputation and credit standing. With the personal information of the victim, the criminal has many options, such as taking out loans, opening credit card accounts, and possibly even impersonating the victim for a length of time (U.S. Department of Justice,).

In one case the criminal impersonated the victim and accumulated more than $100,000 of credit card debt, obtained a federal home loan, and bought various expensive items. To further torment the victim, the criminal called and said he could pose as the victim as long as he wanted. In the end, the criminal filed for bankruptcy under the victim's name; the victim of this fraud spent four years and $15,000 of his own money to clean his reputation. The down fall is the criminal only served a short prison sentence. This case and others similar to it prompted the Identity Theft and Assumption Deterrence Act of 1998. This act provides stronger sentencing and punishment for the people who commit identity fraud (U.S. Department of Justice).

Identity Theft

Identity theft is the process by which the person obtains the personal information about a victim. This does not have to done with a computer; however, computer technology has made it easier for criminals to obtain this information. The most common and oldest method of identity theft is dumpster diving. To obtain information about the victim, the criminal will dive through the victim's garbage and look for documents that have information such as canceled checks and preapproved credit card applications. Other methods of gaining information is "shoulder surfing," where a criminal checks over the shoulder of a person at an ATM to gain the PIN number or listens in on phone conversations that entail credit card or Social Security number information. The following is a list of some of the easy steps that can protect a person's identity from these acts (U.S. Department of Justice):

- Use an ATM in a secluded area so no one can look over you shoulder
- Rear up or shred the preapproved credit card applications received in the mail
- Never give out personal information unless absolutely necessary

If a person is a victim of identity theft or fraud they should immediately contact the Federal Trade Commission (FTC) by phone, e-mail, or mail and report the situation. Next the victim may want to: contact their post office to see if the criminal has submitted a change of address form to redirect the mail; contact the Social Security Administration if the victim's Social Security number is being used fraudulently; inform the IRS if improper use of identification information in connection with tax violations; and call the fraud units of the three major credit reporting companies Equifax, Experian, and Trans Union. The victim also should contact all creditors with whom the victim's name or identifying data have been fraudulently used; and contact all financial institutions where the victim has accounts,and the major check verification companies (U.S. Department of Justice,).

Phishing and Pharming

Phishing and pharming are closely related, however phishing is more commonly used and easier to implement. Phishing is an identity theft attack using technical subterfuge and social engineering to steal consumers' personal identity and financial credentials. Pharming exploits vulnerabilities in DNS server software that allows a cracker to obtain the domain name of the site and then redirects it to another site. Phishing utilizes e-mail to send the consumer to a fraudulent Web site in order to gain the information desired by the attacker. Phishing attacks occur frequently and many times they are successful at gaining the information from the targets. The best way to combat this type of attack is to educate people on what to look for and how to prevent themselves from becoming a victim. The following is a list of simple countermeasures to prevent phishing attacks (Dittrich & Himma, 2006):

- *Do not click the link in an e-mail; instead type the trusted URL into the address bar of a Web browser*
- *Contact the company that is in the subject of the e-mail to check if the message is legitimate*
- *If necessary install and utilize antiphishing software*

A recent example of phishing that was targeted at the Dakota State University faculty, staff, and students involved Wells Fargo Bank. There was a message saying that account information needed to be updated and to click the link below. Fortunately computing services on campus caught this quickly and informed everyone not to follow the link in the e-mail because it was a phishing attempt.

Skimming

Skimming is used to describe a type of credit card fraud where the magnetic stripe on any type of card is cloned and used without the owner's knowledge. Stealing the information from a person's credit card can be done in many different fashions. For example, imagine a person is paying for a meal at a restaurant and use a credit card. Instead of going to a cash register, this person hands it over to the server at the table. While the server is processing the bill, the server may swipe the card a second time to obtain the data stored on the card's magnetic stripe. Another thing a person should be wary of is if the clerk at a convenience store needs to swipe a person's card through two readers; one could be a fake and the clerk is stealing your information (Bruce, 2003).

Restaurants and convenience stores are not the only places people need to be paying attention; ATM machines, where people typically withdrawal money, can be a danger as well. Criminals are able to steal information directly from the ATM transaction itself. They do this by attaching a secondary card reader on top of the current card reader of the ATM. This second reader is connected to a computer or a wireless transmitting device that then stores or sends the information on the magnetic stripe of the ATM or credit card for later use. To obtain the victim's PIN, they may install something that looks like a pamphlet holder and pamphlets near the keypad that contains a spy cam to collect the PIN. This is a more advanced version of shoulder surfing, where the criminal would look over someone's shoulder at an ATM in a public place, such as a hotel lobby or convenience store (Bruce, 2003).

With the sophistication of skimming, there are still simple countermeasures to use to avoid these traps:

- Use an ATM that is in a secluded are, such as one placed a bank
- If the ATM looks like it has been tampered with or just does not look correct, do not use it
- Use cash at restaurants and convenience stores, when possible
- Check bank and credit card statements often to make sure the number of transactions is correct

- Be wary of people at the ATM that want to assist with a transaction

The ATM skimming task force, lead by the Electronic Funds Transfer Association (EFTA), is developing new ATM technology to combat skimming. Currently a new system, called jitter, varies the speed and reverses the direction of the card intermittently and randomly when the card is entered. This system is being implemented in newer motorized ATM card readers (Bruce, 2003).

Critical Infrastructure Protection

The events of Sept. 11, 2001, have brought into focus several security issues that make the nation vulnerable to a host of attacks. In the United States, more than 85% of the critical infrastructure and assets are not owned by the federal government, but rather owned by the private sector (Chabrow, 2002a, b; Garten, 2002; U.S. Department of Homeland Security, 2002; Verton, 2003). Information assurance is a pivotal factor to secure critical infrastructures and assets, so much so that former President Clinton identified a national goal to secure these national private-sector information assets and infrastructures in Presidential Decision Directive No. 63 (1998). This directive identifies eight key sectors that are extremely vulnerable to attack, including telecommunications, electrical power systems, gas and oil storage and transportation, banking and finance, water supply systems, transportation, emergency services, and continuity of government (Presidential Decision Directive No. 63, 1998). Executive Order No. 13231 (2001) identifies several other critical sectors, including manufacturing, shipping, and food. U.S. Department of Homeland Security Directive No. 9 (2004) suggests that security awareness is lacking in the food sector. However, because the critical infrastructures of these key sectors are owned and operated by the private sector, organizations must take ownership in protecting these infrastructures against attack.

The federal government and security experts fear that terrorists will attack these sectors that are vital to the normal operation of the country. For example, the banking and finance industry in the United States safeguards more than $21.5 trillion in credit assets (Allan et al., 2002). What would happen to the markets and consumer confidence, in general, if the stock exchanges were compromised, and the confidentiality, integrity, and availability of the banking infrastructure were disrupted for days?

Money Laundering

Money laundering is the process of using a legitimate business as a front to conceal money from illegal operations. This term came about during the 1930s due to prohibition where the mob ran speak easies, a place that sold alcohol for just five cents. By using laundry mats as a front to hide all the coins collected from the money earned from the nickel beers, the mob was able to hide all its illegal activity. This worked because a person would expect to have a laundry mat with coins lying round and to deposit them at the bank. Today, money laundering uses more advance technology as well does the technology to counter the money launderers. Money laundering is still being practiced today, not only by organized crime but by individuals as well. With the increase in laundering activity, the amount of information to gather is too much for humans, so software has been designed to catch suspicious activity in banking transactions to catch the criminals. Bankers are also to write up suspicious transactions reports for any transaction over $10,000 (Money Laundering, 2005).

Terrorist Financing

Terrorists are stealing information and selling it or using it to fund their terrorist agendas. Beginning July 1, 2003, national banks and federal branches and agencies were required to complete Part III of the suspicious activity report (SAR) that specifically addresses suspicious activity connected to terrorist financing and identity theft (OCC Bulletin, 2003). "Terrorists and terrorist groups require funding ... identity theft is a key catalyst fueling their agenda of terror" (*Terrorist financing identity theft,* 2003, p. 3). In April 2003, the U.S. Treasury issued final rules that required certain financial institutions to establish procedures to verify the identity of new account holders to prevent money laundering, terrorist financing, identity theft, and other forms of fraud, "while also providing financial institutions the flexibility they need to effectively implement the rules." The rules are part of the Bush administration's ongoing work to implement the U.S. Patriot Act to "intercept and obstruct terrorism" (U.S. Patriot Act, 2001, p. 1). This legislation was passed by congress in the wake of the Sept. 11, 2001, terrorist attacks against the United States (U.S. Department of State, 2003) to reduce terrorists capabilities to fund their agenda of terrorism.

Bank Regulation

Banks are highly regulated. This section gives an overview of the regulatory agencies in the United States that enforce its guidance and the bank security law described in a previous section.

Regulatory Agencies

The current regulatory agencies that govern banks in the United States are the Federal Reserve System, Federal Deposit Insurance Corporation, Office of the Comptroller of Currency, Office of Thrift Supervision, National Credit Union Administration, and the FFIEC. Each of these organizations governs a portion of the financial sector, working independently and together to provide supervision to U.S. financial institutions.

Federal Financial Institutions Examination Council (FIEC)

The FFIEC is a council constructed of members from each of the regulating bodies stated above. It was established in March of 1978 as part of the Financial Institutions Regulatory and Interest Rate Control Act of 1978. Its purpose is to promote uniformity in regulation among the regulating bodies (FFIEC,). It is most known for its guidance, which ispublished as part of the variety of handbooks. These handbooks provide very general guidance on topics such as the Bank Secrecy Act, antimoney laundering, information technology, and Check 21. The information technology handbooks were designed to provide a quick introductory resource on a variety of topics. The booklet topics include:

- Audit
- Management
- Business continuity planning
- Operations
- Development and acquisition
- Outsourcing technology services
- E-banking
- Retail payment systems
- FedLine
- Supervision of technology service providers
- Information security
- Wholesale payment systems

These booklets can be downloaded free of charge from the FFIEC Web site (FFIEC,).

Board of Governors of the Federal Reserve

The Federal Reserve System was established as part of the Federal Reserve Act of 1913. This legislation brought all banks in the United States under federal regulation and established the nation's central bank. The Federal Reserve banks were established to furnish an elastic currency and to establish more effective supervision of banking in the United States. (Federal Reserve Board, 1913) The Federal Reserve regulates its member banks across the United States and is also used to provide a stable payment system and to establish monetary policy. The Federal Reserve is broken into 12 districts (see Figure 1 (Federal Reserve Board, 2005))

Governing each of these districts is the Board of the Federal Reserve. This 12-member board, with one member from each district, is appointed by the president and confirmed by the senate to a 14 year term. No two members of the board can be appointed from the same district and the president is ordered by law to select a "fair representation of the financial, agricultural, industrial, and commercial interests and geographical divisions of the country" (Federal Reserve Board, 2003).

Figure 1. U.S. Federal Reserve districts

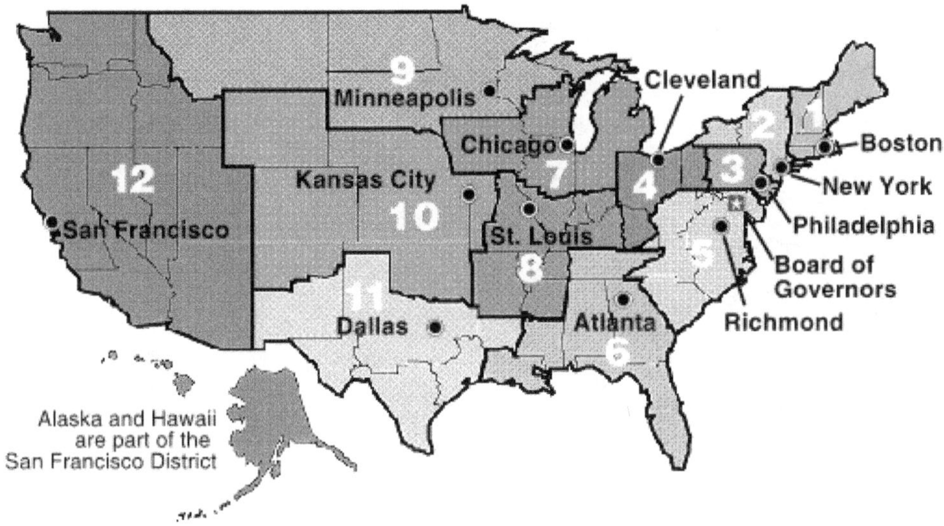

Federal Deposit Insurance Corporation

Established in 1934, during the Great Depression, the Federal Deposit Insurance Corporation (FDIC) was created to promote confidence in U.S. financial systems and to protect investors from the failings of financial institutions that occurred during the 1920s and 1930s. This was done through insuring all deposit accounts up to $100,000. The FDIC also monitors risks in the economy and in its insured institutions though examinations of their operations. The FDIC is governed by a board of five members who are appointed by the president and confirmed by the senate. Currently, the FDIC directly examines and supervises approximately 5,300 banks and savings banks. Banks can be chartered by the states or by the federal government. Banks chartered by states also have the choice of whether to join the Federal Reserve System. The FDIC is the primary federal regulator of banks that are chartered by the state banks that do not join the Federal Reserve System (Federal Deposit Insurance Corporation (FDIC), 2003a).

Office of the Comptroller of the Currency

The Office of the Comptroller of the Currency (OCC) was established in 1863 to oversee the operations of banks with a national charter. The OCC also supervises international banks within the United States. The OCC is led by the Comptroller of the Currency, who is appointed by the president and confirmed by the senate for a five-year term. The comptroller also acts as the director of the FDIC. The OCC has offices across the nation and is divided into four districts (Office of the Comptroller of the Currency (OCC)) (see Figure 2).

Figure 2. U.S. OCC districts

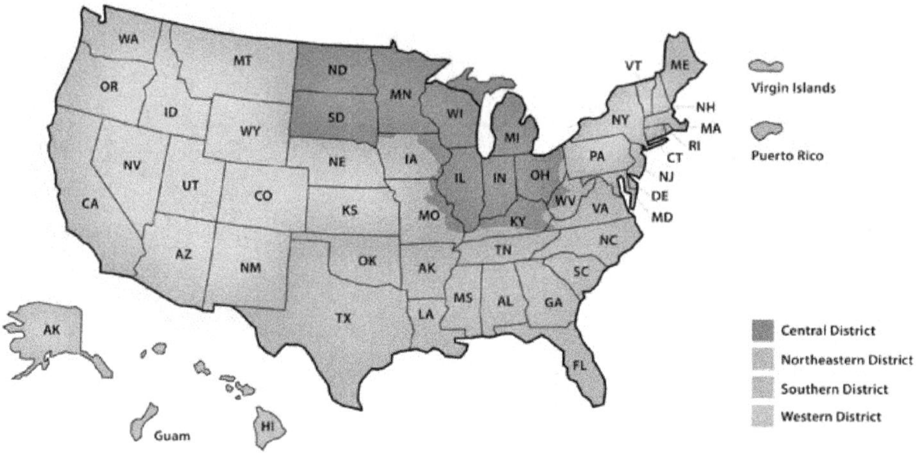

State Banking Regulators

Coming in a variety of names, each state has its own set of bank regulators who handle the chartering and examination of state-chartered banks. Originally, states were the first to offer charters. The state agencies carry out examinations in cooperation with the FDIC.

Office of Thrift Supervision

The Office of Thrift Supervision (OTS) was established in 1989 as a bureau of the treasury department to oversee and stabilize the nation's thrift institutions. Thrift institutions include savings banks and savings and loan associations. OTS also examines, supervises, and regulates state-chartered savings associations belonging to the Savings Association Insurance Fund (SAIF). The OTS has four regional offices in Atlanta, Dallas, Jersey City, NJ, and San Francisco. The OTS is lead by a director who is appointed by the president and confirmed by the senate for a five-year term. The director also serves on the board for the FDIC (Office of Thrift Supervision (OTS), 2006)

National Credit Union Administration

The Federal Credit Union Act was signed by President Roosevelt in 1934, and it established federally chartered credit unions and the Bureau of Federal Credit Unions. The goal of the organization was to promote the availability of credit through a network of nonprofit cooperative credit unions. In the beginning, the Bureau of Federal Credit Unions was part of the Farm Credit Administration but moved under the FDIC, and finally under the supervision of the Department of Health, Education and Welfare. In 1970, the bureau was made a separate federal agency when the National Credit Union Administration (NCUA) was formed. The duties of the NCUA were to charter and regulate federal credit unions. National Credit Union Share Insurance Fund (NCUSIF) is administered by NCUA. This fund insures deposits much like the FDIC insures deposit in its banks (National Credit Union Association (NCUA,). NCUA has a full-time, three-member board appointed by the president and confirmed by the senate. No more than two board members can be from the same political party, and they serve staggered six-year terms (NCUA).

Bank Information Technology Examinations

Banks are required to be examined by a regulator every 12 to 18 months. The regulator will visit the bank and conduct an information technology examination (IT exam). The IT exam will end in a CAMEL Rating that identifies how well the regulator views the bank is securing the technology it uses.

CAMEL Ratings

The CAMEL rating has been a key indicator of a bank's safety and soundness, since it was adopted in 1979. CAMEL stands for:

- C – capital adequacy
- A – asset quality
- M – management quality
- E – earnings
- L – liquidity
- S – sensitivity to market risk

These are the five areas examined by regulators to assess a banks financial operation. Each area is rated from one to five, with one being the highest rating (FDIC, 2003). The CAMEL rating system is an internal supervisory tool for evaluating the soundness of financial institutions. This provides a uniform basis for identifying those institutions requiring special supervisory attention or concern (FDIC, 1996). Out of each of these sections, a composite rating summarizes the examiner's overall rating for the bank. The composite score uses the same scale for each section. A rating of a "1" is deemed excellent, and there is minimal concern with the bank. A rating of a "2" is average with areas for improvement. Anything below a "2" rating is cause for concern and will most likely see the regulating body creating some form of oversight for the institution. If action is needed and the examiner feels it is justified, the examiner may issue a memorandum of understanding (MOU). These memos usually indicate significant problems and are used to alert upper management and the board of directors of the issue. It also outlines what is expected of the bank, and the level of oversight they will be under. A MOU is usually accompanied by an increased examination schedule, depending on the issue.

Uniform Rating System for Information Technology

Adopted in 1978 by all of the governing bodies, the use of the uniform rating system for information technology (URSIT) was established. Originally referred to as the IS rating system until 1998 when modifications were made to better align the system with current operations, URSIT provides a standard rating system for data processing operations, much like CAMEL does for the financial operations of the bank. (FFIEC, 1999) URSIT evaluates the risk to IT operations in four major areas: audit, management, development and acquisition, and support and delivery. (FFIEC, 2003a) As with CAMELS, each section is assigned a rating from one to five, with a one being the highest. Each of these ratings is used to derive a composite score between one and five. This rating generalizes how the bank is doing in terms of managing their information technologies. Appendix A identifies the five rating definitions defined by the FFIEC (2003).

Bank IT Examination Process

All banks are examined minimally every 18 months. If during the exam process the bank is found to have information security issues, this time frame can be reduced to every 12 months or less depending upon the severity of the issues. The bank is reviewed on a variety of topics. Topics include the Bank Secrecy Act, Community Reinvestment Act, loans, deposits, or IT. For the purpose of this chapter, we will focus on IT. As mentioned earlier, there are 12 IT Examination Handbooks. Each of these handbooks is accompanied by a work program to guide an examiner through that portion of the examination (FFIEC, 2003). Each is filled with a series of objectives and each objective contains specific items to be reviewed. The outcome from these work programs will allow the examiner to provide a section and composite URSIT rating.

Examination Reports

When the exam is completed, an initial finding report may be provided during the closing meeting. The meeting will revolve around what actions need to be taken by the bank to correct any issues that were found. Following the exam, the bank will receive the final report. The report is broken into each section that was examined (See URSIT and CAMELS for section breakdowns), and a score is given. The report also will summarize the findings of each of the subsections and give a composite score, or overall rating.

Security Requirements in Banking

Defense in Depth

Defense in depth is a methodology that originated from the military and refers to having multiple levels of defense in place to maximize the amount of time it takes for the attacking party to reach the most valuable assets. Thus, applying the mentality of defense in depth to technology, it is not only protecting a network with a firewall, but with policies governing the use of the firewall and training users on how to correctly administer the actual equipment. International Information Systems Security Certification Consortium, Inc. $(ISC)^2$ identifies 10 domains in the common body of knowledge that also leverage a layered defense in depth approach (Hansche, Berti, & Hare, 2004). A recent report (February 2005) to the president entitled *Cyber Security: A Crisis of Prioritization* identifies a need for "holistic system security," including the need for innovative solutions that promote security awareness in agencies and businesses (NITRD, 2005). Defense in depth includes three levels: people, process, and technology. Controls need to be applied on all three levels for an effective defense in depth approach.

People

Employees can help protect critical infrastructures by being aware of the importance of security and of the techniques attackers use to exploit human, process, and technological vulnerabilities. People are said to be in the front line of defense against attack (Marks, 2002). "Your front line of defense needs to be properly trained for the safety of both the company and their personal well being" (Halbig, 2004, p. 2). Homeland Security Secretary Tom Ridge has declared that people are the "front line of defense for protecting America's food and agriculture" (Stump, 2003, p. 1). The Ernst & Young (2004) *Global Security Survey* identifies security awareness programs as a vital component of any company's strategic plan, clearly stating "Companies should place more emphasis on creating a security-conscious culture" (p.). No matter the amount of money spent or the level of technical controls in place, people are the first line in preventing and detecting security issues. Securing a work station and file server are crucial technological controls, but all these controls are easily bypassed if an employee improperly disposes of a sensitive report. This is why controls are placed on people, such as the requirement for security awareness training to educate employees as to why proper disposal of sensitive information is crucial.

Process

Processes outline the way tasks should be completed. Using dual controls, having two or more people involved in a process to verify the outcome, is an example of a process. Processes are documented in three categories: programs, policy, and procedures. A program outlines high-level objects that are to be carried out by upper management, such as a board of directors. The program will use very general language and cover broad topics. It is then up to management of the bank to implement the program using policy. Policy will further hone the objectives of the program into policy statements. These statements will provide more specific controls on how the program objectives will be carried out in operations. Procedures will spell out, step by step, how to complete a given task. Take the statements below as and example on the different levels of documentation:

- **Program:** The bank wishes to provide the most secure environment for customer information.
- **Policy:** It is the policy of the bank to protect user information. One way this will be accomplished is through the proper disposal of any media, either in print or on digital media, such as CD-ROMs or diskettes.
- **Procedures:** Employees will dispose of digital media, use the following steps...

This breakdown in documentation allows for easier management by all levels of the organization, and it allows those who have the most knowledge on a subject, to have the most influence on the proper way to carry out a control. For example, the board of directors, in most cases, will not understand, or care to approve, the specific steps to ensuring information security, that is why they hire management. The board uses the program to communicate the larger picture for bank management to carry it out.

Technology

Technology is probably the type of control that gets the most attention in any organization. Technology controls can be anything from a firewall to password and session controls on Windows. The nice thing about these types of security controls is that they can be forced on users, and, for the most part, the technology will always enforce the control. The problem is that users, if they do not understand their purpose, will often try to bypass these controls when they are not convenient. It is crucial to understand that the best technical security system in the world can be simply bypassed by users who are careless or unknowingly allow a vulnerability to be exploited. For example, allowing access to critical areas of a building or by attaching their user name and password to a monitor.

Risk-Based Management

A risk-based approach to information security management means that major decisions that are made regarding information security analyze the impact a change will have in either increasing or decreasing the amount of risk there is to informational assets in the bank. This process uses a risk assessment as a key management tool in making choices and prioritizing tasks.

Risk Management Life Cycle

The risk management life cycle is a process in which an organization can manage risk in a repeatable fashion. The risk management life cycle is continual and works toward improving security through mitigating risks to the organization's most crucial assets and measuring their effectiveness. There are nine steps in the risk management life cycle depicted in Figure 3.

The first step of the risk management life cycle is to develop a standard set of policies and procedures. These provide a general set of controls that can be built upon by the remaining steps of the risk management life cycle. If one does not know where to start, it may be helpful to adopt a standard such as ISO 17799 to spring board into policy, best practices, and control development.

Next, the bank needs to create an inventory of the company's assets. An inventory is useful because it is hard to protect assets if you do not know they exist. The asset inventory should be company-wide and involve the proper individuals to ensure nothing is overlooked. This does not only mean that one inventories physical assets, but informational assets also. In today's business world, the information contained on a work station is often more valuable to the business than the work station it is saved on, so it is crucial to inventory the information on the bank's systems in order to apply controls not only to the systems, but also the information they contain. Some organizations also find it useful to assign a monetary value to each asset on the inventory. It is crucial that out of this process the bank knows what its most critical assets are and where they are located. This crucial portion of the process because the asset inventory will drive the risk assessment process in future steps.

The third step is to develop priorities and validate the assigned values for each asset. This is done by pulling together the major stakeholders of the bank and evaluating the criticality and value of each asset. Agreeing upon the priority and value with decision makers in the organization will ease the process of resource allocations and issues of justifying actions in the future.

Figure 3. McAfee risk management lifecycle

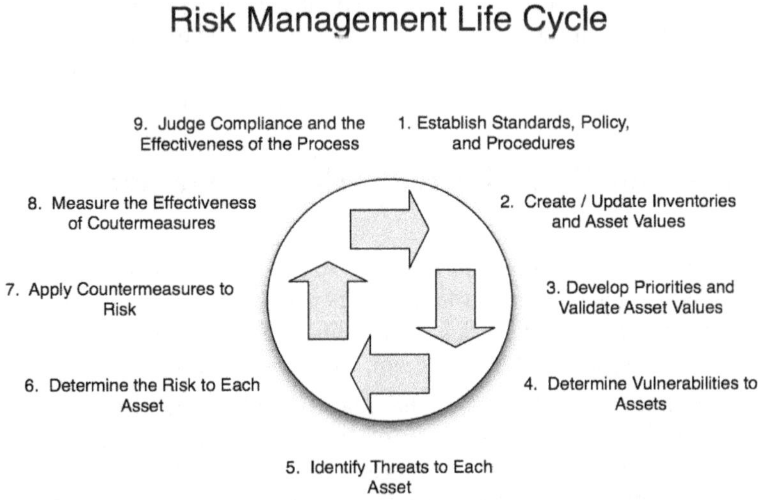

The fourth step of the process is to determine if vulnerabilities exist in the assets identified. Vulnerabilities are defined as a condition or weakness in a system or the way information is being handled. An example of vulnerability is a computer bug that allows for information disclosure. It is also important to remember that information is vulnerable in all of its states. There are typically three states for data: transmission, storage, and processing. Transmission occurs as information is sent or broadcast across a network or the Internet, for example. Storage is when information is held in memory or on a disk for later access. Processing is when information is being manipulated, calculated, or changed. For vulnerabilities to be a risk though, it must also have a threat to exploit the vulnerability. Step five is identifying if vulnerabilities are exploitable by a threat. Thus, if there is a known exploit for a threat, then there is risk to that system and information.

The sixth step is to determine the amount of risk for each system. A general equation is used to determine total risk. It is generalized as: Asset Value × Vulnerabilities × Threats = the associated risk level. This can be a number-based calculation or casual rating, based on the approach used to conduct the risk assessment, either quantitative or qualitative, which is explained in the next section.

Now that the level of risk is established, what is the bank to do to mitigate such risks to acceptable levels? Apply mitigating factors or controls to reduce a threat, thus reducing the overall risk. For example, if computer virus outbreaks are a highly likely threat, then the bank would mitigate the risk by applying a managed antivirus solution to its network. Different mitigating factors also carry different weights. For example, if a bank has the threat of a power outage affecting its daily operations, a viable solution would be to use uninterrupted power supplies to mitigate the risk. This solution only mitigates part of the risk, as uninterrupted power supplies can only maintain operations long enough to safely shut down the systems. To fully mitigate this risk, if deemed appropriate, the bank would want to arrange for the use of a back-up generator. These two solutions combined, mitigated more risk, than the one solution alone. After countermeasures are established to reduce risk, the effectiveness of the measures needs to be assessed. This will then give the bank an idea of its residual risk or risk that has not been fully mitigated. More importantly, is the residual risk at a level that the bank can safely accept or does more need to be done to mitigate this risk? The last step in the process is to check compliance with legal regulations. Is the bank meeting these requirements as they work to reduce risk in the organization? The risk management life cycle is an ongoing process and should be completed minimally on an annual basis, or when major changes are made to the bank's operations for infrastructure.

Qualitative and Quantitative Risk Management

There are two schools of thought when it comes to conducting risk management—qualitative and quantitative. Each has its positives and negatives and each approach lends itself to certain applications. Quantitative is based on numbers and equations to calculate risk, while qualitative uses scales, such as high, medium, and low to measure risk.

Quantitative approaches to risk assessing have been popular, especially in banking, because they are very useful for assessing the value of assets and assigning a number the risks. The issue with this approach is that there currently are no standards in terms of developing metrics for measuring risk. An up side to this method is also its weakness. Using a numeric approach to risk allows the calculation of a wealth of information, but developing an appropriate scale has proven to be quite difficult. Also, using a quantitative method may cause users to get too wrapped up in the math and numbers. The idea behind a risk assessment is not to know if a threat is a 2 or 2.5, but rather to come out with an understanding of where the organization's risks are and then coming up with solutions to mitigate such risk.

The other approach is qualitative, or using general scales of highs, mediums, and lows to generate risk ratings. The issue with this approach is that even though it may be easy to rank systems, threats, vulnerabilities, and risk, it often is not granularly enough in larger operations to differentiate all the systems that are ranked highs and make a meaningful judgment on their level of risk.

Information Security Programs

The term information security program (ISP) has been a major focus for banking recently. With the FDIC recently revising its examination procedures to focus on a top-down management approach to information security within the bank, ISPs have a new-found focus and emphasis. An ISP's purpose is to layout the way a bank's management perceives information security within the bank. It also centralizes and describes the activities that are used to test, improve, and monitor information security. The program is supported by a set of policies that govern the activities that are part of the ISP. These activities may vary by institution and are based on the specific needs of the bank. Generally an ISP will require the following activities:

- Risk assessing
- Vulnerability and penetration testing
- Social engineering testing
- Security awareness training
- Business continuity planning
- Incident response planning
- Auditing it functions

Next we will discuss what each of these activities are and how they fit into the ISP.

Risk Assessment Program

The risk assessment is the first step in setting up an ISP. As stated earlier, the risk assessment will help the bank assess where its critical assets are located, what controls are in place and what risks still remain. The outcome of the risk assessment will show the areas of weakness, where controls, either technical, procedural, or personnel, will be needed to be implemented to reduce the risk to the bank. As stated earlier, the risk assessment is not a one-time activity. The risk assessment life cycle is ongoing. When system changes are made, new systems are acquired, or when there are major changes to operations, it is critical that these activities be assessed for the amount of risk they present. The bank should try to address the risks prior to implementation to avoid rushing the process after implementation or right before an examination.

The risk assessment process also drives other portions of the ISP because of its use of prioritization. One of the first steps in the risk assessment process is to inventory all of the assets of the bank, both informational and physical, and assign them a value. This process will be used in future activities when making key decisions regarding information security, such as where to apply controls, what controls to audit most often, and what topics to educate users on.

Vulnerability and Penetration Testing

The purpose of vulnerability and penetration testing is to build an understanding of where technical weaknesses lie on a bank's systems and network. Often confused, vulnerability and penetration testing are two different types of tests. A vulnerability assessment is an internal scan of the network for vulnerabilities. Often full access is given to systems so that testing can be completed accurately. Outcomes from a vulnerability assessment will be highly technical findings about specific vulnerabilities or configurations on internal systems. A penetration test, on the other hand, is an attempt by an entity to attack a network from the outside, with no prior knowledge of system and network layouts. The goal of a penetration test is to gain access to a system externally and actually exploit a weakness. Both tests can be completed by a variety of products on the market, but automated penetration testing is much more costly to obtain due to the complexity involved with "hacking" a system and exploiting a weakness.

Social Engineering Testing

Social engineering is the "art" of using people, mostly likely bank employees to gain access to restricted information or systems. This can be done a variety of ways: via phone, e-mail, phishing, Dumpster diving, or impersonation. This type of testing can be used to educate and test employee's compliance with policies and training.

Security Awareness Training

Since we have learned that people are the weakest link in a security system, an appropriate risk reduction control is to train users on topics that introduce the most risk. This includes reviewing applicable polices and current security topics to educate users and enable them to better understand the security controls in the bank. It also important to emphasize how to spot attempts to gain access to bank systems or information and what should be done to report such incidents.

Business Continuity Planning

Often overlooked, business continuity planning (BCP) is a crucial process that must be completed to protect customer information and the business, in general. BCP is the process of developing policy and procedures to restore bank services in the event that there is a disruption in a portion of the business. Disaster recovery also is included within the topic of BCP. Disaster recovery is the process of restoring a business after a catastrophic event that has effectively destroyed the bank or one of its locations.

The first step in developing a BCP is conducting a business impact analysis or BIA. The BIA takes each of the bank's critical systems and analyzes the impact of loosing a specific system and what affect it would have on the organization. The BIA together with the risk assessment will allow management to determine which systems are the most critical and should be the focus of their planning. Once the BIA is complete, procedures are developed and agreements are put in place to help in the restoration of that specific system. For example, in most banks the system with the largest impact on operations is the core banking system, thus the bank would plan for quickly rectifying issues with the system or replacing that system in an emergency. This is done by establishing agreements for hardware support, off-site backups, and data restoration services. Procedures would outline what the appropriate employee must do and who they must contact to restore the service. Having a plan of action for each critical system is crucial because often confusion will take over in an emergency or on an issue that is disrupting operations. Having the process documented and agreements in place for support and back-up sites will mitigate the risk of going without a system for an extended period of time. The same approach is used when developing disaster recovery procedures, but rather than looking at a single hardware vendor, the bank will incorporate infrastructure vendors, such as a contractors, security personnel, utility providers, back-up locations, and law enforcement.

Items that should be included in a business continuity plan vary from plan to plan. In general, a procedure on a chain of command for the bank is a minimum. This document will outline who in the bank needs to be notified of a continuity issue and who the decision makers are in each situation. The procedures also should outline how notification of the issue is handled and what media outlets, such as radio or television, are contacted. A BCP also should include a physical inventory of all the items needed to complete a specific task. Items, from a listing of all the workstations and their specifications to the forms needed to take deposits, should be documented. Vendor lists, employee's contact information, and vendor agreements also should be included in the plan. The general train of thought in BCP is to provide everything an employee would need to reestablish a specific service in one document.

Testing of the BCP is an aspect that is often overlooked. At least annually, all the business continuity processes should be tested. This will facilitate changes and improvements to the plan. A plan that is not tested is more likely to fail and be useless in the actual event it is needed.

Incident Response

Incident response is planning what actions need to be taken in response to specific events. Most often associated with negative events, such as a virus outbreak or system compromise, incident response can be used for any event that needs a planned and thought-out process. For example, a bank may have an incident response procedure for a virus infection and a request for information from a third party. Both are valid and can be planned for. The incident response process should focus on the most likely events and systems for the bank. Just as with the BCP, all the information an employee will need to respond to an incident should be in the procedures, including contact information, contract numbers, or the chain of command for a specific incident.

Auditing

Auditing is the final step in any ISP. The audit is a systematic checking of the controls in place in the bank. Basically, it is an independent assessment if the wishes of upper management are being carried out in operations, that is, if the directives in the ISP and the associated policy are actually being done. The audit process is driving by three documents: the audit policy, audit program, and audit schedule. The audit policy establishes the general controls around the audit function. For example, the policy will outline that an audit will need to be completed annually by both the internal audit department and an external auditor. It will outline what types of controls and the methods used to test the controls. It will also outline the type of report that will be generated out of the audit and how the audit findings are to be reported to the board of directors. The audit program is the next document. The program establishes what controls will be tested and the process for testing them. Lastly, there is the audit schedule. This document outlines when controls will be tested. Often it is too long of a process to test each control every time an audit is conducted. Plus, the audit schedule also needs to be tied to the risk assessment, so that controls that are around the most critical systems are tested the most often.

Two types of audits exist, controls-based and standards-based. A controls-based audit will use the controls stated in policy to build the audit program. The approach works well for testing if what the board has approved in policy is being implemented in operations. A controls-based audit will audit the policies and procedures that fall within the scope of the audit. A standards-based audit uses a set of controls approved as an industry standard to build the audit program. Thus, operation's performance is matched up against a standard set of controls such as ISO 17799 or control objectives for information and related rechnology (COBIT).

Conclusion and Future Directions

Bank security is serious business. Technology is exploding in banks and criminals understand that information is worth money. A plethora of information security law requires banks to safeguard confidential customer information. This chapter reviewed what banks need to do to protect the confidentiality, integrity, and availability of information, including the presentation of an ISP design that community banks should use as a framework for information protection. Future directions include expanding the information security framework provided in the chapter. Future directions also include working with bank regulators to revise their regulatory processes to be in line with the aforementioned information security framework.

References

Allan, C. A., Anderson, C., Axelrod, C., Bender, M., Callahan, R., Gerbracht, F. W., et al. (2002). *Banking and finance sector: The national strategy for critical infrastructure assurance*. Washington, DC: U.S. Department of Treasury.

Bruce, L. (2003, March 26). *Skimming the cash out of your account.* Retrieved July 6, 2006, from http://www.bankrate.com/brm/news/atm/20021004a.asp

Chabrow, E. (2002a). Businesses urged to share. *Insurance & Technology, 27*(8), 14.

Chabrow, E. (2002b). Businesses urged to share data about security holes. *InformationWeek,* (888), 36.

Coolidge, S. (2006). *About SAS 70.* Retrieved April 12, 2006, from www.sas70.com/index2.htm

Dittrich, D., & Himma, K. E. (2006). Hackers, crackers, and computer criminals. In H. Bidgoli (Ed.), *Handbook of information security: information warfare; social, legal, and international issues; and security foundations* (pp. 154-171). Hoboken, NJ: John Wiley & Sons, Inc.

Ernst & Young. (2004). *Global information security survey 2004.* Retrieved March 5, 2006, from http://www.ey.com/GLOBAL/content.nsf/International/Press_Release_-2004_Global_Information_Security_Survey

Exec. Order No. 13231, 86 C.F.R. 53063-53071 (2001).

Federal Deposit Insurance Corporation (FDIC). (2003a). *Who is the FDIC?* Retrieved April 20, 2006, from www.fdic.gov/about/learn/symbol/index.html

Federal Deposit Insurance Corporation (FDIC). (2003b). *Banking review.* Retrieved April 22, 2006, from www.fdic.gov/bank/analytical/banking/2003sep/footnote1.html

Federal Financial Institutions Examination Council (FFIEC). (). *About the FFIEC.* Retrieved April 20, 2006, from www.ffiec.gov/about.htm

Federal Financial Institutions Examination Council (FFIEC). ().*Glossary d to h.* Retrieved April 4, 2006, from www.ffiec.gov/ffiecinfobase/html_pages/gl_01a.html#E

Federal Financial Institutions Examination Council (FFIEC). (1999). Uniform rating system for information technology. *Federal Register, 64,* 3109.

Federal Financial Institutions Examination Council (FFIEC). (2003). *Audit work program.* Retrieved April 22, 2006, from www.ffiec.gov/ffiecinfobase/booklets/audit/audit_work-program.rtf

Federal Financial Institutions Examination Council (FFIEC). (2003). *Supervision of technology service providers.* Retrieved April 22, 2006, from www.ffiec.gov/ffiecinfobase/booklets/tsp/TSP_01_risk_based%20_supervision.htm

Federal Financial Institutions Examination Council (FFIE). (2003). *Supervision of technology service -roviders—Appendix D.* Retrieved April 22, 2006, from www.ffiec.gov/ffiecinfobase/booklets/tsp/TSP_08_appendix_d.htm

Federal Financial Institutions Examination Council (FFIE). (2004). *Outsourcing technology services.* Retrieved April 4, 2006, from www.ffiec.gov/ffiecinfobase/html_pages/outsource_book_frame.htm

Federal Financial Institutions Examination Council (FFIE). (2004). *The automated clearing house.* Retrieved April 5, 2006, from www.ffiec.gov/ffiecinfobase/booklets/Retail/retail_02d.html

Federal Reserve Act, (1913). Retrieved April 20, 2006, from www.federalreserve.gov/generalinfo/fract/

Federal Reserve Board. (2003). *The structure of the Federal Reserve System.* Retrieved April 20, 2006, from www.federalreserve.gov/pubs/frseries/frseri.htm

Federal Reserve Board. (2005). *The twelve Federal Reserve districts.* Retrieved April 20, 2006, from www.federalreserve.gov/otherfrb.htm

Fisher, D. (2004, May 24). Tales of cyber-crime running rampant. *eWeek*, Retrieved July 18, 2006, from http://www.eweek.com/article2/0,1895,1597360,00.asp

Garten, J. E. (2002). Homeland security could really shake up business. *Business Week,* (3797), 24.

Halbig, W. W. (2004). *What is your first line of defense?* Retrieved February 4, 2004, from www.nisws.com/article013.html

Hansche, S., Berti, J., & Hare, C. (2004). *Official (ISC)2 guide to the CISSP exam.* Boca Raton, FL: Auerbach.

Hayashi, F., Sullivan, R. & Weiner, S. E. (2003). A guide to the ATM and debit card industry. *Federal Reserve Bank of Kansas City,* 6-8, 12-15.

Money Laundering. (2005). In J. Lehman & S. Phelps (Eds.), *West's encyclopedia of American law*(2nd ed.) (Vol. 7, pp. 101-102). Detroit: Thomson Gale.

National Credit Union Administration (NCUA). *About NCUA.* Retrieved April 22, 2006, from www.ncua.gov/AboutNCUA/Index.htm

National Credit Union Administration (NCUA). *NCUA board and actions.* Retrieved April 22, 2006, from www.ncua.gov/NCUABoard/index.htm

National Strategy to Secure Cyberspace, The President's Critical Infrastructure Protection Board. Retrieved February 14, 2003, from http://www.whitehouse.gov/pcipb/

NITRD. (2005). *Cyber security: A crisis of prioritization.* Retrieved March 7, 2006, from www.nitrd.gov/pitac/reports/20050301_cybersecurity/cybersecurity.pdf

OCC Bulletin—Comptroller of the currency administration of national banks: 2003—Suspicious Activity Report. Retrieved from http://www.occ.treas.gov/ftp/bulletin/2003-27.doc

Office of the Comptroller of the Currency (OCC). *About the OCC.* Retrieved April 20, 2006, from www.occ.treas.gov/aboutocc.htm

Office of the Comptroller of the Currency (OCC). *About the OCC—District map.* Retrieved April 20, 2006, from www.occ.treas.gov/district.htm

Office of Thrift Supervision (OTS). (2006). *About the OTS.* Retrieved April 20, 2006, from www.federalreserve.gov/otherfrb.htm

Presidential Decision Directive No. 63, 150 C.F.R. 41804 (1998).

Smith, D. (2005). *Customers vs. Bank of America: Who's to blame?*. Retrieved April 20, 2006, from http://searchsecurity.techtarget.com/columnItem/0,294698,sid14_gci1062440,00.html?track=NL-358&ad=506214

Stump, J. (2003). *Food security—Protect and prevent.* Retrieved February 1, 2004, from www.vdacs.state.va.us/foodsafety/advisory.html

Terrorist financing identity theft: Homeland security and terrorism threat from document fraud, identity theft and social security number misuse, 208th Cong., (2003) (testimony of John S. Pistole). Retrieved June 10, 2006, from: http://www.senate.gov/~finance/hearings/testimony/2003test/091003jptest.pdf

Tommaso, P. (2003). Bank for international settlement: Committee on Payment and Settlement Systems, payment and settlement systems in selected countries. *Press & Communications.*

U.S. Department of Homeland Security. (2002). *The Department of Homeland Security.* Washington, DC.

U.S. Department of Homeland Security Directive No. 9 (2004).

U. S. Department of Justice. (n.d.). *Identity theft and fraud.* Retrieved July 10, 2006, from http://www.usdoj.gov/criminal/fraud/idtheft.html

U.S. Department of Justice. (2003). *Public advisory: Special report for retail businesses on identity theft (1).*

U.S. Department of State. (2003). *New customer identification rules target terror financing.* International Information Programs. Retrieved July 17, 2006, from http://www.iwar.org.uk/news-archive/2003/04-30-5.htm

U.S. Patriot Act of 2001, P.L. 107-56.. Retrieved July 19, 2006, from http://frwebgate.access.gpo.gov/cgi-bin/getdoc.cgi?dbname=107_cong_public_laws&docid=f:publ056.107.pdf

Verton, D. (2003). Protection of critical systems still haphazard. *Computerworld, 37*(36), 4.

Appendix A

Composite 1

"Financial institutions and service providers rated composite 1 as exhibiting a strong performance in every respect and generally have components rated 1 or 2. Weaknesses in IT are minor in nature and are easily corrected during the normal course of business. Risk management processes provide a comprehensive program to identify and monitor risk relative to the size, complexity, and risk profile of the entity. Strategic plans are well defined and fully integrated throughout the organization. This allows management to quickly adapt to changing market, business, and technology needs of the entity. Management identifies weaknesses promptly and takes appropriate corrective action to resolve audit and regulatory concerns. The financial condition of the service provider is strong and overall performance shows no cause for supervisory concern."

Composite 2

"Financial institutions and service providers rated composite 2 as exhibiting a safe and sound performance, but it may demonstrate modest weaknesses in operating performance, monitoring, management processes, or system development. Generally, senior management corrects weaknesses in the normal course of business. Risk management processes adequately identify and monitor risk relative to the size, complexity, and risk profile of the entity. Strategic plans are defined but may require clarification, better coordination, or improved communication throughout the organization. As a result, management anticipates, but responds less quickly to changes in market, business, and technological needs of the entity. Management normally identifies weaknesses and takes appropriate corrective action. However, greater reliance is placed on audit and regulatory intervention to identify and resolve concerns. The financial condition of the service provider is acceptable, and, while internal control weaknesses may exist, there are no significant supervisory concerns. As a result, supervisory action is informal and limited."

Composite 3

"Financial institutions and service providers rated composite 3 as exhibiting some degree of supervisory concern, due to a combination of weaknesses that may range from moderate to severe. If weaknesses persist, further deterioration in the condition and performance of the institution or service provider is likely. Risk management processes may not effectively identify risks and may not be appropriate for the size, complexity, or risk profile of the entity. Strategic plans are vaguely defined and may not provide adequate direction for IT initiatives. As a result, management often has difficulty responding to changes in business, market, and technological needs of the entity. Self-assessment practices are weak and are generally reactive to audit and regulatory exceptions. Repeat concerns may exist indicating that management may lack the ability or willingness to resolve concerns. The financial condition of the service provider may be weak and/or negative trends may be evident. While financial or operational failure is unlikely, increased supervision is necessary. Formal or informal supervisory action may be necessary to secure corrective action."

Composite 4

"Financial institutions and service providers rated composite 4 as operating in an unsafe and unsound environment that may impair the future viability of the entity. Operating weaknesses are indicative of serious managerial deficiencies. Risk management processes inadequately identify and monitor risk, and practices are not appropriate given the size, complexity, and risk profile of the entity. Strategic plans are poorly defined and not coordinated or communicated throughout the organization. As a result, management and the board are not committed to, or may be incapable of ensuring, that technological needs are met. Management does not perform self-assessments and demonstrates an inability or unwillingness to correct audit and regulatory concerns. The financial condition of the service provider is severely impaired or deteriorating. Failure of the financial institution or service provider may be likely, unless IT problems are remedied. Close supervisory attention is necessary and, in most cases, formal enforcement action is warranted."

Composite 5

"Financial institutions and service providers rated composite 5 as exhibiting critically deficient operating performances that are in need of immediate remedial action. Operational problems and serious weaknesses may exist throughout the organization. Risk management processes are severely deficient and provide management little or no perception of risk relative to the size, complexity, and risk profile of the entity. Strategic plans do not exist or are ineffective, and management and the board provide little or no direction for IT initiatives. As a result, management is unaware of, or inattentive to, technological needs of the entity. Management is unwilling or incapable of correcting audit and regulatory concerns. The financial condition of the service provider is poor and failure is highly probable due to poor operating performance or financial instability. Ongoing supervisory attention is necessary."

Chapter V

Security Risk Management Strategy of Financial Services Institutions

Guoling Lao, Shanghai University of Finance and Economics, China

Liping Wang, Shanghai University of Finance and Economics, China

Abstract

This chapter is about a new security risk management strategy for financial services institutions. The proper strategy presented here takes the systematic and cybernetics theory as the instruction, regards the risk analysis process, the management strategy implementation, and the monitor and audit as an organic security management system. Thus the strategy is an autoadapted open system to defeat various safety threats dynamically. By comparing management of electronic commerce (e-commerce) security risks with that of traditional financial risks, this chapter suggests accurate security risk measurement using quantitative analysis and further integration of the e-commerce security risk with traditional financial risks.

Introduction

Along with the high-speed development of the Internet, e-commerce is attracting more and more users owing to its characteristic of openness, liberty, and internationality, but, at the same time, the safety and security problems are becoming more and more serious. In an online investigation of e-commerce by a world investigation company, when asked why people don't prefer the online payment, the majority replied that they worry that hackers may steal their credit card information. And according to the FBI's 2005 Computer Crime Survey, "Over 64% of the respondents incurred a loss. Viruses and worms cost the most, accounting for $12 million of the $32 million in total losses." Internationally, this situation is not an exception.

In China, CNCERT/CC, which is the central institution collecting reports of security incidents for China's inland network, received 65,679 reports in the first two quarters of 2005, more than the total number in 2004. Among these reports, 45.91% were home page tampers; 29% were network fraud; and others included DoS, junk mails, worms, Trojan horses and so on. Since 2004, threats of network fraud in China have been more terrible, and the victims are mainly financial and e-commerce Web sites. E-commerce and financial Web sites are the main targets of attacks by hackers and their security urgently needs to be strengthened. How to establish a secure, reliable, and convenient e-commerce application environment and provide enough protections for information security has already become the hot topic for financial services institutions as well as their customers.

Whether in the academic, industrial, or practical field, there are many studies about e-commerce security risk management at financial services institutions. Rich experiences have been accumulated, and some standardized regulations and codes have been formed, but several problems still exist. For instance, security risk management strategy does not possess the capability of integrity and adaptation without systematic and cybernetics theory as a guide; risk assessment still settles at a grading stage. Security risk management does not comply with the traditional risk management of financial services institutions and so on. In view of these points, this chapter attempts to make improvements on the basis of existing research and studies and provide a proper security risk management strategy for financial services institutions engaged in e-commerce.

Background

Different Angles of E-Commerce Security Research

It is taken for granted internationally that security is the key and core problem in the field of e-commerce. Wang (2005) gives a generalized definition of e-commerce security: "E-commerce security means to protect the organizational and individual assets (including physical and electronic assets) in e-commerce system from unauthorized access, use, distortion and destroy. E-commerce security covers every part of the whole e-commerce chain, such as client terminal, communication channel, as well as relative internal information system of the organization" (p. 11). E-commerce's core problem is security, which includes information security, transaction security, system security, application security, and so on.

Two Primary Study Angles

A conclusion can be drawn from the above definition: e-commerce security actually contains physical security and information security, if classified from the material modality. Therefore, the study of e-commerce can be carried out from two angles: physical security and information security. Most studies and research focus on the information security. In fact, both data loss and device breakdown come down to the damage of e-commerce information. So we can say the core problem of an e-commerce security study is essentially information safety.

At financial services institutions, the study of e-commerce security usually starts with an e-commerce operational platform. In this way, e-commerce security may include the security of the physical environment, application platform, system platform, network platform, and communication platform. In September 2003, the World Bank held the Financial Sector Policy Global Dialogue, which included the topic Electronic Safety and Soundness. In this dialogue, Nelms, chief security officer of the World Bank Treasury, emphasized the five layers of network data flow: application layer, intermediary device, database management, operational system, and network. Each layer has the ability to influence information security, so access control measures must be deployed in each layer. The business process is horizontal, while information flow is vertical, so risk assessment must be analyzed from each layer, when data transmission needs cross-technology.

In recent years, the study of how to carry out information technology (IT) risk inspection and bank supervision in the open environment, especially how to appraise whether each layer of a multilayer e-commerce system is secure, has drawn much attention.

Diversified Definitions of Information Security

Since any kind of e-commerce security problems eventually result in the damage or loss of e-commerce information, it is reasonable that various studies of e-commerce security concentrate on information security. The definition of information security affects the scope of the study of e-commerce security risk management directly and deeply.

There are multifarious definitions of information security both in academic field and in industry. Chen(2000) says that e-commerce security elements include validity, confidentiality, integrity, nonrepudiation, and accountability. Laudon and Traver (2003) conclude that there are six key aspects of e-commerce security: integrity, nonrepudiation, authenticity, confidentiality, privacy, and availability. In Guidelines for the Management of Information Technology Security (GMITS), the properties of assets (information) are extended from the classical confidentiality, integrity, and availability to accountability, authenticity, and reliability. (GMITS: ISO/ IEC 13335 Information Technology—Security Techniques—Guidelines for the Management of IT Security. This ISO/IEC technical report, published in 1995, was written to be usable and useful in the worst-case scenario environment; that is, a hostile environment, such as the Internet.)

International Federation of Accountants considers that information security is to protect people and communication infrastructure that transmit information and depend on information and information system against loss incurred by failure of information confidentiality, integrity and availability (International Federation of Accountants, 1998). ISO defines information security as technological and managerial security protection established for data processing systems that aims to prevent computer hardware, software, and data from incidental or vicious damage, distortion, and leak. In ISO/IEC17799, information security is described as an asset with value to an organization that needs proper protect; information security has the following characteristics: confidentiality, integrity, and availability. Latham D.C, chairman of National Telecommunications and Information Systems Security Committee (NTISSC), principal of American C3I, and former deputy secretary of defense, insists that information security should include six aspects: communication security, computer security, TEMPEST, transmission security, physical security, and personnel security.

The above definitions and descriptions are only small parts of the exciting information security definitions. Different research institutions, organizations, and individuals have their own standards and points of view, so a universal definition seems not to be found. But they still have some things in common. Generally, the elements of information security that are used in practice are different from those in theory.

Evolution of E-Commerce Security Management Strategy

Information security strategy continuously evolves and develops. Reviewing the evolution process of security management strategy, we can divide it into two stages: scattered supplement stage and standardization stage. The middle 1990s may be thought of as the boundary between the two stages (Zhao, 2004). Security management strategy generally follows the following path of progress: driving by event; gradual standardization; security risk management.

Initial Stage: Driven by Event

Thirty years ago, security mainly meant physical security, such as a guard, door, and window with an alarm, security medal, and vidicon serving as monitors. At that time, the dump terminals in use had limited access, so computer security was only concerned with a few people and was a simple question. With the development of computer technology and networks, especially after e-commerce began to hold an important position in the financial business, security management began to draw much more attention and gained its way to develop.

At the initial stage, security management attached too much importance toIT and pursued a high level of technology ignoring the economic cost and real security needs, which led to multiple resource wastes and still left many security weaknesses. This action proved to be wrong and organizations began to shift to management methods. In this course, technology methods and management solutions were separate and divided.

Many financial services institutions also made great efforts to keep information security in good status besides the high technology investment. But information security management took only static, partial, few-people involved, afterward mode. Only when some threats brought loss or damage did the organization begin to amend and adapt security management solutions. That is why this phase is called driven by event.

Such security management has obvious defects. Its structure is too incompact and scattered and left many security leaks and blind spots. Once the configuration of the enterprise's system changes, the size of enterprise expands, or the number or the scope of assets needed to secure increases, security solutions would likely fail to quickly change accordingly, and therefore induce a series of security problems.

Stage of Standardization

Organizations began to regard security problems as a whole and formed a relatively integrated security management strategy at this stage. The security management strategy generally contained technology and management system (or sometimes referred to as operation management) methods. Almost all of the organizations engaged in e-commerce had their own security strategy, which included technology solutions, management solutions, faculty training for security, and so forth. These solutions and rules joined together, but in the security risk analysis, defects and limitations still remained.

The Main Trend: Security Risk Management

During the evolution process of security management strategy, technology and management methods were integrated and risk analysis and control were introduced. Thereby security management entered the era of security risk management.

Common Sense Approach to Security Risk Management

Risk indicates a likelihood of economic loss, other interest loss, and natural damage or harm, which are induced by uncertainty existing in the course of some activities. In economics, risk is also thought of as an uncertainty, including the quantifiable likelihood of loss and profit. But here we only discuss the harm brought on by security problem, so it is reasonable to limit risk to likelihood of loss. This definition is widely used in the field of risk management and insurance.

Risk is very familiar to financial services institutions. The traditional business mode of the financial services institutions is confronted with risks in many aspects of routine operations: competition risks led by the intensive market competition; transformation risk resulting from the social development and technical innovation; and financial risk, credit risk, as well as operational risk, and so on. The rise of e-commerce increases the probability and the degree of damage of the above risks, since most e-commerce activities depend on computer networks and systems. New risks, which never appeared in traditional financial businesses, also are created by the combination of open networks and complicated business operations. Therefore it is important to make out the category of risk, risk characteristic, and scope of effect, and analyze and assess e-commerce security risks correctly to avoid and control

Table 1. Process flow of information security risk management recommended by IS-One (Source: IS-One China, n.d.)

Demand analysis and extension definition
• assets differentiation and classification • threats analysis • definition of demand level of security protection(optional)
Detailed risk assessment and analysis (not full quantitative)
• weakness analysis • current security control measurement analysis • combined risk analysis • risk quantification and classification
Security measures design and implementation
• choosing security measures • design and improvement of security strategy • identification of security solutions • implementation of security measurements
Check and re-examination
• residual risk analysis • periodic reassessment of the contents in first two phases

risks. More and more financial institutions realize this problem and are working to manage the e-commerce security risk.

Risk management theory and method have made continuous progress in last few decades, which contributed a lot to security management. Risk management is a management process that reduces the probability of risks or limits loss brought on by risks, including the activities of programming, organizing, leading, harmonizing, and control necessary for the effective ways to prevent loss. Risk management takes the existence of successful attacks for granted but will control and minimize the probability and degree of influence, which is the substance of risk management. The management of security risk just follows and abstracts the soul of risk management, and forms its own features.

For instance, IS-One, a famous corporation in the information security field in China, provides information security services. IS-One considers that information security problem as well as other security problems, such as asset problem and finance problem, can be summarized as the problem of risk management. So the risk management is the essence and basis to provide sound security solution for customers and establish healthy secure technical and managerial system. Table 1 describes the basic process of information risk management followed by IS-One.

Various Standards and Regulations Forming and Improving

In recent years, the standard and criterion of security risk management continue to come on internationally, such as *Risk Management Principles for Electronic Banking* by the Basel

Committee on Banking Supervision, BS7799 by British Standards Institution, and so forth. The first part of BS7799 formed the international standard ISO/IEC17799, which is accepted globally and taken as national information security standard by many countries.

Besides the international criteria, a lot of countries have gradually recognized the importance of security risk management and made some country standards and regulations, such as the Electronic Banking: Final Rule by the Office of the Comptroller of the Currency and the Management of Security Risks in Electronic Banking Services by the Hong Kong Monetary Authority. In March 2006, the China Banking Regulatory Commission promulgated Administrative Measures on Electronic Banking, giving suggestions for e-commerce security risk management of Chinese financial enterprises.

Comparatively, standards about security management strategy are less than security information technology. Current research basically focuses on practice, and theoretic studies are scarce.

Depending on External Professional Institutions to Assess Security Situation

The financial services institutions engaged in e-commerce generally make security risk management. The very popular mode is depending on professional institutions to assess the status of security risk management. The e-commerce security and technology risks have tight connection with the advance of information technology (IT), the level of system design and development, and selection of equipments and suppliers, so financial institutions cannot identify, inspect, control, and manage correlative risks, only depending on own resources and strength. Similarly, the supervising institutions cannot assess and inspect the e-commerce security of financial services institutions correctly just by themselves either. So in most countries, financial supervision institutions introduce external professional organizations to assess e-commerce security to assist and improve the inspection and administration of the e-commerce security and technology risk. And many financial services institutions employ the similar organizations to provide objective security risk assessment.

Because of such a demand, information system audit (ISA) prevails widely as an IT service in many countries. Almost every famous consulting corporation will provide likely service of ISA.

ISA with information technology audit (IT audit) as another name, is a kind of information service. In the early stage of development, ISA was called as electronic data processing audit (EDPA), which means the audit to IS whose core is computer. In 1960s, along with the popularization of computers, especially after the computerization of accountant, ISA came forth.

In Japan ISA is defined as: a serious of activities performed by an independent IT auditor, including comprehensive check and assessment of IS which core is computers and giving suggestions and advices to the highest leader of the audited objects, in order to ensure the security, reliance, and availability of IS. Some Chinese scholars consider IT audit should cover the entire process of examination and assessment of IS, including programming, development, implementation, operation, and maintenance, so that it can audit the security, reliability, and availability of the IS and assure the soundness and accuracy of data.

In brief, ISA can be defined as: serious activities of examination and assessment of security, stability, and availability of IS which has close relation with the audited organization and then providing suggestion of improvement to the audited objects. And professional auditing institutions and auditors carried out these functions. Comparatively, the definition of ISA would cover more contents than IT audit.

Box 1. China Information Technology Security Certification Center (Source: Based on China Information Technology Security Certification Center, n.d.)

China Information Technology Security Certification Center (CNITSEC) is a functional institute that is professional in information security assessment and certification in behalf of the government in China. CNITSEC administrates and functions the national information security certification system which complying with the national laws and regulations of product quality and information security management.

CNITSEC is the unique assessment and certification institute authorized by China government in the field of IT security. It can provide following product certification:

- Certification to information security products: assessment and certification to national and foreign IT products, including information security products, such as firewall, intrusion monitor, security audit, network isolation, VPN, smart card, card terminal, safety control, and so on; as well as IT products used in other areas like operating system, database, switch, router, application software, and so on.
- Information system certification: test, assessment, and certification to the security of national IS.
- Certification to the quality of information security service: testing, appraisal, and authentication to the qualities of organizations and institutes who provide information security services.
- Certification to the quality of information security professional: examination, appraisal, and authentication to the quality and capability of information security professional.
- Standards and criteria of the assessment and certification: the basic standard of information certification is the Chinese standard GB/T18336-2001, which equal to international standard ISO/IEC 15408(CC).

In addition, the standards complied still include security technology rules, standards, and certification criteria authorized by China National Information Security Certification Administration Committee:

- System certification: Information Technology—Code of Practice for Information Security Management, (ISO/IEC 17799-2000), Information Technology—System Security Engineering—Capability Maturity Model (ISO/IEC 21827-2002), Code of Information System Assurance Assessment, Administration Specification of Information Security Engineering Quality, Code of E-Government Information System Security Assurance Certification, and Security Technology Specification of Online Securities Entrust System;
- Service quality certification: Evaluation Criteria for Competence of Information System Security Service Provider; and
- Professional certification: Evaluation Criteria for Competence of Certified Information Security Professional.

Many Chinese financial institutions pass the information security assessment and get the certification. Among commercial banks, both China Merchants Bank and Industrial Bank, have gotten the certifications of online banking.

Considering the evolution and current status of security risk management, we can find that although financial services institutions have thought much of the e-commerce security risk management and accumulated a lot of experiences and rules, these achievements of research are solely practice guides or assessment rules, not offer details about how to realize the successful security risk management. The external risk management services can indeed give assurance suggestions and references of e-commerce security management, but many enterprises would not disclose entire security problems and status of internal security management to outer organizations in view of the sensitivity and significance of the security. Just like the outsourcing of IS of the financial services institutions, if these critical resources are delivered to another party completely, it is undoubtedly that the party possesses the power to affect the continuity of organization's business and the organization's survival and development would potentially be under control of outer parties. At present, most financial services institutions begin to reject outsourcing (PricewaterhouseCoopers, 2006). This trend can make us believe that financial services institutions would manage their e-commerce security risk by itself in the future except the necessary external authentication.

PricewaterhouseCoopers and CIO Magazine have conducted a worldwide study *The Global State of Information Security 2005*. In the Next Year's To-Do List of the study lists 10 common answers of the top strategic priorities. The fourth is "overall information security strategy" and the sixth is "centralized security information management system." Thus it can be seen that information security management strategy is a universal and even critical problem to enterprises.

So it is urgent to give an e-commerce security risk management strategy on the level of enterprise, making full use of the enterprise's own resource and current research production.

Study of E-Commerce Security Risk Management in Financial Services Institutions

Problems of Current E-Commerce Security Risk Management Strategy

Lack of Theory of Systematic and Cybernetics

Whether the security risk management strategy in practice or the rules and codes serving as a guide, such as Code of Practice for Information Security Management(ISO17799), Evaluation Criteria for IT Security(GB/T18336.1, China, based on CC – Common Criteria for Information Technology Security Evaluation), Risk Management Principles for Electronic Banking by Basel Committee on Banking Supervision, cannot act as a risk guard system that can be implemented directly in the enterprise, even if these rules all give solutions of security risk management, and may include specific principle and detailed program of risk management.

In practice, the organization engaged in e-commerce is a complicated system. The framework and process of e-commerce security risk management is also a delicate system. The advantage of systematic is solving problems of organization management, and in the system management the cybernetics will work inevitably. So the idea of systematic and cybernetics is absolutely necessary in e-commerce security risk management. But in the course of project and implementation of the existing e-commerce security risk management strategy, we nearly cannot find the use of systematic and cybernetics methods. The entire system appears evidently to lack support of scientific theory.

If the security risk management strategy just simply lists a lot of security control methods, then the security assurance cannot be realized to deal with risk dynamically. Moreover, it also will be inconvenient for internal employees to grasp and follow the security strategy because of the wide scope and numerous kinds of these security control methods. Without the guide of the theory of systematic and cybernetics, the strategy cannot form a comprehensive and orderly security network and security weakness would be attacked easily when the organization meets multifarious security attacks. This is an apparent limitation of the current e-commerce security management of the financial services institutions.

Immaturity of Method and Model and Insufficiency of Quantitative Analysis in Risk Analysis

The traditional e-commerce security risk management strategy of a financial services institution is confronted with the problems, such as immaturity of risk analysis model and insufficiency of quantitative analysis. In general, the financial services institution would employ technology solutions and management solutions when control the e-commerce security risk. In the aspect of technology solution, encryption, firewall, authentication, secure network protocol, and other technology will be used usually. As for the management methods, there may be only employee management, routine operation limitation, device and equipment management, data management, and so forth. But a formal management scheme is absent to integrate both solutions. And in most financial services institutions, the e-commerce security risk management strategy still stays at the stage of focusing on relative risk level. The quantitative analysis method does not appear in the risk analysis and assessment. This fact directly results in the absence of formal evaluation model. At the same time, the e-commerce security risk analysis method in use is simple and not rich in category.

Comparing the security risk management strategy of commercial bank with that of the traditional business, we can see the problem more clearly. Commercial banks accumulate a lot of the methods in risk analysis and risk control and form many quantitative models to measure and estimate the risks during the long time research and study of the traditional business (The credit risk may be the proper example, about which there are many mature models and formal methods universally accepted). These models and methods can serve as the reference of the e-commerce security risk management strategy.

Firstly, uses a lot of scientific methods in the risk identification process, such as risk tree analysis, expert forecast, flow chart analysis, screening monitor diagnostic, and so forth.

- **Risk tree analysis:** This method uses the graphic form to decompose the risk step by step and find the concrete state of the risk finally. Since the figure of the decomposed risk is like a tree, so this method is called risk tree scavenge.
- **Expert forecast:** The expert acts as the object from which the information is obtained in such a method. Commercial banks constitute a scheme and gather experts of various fields to find the rules and forecast the future development on the basis of overall analysis of the historical and current problems.
- **Flow chart analysis:** By the aid of flow chart system, flow chart analysis is suitable to find out the potential problems and the headstream of the risk, since each node of the concrete trade process of the bank can be analyzed.
- **Screening monitor diagnostic:** Estimates and identifies the risks commercial banks faced according to the results of screening, observing, recording, and analyzing of various risk factors.

Secondly, uses a lot of quantitative analysis in the risk measurement. In usual risk analysis, the process of risk identification, risk measurement, and risk analysis belong to one process. Risk measurement is the continuance of the risk identification, so these two stages are not necessarily divided clearly. Risk analysis and assessment to the commercial bank includes measurement of the loss probability, degree, and extension of each risk factors

In the market risk measurement, the value at risk (VaR) method becomes the mainstream gradually, which is the expected maximum loss of the financial assets or security portfolio at a given confidence level. In the process of credit risk measurement, some mature quantitative models, like CreditMetrics, RiskMetrics, KMV, are popular. In the advanced field of the operational risk measuring, the Basel Committee regulates the commercial banks should take the quantitative analysis to evaluate the operational risk. The quantitative analysis methods for measuring the operational risk develop and progress continuously.

Thirdly, uses a lot of quantitative analysis in the assessment to the traditional business risk.

On the basis of risk identification and measurement, commercial banks also acquire the risk probability of the bank system and the degree of damage by combining the probability of the risk event, loss, and other factors. And, then, commercial banks make decision about what measures should be adopted to control risk, to what extent the risk control is proper, and so on. Some methods, like cost benefit analysis, risk benefit analysis, risk trade-off analysis, comprehensive analysis, and statistical appraisal analysis, are in common use.

- **Cost benefit analysis:** This analysis considers what cost can afford and what result can achieve, under the precondition of some actions.
- **Risk benefit analysis:** This considers how much risk will undertake and how much benefits can obtain under the precondition of some actions.
- **Risk trade-off analysis:** This compares each sequent result of risk quantitatively and measures the influence of risk.
- **Comprehensive analysis:** This analysis adopts the statistical analysis method, divides the risk factors into different categories, uses expert survey to give scores in each category, and then calculates the ratio of actual score versus possible maximum score,

according to the scores and weight of each element. The ratios serve as the foundation of the risk assessment.

- **Statistical appraisal analysis:** This compares and analyzes the costs and benefits for further assessment under the condition that history probability and value of loss are known.

But in the e-commerce security risk management, commercial banks scarcely use precise quantitative analysis. What is the reason? On one hand, security risk emerges accompanied with the new business mode of e-commerce, and the history of e-commerce mode itself is only about two decades. So it is natural that the quantitative technology is not mature. On the other hand, different from the traditional business risk, security risk often has not the direct and clear link to the return or loss of assets. But as for the credit risk, which measures the risk of an economic loss brought by the counter party's failure to fulfill its contractual obligations, there are lots of calculation methods and quantitative measurement. Because the credit risk directly connects certain benefit or loss, the measurement is comparatively convenient. While the security risk usually affects the enterprise's return or loss indirectly through the conduction of information or entity, and even through a much longer conductive chain. Thirdly, security risk may cover most business flow in which there are many different kinds of operations. Each operation has its own features and the relative risks and loss may not be calculated by a universal way. So the quantitative method is scarcely used in the management of security risk.

Ignorance of Integrity with Original Traditional Risk Management Strategy

Most existing research about security risk of e-commerce focus on IT or the computer technology. There is little research about security risk of e-commerce from the angle of financial services institutions themselves. This situation results that the research about security risk cannot be established at a high level. If the research about e-commerce security risk ignores or departs from the integrality of commercial bank risks and only focuses on information technology, it will lag behind and further affects the research of traditional business risks. But in most commercial banks, one side is risk control about traditional business, and the other side is the security risk control about e-commerce business; and the two sides are separated.

In essence, the security risks of e-commerce are no more than the changed traditional business risk by new business mode and the new risk which in the field of traditional business risk cannot be perspicuous for a while. Security risk of e-commerce and the risk of traditional business belong to the risks of the same commercial bank, which should be integrated according to the management theory. While the separate manage strategies will results in inefficient actions, such as many heads to manage one thing, resource waste, departments' wrangling, and even absence in management body. So from the point of view of the total enterprise's management, the integration of e-commerce security risk and the risk of traditional business is a feasible and necessary trend.

In the New Basel Capital Adequacy Standards, the risk of commercial banks can be catalogued to market risk, credit risk, operational risk, interest risk, and national risk, and so forth. British Bankers Association (BBA), International Swap and Derivatives Association (ISDA), Risk Management Association (RMA)(1999), and the Basel Committee eventually defined operational risk as "the risk of direct or indirect loss resulting from inadequate or failed internal processes, people and systems or from external events". This universal definition includes legal risk, but excludes strategic and reputational risk. According to the different risk resources, the operational risk can be catalogued to the trade execute risk, fraud, IS risk, technology failure risk, model risk, accountant risk, legal risk, and so on. In the existing definition about operational risk, the security risk of e-commerce belongs to the operational risk field, in practice, while many traditional risks of financial institutions are classified to operational risk, too. Thus the integration of security risk of e-commerce and the risk of traditional business is well regulated; and the gap between the two risks is not large as apparent. And information security is a business responsibility shared by all members of the management team, more than the technology department.

E-Commerce Security Risk Management Strategy of Commercial Bank

Commercial banks are always important research objects in the academic field because commercial banks were one of the first financial institutions to adopt e-commerce mode, at the same time its business scope expands most widely and has highest requirements for security. So in this chapter, commercial bank will serve as the typical representative. The introduction of e-commerce security risk management strategy will take commercial bank as an object. The security risk management strategy of other financial services institutions is alike and can be analogized.

Information security shows new characteristics, along with the development of international e-commerce of banking. In both the developed and the developing countries, the advanced financial service through networks expands the scope of the traditional banking service, whereas great challenges confront the information security of commercial banks. The current progress of IT also raises more diversified security threats, which requires more powerful and effective security protections and controls to deal with. The demand for communications across branches inside the commercial bank and transactions between the internal business network and the Internet grows rapidly. It makes the security control more complicated. In developing countries, financial data consolidation also concentrates the technology risks and defies the original security management. At the same time, many commercial banks in developing countries introduce the service of the third party because of the lag in security technology and management, which brings the new security problems of administration and control.

It becomes the mutual issue facing the global commercial banks about how to propose a set of e-commerce security risk management strategy, based on the theory of systematic and cybernetics, strengthen the quantitative analysis during the e-commerce security risk management, and promote the integration of risk management of traditional business and e-commerce.

Box 3. The availability of China Union Pay failed and affected several banks (Source: Zhe, Langran, Yanxia, Jiang, & Yuandan, 2006, April 21)

On April 20, 2006, the communication system and host computer of China Union Pay broke down, which made the transactions within its service scope entirely intermit. This failure influenced its 18 subsidiary companies, covering majority of areas in China, including Guangzhou, Shenzhen, Beijing, Shanghai, Nanjing, Tianjin, Fujian, Xiamen, Yunnan, Dalian, Qingdao, and so forth. The main appearance of the failure included: failure to draw money across different banks in automated teller machine (ATM); invalidation of consumption by credit card; and unsuccessful online transaction across banks. This failure of service lasted nearly eight hours.

The supermarket cashier suffered big pile of abandoned commodity because the credit card could not be used for payment. At noon, the Wuyang branch store of Wanjia supermarket repeatedly broadcast the announcement, "because of the system failure of China Union Pay, we cannot accept the bank card temporarily for payment, please use cash." Mr. Gao entered the supermarket. Hearing the notice, he turned out and complained: "I could not draw cash, now the card failed either."

In the afternoon, in the Wuyang branch of the Communications Bank, the "national usable" business suspended because of the network breakdown. A customer looking very anxious, he said that he must perform the liability of payment according to contract otherwise he would compensate the opposing party 100,000 RMB. He explained ceaselessly by mobile, "today bank network has gone bad, not I would defy the money, you must understand."

In the Bank of China, and the Construction Bank in Tianhe district, the massive residents lined up to draw money in front of the counter. Customer only can choose the respective bank ATM that issued the bank card to draw money.

It was the last day of the first Guangzhou Export Commodities Fair, so many guests prepared shopping to bring gifts to family, while encountered the dilemma of "cannot use the card." Many merchants originally thought to make money in that day, therefore they complained, "it does not crash usually, but go bad in the critical moment."

Although the security assurance system of certain bank was in operation, the breakdown of availability of the national bank network still made the bank fail to provide qualified service, indirectly affecting normal transactions between banks and brought some influence and loss to both customers and merchants.

Construct Framework of E-commerce Security Risk Management Strategy in Commercial Bank

Targets of Security Risk Management

In the point of view of information security, the target of e-commerce security risk management in commercial banks should be: assure the integrity, nonrepudiation, authenticity, confidentiality, privacy, and availability of the related information.

It is in the first place to ensure the availability in high level. The commercial bank must guarantee reliable and stable function of bank system in 365 days of a year and in 24 hours of a day in order to provide the customers with qualified service and ensure the system can resist and recover when encounters incidents or damages.

The integrity, nonrepudiation, authenticity, and confidentiality of information holds the next place. Compared with other e-commerce enterprises, commercial banks should meet higher demand of data security. Each transaction will contain the flow of fund. If the data was tampered, commercial banks might suffer unaffordable loss. Therefore commercial banks must ensure that all the business information cannot be accessed or tampered by unauthorized person, that is, guarantee the integrity and confidentiality. In order to keep these aspects of

Figure1. Priority of the key aspects of information security

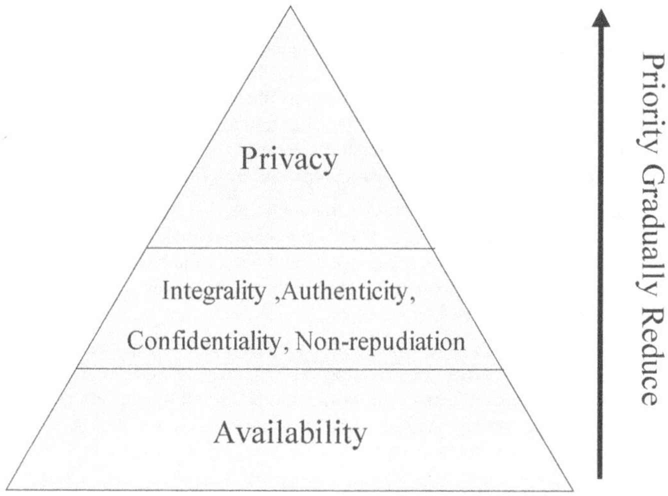

information security, commercial banks, of course, should authenticate the identity of the person who makes data operation and prevent the operator from denial. In this way, these four aspects connected with each other tightly.

The last is the demand to privacy. The bank must make sure that no unauthorized person read or use the individual information of customer. This is not only a demand of security but also a necessity to keep image of the institution and maintain the customer group. Figure 1 is the priority order of the six aspects.

Principle of Security Risk Management

Usually, a security strategy is defined as a formal statement of the rules that people who are given access to an organization's information and technology assets must abide to. The strategy firstly communicates the security goals to all of users, administrators, and managers and informs them of their obligatory requirements for protecting technology and information assets. The strategy also should specify the mechanisms through which these requirements can be met. (This section is an abstract of the security policy section of RFC 2196, Site Security Handbook.)

Gao and Zou (2005) think that, in general, a security strategy virtually indicates what is permissive and what is inhibitory in virtual of security when the person makes routine operations. And the strategy would not give detailed specification, it can only point what is the most important without explaination of how to realize. The strategy is the highest level of the rule of security management.

About the details of implementation, there are different opinions in the above two presentations, which are representative. Financial services institutions can make proper arrangement according to its unique situation.

For a competent institution, security strategy should contain the comprehensive and detailed descriptions about the security control, management, and use of the whole network. The security strategy is the foundation of network security. Different networks need different strategies, and the strategy should give solutions to all problems concerned with security in the network, such as how to realize the security at network level, how to control remote users' access, how to employ authentication and secure encryption transmission, and so forth. After these questions are solved and corresponding methods are determined, a complete security strategy of the whole network is obtained.

No matter from what aspect the strategy is defined, the aim of security strategy is to make users and managers keep their compulsory liability and responsibility in mind to protect enterprise's technology and information asset, and make a limit of the expected loss induced by security problems. An excellent security strategy should specify the responsibility of each user and administrator, flexibly adapt to the changeful network environment, and be able to put into effect. What is most critical is that security strategy must be implemented and followed once it is in operation.

Any security management strategy must satisfy the compliance to law and rules, targets of organization, and economic principle. The security risk management strategy in the first place is a guideline of security management, whether or not it contains detailed principles of implementation. All the limitative factors in the outer environment should be taken into account. Law and regulations must be abided to by the organizations in the jurisdiction scope, otherwise the organization cannot operate. The targets and the rules of the organization are the basis of organization's existence and development. The e-commerce mode is only a way to realize the targets, so e-commerce security risk management should contribute to the whole aim and cannot ignore the targets. Economic principle is the key rule for all the organizations that aim at profit. Commercial banks must consider the trade off between cost and profit. Thus security risk management cannot pursue highest level security without considering costs.

Framework and Content of Security Risk Management

The strategy put forward in this chapter has the following distinguishing features.

In the first place, the process of security risk management defined in the strategy is an open system with capability of adaptation.

The e-commerce security risk management strategy in this work is an open adaptive system. Guided by systematics and cybernetics, in general, it takes full account of the dynamics, systematic, and relativity of the e-commerce security risk. All the risk control methods are selected on the basis of real and all-around risk analysis; in the strategy, both the problems found during the implementation of strategy and the new emerging risks would be contained in the new risk analysis, while this process is a circulation with upward spirals. As the elements of system, steps of security risk management influence each other, integrate seamlessly, and form a system with complete function.

Systematics, in essence, researches the function, behavior, and dynamic characteristic of the objective. Systematic studies not the isolated system but groups of connected systems. The study of the object is carried out not only in the static state but also in the development and movement. This conforms to the characteristic that the e-commerce security risk environment changes unceasingly. Since systematics takes systems as research objects and every management aims as a system, the method of systematic inevitably takes the first place in solving problems of administration and management. E-commerce security risk management strategy deals with the security risk management, and itself is a system consisted of various technology and management solutions.

Systematics regards the system as an organic functional integration composed by several elements that act and relate to each other. Each system possesses the structure and function, that is, the system is an entity of the combination of structure and function, among which the structure decides the function, but different structure can realize the same function.

The dominant character of systematics is the relativity in research. When the object is treated as a system, whatever outside it would be regarded as environmental influential factor. The division of the system and its external environment is also relative. Because of this feature, it is proper to utilize systematic to study e-commerce security. We can study some object in the system and consider the other parts in the system as influential factors. In this way, not only the function of certain security control method can be understood clearly but also the system performance as well as the combination with other methods cannot be neglected.

With systematics as a guide theory, all kinds of conceptions and characteristics, as well as axioms and laws in the framework of system, can be used directly without further explanation; and many conclusions will gain strong logical and theoretical support and are no longer pale and weak.

No matter what system it is, there are some features in common:

- **Integrity:** The system as the organic combination of relative and connective elements forms an integration with the certain structure and function. Its essential characteristic was the organic integrity. The integrity also is embodied in that the rule of system is a rule for whole entity, its nature and law of motion can only be demonstrated from the whole. The integrity also expresses in the integrity of the system function, which was not equal to the s simple summation of element's functions.
- **Order:** The level of the system is orderly. And the development of system is also in order. System changes and evolves complying with certain laws and limited or affected by the internal and external factor of the system.
- **Relevance:** Subsystems in a large system restrict and relate each other. These dependence and restriction are realized through the large system.

The systems, such as financial services institutions and management strategies, still have some special features:

- **Purpose:** The system has an explicit purpose, and the subsystems work mutually for the purpose of the large system.
- **Environment adaptability:** In the large system, other subsystems relative to certain subsystems is the environment of the subsystem. There are transmission of substances, energy, and information between the subsystem and other subsystems.

There are some basic techniques in systematics that are helpful to the security risk management strategy: information method and feedback method.

Figure 2. Purposive movement of system can be abstracted as an information conversion process

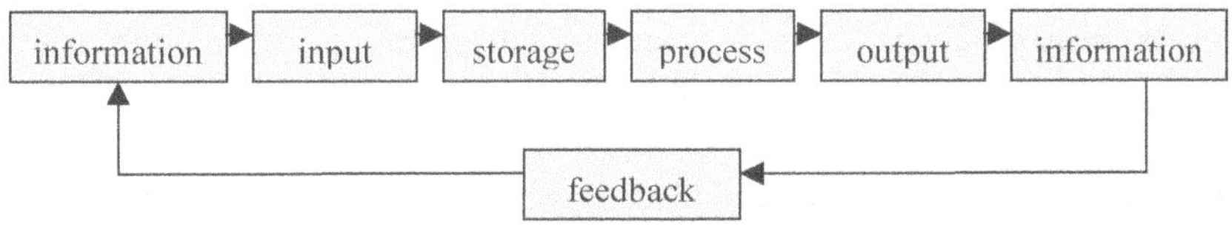

- **Information method:** The so-called information method is with the information viewpoint, regards that the system realizes its purposive movement by aid of acquirement, transmission, processing, and dealing of information. Its characteristic is that when analysing and dealnig with specific problems, people may put aside the concrete configuration and constitution of the system object completely, and abstract the purposive movement of system as an information conversion process as seen in Figure 2.

  From the information method of systematic, it can be easily concluded that the whole process of e-commerce security risk management strategy from program to implementation should keep to such a transform of information. In this way, it is no doubt that e-commerce security management is always studied as information security management.

- **Feedback method:** In order to make the security risk management strategy react effectively to the changeful environment, we must provide the result information of its action to the system as part of necessary information to guarantee its forward actions. The feedback is a control mode in which output information of system is led to the input end and influences the information re-exportation. It also can be described as a way to collect response information of performance and then compare the result with original goal during the control. In brief, the method of using result of system function to adjust system actions is feedback method. There are two kinds of feedback. If the feedback causes the system instable, even leads to system destruction, makes the system collapse, it is positive feedback; another kind of feedback that can make system tend to steady status is negative feedback. In the control system, the negative feedback is commonly used to adjust and dominate the system to act towards the goal because for any system in operation, its movement will be affected apart from its correct state by outside and inside factor. When system is interfered, the certainty decreases while uncertainty increases. Feedback method just makes use of the difference between these two states to solve the conflict of certainty and uncertainty and make the system achieve stabilization.

Feedback is a necessity if a system wants to survive and adapt to the environment full of changes. Guided by this rule, the e-commerce security risk management strategy introduces monitor and audit to provide feedback to persons who makes and implements the strategy. The strategy has the ability to reduce the gap between aims and performance reasonably so as to keep the vitality and adaptation of the system. Moreover the circulation of the course is absolutely necessary because of the continuous changes of risk environment.

It must be emphasized that feedback not only needs the information connection of the control system but also the correct direction of the control course. Thus the strategy can ensure the direction of institutes in the random environment by revising the original actions. That returns to the early problem, that is, whether or not detailed implementation is contained in the security risk management strategy, it must be a correct and reliable guideline. Thus it can guarantee the validity of the following feedback and adjustment.

The actions needed by the system are realized through the mechanisms of control, feedback, and adjustment. The system possessing these mechanisms is a cybernetics system and thus a purposive system. According to the theory of cybernetics, the mutual feature of all the cybernetic systems is the course of information transform and feedback principle.

During the management, actual operation often departs from schedule, so the method of control and adjustment is needed to revise and correct the actions or the project to reach the aim of organization, while feedback will point out the direction for this process. Once people neglect feedback, adjustment, and control, problems will appear.

In the system, especially in the system of e-commerce security risk management, feed forward control as well as the feedback control is necessary, because many risks could be eliminated before they induce loss depending on this method. Feedback control is usable to solve the unforeseeable problems.

Guided by systematics and cybernetics, security risk management strategy functions as a large system, including both technology solution and management solution. As two vital components to guarantee the operation of system, management and technology methods effect and influence each other and integrate seamless into the security risk management system of the enterprise. In this system, the ideas and theories of systematics and cybernetics are extremely helpful.

Figure 3. Technology and management combine seamlessly in the system of security management strategy

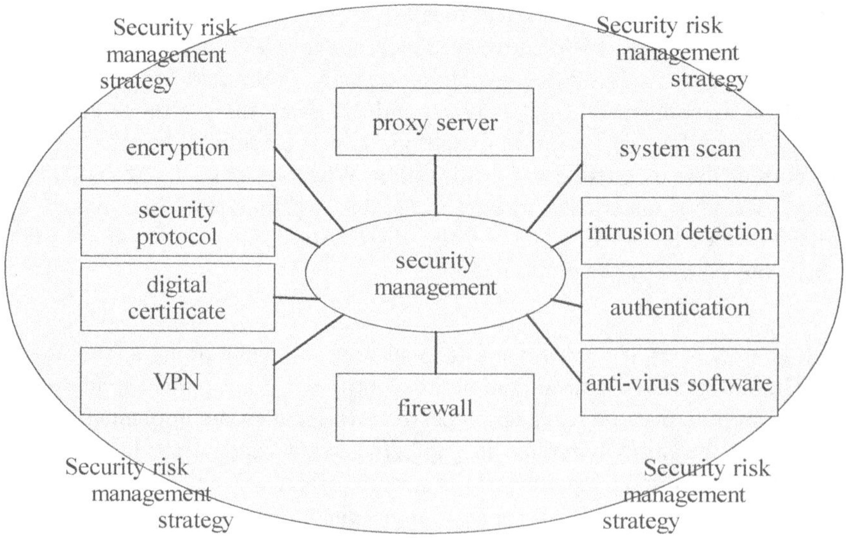

Then what is the security management strategy? If we say the common technology and management are still solutions of e-commerce safe problems, the security risk management strategy is a layout about how to use these means to achieve the goal then. The strategy standing on the overall situation, gives a pool solution to the security threats encountered in the e-commerce activity, demonstrates the essence of the problems, the concrete steps and direction of solving the problems at the same time, and so on. So we say that the security risk management strategy is both the overall scheme and concrete implementation regulations. Through the security risk management strategy, the technology and management are integrated organically, interweaving into a safe network.

Secondly, e-commerce security risk management strategy integrates with the management strategy of traditional risks.

Since the process of risk analysis, assessment and control all involve the ideas and methods of traditional risk management in commercial banks and all the risks of banks are considered in the same framework, this security risk management strategy has more advantages than the original strategy and can benefit the integration of various risk management strategies. Moreover, the strategy also embodies the idea of IT governance. IT governance is a new concept of the domain of IT, economics and management. It mainly studies whether the government or enterprise has employed effective mechanism so that implication of IT can achieve its aims, and balances risks during computerization to guarantee the strategic goals

Figure 4. Framework of security risk management strategy in commercial banks

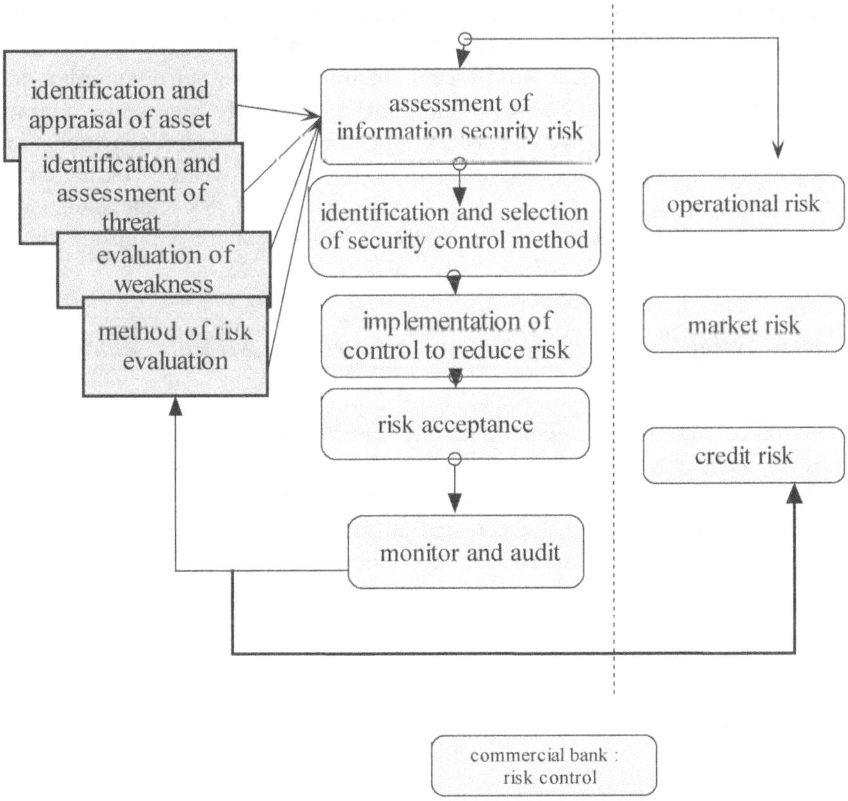

of the organization. The main task of IT governance is to: make IT consist with business targets, prompt business development, maximize profits, use IT resource rationally, and manage risks relevant to IT properly.

In fact, according to the theory of systematics, the management of total risks of commercial banks can be regarded as a large system, while the traditional risk management as well as the security risk management is a subsystem. These two subsystems react and relate to each other. Since the function of the system will exceed the total functions of the subsystems, theoretically, the combination of traditional risk management strategy and management strategy of e-commerce security risk is necessary and profitable.

From the point of view of practice, integration of management strategy of e-commerce security risk and traditional business risk is essential and feasible. There are rich experiences and mature methods in the field of risk management of traditional business. E-commerce security risk management substantially is a kind of risk management, although it takes a new form. Therefore, the basic risk management process can be treated together with traditional risk management; while the concrete quantitative methods are optional considering different risk field. In this way, all the risks facing commercial banks can be integrated and analyzed as a whole.

The framework of security risk management strategy in commercial banks is expressed by Figure 4. A dashed line divides the figure into two parts. The control of e-commerce security risk concentrates in the left part. In this part, the process of e-commerce security risk control includes evaluation of information security risk, identification of security control, implementation of risk control, risk acceptance, as well as monitoring and auditing, while the assessment of information security risk include appraisal of asset, identification of threat, and identification of weakness. In this process, the information got from monitor and audit is input to new turn risk assessment. The left part of the figure represents the traditional risk of the financial business. We can see e-commerce security risk management has connections with these traditional risks, and there is overlap between e-commerce security risk and operational risk of commercial banks. These kinds of risk managements together constitute the bank's total risk management process. In the next, we will discuss the specific methods of risk analysis.

Risk Analysis Method in E-Commerce Security Risk Management

The e-commerce security management includes the security risk identification, evaluation, and analysis, and on the basis of which realizes the most effective security assurance with lowest cost. In this part, we introduce the normal means of risk analysis in e-commerce security risk management, and then present an idea of improvement about quantitative analysis that benefit from the measurement of operational risk in the New Basel Capital Adequacy Standards.

General Way of E-Commerce Security Risk Management

Three Phases of Risk Management

In general, security problems do not necessarily appear in weak e-commerce systems. Likewise, e-commerce systems confronted with a security threat are not necessarily doomed to suffer losses. Only when the e-commerce system has a weakness and that weakness is exploited by an outside threat can the security problems occur. The relationship of security risk and various elements affected by risk or inducing risk is expressed in Figure 5.

In the figure, threat means the potential factor that can damage the asset or organization. Weakness is the failing or defect can be successfully attacked by threat. Information asset contains all information concerned in the operation of the bank e-commerce. According to the figure, threat and weakness co-determine the intensity of the risk facing the bank, and their mutual actions raise the possibility of loss of information asset. Information as a kind of asset has certain value, and the value should be protected. Assets with higher value will suffer greater risk and need more considerable protection if the probabilities of risk are same. The existence of risk and assets that need protection result in security demands of enterprise. While the security method is a solution against the security demand and can decrease risk to the acceptable level.

We can summarize the general steps or phases of security risk management from the figure as followed: risk identification, risk evaluation, and risk control.

Figure 5. Relationship of key elements of risk control

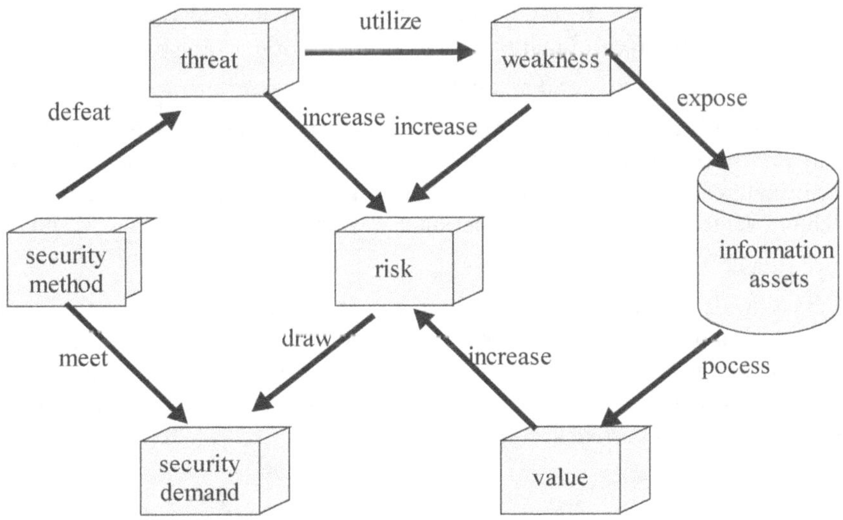

- **Risk identification.** Security risk identification and analysis covers the actions of information collection, identification of weakness, and threat in the e-commerce system and appraisal of possible loss. The main task of this stage is making security risk analysis and sufficient evaluation of the status of e-commerce, information, and other assets. Since the assessment of e-commerce status is the foundation of risk management, in order to find out potential security risk as much as possible, relevant information of threat, weakness, and solution should be gathered for further analysis.
- **Risk evaluation.** The evaluation to information and asset means the appraisal of the value of information and asset that possibly suffer loss. This step is the course of determination of the bank's security demand. After identifying and analyzing the risk, the bank should use appropriate measurements and tools to make out the risk level and intensity, in order to determine correct and proper security control methods and avoid that the investment does not match the protection demand.
- **Risk control.** The task of risk control is reducing the risk to acceptable levels through a series of security control methods. Under the principle of balance between cost and risk level, many ways can help to realize the acceptance of risk, such as risk avoidance, risk transmit, threat reduction, weakness reduction, decrease of possible effective extent of threat, and damage detection.

Risk Identification

Common Steps of Risk Identification

It is very critical to identify risk and give objective appraisal of risk in risk management. This phase is the basis of the risk control. In general, the risk identification in e-commerce security risk management should include following steps.

The first step is identification and appraisal of information assets.

Data and file, document contract, software, personnel, service, physical assets, and other assets are all in the scope of identification. Each asset will be given a value for further appraisal. Usually the value is determined as relative importance degree of the real value of asset since the quantitative difficulty in practice.

The second step is to identify and assess the threat.

The objects of this identification are all the crucial information assets. After identification the probability of threat should be made out. Commercial banks can estimate the frequency or probability of threat according to historical or statistic data. Usually each level of risk is given a probability value, ror example: very possible, 1; possible, 2; impossible, 3; and so on.

The third step is assessment of weakness.

Weakness is the defect of information asset that can be made use of by threats. Commercial banks should find out all the weaknesses of each information asset to protect and assess the reasonable importance of every weakness, for example: very possible, 3; possible, 2; not extremely impossible, 1; and absolutely impossible, 0. Moreover, commercial banks should examine the validity of current security control.

In the last two steps, the process of assessment can be separated into two phases. In the first phase, the threat or weakness is identified, and the possibility, scope, and degree of effects of the threat or weakness are analyzed in the second phase.

Common Methods in Risk Identification

Risk survey and analysis table. In this method, risk administrators and relevant experts together scheme various survey tables for an enterprise's reference after comprehensive investigation and analysis. The survey table should involve comparatively detailed questions. This method is usually used in the risk management of traditional business in commercial banks and other financial institutions.

The contents of a survey table can be classified by asset, threat, and weakness, and some key questions can be given in each category. The risk status is concluded according to the final results of survey. Table 2 is an example of asset risk survey and analysis.

Accident tree analysis (ATA). Accident tree analysis studies the accident that may induce damage and investigates the reason and result of the accident. An accident tree is a kind of chart. It can be used to figure the risk accidents potential to bring loss. Each node of the accident tree represents a concrete accident, while the line is the relationship between the nodes. It is a kind of deduction, starting from the results to find reasons. Many risk elements can be identified by accident tree analysis. In this way, the probability of accidents can also be calculated. This method combines qualitative and quantitative techniques and prevails in risk management.

Table 2. Risk survey and analysis

Risk survey and analysis of assets	Yes	No
1. Network equipments		
a. Is there a regular examination and maintenance?	✓	
b. Is there some relevant rule or regulation?		✓
c. Is there some back up for key device?	✓	
d. …		
2. Severs		
a. Is there some isolation from outside network?	✓	
b. Is there a back up?	✓	
c. Is there a specification of access?		✓
d. …		
3. Database		
a. Is there a renew standard?	✓	
b. Is there a data back up?	✓	
c. Is the important information kept separately?		✓
d. …		

Figure 6. Accident tree analysis

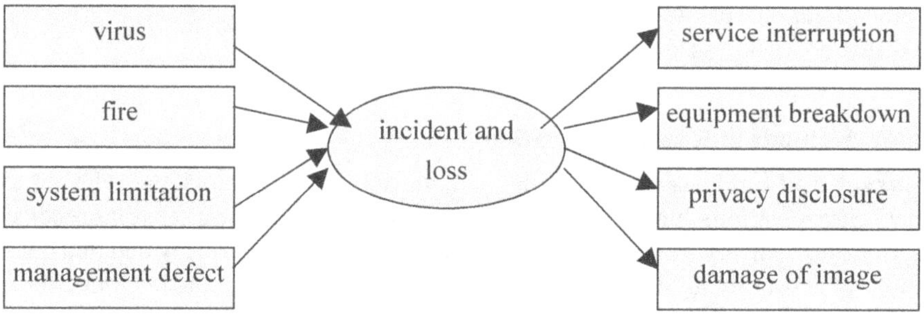

Usually during the risk identification, the validity of the current measurement of security risk control must be revalued because many security management methods can continue to effect and prevent risk, but some are invalid. In addition, the current risk control solutions have connection with the analysis of risk status. So this identification to current risk management system cannot be omitted.

Risk Evaluation

After the identification and appraisal of asset, assessment of weakness and threat, and determination of the effectiveness, proper methods and tools for risk evaluation should be employed to identify the value and level of risk. The following contents will discuss normal risk quantitative methods and determination of risk priority.

The risk evaluation needs risk appraisal by risk measurement and tools. We can calculate risk in this way: risk can be regarded as the result of mutual effect by threat to asset, weakness, and potential influence of threat to weakness, defined as:

$R = R(P_T, P_V, I)$

R = risk when asset meets threat;

P_T = probability of threat;

P_V= probability of threat to weakness;

I = potential influence of threat;

where $I = V \times C_L$;

C_L = extent of loss;

V = comparative value of asset.

Example 1

Supposing C_L= 1, that is, the loss is 100%. The risk measurement of asset can be rewritten as:

$R = R(P_T, P_V, V) = R(P_{TV}, I) = P_{TV} \times I$, where P_{TV}—the real probability of threats.

Table 3. Risk calculation

Threat	Potential influence of threat (I)	Probability of threat (P_{TV})	Risk (R)	Level of threat
Threat A	5	2	10	3
Threat B	3	4	12	2
Threat C	1	2	2	5
Threat D	2	3	6	4
Threat E	4	1	4	4
Threat F	3	5	15	1

The risk is evaluated by the real probability of threats and the potential influence of threats. Divide both the probability of threats and the potential influence of threats into five grades, while the concrete standard of division can be acquired from the practical experiences. Here we define the final results 1-3 as level 5; 4-7 as level 4; 8-10 as level 3; 11-14 as level 2, and equal and larger than 15 as level 1. Table 3 gives the risk values and levels of threat.

Example 2

According to the vital importance of the system (the comparative value of system), V, the probability to prevent threat, P_O, and the probability to prevent performance decline after the threat, P_D, these three factors are used to appraise the risk.

$$\begin{aligned} R &= R(P_{TV}, I) = I \times P_{TV} \\ &= V \times C_L \times P_{TV} \\ &= V \times (1 - P_D) \times (1 - P_O) \end{aligned}$$

V = the vital importance of the system, can be measured by C (confidentiality of the system), IN (integrity of the system), and A (availability): V=C*IN*A.

P_O = the probability to prevent threat, is affected by numbers of users, original trust, the rate of back up, and satisfaction of the demand of compulsory security control.

P_D = the probability to prevent performance decline, concerned with the existing protective control.

Supposing there is a network system in the e-commerce business of the commercial bank: management subsystem, engineering subsystem, and e-commerce subsystem. According to the confidentiality, integrity, and availability of system, the security of system can be divided averagely to three grades: low, 1; general, 2; and high, 3. Both P_O and P_D can be divided to five grades, and values in each grades as followed:very low, 0.1; low, 0.3; middle, 0.5; high, 0.7; and very high, 0.9.

The results of risk calculation are listed in Table 4.

Table 4. Result of risk calculation

Name of network system	Management subsystem	Engineering subsystem	E-commerce subsystem
Confidentiality (C)	1	2	3
Integrity (IN)	3	3	3
Availability (A)	2	2	2
Vital importance (V)	6	12	18
Probability to prevent threat (P_O)	0.1	0.5	0.3
Probability to prevent performance decline (P_D)	0.3	0.5	0.3
Risk (R)	3.78	3	8.82
Risk order (r)	2	3	1

Table 5. Example of risk level determination

Numeric span of risks	Risk level
6,7,8	First level, with high risk, needs prior and strict control
3,4,5	Second level, with general risk, needs proper control
0,1,2	Third level, with low risk, can accept

The relevant priority order of the asset risk can be obtained from the risk evaluation. The assets with a high-risk level should be given more protection and assigned resources in priority. Table 5 gives the determination of risk level according to the span of risk value.

Risk Control and Risk Acceptance

After the risk evaluation, a commercial bank should adopt proper solution for security control. The security control determination should be in accordance with the results of risk assessment, decide what asset needs protection, and what method should be employed to cut down or eliminate loss of risk and reach the acceptable level. The risk controls can include: isolate the key computer system from Internet to avoid risk; transfer risk through insurance; reduce extent of threats by using professional software; train employees to improve their security technique; understand to reduce weakness; and so on.

The absolute security of e-commerce in commercial banks is impossible, in fact. The residual risk will always exist even if excellent security controls are implemented. The residual risk should be limited in the acceptable scope to assure information security. There is such a relationship:

Figure 7. The process of risk assessment

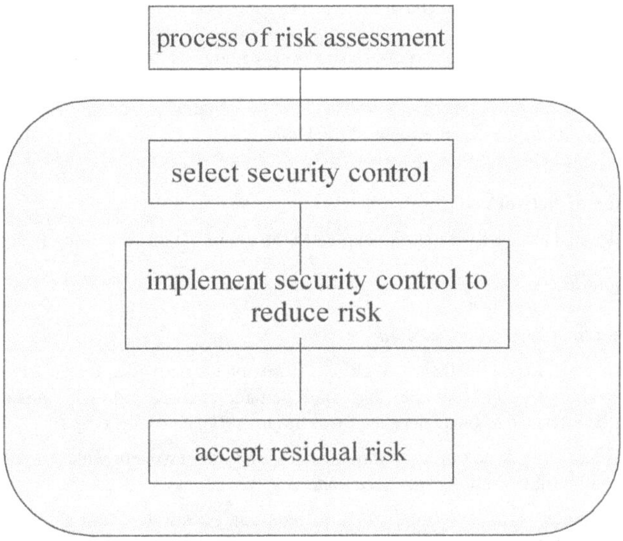

$R_r = R_0 - \Delta R$

$R_r <= R_t$, where

R_r is residual risk;

R_0 is original risk;

ΔR is reduced risk through control;

and

R_t is acceptable risk.

The above process of risk management is expressed in Figure 7.

In the traditional risk management of commercial banks, the basic methods of risk control include risk avoidance, risk prevention, and risk diversification and, from the angle of financial control, may include risk retain and risk transmit. These methods can be used or referred to in the e-commerce security risk management of commercial banks. For instance, the risk transmission in fact transfers the risk from one part to another to reduce the intensity of risk. When control the e-commerce security risk, insurance, and outsourcing can help to transfer part of risk to others and limit the loss within the acceptance scope.

Monitor and Audit

The process of monitoring and auditing provides feedback to the performance of risk analysis according to systematics and cybernetics.

As long as the inside and outside environment changes ceaselessly, risks from the environment can hardly keep static. Therefore through monitor and audit the commercial bank can

Box 4. Security risk management strategy implementation of the Guangdong Development Bank Source: China Computer World (2005, August 23)

Guangdong Development Bank (GDB) was established in 1988 and has owned more than 400 branches all over China. With the trend of computerization and automation of banking, GDB continued to expand the business scope in e-commerce. But the new opportunity also brought new challenges, among which the network security became the key factor to limit the development of the bank.

First Reconstruction of Network

In 2001, GDB constructed a security network adapted to the environment, according to security threats at that time.

Problems Discovered from Security Risks Analysis

The GDB needed a firewall to isolate the key interfaces from outside networks. Because of the special distribution of the bank's headquarters and branches, they both demanded connection with outside networks such as the Internet. While the interface to outer networks was the main object of hackers.

Unauthorized access to the inside resources within the network system were prevalent and serious. So real-time scan and monitor to network operations was necessary.

Original network technology was too complicated, difficult, and costly to maintain, causing difficulty and a blind spot in security management.

Total Solution of Security Risk Management Strategy

In the whole network design, GDB made a general security risk management strategy, using the Cisco secure policy manager (CSPM) to appoint the whole security strategy and implement regularly control and improvement.

Technology and Management Solutions

What GDB used then was the security solution of Cisco and relevant online security products. The main security module included whole security strategy, firewall, intrusion detection system, and VPN. This module method offered the great flexibility for the bank.

On management solutions, GDB made relevant regulations about the connection between LAN, WAN, and public networks.

Performance of New Security Risk Management Strategy

As to the problem of network link, GDB realized security isolation between application server, other system servers, official automation system and the management information system adopting the inside firewall, and the security of the host computer got a better guarantee.

To deal with the external illegal access, the reconstructed network set up a special router in WAN center. All routers were placed in both sides of the high-performance firewall preventing the illegal outside operations from the host computer. At the same time the network's ability to treat with system network architecture (SNA) protocol improved.

The bank's network realized security isolation from external networks owing to the firewall. Address interpretation shielded inside network's address and structure.

Explicit and specific security requirements were fulfilled in this reconstruction. The whole bank held an intact security system. The potential and existing security defects related to system and subsystem were eliminated. This implementation of the security management strategy got perfect effects.

Reconstruction for the Second Time

With the continuous expansion and innovation of bank's own business and the development of the serious online security risks, original safe solutions of e-commerce could not keep up with the new demands. On the basis of

continued on following page

Box 4. Continued

analysis in an all-round way of the emerging risks, GDB improved the existing security management strategy and employed a security management strategy that met the new environment requirements.

Security Risk Analysis

The hacker's technology developed constantly, and the challenge to the bank's security was more and more severe. The bank's network needed more security protections.

In recent years, the inside job prevailed. As for the former security system, it was very easy for staff members to enter the system and carry on crime or breakage. So GDB needed stricter authorization management and access control.

The reliability of the network needed urgent improvement.

Whole Strategy

In order to better resist the illegal access from network, manage the online authentication of key users, and guarantee the high-quality financial services for users, GDB must strengthen the arrangement in online security further. A unified, three-dimensional online security strategy for the whole bank was designed to deal with the potential security risks.

Technology and Management Solutions

At the beginning of 2003, GDB implemented integrated security protections in the whole scale, protected the e-commerce assets from the four aspects: defend, filter, block, and detect, forming the three-dimensional integrated security system. The solutions were as follows.

In order to improve reliability of the network, GDB used dual back up, adopted the router to connect with the outside through a lot of WAN ports, and offered certain security controls to prevent illegal accesses and operations.

On core of the network, disposed many private branch exchanges (PBXs) to control key network sections through the firewalls and intrusion detection module. More intelligent abrupt incidents monitor and unusual data transmission controls realized.

In addition to log analysis and management, GDB strengthened the inside user's operations and access authorization.

Particularly, GDB employed the integrated security defensive system, including router, firewall, and PBX, which together formed a firmly three-level protection.

Performance of the New Security Management Strategy

The overall upgrade success of the security management strategy had dispelled the potential online security hazards towards the bank, cleared away the obstacle for the development of e- commerce. The GDB online security system was promoted to a three-dimensional, large-scale unified online security defensive system. The network after reconstruction hold higher security, easy to manage, and could meet the needs to launch the new type business and the needs to provide reliable services for users.

find the new problems that are not covered in the security risk management. In this way, all the steps of e-commerce security risk management of commercial bank form a dynamic circular system. When one circulation completes, the effect of security risk management will reach a higher stage, and the performance of security management of the commercial bank can improve continuously.

Some Ideas for Quantitative Analysis Improvement in Security Risk Management

Just as discussed above, the methods of e-commerce security risk management in current stage lag behind the risk measurement of traditional business. It can be found that the steps of risk assessment and control of both kind of risk are in accordance. The quantitative measurement of former still stays on the level of appraisal of not risk but asset, and mainly aims to provide theory evidence for the design of risk management and risk control in the way of combination of less qualitative and more quantitative methods. The risk assessment of the latter achieves detailed and delicate appraisal and quantitative means. At present, the commercial bank accumulates various methods of risk analysis, such as risk probability/influence appraisal matrix, sensitivity analysis, simulation, and so on. Moreover, with the development of econometric maturation of relevant software, quantitative risk analysis becomes a trend and a necessity. Original expert grading and judgment according to experience cannot take the dominant position for the reason of subjectivity and imprecision.

The commercial bank can adopt some mature measurement in traditional financial risk management to alter the rough method of grading by priority in the management of e-commerce security risk. In the classical e-commerce security risk management, the possibility of threats often is divided into some grades and the same to threat influence. This way is easy but not precise, especially for the continuous events. For instance, supposing the original risk level is 3, after the risk control according to the above process of security risk management, the improved status is still at level 3. Then we would be confused whether the risk has been reduced even if the real risk level, in fact, has been lowered. This results from the inaccurate appraisal of risks. Especially, when calculating the total risk, each risk may multiple a weight factors before added up, and thus the error will be expanding and the precision decreases further.

In practice, the management of operational risk in commercial banks has some in common with the security risk management. So the methods used in management of operational risk can be introduced after some necessary adjustment. Basel Committee on Banking Supervision regulates the method of operational risk management. For instance, the basic indicator approach can only make simple measurement by multiplying the total income with an indicator to get the number of required capital; while the advanced measurement approach (AMA) may involve estimation of the parameters and capital requirement through internal database. Referring to the quantitative measurement in operational risk management, we can make a small improvement of measurement of the security risk.

The commercial bank mainly uses the statistic and actuarial technology to measure the distribution of the lost. Zhao (2004) gives a kind of method to measure the loss distribution. We introduce it here.

Let i, j represent the types of the work and loss; Stochastic variable $\varsigma_{(i,j)}$ represents the loss at the work type i, loss type j. $F_{i,j}$ is the distribution function of $\varsigma_{(i,j)}$.

Suppose the stochastic variation, $N(i, j)$, is the frequency of the lost between time t and t + τ; $P_{i,j}$ is the probability of the $N(i, j)$; and $P_{i,j}(n)$ is the distributed function of loss frequency and $P_{i,j}(n)\sum_{k=0}^{n} p_{i,j(k)}$.

The loss with the work type i and loss type j between time t and $t + \tau$ is:

$$\theta_{(i,j)} = \sum_{k=0}^{n} \varsigma_{n(i,j)},$$

Let $G_{i,j}$ be the distribution function of $\theta(i, j)$, so the compound function $G_{i,j}$ can take the form of:

$$G_{i,j}(x) = \begin{cases} \sum_{k=0}^{n} p_{i,j(n)} F_{i,j(x)}^{n*} & x>0 \\ p_{i,j(0)} & x=0 \end{cases}$$

In above function, $F^1 = F$, $F^{N*} = F^{(N-1)*} \times F$, F^{N*}represents the n degree convolution of F, the mark * is the convolution operator of the distribution function.

In the security risk management of the e-commerce, if the database can record precisely the probability and degree of threat, the existing methods for risk measurement will do favor of the precise risk analysis and comparison, the summation of the total risk as well as the performance comparison between original risk control strategy and the improved strategy can be obtained.

For example, by precise measure, the results in Example 1 will be revised as shown in Table 6.

Table 6. Risks calculation

Threat j	Potential influence of threat i	Realization probability of threat $P_{i,j}$	Loss of risk θ	Level of risk
Threat A	5	$P_{1,5}$	$\theta_{(i,j)} = \sum_{k=0}^{n} \varsigma_{n(i,j)}$	3
Threat B	3	$P_{2,,3}$	$\theta_{(i,j)} = \sum_{k=0}^{n} \varsigma_{n(i,j)}$	2
Threat C	1	$P_{3,1}$	$\theta_{(i,j)} = \sum_{k=0}^{n} \varsigma_{n(i,j)}$	5
Threat D	2	$P_{4,2}$	$\theta_{(i,j)} = \sum_{k=0}^{n} \varsigma_{n(i,j)}$	4
Threat E	4	$P_{5,4}$	$\theta_{(i,j)} = \sum_{k=0}^{n} \varsigma_{n(i,j)}$	4
Threat F	3	$P_{6,3}$	$\theta_{(i,j)} = \sum_{k=0}^{n} \varsigma_{n(i,j)}$	1
...	...	...	...	...
Total risk			$\theta = \sum_{i=1}^{I} \sum_{J=1}^{J} \theta(i,j)$	

The total risk assessment in the last line is the summation of quantitative risks.

Likely, in Example 2, we can also get three grades – low, 1; general, 2; and high, 3 – according to the confidentiality, integrity, and availability. P_O, P_D also can be divided into five grades: very low, 0.1; low, 0.3; general, 0.5; high, 0.7; and very high, 0.9. In practice, it will contribute to the accurate risk assessment, if the arbitrary variable can be calculated with continual value or probability.

It cannot be ignored that there still exists huge difficulties to accurately appraise information assets and evaluate the probability of risks because of the particularity of e-commerce security. Whereas the operational risk it is a hard node of the risk control in commercial banks. Hence further study is necessary to promote the quantitative analysis of e-commerce risk management.

Implementation Project of Security Risk Management Strategy

In this part, mainly discuss the implementation of e-commerce security risk management strategy. When bring forward implementation policy, we refer to the traditional management strategy of financial business risk in commercial bank.

Information Technology Solutions

As the administrator of Chinese commercial banks, the People's Bank of China gives a reference model for the security technology framework of the bank's computer system (see Figure 8). So in China, commercial banks usually start from these points to make their own specific security technology policy. Among the three aspects, the "component units of information system" has more maneuverability. In the following content, we analyze the technology solutions from this angle.

Security of Physical Environment

The availability of the whole system should be guaranteed firstly. Nice physical guard against theft is inevitable. Make redundant design of key equipments and communication facility, and fulfill the requirements of system back up and recovery. Establish implementation scheme of the system usage and maintenance to reduce possible losses to lowest extent.

Security of Application Platform

Authentication and identification mechanism are necessary to guarantee integrity, authenticity, confidentiality of the information. Effective encryption and antivirus software are essential security control methods. As for database, the audit function of database management systems (DBMSs) can be used to monitor the users' operations. Upgrade the application software and download the patches offered by the manufacturers in time, and these methods can brought down risks caused by system defects to minimum.

Figure 8. Three-dimensional model of security technology

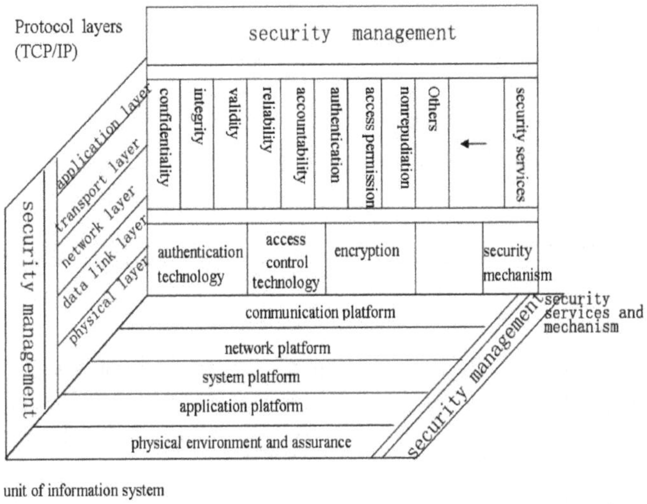

Security of System Platform

Keep management of users' identification and monitor system attacks by appropriate tools. Use the firewall and technology of invasion detects to realize the combination of static and dynamic protections. Set security grade to high level and do not use system defaults value at will. Manage the access to data and information, which can be aided by one-off password authentication system basing on token. Control system defections and forbid mistaken or malicious operations by scanning tools.

Security of Network Platform

According to the different outside networks linked, adopt different kinds of connection and protocols. Through the physical isolation card or entire disconnection from outside networks, the bank's operation system network can be isolated from the public network. Firewall can be used to realize the access control between the internal system and external network. For the remote users, the firewall provides one-off password to authenticate the identity. In addition, the bank can use switch to divide VLAN inside the LAN in order to control the connection between different departments and users with different privilege. Professional access control software can realize more delicate management of various applications.

Security of Communication Platform

Guarantee data security in the channel through encryption and security network protocols. secure electronic transaction (SET) and SSL is suitable for users from public networks. For the ordinary business system of the bank, VPN can be employed, while for the main links in the way of ATM and digital data networks (DDNs), such as connections between headquarters and other branches, the encryption machine irrelevant of protocol may work. The connections by the means of asymmetrical digital subscriber loops (ADSLs), integrated services digital networks (ISDNs), and dial up with superior banks can be protected by IP encryption machine, which can encrypt IP data packets in the TCP/IP protocol. The connection between banks with less sensitive information can adopt node encryption machine. In addition, the technology of digital signature, time stamp, digital certificate, and authentication are also in common use in commercial banks.

In addition, pursue physical methods to reduce the chances of interception.

Management Solutions

Faculty Management

Keep a security management system, including the rules and regulations about access ranges, terminations, obligations, and so on. A balance should be found between security and work performance to avoid inside job as well as inefficiency raised by faculty exchange. Set up a special security management organization or training center to guarantee the renewal speed of staff's security knowledge.

Equipment Control

Make the detailed strategy of emergency response, back up, and recovery. Set up regulations of the hardware and software maintenance, and check the performance regularly. Regulations of computer lab management are necessary. Manage system of equipments accessed to the outside networks and limit the operation to inside network.

Routine Operation Management

Control the access to key medium equipments and confidential information and establish specification of identity card management, regular inspection, and so on. Set up an authorization management system. Keep periodical inspection regulations, including the rules for confidential information, information operation, and information storage. Make detailed regulations about the application software design, modification, and realization, specifying the scope and time of these operations. Analyze and track the logs, and so forth.

Data Management

Establish regulations of deletion and modification of important program and data, including what need preserve, how to preserve, how long to preserve, who executes deletion, how to delete, and so on. Back up and preserve important data and data access authorization. There also should be a description about the usage of different data.

Strengthen Internal Control

According to the 2005 information security survey by PricewaterhouseCoopers and CIO Magazine, the inside job becomes the most importance problem of all the risks relevant to IT. It is a vital task for banks to strengthen internal control. E-commerce mode changes the traditional internal control; labor and transparent audit trace of the bank. The bank needs new professional technology and skill to cope with operation and audit in new position. So it is necessary to strengthen the internal control and improve its performance in the bank, especially to the branches engaged in e-commerce.

When make management regulations, convenience to operate and administrate must be kept in mind. No matter how powerful the security management strategy is, it will be useless and meaningless unless it is implemented correctly in practice. In many circumstances, it is not because of the absence of regulations but for the reason of implementation that the security solution or strategy fails. Carelessness of the operator, complexity of security strategy and inconvenience to implement can all lead to this failure. Thus the degree of acceptance and feasibility of implementation must be pay enough attention when design the specific rules of security risk management strategy.

Routine Monitor and Security Audit

Security monitor refers to real-time inspection of the network, which can realize by scan. As an important element of classic security model, audit can protect the network by recording all the data packets transmitted through network and analyze the packets to find out attacks and suspect actions. Security monitor and audit belong to the real-time protection and aim to fulfill the dynamic security.

Monitor and audit is an extremely significant part of security risk management strategy in commercial banks. This method provides the feedback of the strategy and offers the input for new turn of risk analysis in the circulation of risk management. Owing to the information feedback, security risk management strategy has ability to adjust specific solutions and even the strategy framework to lessen the difference between goals and real effects of the strategy. The method of monitor and audit is crucial for the security risk management strategy to become an open system with adaptation.

Monitor

Commercial bank should examine the announced situation of system security implementation periodically. Make comprehensive audit to the security reports, strengthen the daily inspection of internal network besides the monitor of network attacks, and control the usage of network resources to prevent the bottleneck. The usual methods of monitor include scan of network security, scan of system defects, autoscan of database, and monitor of user's operation. The normal methods for scan in practice may consist of scan with security tools, artificial security check, and penetration test.

- **Scan with security tools:** In the construction of network security system, the security scan tools are very effective, whereas cost less. It is relatively independent with the operation of network and its installment is simple, which may reduce the security manager's manual labor massively and benefit the unity and the stability of the security policy. This method is powerful and useful in the risk analysis. The security scan technology basically contains two kinds: based on host and based on network. The former mainly pays attention to the risks and weakness of the host where the software installed, while the latter aims to find other hosts' security risks and weakness through remote network detection.

- **Artificial security check:** The system scans means using security evaluation tools to scan the weakness of host and network device in the domain of examination. But the security policy weakness of network equipments and the disposition mistakes of some hosts and so on cannot be discovered by the scanner, so the artificial security check to the system and device beyond the reach of scan tools is necessary. During the artificial check, the following aspects should be taken into account:
  - Whether the division of VLAN and the different segments is optimized, and whether each user's smallest privilege principle is guaranteed
  - Are there necessary isolation between inside and outside network, and important segments
  - Whether deployment of equipments, such as router, switch, host is optimized, and whether the essential security parameter is set
  - Whether the way of connection of security equipment is correct, whether it maximizes its security function at the cost of least system resources, and whether it affects the business and the normal system operation
- **Penetration testing:** Penetration testing is a security testing method. In this method, user should authorize the operator firstly, and then use hacker's tools and analysis approaches to imitate attacks to find factual defects and problems. The testing method is very helpful to find serious security problem. Especially it is more efficient and uses less time than the whole-code audit.

  During the testing, users can select the intensity. For instance, user can forbid operator to test some servers and applications in order not to influence the normal operation. But the all-around and correct testing to some key servers would be helpful to find the weak part of system, and people can make timely repair and amend to avoid loss.

Audit

The security audits of the bank include the audit of the application system, equipments, network application, information and data involved in operation system, and so on. The special audit assessment systems can be of great help. The audit can make following benefits: provide powerful evidence of the destructive operations for further actions; provide valuable system usage log and contribute to find out invasion and potential insecurity; provide statistic log of system function; and make it clear what is deficient, and what needs improvement or reinforcement.

The security audit and assessment should obey the rules of information security management. To investigate the security status of the IS, the methods of questionnaire survey and expert interview can be effective and useful.

Assessment of Security Risk Management Strategy

Monitor and audit still aim at the elements or subsystem of the security risk management strategy that is a large system, while the assessment of security risk management strategy is the general systematic appraisal to existing network security strategy. In the point of view of systematic, to examine the performance of a system, we should focus the unique functions of each element, and in addition, much importance ought to be attached to the elements as a whole. The assessment of security risk management strategy also is composed of technology and management appraisal. The contents of assessment may include following:

- Whether the strategy covers all the security aspects of the whole system completely
- Whether the security control, management, and measure specified in the strategy are correct and effective
- Whether content in the strategy has been identified and implemented

The problems obtained from monitor and audit as well as the data and results got from the assessment should serve as new security threats or weakness, and should be brought into the next new risk analysis. Security management strategy ought to be improved accordingly in the new turn.

Guarantee Implementation of Security Risk Management Security with the Aid of Bank Re-Engineering

Nowadays, bank re-engineering has become the common strategic thought of international banking. The bank re-engineering adjusts the long-standing organizational structure, operation strategy, and business flow in the new environment, increases the value of current operations of the bank to acquire huge profit, and forms core competitive power. In the course of business flow re-engineering and organization re-engineering, the information security must be fully considered to smooth the implementation of security risk management strategy of e-commerce business and improve the information transmission inside the bank. Whereas

Box 5. Online security protections provided for the customer by the Industrial Bank (Source: The Industrial Bank, n.d.)

The implementation of e-commerce security risk management strategy must not only provide the reliable safety control for bank itself, but must also offer the customer with considerate security services. The Industrial Bank as one of the Chinese earliest joint stock commercial banks, in the aspect of e-commerce security management, has made certain achievements. The Industrial Bank provides 12 security controls for the customers of the online finance to enable the customers to enjoy the diversified high level finance services.

The First Protection: The security of the electronic bank (e-bank) system passed certification by authority institution.

Online Industrial Bank is one of the e-bank systems which passed the authentication of the China Information Technology Security Certification Center and the security performance achieves the state-level standard.

continued on following

Box 5. Continued

The Second Protection: Certificate by the China Financial Certification Authority (CFCA).

The Industrial Bank adopts digital certificate issued by CFCA, which is the sole state-level electronic authentication organization, to provide security assurance for e-bank business.

The Third Protection: Movable digital certificate.

The movable digital certificate is very small and convenient to carry. It can use the USB interface. Comparing with the document digital certificate, it is nonreproducible, so it can avoid theft of certificate by hacker or Trojan horse and the influence of format of hardware and reinstallment of system.

The Fourth Protection: SSL128 encryption.

The user of online individual bank can enjoy the protection of international encryption standard SSL128 to ensure the safety of the transaction even if he does not employ the digital certificate.

The Fifth Protection: Password lock.

If the password is wrongly input more than six times, the system would automatically lock the operator of online enterprise bank or account of online individual bank to prevent the vicious attempt of password or key of account.

The Sixth Protection: Automatic exit when overtime.

If the user ceasing operation for more than 15 minutes after log in, the e-bank system will exit itself automatically to avoid the wrong operation by someone else.

The Seventh Protection: Short message service of fund changes.

The customer can register a mobile number for certain account he possesses in the Industrial Bank. And then if any fund change appears in the account, the bank will send a short message to the registered mobile. In this way, the customer can master the fund changes anytime and anywhere.

The Eighth Protection: Key input using soft keyboard.

The unique disordered soft keyboard permits input of key information by click of mouse to avoid the Trojan horse and virus which can monitor the normal keyboard.

The Ninth Protection: Intelligent modularization technology.

The online enterprise bank provides flexible and strict internal control system which can automatically deploy different operation interface and contents for operators with different privilege, and the system can give more security protection, such as restrained business range, daily transactions limit, and limitation of one transaction.

The Tenth Protection: Individual transaction protection by short message.

If the individual user applies this service, he will input the authentication code sent to the user's mobile by Industrial Bank besides the account password. This service is selective.

The Eleventh Protection: Dynamic additional code.

The register page adds the certification of one-off dynamic additional code, protecting the password from the malicious software by unauthorized users.

continued on following

Box 5. Continued

The Twelfth Protection: Complete operation prompt service.
The system can prompt the time of last successful register and last failed register as well as information of this time. There are still complete historical operation records for inquiry. This kind of trace management can give more considerate protection.

the e-commerce security risk management and traditional risk management also will affect the bank re-engineering. So the commercial bank should not neglect the relationship of security risk management and bank re-engineering.

Future Trends

The development history of network and e-commerce tells us it is a doubtless trend that financial services institutions adopt the mode of online promotion and e-commerce. Further more, with the advance of technology methods and pursuance of the convenient shopping mode by customer, e-commerce security management will consequentially draw great attention of the financial institutions and share the same state of the traditional financial risks. So the study of e-commerce security problems in financial services institutions has the meaning of practicability and foresightedness. In the near future, this research area will of course remain a hot spot of the subject of e-commerce.

The e-commerce security risk management strategy proposed in this article guided by the systematic and cybernetics theory has the character of adaptation system and has the formidable vitality in the environment that security threats unceasingly renew, so it is suitable and proper to be used in the current and future risk-changing circumstance. The risk analysis of the strategy refers the quantitative methods and models of traditional financial risks. In this way the financial services institutions can spare great manpower and physical resource for other necessary tasks. And the integration of e-commerce security risk and the traditional financial risks can be realized more easily. As to the strategy itself, it emphasizes the consistency and harmony with the traditional risk management strategy, so it has more soundness and adaptability than the existing security risk management strategy.

The existing security risk quantification method, due to its simple and rough measure, only adapts in the present stage which safety control requests are not extremely high. Once the security risk management obtains further regards and development and necessary data accumulation is completed, the precise quantification and the experience model will inevitably take the place of current method. While under the framework of financial organization's whole risk management, it is certain that the e-commerce risk should be considered together with other traditional financial risks. Since the study will involve the combination with other risks, and the risks influence each other, therefore e-commerce security risk management will have to emulate precise quantification methods of other risks. The precise risk evaluation as well as appraisal will become a research direction of the e-commerce security risk management in the future.

About e-commerce security risk management of the financial services institutions, another research opportunity is the new trend of the traditional risks of the financial institutes under the e-commerce pattern. In fact, according to the New Basel Capital Adequacy Standards, all the other risks except the market risk and the credit risk should belong to operational risk. Therefore the e-commerce security risk should also be interpreted as operational risk. But since this kind of new business model may bring various influences to the characteristic as well as the type of traditional operational risk, the risk evaluation, risk control, risk strategy of the e-commerce security risk will change necessarily. At the same time the e-commerce security risk and the credit risk as well as market risks also have overlapping. How to divide the changed risks in detail, and appraise the traditional risks regarding influences of the e-commerce security risk will have a very broad research space.

Conclusion

This chapter analyzes the background of e-commerce security risk management and the limitation of current security management strategy, and then proposes a new security risk management strategy. The security risk management strategy takes the systematic and cybernetics theory as the instruction, regards the risk analysis process, the management strategy implementation, and the monitor and audit as a complete security management system, integrating each safety control step organically. At the same time, the new problems obtained from audit serve as the input content of the new turn of risk analysis. Therefore this system processes the power to exchange information unceasingly with the outside environment and reduce the difference between whole target of the strategy and the practical results in virtual of feedback and control. Thus the strategy is an autoadapted open system, defeating various safe threats from both internal and external environment that changes unceasingly.

Security risk analysis, which contains risk identification, risk assessment, and risk control, is a very important part of the security risk management strategy. The chapter compares common assessment methods of e-commerce security risk with those of traditional financial risk, when introducing the risk analysis, and gives suggestion to make further accurate risk measurement in the way of quantitative analysis. This idea enriches the study contents of e-commerce security risk management and integrates the e-commerce security risk and traditional financial risks tightly as well.

Additionally, about the management strategy, this chapter tries to look the financial services institution as a whole and adapt the e-commerce security risk strategy to the original general risk management strategy. In this way, some departments in the financial institutions can be reformed or combined to avoid both overlapping and separation between security and business.

References

Bank for International Settlements (BIS). (2002). Basel Committee on Banking Supervision. *Operational risk supporting documentation to the new Basel Capital Accord.* Basel: BIS.

Chen , J. (2000). *Finance and security in e-commerce.* Beijing: Qinghua University Publishing House.

China Computer World (2005, August 23). *Cisco help the industrial bank build an advanced network security system.* Retrieved from http://tech.sina.com.cn/t/2005-08-23/1426701403.shtml

China Information Technology Security Certification Center (n.d.). *Table of contents of testing and authentication.* Retrieved from http://www.itsec.gov.cn/webportal/portal.po?UID=DWV1_WOUID_URL_175271

Gao, X., & Zou, J. (2005). Risk analysis and management of e-commerce security. *Journal of Wuhan University of Technology (Information & Management Engineering), 27*(4), 254-258.

IS-One China (n.d.). *Security service - Theory and standard.* Retrieved March 20, 2006, from http://bj.is-one.net/safe/standard/manage/

Laudon, K. C., & Traver, C. G. (2003). *E-commerce: Business, technology, society (update).* MA: Addison Wesley Professional.

PricewaterhouseCoopers. (2006). *IT governance survey 2006.* Retrieved March 20, 2006, from http://www.pwc.com/extweb/pwcpublications.nsf/docid/D3E2997D370F3C648025713300511A01

The Industrial Bank (n.d.). *Online industrial bank: More security protections.* Retrieved March 20, 2006, from http://www.cib.com.cn/netbank/netbank.portal@_nfpb=true&_pageLabel=index_aqsm

Wang, Z. (2005). *E-commerce security.* Beijing: Mechanical Industry Publishing House.

Zhao, Z. (2004). *Trends of standardized information security management.* The State Key Laboratory of Information Security.

Zhe, F., Langran, L., Yanxia, X., Jiang, X., & Yuandan, S. (2006, April 21). *System failure—The first-time transaction interruption across banks of China Union Pay.* Retrieved from http://www.nanfangdaily.com.cn/southnews/jwxy/200604210168.asp

Appendix: Additional Reading

Cai, S. (2004). *E-commerce security risk management and control.* Shenyang, Liaoning: Dongbei University Publishing House.

Cofly Management Consulting. (2002). *Information security management introduction–BS7799 understanding and implementation.* Beijing: Mechanical Industry Publishing House.

Glaessner, T., Kellermann, T., & McNevin, V. (2002). *Electronic security: Risk mitigation in financial transactions public policy issues*. The World Bank.

Greenstein , M., & Vasarhelyi, M. (2002). *Electronic commerce: Security, riskmanagement, and control.* Boston: McGraw-Hill/Irwin.

Lu, H. (2001). *Internal control system of modern commercial bank.* Beijing: Chinese Finance Publishing House.

Ong, M. K. (1999). *Internal credit risk models: Capital allocation and performance easurement.* London: Risk Books.

Qiang, S., Chen, W., & Wang, D. (2004). *Information security management—The best global practice and implementation guide.* Beijing: Qinghua University Publishing House.

Wang, F., & Zhang, Z. (1998). *Banking risk and risk guard.* Beijing: Economic Science Press.

Xianxin, Z. (2003). *Internal models and regulation models of bank-risk measurement and capital assignment.* Shanghai, China: Shanghai People's Publishing House.

Zhenghui, F. (2005). *Capital management and risk control in commercial bank—-Explains "Barthel New Capital Agreement."* Beijing: Economics Daily Publishing House.

Zhou, J., & Chen, W. (1985). *Managerial philosophy—Systematic.* Shanghai, China: Shanghai Jiaotong University Press.

Greenstein , M., & Vasarhelyi, M. (2002). *Electronic commerce: Security, riskmanagement, and control.* Boston: McGraw-Hill/Irwin.

Section II

Technologies and Countermeasures

Chapter VI

New Technologies in E-Banking: Convenient and Trustworthy?

Niels Jørgensen, Roskilde University, Denmark

Abstract

In e-banking, user authentication with mobile phones and special-purpose cryptographic tokens is a promising alternative to conventional approaches, such as digital signatures on a personal computer (PC). Special-purpose tokens that do not have external connections avoid viruses transmitted via the Internet. Moreover, phones and tokens are mobile. The chapter assesses the potential of new technologies for user authentication (verification of the user's identity) on the basis of a practical test and an analysis of trust. The practical test comprises a password generator, mobile phones with short message service (SMS), wireless application protocol (WAP), and third generation (3G), and (conventional) PC-based authentication, using digital signatures—all as used by a Danish e-bank. On the one hand, the test indicates that in some ways the hardware-based technologies are indeed easier to use. On the other hand, the trust analysis indicates that the secrecy of the new approaches may be a weakness, since there is no publicly available analysis of their security. The secrecy of the hardware-based technologies may be justified by the need to prevent various attacks, such as physically opening a password generator to determine its secret key. A prerequisite for consumer trust in the hardware-based technologies may be the introduction of security evaluation methods that do not disclose the secret parts of the technologies to the public and are conducted by public authorities or independent third parties.

Introduction

A dilemma is facing systems for Web-based electronic banking (e-banking). E-banking must be secure and easy to use, but the two goals are in conflict. Passwords provide an illustration of the dilemma. On the one hand, a strong password such as x7h!t%C9 is less vulnerable to attack than a simple password, such as a person name. On the other hand, a strong password may be difficult to remember, so the user is tempted to write the password on paper attached to the computer screen. The dilemma of passwords is widely acknowledged (Morris & Thomson, 1979; Schultz, Proctor, Lien, & Salvendy, 2001).

Digital signatures provide much better security than passwords but do not solve the basic conflict between security and ease of use. In their best practice recommendations, Claessens, Dem, De Cock, Preneel, & Vandewalle (2002) noted that in principle, digital signatures are the most secure method for authentication, but when stored on a user's PC, a signature file requires the user to protect the PC against intrusion from the Internet, which requires skills and time. Therefore special-purpose cryptographic hardware tokens were recommended as a best practice.

A recent event in Denmark highlights the risks of storing digital signatures on Internet-connected computers. In 2004, a person stole 25,000 DKR (approximately $4,000 (US)) from a private e-bank account in Nordea, which holds the second largest market share in Denmark. The attacker managed to transfer, via the Internet, a Trojan-horse program to the account holder's computer. The program obtained the signature file and the password and transmitted them to the attacker's computer. The signature file was copied from the hard disk, and the password was intercepted when the user typed it on the keyboard. In this case, the attacker was caught easily, since he transferred money from the victim's account to his own (RB-Børsen, 2004).

E-banking is widely used in Denmark. In 2006, 83% of the population had access to the Internet from home, and in a given month, 56% of the population had logged on to a private e-banking account (Danmarks Statistik, 2006). Recently, several Danish banks have introduced alternatives to digital signatures. These are a password generator called ActivCard® and GSM mobile phones with SMS, WAP, or 3G. This provided the opportunity to conduct the practical test of the new technologies that is reported in this chapter.

Picture 1. Hardware tokens of the test: From left are a 3g mobile phone (Nokia 6680), a password generator (ActivCard®), and a 2g mobile phone (Nokia 7650)

New Technologies for User-Authentication

Password generators and other new hardware technologies for user authentication define a new generation of e-banking, based on processors that are very small, yet powerful enough to conduct cryptographic operations in a fraction of a second. Such a processor is embedded in the ActivCard®, a password generator the size of a credit card, as well as in the SIM card of a GSM mobile phone. A related development is the introduction of chip-based credit cards. Visa, MasterCard, and other credit card companies are currently deploying credit cards based on the EMV®-standard, replacing the magnetic strip technology. The processor of an EMV®-compliant credit card is capable of computing a digital signature (EMV®Co, 2005).

The ActivCard®, which is part of the test, has a small keyboard for input and a small display for output. It has no network connection facilities. The card is used as follows for authentication in e-banking: The user types a personal identification number (PIN) code to begin using the card. In response, the card displays a password. The user reads the password and types it into the browser. If the password is accepted by the e-bank, the user is authenticated. The ActivCard® is marketed by the ActivCard company (see http://www.activcard.com). A related product is SecurID®, which is marketed by the RSA company (see http://www.rsa.com).

Previously introduced technologies for e-banking include ATMs, phone banking, PC banking, and electronic banking. In this terminology, PC banking is the sort of electronic banking that requires the user to install software from a CD or other physical medium and use a modem to connect the user's computer directly to the bank. Advantages of e-banking over PC banking is that the Internet is used for data transfer and download of software. This has a potential for simplifying deployment (by not requiring a physical medium for software distribution), reducing maintenance cost (for the bank), and providing the familiar browser user interface (to the user). The new generation that uses an independent token may be termed hardware-based authentication, and the contemporary approach of using a key stored in the PC may be termed software-based authentication. (The term may be an abuse of language, since each of the technologies is a combination of hardware and software.)

Table 1. Two-factor authentication with PC, ActivCard®, and GSM mobile phones. If the e-bank trusts the mobile network operator, authentication to the network can serve as (partial) authentication to the bank.

Technology	Two factor authentication	
	A secret the user has	**A secret the user knows**
PC with signature file	A secret key stored in the signature file.	A password. The password is required for each use of the private key.
ActivCard®: Processor capable of cryptographic operations	A secret key stored on the ActivCard®.	A PIN code. The PIN code is required each time the card is used to generate a password.
GSM mobile phone: Processor on SIM-card is capable of cryptographic operations	A secret key stored on the SIM-card.	A PIN code. The PIN code is required when the phone is switched on.

Table 1 summarizes two-factor authentication for two hardware-based and one software-based technology. Two-factor authentication is commonly recognized as good practice (e.g., Claessens et al., 2002). In Denmark, it is mandated by the Danish Bankers Association's industry code. One factor is a secret the user *has*. This is a key stored in hardware. The user invokes a cryptographic operation with the key, the result of which is sent to the authenticating authority to prove that the user is in possession of the key. (Sometimes the key the user has is referred to as the *possessed* key.) The other factor is a secret the user *knows*. This is a PIN code or password of a limited length so that it is feasible for the user to type the secret manually. A user may or may not be able to memorize the known secret. If not, the user should be careful not to defeat the purpose of two-factor authentication by keeping a piece of paper with the PIN code for an ActivCard® in the same pocket as the ActivCard® itself.

With regard to GSM mobile phones, two-factor authentication is used to authenticate the user to the GSM network. Authentication establishes which user account to bill for phone calls, SMSs, and other services used. The mobile e-banking application in the test uses additional authentication (based on a secret the user knows). In addition to something the user has or knows, there are schemes for biometrical authentication, for example, using fingerprints. These schemes, which are not part of the test, can be said to use something the user *is*.

Usable Security in E-Banking

The security goals of the most relevance to e-banking are user authentication (as discussed in the previous section), confidentiality, and integrity.

The significance of **user authentication** is that the bank must be able to verify the identity of the user prior to completing transactions. User authentication may be required already at log on, because the logged on user has access to account listings and other confidential information. Reauthenticating an already logged on user at transactions completion protects the user who has left the computer and forgotten to log out.

Confidentiality is the security goal of protecting from disclosure transaction or account data communicated between the user and the bank.

Integrity is the goal that such data is not altered during transmission, for example, that a change is not made to the account number of the recipient of a payment. For confidentiality and integrity, contemporary Web browsers implement the secure socket layer (SSL) and similar protocols, so these goals can be attained by means of the existing Internet infrastructure. SSL is used in both PC-based solutions in the test, as well as the mobile 3G solution.

Additional security goals are mutual authentication and nonrepudiation. **Mutual authentication** is when both parties are authenticated, that is, not just the user but also the bank. Mutual authentication aims at protecting against attackers that set up a Web site that looks like the user's e-bank. As with confidentiality and integrity, there is support for mutual authentication in current Web browsers. **Non-repudiation** is when a user cannot deny having made a given transaction. Non-repudiation is provided by public key algorithms, where the user possesses a key (the so-called private key) that is not known to the other party (for example, the e-bank). The ability of public key-based systems to provide nonrepudiation is the reason that they are, in principle, the most secure. In contrast, the known secrets stored on ActivCards® and GSM phones (as well as credit card PIN codes) are known to the other side, and so do not provide nonrepudiation.

Tamper resistance is the ability of a token to hide the (possessed) secret stored on it to anyone who does not have the (known) secret used for access to the token, for example, a PIN code. The scenario where tamper resistance is relevant is when an attacker steals the token and subsequently applies various means, such as drilling, to gain access to the token's memory. An example defense is for the token to be able to detect an attack and, in the event of an attack, delete the possessed secret (Kömmerling & Kuhn, 1999).

Cryptographic tokens with external connections must be protected against attacks that use the connection. This is the equivalent of protecting a PC against viruses transmitted via the Internet and applies to, among others, mobile phones with network facilities (for example, Bluetooth) and chip-based credit cards (which can exchange data with a card terminal).

Usable security has been proposed as a concept for capturing usability of security-sensitive systems. Contributions to a better understanding of usable security include the set of characteristics proposed by Whitten and Tygar (1999) of such systems, including the **weakest link property**, the **unmotivated user** property, and the **barn door property**. The latter is the property that once a secret, such as a private key has been compromised, then closing the barn door, for example, setting up a firewall, does not restore security. One consequence of the barn door property is that typically, it is not feasible to learn a system by playing with it; security mechanisms must be turned on from start.

Whitten and Tygar (1999, p. 3) suggest the following definition of usable security, against which the e-banking systems will be measured in this chapter: *"Security-related software is usable if the people who are expected to use it:*

1. *Are reliably made aware of the security tasks they need to perform;*
2. *Are able to figure out how to successfully perform those tasks;*
3. *Don't make dangerous errors; and*
4. *Are sufficiently comfortable with the interface to continue using it.*"

From the point of view of usable security, some e-banking systems based on software-based authentication are simply not satisfactory. Initialization may be quite complex, because the user must download and install software to generate a public and a private key. The initial phase may require the user to press "OK" to a number of messages that the ordinary user does not understand. Of course, it is an unsound habit to press such buttons blindly—indeed, this will make the user's computer vulnerable to attacks via the Internet. For the user to act "reliably" and not make "dangerous errors," it would appear that the user needs more technical insight than one can reasonably expect. An analysis of this and other inherent weaknesses of software-based user authentication is reported in Hertzum, Juul, Jørgensen, Nørgaard (2004).

In contrast, tokens for authentication, which have no external connections, have a potential for attaining usable security, because complex measures, such as firewalls, are not required to protect the possessed secret. Moreover, the new technologies offer mobility, because the user is not required to use a particular PC.

Evaluation Method

The test covers the following ways of authenticating a user in e-banking:

1. PC with signature file (the "traditional" approach)
2. ActivCard® for use with a PC
3. GSM mobile phone with SMS. Provides account listing
4. GSM mobile phone with WAP (with a GPRS "generation 2.5" connection). Provides account listing and money transfer among one's own accounts
5. GSM mobile phone with UMTS (ie. a 3rd generation GSM phone) in combination with an ActivCard®. Provides money transfer to arbitrary accounts

The five authentication methods were tested using e-banking accounts in Danske Bank, the largest Danish bank (www.danskebank.dk). The mobile solutions in the test (nos. 3-5) require that the user already has a PC-based solution (nos. 1-2).

The test covers the following five e-banking user tasks: initialization (such as defining a PIN code for the ActivCard®), log on to the e-bank account, generating an account listing showing the most recent transaction, money transfer, and log off. The test was carried out by the author as follows: for each task and each type of authentication, a table was constructed. The table recorded the information displayed by the system and the actions undertaken by the user/tester as the tasks were conducted. These so-called sequence tables are inspired by Beyer and Holtzblatt (1998). Following the practical test, the sequence tables were analyzed. To attain an approximate, quantitative measure of the complexity of the user interfaces, the following data was computed from the tables.

- **Steps:** The number of steps carried out by the user. A step is an action the user must perform, either typing a text or pressing a button (perhaps virtually with the mouse). Typing a string is typically followed by some indication of termination, say pressing the enter key or pressing a (graphical) OK button. Such an act is counted as an additional step, if it is not required by convention in the context of the given user interface (the Web or WAP browser, SMS user interface, etc.) Loading the URL of the e-bank counts as the first step in the log on task.
- **Codes:** The number of codes the user must manage. A code is a string such as a password, PIN-code, or account number.
- **Concepts:** The number of concepts the system presents to the user. A concept is a security-related term such as signature file, private key, and so forth.

A similar method was used by the author and coauthors in Hertzum et al. (2004) to evaluate software-based user authentication of e-banking solutions, based mainly on digital signatures.

The PC in the test was equipped with the Windows XP operating system (with Service Pack 2) and the Internet Explorer Web browser (version 6.0). The user account was granted administrator privileges, and the browser privacy level was set to medium. Java and other plug ins to the browser were downloaded prior to the test, so that the browser complied with the requirements defined by the bank. The UMTS phone was a Nokia 6680, and the phone used for testing the WAP and SMS solutions was a Nokia 7650, using a GPRS connection (i.e., GSM "generation 2.5"). The display was 176x206 pixels on both phones. There was some work in setting up the PC as indicated above, but this was not assessed in the test. Details about the test can be found in Jørgensen (2006).

Test Results: Ease of Use

The test results are presented in two subsections. First, initialization of the two PC-based solutions is compared in detail. Initialization is important because the task may be overly complex with a signature file solution. Second, the overall performance of the five solutions is compared, especially with respect to daily use.

Initialization: The PC-Based Solutions

For the PC-based solutions, the main results with regards to ease of use are that initialization is the easiest with the new technology (the ActivCard®). Table 2 below provides details about initialization of the two PC-based solutions.

- **Steps:** The signature file solution requires more initialization steps than the ActivCard® (12 vs. 6). The extra steps are due to a more cumbersome procedure for defining (and confirming) a new password and a path to the back-up copy of the signature file. With the ActivCard®, although defining and confirming a new password is logically the same procedure as with the signature file, the ActivCard® is preprogrammed to present the password definition dialogue. Therefore, the ActivCard® variant of the password initialization procedure is more direct than with the signature file, where there is overhead involved in browsing to the proper window, as reflected in the higher number of steps. This may reflect that the ActivCard® is a special-purpose token, while the browser is a generic tool.

Table 2. Steps, codes, and concepts in initialization of the two PC-based user-authentication methods

Complexity of initialization	Signature file	ActivCard®
Steps	12	6
Codes	4	3
Concepts	8	4

- **Codes:** Both solutions require the user to manage a user ID and an initial and user-defined password. In addition to these three codes, we count the path to the back-up signature file as a fourth code. In return for dealing with the back-up file path, the user of the signature file solution does get some useful functionality. In particular, the user may create a back up on an external medium, such as a USB stick, which can then be inserted into a different PC, providing some of the mobility of the ActivCard®.
- **Concepts:** Finally, the number of security-related concepts presented to the user during initialization is also higher in the signature file case. The concepts presented to the user include the names of the four codes and a set of concepts, such as "secure connection," displayed in the pop-up browser windows shown in Figures 1 and 2. The browser messages indicate another aspect of the trade off involved in using a standardized tool (the browser), namely that the e-banking system is unable to control the warning messages, some of which may be difficult to understand (in particular, the message in Figure 2). The ActivCard® is initialized without using the browser, so the user avoids the browser messages altogether. (The ActivCard® user is confronted with the messages during the log on task, though, as discussed below.)

Interestingly, the concepts presented to the user during initialization of the signature file solution do not include concepts related to public key cryptography. A previous test by Hertzum et al. (2004) of Danske Bank and five other e-banking solutions reported that all signature file-based banks would mention concepts, such as "private key," or merely "key." Now, in Danske Bank's contemporary solution, the signature file is referred to as a "User ID." The fact that the system is based on public key cryptography is explained to the user in additional online help files but not in the initialization dialogue. Also, the downloading and execution of a program to generate the keys is transparent to the user. To the author, this radical approach to simplifying an interface to a cryptography-based system appears to be successful. The simplification may be seen as legitimate as long as the additional help files explain the matter and also provides relevant instructions for protecting the "User ID" (i.e., signature file), namely by using an antivirus program, a firewall, and regular software updates.

Figure 1. Incomprehensible browser messages

continued on following page

Figure 2. Continued

All in all, while both PC-based solutions are relatively easy to initialize, the ActivCard® is markedly easier than the signature file solution. This holds despite the fact the ActivCard® is reminiscent of PC-banking, in the sense that deployment involves sending a token to the user. (Recall that in PC-banking, the software is distributed on a physical medium.) The special-purpose cryptographic token outperforms the generic, Web-based solution when it comes to initialization, because the generic solution requires more user involvement in the process.

Daily Use: PC-Based and Mobile Solutions

Table 3 gives an overview of the five tasks in the test by listing the number of steps in each task for all five access methods. On the basis of Table 3, firstly the two PC-based solutions are compared (listed as solutions 1 and 2 above) and secondly the mobile technologies are discussed (solutions 3-5).

Table 3. Number of user steps required for the five e-banking tasks in the test

Technology for user authentication		Initialization	Log on	Account listing	Money transfer	Log off
PC-based	Signature file	12	7	3	6 + payment details	2
	ActivCard® (PC)	6	12	3	10 + payment details	2
Mobile phone-based	SMS	0	n/a	3	n/a	n/a
	WAP	0	2	6	4 + payment details	1
	3G (ActivCard®)	0	7	6	10 + payment details	1

PC-based solutions. With the signature file solution, the ordinary tasks, such as log on and money transfer, require only a few navigation steps in the browser and typing a password (the *known* secret). In comparison, the ActivCard® is somewhat cumbersome. Log on and money transfer each require that the card is activated with the PIN code and a password is read and typed into a browser field. In the author's opinion, the difference with respect to convenience is significant. It is even greater if the user must conduct several payments. There is a facility for bundling of payments, so that a set of payments can be confirmed with a single use of the ActivCard®. This is attractive for the ActivCard® user, while for the user of the signature file, signing the individual transaction is so simple that bundling does not even appear to be a significant time saver. Account listing is the same in the two PC-based solutions, because when the user is already logged on, the account listing does not require authentication, and the Web pages are the same for the PC-based solutions, except for authentication. Also, the browser messages shown in Figures 1 and 2 are displayed at log on with both PC-based solutions and contribute to the number of steps because the user must press the OK and Yes buttons.

Mobile solutions. A general observation about the mobile technologies in the test is that they are not more difficult to use than the PC-based solutions. The various tasks require about the same number of steps (except for account listing). One might suspect that navigation would be cumbersome because the displays have room for only a limited number of links, but this was not the case. On the contrary, navigation is convenient, and there is some relief in working with the simplified pages, where one is not distracted by various advertisements for additional banking services and financial and other news. The graphical design of the 3G and WAP solutions consists of simple pages with text and a few miniature icons, all directly related to the e-banking tasks.

Technically, the WAP and 3G solutions are similar in the sense that the user interacts with the bank's Web server via the mobile phone's browser. They are different in the sense that the 3G solution uses HTML and scripting languages understood by conventional Web browsers, while WAP has its own set of mark up and scripting languages. WAP is tailored for mobile phones, particularly their display and keyboard (WAP, 2000). In the test of the WAP solution, only a single instance of mobile tailoring was observed, namely using a key (the "back" or rightmost navigation key) as a shortcut to an account overview page.

In the detailed evaluation of the mobile solutions, the features provided by each method should be taken into account.

- **Detailed evaluation of SMS-solution:** SMS allows for sending text messages from one mobile phone to another. The SMS access method in the test provides only a single feature: account listing. It is implemented by means of two SMS messages: a request sent by the user, and a reply sent by the e-bank. There is no session to log on to (or out of) and no initialization. To list account data, the user activates the phone's ordinary SMS interface and sends an SMS message to the bank's SMS number, supplying the account number and a service code. Within a few seconds, the user receives a balance and a summary of the three most recent transactions. Viewing the full listing requires some scrolling through the SMS message, as shown on the phone's display. Of the five access methods, SMS is the quickest way of getting an account balance. The SMS solution may be convenient in scenarios such as traveling or shopping, where a PC may not be available as a means of verifying, say, that the balance is positive. Thus it may be a useful add on to an ordinary PC-based access method. The SMS service does introduce a security weakness, however. The service code is a generic, four-digit number, and the SMS service is available between any account subscribing to the service and any (SMS-enabled) phone. Thus there is no user authentication. Therefore, the service violates confidentiality of account information (see the listing of security goals above).

- **Detailed evaluation of WAP solution:** The WAP-access method in the test provides account listing and money transfer, restricted to transfers among the account holder's own accounts. There is no session concept. Thus, the two steps listed in Table 3 for log on merely represent browsing to the appropriate URL. Account listing and money transfer supplies the same information as in the SMS case. Since there is no session concept, the information (including account number) must be supplied in each task, so account listing requires more steps (6), than in the PC-based solutions (3). Similar to the SMS case, overall usage is convenient, reflecting lack of proper user authentication. In fact, the WAP service introduces the same security weakness as with SMS, and moreover a new risk that transfers can be abused. As long as money transfers are restricted, the risk is limited, but because of the limited functionality, it is difficult to see a significant advantage of the WAP solution over the SMS solution.
- **Detailed evaluation of 3G-solution:** The 3G solution provides features for conducting all five tasks in the test. User authentication is by means of an ActivCard® and takes place at log on and transaction confirmation. Table 3 lists 0 steps for initialization, which assumes the user already has an initialized ActivCard®. Log on requires more steps (7) than with WAP, and this is because the user is authenticated with the ActivCard®. The most striking difference between PC- and mobile-based ActivCard® is the log on. Log on is simpler with 3G mainly because the mobile Web browser does not display warning messages, such as those in Figures 1 and 2. This is convenient, but reflects that the mobile browser, though providing SSL, is not configured to issue such warnings. This is permissible from the point of view of security, if one assumes that the mobile phone is less vulnerable to attacks from the Internet. On the one hand, this assumption would seem to require that mobile Web browsing remains a marginal phenomenon. On the other hand, as long as one of the user's secrets is stored on an independent token (the ActivCard®), the issue of protecting the Internet-connected phone (or PC) is less critical. Although not part of the formal test, it may be noted that the 3G solution does not provide features for "bookmarking" frequently used account numbers. Such a feature is possible even given the limited display size and would enhance usefulness.

The test results are summarized in Table 4. Among the new hardware-based technologies, the PC-based ActivCard® solution may seem to perform best, but it is not clear that it outperforms the "traditional" signature-based method. Since typing account numbers and so forth on a mobile keyboard is cumbersome, mobile technologies are perhaps best viewed as optional supplements to PC-based access, and then perhaps the simple account listing features of SMS (and WAP) are of the most interest.

Table 4. Summary of advantages and disadvantages of the five technologies, based on the practical test and the security assessments made above

Technology for user authentication		Main advantage	Main disadvantage
PC-based	Signature file	Simple authentication at log on and money transfer.	Requires firewall and other protective measures.
	ActivCard® (PC)	Firewall and other protective measures not required.	Execution of ordinary tasks is less convenient.
Mobile phone-based	SMS	The simplest way of obtaining an account listing.	No proper user authentication.
	WAP	The ability to conduct (restricted) money transfer (not significant).	No proper user authentication.
	3G (ActivCard®)	Supports all tasks in the test.	Typing of account numbers is cumbersome, especially without "bookmarking."

Trust Analysis

Assessing the usable security of the new hardware-based technologies requires the examination of issues related to trust. This includes the issue of trusting a technology based on mechanisms that are not publicly available (for example, for tamper resistance of a token) and trusting another organization's procedures (for example, about access to sensitive information by network operator employees). This may be of relevance in evaluating the ActivCard® as used in the test and in evaluating the feasibility of some obvious improvements to the SMS and WAP solutions, which are indicated below.

ActivCard®. A user who has lost an ActivCard® should trust that the card cannot be used without the user-defined PIN code. This is the rationale of two-factor authentication (see Table 1). The mechanisms used in the ActivCard® to attain some degree of tamper resistance are kept secret. In practice, many tamper resistant designs have been broken, although frequently only by means of expensive equipment (Kömmerling & Kuhn 1999). Keeping the design of a tamper resistant mechanism secret is likely to make tampering more difficult but also makes it difficult to trust the mechanism.

SMS. Account listing as provided by the SMS solution in the test violates confidentiality, as discussed above. An obvious improvement is for the account holder to register a particular phone number with the SMS service. Then the confidential information would be sent only to the user as authenticated by the GSM network. This raises the issue of the trustworthiness of GSM user authentication. The issue also arises where SMS is used for micropayments, such as purchasing train tickets (Mallat, Rossi, & Tuunainen, 2004). User authentication in GSM relies on the security provided by the SIM card (as sketched in Table 1). Previously, the SIM cards deployed by most operators of 2G networks used an algorithm called Comp128-1, which was originally kept secret. When the algorithm eventually became publicly known, it was subjected to public analysis and deemed insecure (e.g., Schiller, 2000). For a party such as a bank, it is difficult or impossible to establish, given a user that sends an SMS request to the e-bank, by what method the user has been authenticated to the GSM network—by the old

Table 5. Trust issues related to the ActivCard® (as tested) and to WAP and SMS (pertaining to suggested improvements of the solutions tested)

Technology	Trust issue
ActivCard®	Trusting a secret tamper-resistant token design.
SMS	Trusting an authentication mechanism used by a GSM network operator.
WAP	Trusting the internal procedures of a network operator running a WAP gateway.

insecure method or a newer, more secure method. However, for SMS access to e-banking, the degree of security provided by SIM-card authentication may be acceptable as long as the security goal is merely that of confidentiality of account listing information.

WAP. An obvious improvement of the WAP solution in the test is to allow money transfer to arbitrary accounts so that the WAP solution would provide the same full set of features as the 3G solution. This would be of interest because WAP is available on 2G and "2.5G" (GPRS) networks, and is more adaptable to the specific characteristics of mobile phones (as discussed in the previous section). For security, the WAP protocol provides SSL connections (WAP Forum, 2000). However, a trust issue arises between the e-banking parties (the user and the bank), on the one side, and the network operator on the other side. The secure connections provided by WAP are such that messages are not encrypted while passing through the WAP gateway. The gateway links the mobile network to the ordinary Internet. The gateway is normally under the control of the network operator, so in theory, data may be disclosed to and modified by employees at the operator, or rather, by software operating under their control. This would violate confidentially and integrity, of course. The dependency on the network operator is avoided by WAP version 2.0, however the most widely deployed version of WAP is 1.2.1, which has the problem. Some financial institutions that provide WAP services use another work around: they operate their own WAP gateway. This may incur extra maintenance costs for the e-bank; moreover, it may cause inconvenience to the user of multiple WAP-services, because if each service uses its own gateway, the phone's WAP setting must be changed frequently. These weaknesses of WAP may have contributed to the failure of WAP being widely used in security-sensitive applications, as discussed by Juul & Jørgensen (2003).

Table 5 summarizes the trust issues raised by the three technologies.

Trust Discussion

A common theme of the trust issues raised by new technologies is the problem of trusting a third party: a third party's secret tamper-resistant design, choice of GSM authentication algorithm, or internal procedures for employees' access to a WAP gateway.

For the bank, the trust issues may add complexity to the task of providing a secure e-banking service and convincing customers and relevant authorities that the service is indeed secure. This is already difficult when no third party is involved. Anderson (1994) gives examples of legal cases in the United Kingdom, where banks have accused an account holder of fraud because of withdrawals that the customer denied having made. When the court demanded that the bank present documentation, such as security manuals and audit reports, in order to prove that only the customer would have access to the relevant secrets, such as PIN codes, typically the bank would withdraw its case. It is clearly even more difficult to provide proof of proper organizational procedures when a third party organization is involved.

For the customer, the trust issues may raise concerns as well. Danish citizens tend to trust the security provided by Danish e-banks, as indicated by the high percentage of the population that uses e-banking (56% in a given month in 2006). Among those that have Internet access, but never used it for e-banking or other types of e-business, less than one-fifth indicate that security concerns are the main reason (Danmarks Statistik, 2006). It may be noted that these statistics reflect usage of the conventional Internet, including conventional e-banking, such as the signature file solution, which was evaluated in this study, so it may reflect the open, public culture of the Internet, with a tradition of open source and open standards (Schmidt & Werle, 1999). To attain confidentiality, authentication, and other relevant security goals, e-banking systems with software-based user authentication rely on publicly available protocols and algorithms, such as SSL, Rijndael, and RSA. It is reasonable for customers and citizens to trust the security community's consensus that nobody knows how to break these publicly available protocols and algorithms (Kaufman, Perlman, & Speciner, 2002).

With regard to the technologies used by conventional e-banking systems, there are even developments that will lead to a higher degree of public insight. A notable example is the standardization of the Rijndael algorithm by a U.S. government organization in 2001 (National Institute of Standards and Technology, 2001). The standardization organization invited candidate algorithms from independent experts, and organized an evaluation process where the proposed algorithms were subjected to public scrutiny by the international cryptology community. Rijndael supersedes the encryption algorithm DES, which was standardized in 1976, and has been widely used for encryption in the financial sector. Contrary to Rijndael's open design, the design considerations underlying the DES algorithm were kept secret. This led to suspicion that the DES algorithm was designed to include certain weaknesses, for example, to allow American intelligence agencies to intercept encrypted messages. Although the cryptology community now believe the suspicion was not justified (Kaufman et al., 2002), the development from DES to Rijndael does indicate that customers and businesses prefer a fully disclosed technology.

For the new hardware-based authentication technologies to rely on designs and procedures that are not public is a deroute from the openness of the Internet technologies underlying conventional e-banking. While the information technology industry has established its own practices of independent evaluation, such as those sketched above, the industry may also look to traditional, manufacturing industries for methods to evaluate products and services sold to the general public.

In the airline industry, there is an established tradition of inspection of aircraft production and airline operation. For example, inspectors from the U.S. Federal Aviation Agency (FAA) demand to be present at mandatory evacuation tests of commercial passenger aircraft, such as the test of Boeing's latest passenger aircraft in 1994 (Sabbagh, 1995). This tradition may be among the factors behind the improvement by a factor of more than 30 in the passenger fatality rate from the 1950s to the 1990s (Savage, 1999). In the auto industry, crash tests are performed by independent institutions (such as the National Highway Traffic Safety Administration and Insurance Institute for Highway Safety in the United States), and at least a segment of customers look to the results of the crash tests when making their purchasing decisions (Burns, 1999). The aviation and auto industries have a history of increasing customer concerns over safety issues, and the practices developed in the industries may be of interest in addressing the trust issues associated with new technologies in e-banking.

Conclusion

A selection of hardware-based technologies for user authentication has been tested with a view to usable security. The most promising may be the password generator ActivCard® as used with a PC (for daily use), and SMS-based access for occasional access to account listings. The 3G GSM phone also appears to be secure and (relatively) easy to use. The new technologies raise new issues of trust, due to interoperation of the mobile and fixed networks (where WAP raises the issue of trusting a third party's internal procedures), reusing GSM authentication (where SMS raises the issue of trusting a GSM operator's authentication mechanism, which may be secret), and tamper resistance (the design of which is typically secret). Traditions of independent inspection and review in mature industries, such as the aviation and auto industries, may be of interest in addressing these new trust issues.

References

Anderson, R. J. (1994). Liability and computer security: Nine principles. In *Computer Security—ESORICS '94. Lecture Notes in Computer Science, 875,* 231-245.

Beyer, H., & Holtzblatt, K. (1998). *Contextual design: Defining customer-centered systems.* San Francisco: Morgan Kaufmann,

Burns, R. G. (1999). Socially constructing an image in the automobile industry. *Crime, Law & Social Change, 31*, 327-346.

Claessens, J., Dem, V., De Cock, D., Preneel, B., & Vandewalle, J. (2002). On the security of today's online electronic banking systems. *Computers & Security, 21*(3), 257-269.

Danmarks Statistik. (2006). *Statistiske Efterretninger, Serviceerhverv* [Statistical Messages, Service Sector].(Vol. 33, pp. 1-24). Copenhagen: Danmarks Statistik.

EMVCo. (2005). *EMV issuer and application security guidelines. Version 1.3, April.* Retrieved July 14, 2006, from http://www.emvco.com/cgi_bin/terms.pl?action=download&fichier=documents/specification/download/0420_EMV-SWG-N420IssuerSecurityGuidelinesUpdate9a_PU.zip

Hertzum, M., Juul, N. C., Jørgensen, N., & Nørgaard, M. (2004). Usable security and e-banking: Ease of use vis-à-vis security [Special issue]. *Australasian Journal of Information Systems, 11*(2), 52-65.

Jørgensen, N. (2006). *New technologies in e-banking: Test documentation.* Retrieved July 14, 2006, from http://www.ruc.dk/~nielsj/research/publications/ebanking-tr-nt.pdf

Juul, N. C., & Jørgensen, N. (2003). The security hole in WAP: An analysis of the network and business rationales underlying a failure. *International Journal of Electronic Commerce, 7*(4), 73-92.

Kaufman, C., Perlman, R., & Speciner, M. (2002). *Network security. Private communication in a public world* (2nd ed.). Englewood Cliffs, NJ: Prentice-Hall.

Kömmerling, O, & Kuhn, M. G. (1999). Design principles for tamper-resistant smartcard processors. In *Proceedings of USENIX Workshop on Smartcard Technology* (pp. 1-13). Chicago.

Mallat, N., Rossi, M., & Tuunainen, V. K. (2004). Mobile banking services. *Communications of the ACM, 47*(5), 42-46.

Morris, R., & Thomson, K. (1979). Password security: A case history. *Communications of the ACM, 22*(11), 594-597.

National Institute of Standards and Technology. (2001). *Advanced encryption standard.* ((Pub. No. 197). Washington, D.C.: Federal Information Processing Standards. Retrieved July 14, 2006, from URL:http://csrc.nist.gov/publications/fips/fips197/fips-197.pdf

RB-Børsen. (2004, June 18). *Første indbrud I netbank i Danmark* [First break-in to an ebank in Denmark]. Retireved July 14, 2006, from http://www.valutakurser.dk/News/ShowNewsstory.aspx?StoryID=8852495

Sabbagh, K. (1995). *21st century jet. The making of the Boeing 777.* London: Macmillian Schribner.

Savage, I. (1999). Aviation deregulation and safety in the United States. The evidence after twenty years. In M. Guadry & R. R. Mayes (eds.), *Taking stock of air liberalization* (pp 93-114). Boston: Kluwer Academic Publishers.

Schiller, J. (2000). *Mobile communications.* Boston: Addison-Wesley.

Schmidt, S., & Werle, R. (1999). Coordinating technology. Studies in the international standardization of telecommunications. Cambridge, MA: MIT Press.

Schultz, E. E., Proctor, R. W., Lien, M.-C., & Salvendy, G. (2001). Usability and security: An appraisal of usability issues in information security methods. *Computers & Security, 20*(7), 620-634.

WAP Forum. (2000). *Official wireless application protocol. The complete standard with searchable CD-Rom.* Wiley Computer Publishing.

Whitten, A., & Tygar, J. D. (1999). Why Johnny can't encrypt: A usability evaluation of PGP 5.0. *Proceedings of the 8th USENIX Security Symposium*, (1-16). Berkeley, CA: USENIX.

Chapter VII

Stronger Authentication: Responding to the Crisis of Confidence

Alvin Y. C. Yeo, SIM University, Singapore

Abstract

Authentication is a prime challenge for banks today as end users' digital identities are being compromised through increasingly sophisticated means. This chapter provides a timely review of the authentication concept and key authentication technologies, namely password tokens, biometrics, smart cards, smart tokens, and out-of-band authentication. An integrative model is proposed, which frames three key considerations in choosing an authentication solution—cyber threat types, regulatory requirements, and business considerations. Each of the implications is considered in turn. Finally, to guide future deployments of authentication solutions, the chapter concludes with pragmatic suggestions by proposing a set of evaluation criteria for choosing authentication solutions and key legal considerations.

Introduction

The use of infocomm technology is pervasive in today's wired world. Mainstream consumer services, such as health care and education, are migrating online. In the banking sector, this process has been going on for some years, beginning with automated teller machines (ATMs) and over, the past decade or so, telephone banking and personal computer (PC)-based proprietary systems. The Internet significantly expanded the banks' distribution scope, no doubt catalyzed by the fact that an Internet bank user is substantially cheaper to serve than a branch bank customer is.

However, the extent and maliciousness of cyber threats steadily have been escalating, in tandem with the evolving infrastructure landscape. With ubiquitous connectivity, data, such as bank account numbers and credit card details, may be available on networks. If someone can steal such vital identity-related information, that person may be able to access another's bank account or credit information. This makes online bank users prime targets.

Lured by high profits and low risks, organized crime syndicates are quickly replacing casual hackers in perpetrating acts like cyber espionage, cyber extortions, and identity thefts. End users, who previously were not prime targets, have become targets of opportunity, when their security posture is not maintained.

In particular, identity theft is flourishing, and one easy and increasingly popular way of capturing personal data is called "phishing" (Lepofsky, 2004). This scam involves e-mail messages that purportedly come from legitimate businesses (e.g., ABN Amro, Citibank), asking for verification of certain information, such as account numbers and passwords, allegedly for auditing purposes. In particular, the Anti-Phishing Working Group found that 85% of the 14,000 unique phishing attacks in August 2005 were directed against customers of financial institutions (Marlin, 2005). This places an increasing importance and burden on authentication mechanisms and banks for validating those identities.

These phenomena, perpetuated in stealth, undermines consumer confidence in online services and, at the same time, deters the innovation of value-added services by banks. Lee and Turban (2001) argue that the lack of trust is increasingly a key impediment to the growth of Internet banking. According to a survey conducted by market research firm Gartner of 5,000 U.S. Internet users, 28% of the respondents said concerns about cyber attacks have affected their online banking behavior; 14% have stopped paying bills via online banking; and about 4%have completely given up on online banking.

The online environment does not allow customers the natural benefits of face-to-face communications (Ba, Whinston, & Zhang, 1999; Citera, Beauregard, & Mitsuya, 2005). This temporal and spatial separation increases fears of opportunism arising from product and identity uncertainty. As Dellarocas (2001) noted, "... the more the two sides of a transaction are separated in time and space, the greater the risks" (p. 2). Overall, these unique differences decrease customers' perceptions of control over their online transactions and erode consumer confidence in online banking.

Financial regulators worldwide are responding to these challenges. For example, in the United States, the Federal Financial Institutions Examination Council (FFIEC) has given banks until the end of 2006 to implement two-factor authentication, which relies on something the consumer has, such as hardware tokens or smart chards, as well as something the consumer knows, such as password. The Monetary Authority of Singapore has similarly given local banks until December 2006 to comply.

To meet stipulated deadlines, many banks are scrambling to choose an appropriate authentication solution. In the United Kingdom, Lloyds TSB Bank plc is piloting a device that generates a one-time, six-digit number every time a customer logs on to its banking site (Marlin, 2005). Bank of America unveiled SiteKey, in which an image picked by the customer appears when a person signs on, indicating that the bank recognizes the computer from which the customer is signing on and tells the customer that the site is legitimate. Bank Koper in Slovenia has issued cards and readers to all of its retail and commercial customers, while the National Bank of Abu Dhabi has provided 19,000 hardware-based tokens for its Internet banking customers. Nine Hong Kong-based banks, including Bank of China and Dah Sing Bank, will be deploying smart card readers to read electronic certificates embedded in the Hong Kong national smart ID card for two-factor authentication purposes.

Service providers from other verticals are beginning to jump on the strong authentication band wagon. Korea Telecom has partnered with a major security solution provider to allow its mobile phone customers to secure electronic commerce (e-commerce) transactions by using their phones to generate unique one-time passcodes.

Against such a backdrop, the chapter begins with a review of the authentication concept and key authentication technologies. Next, we propose an integrative model that frames three key considerations in choosing an authentication solution—cyber threat types, regulatory requirements, and business considerations. The respective implications to financial institutions also are explored. Finally, the chapter concludes with pragmatic suggestions to guide future deployments of authentication solutions.

A Brief Literature Review

The Concept of Authentication

At the core of performing online transactions is the need for mutually recognized identities. Users need to feel confident that they are transacting with the intended organization. Likewise, the organization needs to have confidence in the identity of the user. Without this mutual trust, online transactions cannot be completed without significant risk of misinterpretation and fraud.

Authentication thus refers to any process, either online or off line, by which one party determines whether the other party is who the other party claims to be. A common example is the use of a user ID and password that are known only to the customer and the financial institution (Hayes, Judy, & Ritter, 2006). There are three basic authentication categories or factors:

- **Something a person knows** (e.g., a secret password)
- **Something a person has** (e.g., an ATM card)

- **Something a person is** (e.g., fingerprints)

In the past, username and password authentication has been deemed sufficient to meet the needs of many online transactions. However, the rapid increase in online identity-related fraud shows that passwords alone can no longer counter the ever-increasing sophistication of online identity attacks.

In this respect, an authentication process that requires the entry only of a user ID and password is commonly referred to as single-factor authentication because both of its elements are things that the person knows. ATM transactions commonly require two-factor authentication because they require the use of an ATM card (something that the person has) and a personal identification number (PIN) (something that a person knows).

Key Authentication Technologies

This section briefly reviews five key authentication solutions that are commercially deployed today: password generating tokens, biometrics, out-of-band authentication, smart cards, and smart tokens.

Password Generating Tokens

A password generating token reveals a unique password to its owner each time it is used. The token removes the need to memorize passwords and ensures that the same password is never used twice. The secret password is generated from a secure algorithm that is based on both a unique user ID and the current time. In some form factors, a PIN is used to activate the card and assure that it becomes useless if it is lost or stolen. This type of authentication is sometimes called "session-based" authentication, since the authentication lasts for a period of time. Form factors include key chain devices and credit card-sized generators. They normally have a life expectancy of two to six years.

Advantages. Password generating tokens are reliable, very easy to use and can withstand physical abuse. In a consumer environment, the one-time password (OTP) tokens offer high simplicity and cross-channel utility. Moreover, no special client hardware or readers are needed to use a password generator.

Disadvantages. User error is a common problem with password generators because users must manually enter each password during the authentication process. This extra step can be cumbersome when repeated many times and can increase the likelihood of repeated errors. Session-based authentication is vulnerable to "session hijacking" because the end user is able to leave the computer unattended while the authenticated session is still active. Tokens are a bit cumbersome to carry, especially if customers are required to manage tokens for multiple banks with whom they have accounts. Finally, password generating tokens suffer in manageability and cost because of the relatively high cost of the unit and the efforts in dealing with loss replacement. Back-end management of password generation environments is time consuming and costly as databases and servers must be retooled to accommodate changing password requirements.

Biometrics

Biometrics refers to the measurement of unique physical or physiological characteristics of the human body. Biometric authentication covers a broad spectrum of measurement techniques, from retinal scanning to voice verification. Examples of the biometric methods employed today include (Langenderfer & Linnhoff, 2005):

- **Fingerprint verification:** Used by police organizations around the world, fingerprint verification is the most common biometric authentication method in use. Improvements to scanning techniques and enrollment methods have reduced the instances of false rejection experienced in many early fingerprint verification systems.
- **Retinal and iris scanning:** These biometric processes involve examination of patterns found in the human eye. Retinal scanning is very accurate but requires a user to place his or her eye very close to a scanner.
- **Voice verification:** This form of biometric requires a user to speak a specified phrase into a microphone. Speech patterns are analyzed and compared to the user's prerecorded voiceprint.

Advantages. Unique physical or physiological characteristics of the human body cannot be easily transferred between individuals, reducing the likelihood of fraud.

Disadvantages. Biometric systems are relatively more costly, difficult to use, and may suffer from identification inaccuracies. It is possible—depending on the user group size—for biometric systems to falsely reject real registered users or to not be able to distinguish between the subtle differences of two similar individuals. Intrusiveness and privacy-related issues compound the usage of such systems. Some systems actually store the original biometric image in the reader itself, instead of using a remote server for authentication. This could become a security loophole unless properly protected.

Smart Cards

One of the most pervasive authentication devices, a smart card, is a credit card-sized device with an embedded computer chip. It contains tiny computer chips that store information and, in some cases, perform encryption techniques. Smart cards may contain active components that can be frequently interrogated by software, cards, and tokens to provide "always-on" authentication. Generally, smart cards must be inserted into a reader device for use.

There are two types of smart cards—memory cards and microprocessor cards. Memory cards are less expensive than microprocessor cards and rely on the card reader for securing the data on the card. Memory cards tend to be used in lower-security environments because of their inability to perform encryption algorithms. A microprocessor smart card can store, add, delete, and process data much like a tiny computer. A microprocessor smart card can download data and applications. The card itself offers security independent of the reader device.

Advantages. Smart cards are small, easy to transport and difficult to replicate. Smart card applications range from mobile phone identification to satellite television control, making their use straightforward. Smartcards can safely store digital certificates and private keys, making them extremely secure devices.

Disadvantages. Smart cards require expensive readers, making them inconvenient in use. Smart cards also require drivers in order to execute an application. These solutions are most appropriate for organizations already distributing smart cards to its consumer community—specifically, that applies to European and other financial institutions today undergoing conversion to smart cards under the Europay-Mastercard-Visa (EMV) initiative.

Smart Tokens

Smart tokens are technologically identical to smart cards with the exception of their form factor and interface. Smart tokens are designed to interface with theUSB ports found on millions of computers and peripheral devices. Like smart cards, smart tokens are available in both memory and microprocessor variations.

It is a hardware device with associated software that has the ability to perform private key operations without the private key ever being vulnerable to compromise. A smart token represents a trusted node on an untrusted network that carries secret data. It must be tamper resistant, which means it must not be possible to open a smart token without breaking it. In addition, a smart token must be password protected, so even if it gets stolen, it will be difficult to impersonate its owner.

Advantages. Smart card readers are not required because smart tokens simply plug into USB ports. USB smart tokens can be much faster due to the higher speed of USB, compared to the traditional parallel or communication port-connected smart card reader. In addition, USB smart tokens are easy to use and designed to fit on a key chain. USB tokens have an estimated life expectancy of 10 years and can deal with changing weather circumstances.

Disadvantages. USB tokens often require drivers in order to execute an application.

Out-of-Band Authentication

Out-of-band authentication involves establishing a second communication channel outside the Web session used to log on, either to communicate an OTP or to perform a second level of authentication directly. There are several approaches. Typically, a correct user ID and password entry generates an automated phone response to the customer. In one method, the customer receives an OTP via short message service (SMS) to a cell phone and then uses it to gain entry to the Web site. In another method, a phone call prompts the customer to speak a phrase for voiceprint authentication.

Advantages. The solution offers excellent manageability; customers already own the device, and it only requires they register the phone number(s) to call. It is fully portable, if using a cell phone; otherwise, it is limited to the phone number registered (the ability to register multiple phone numbers improves portability). It is an effective defense against the Internet threats of primary concern, and it can be used across multiple channels of interaction.

Disadvantages. Inconvenience and the lack of availability may impair ease of use. For example, customers must register their cell phone numbers with the business. Additionally, cell phones may not support SMS or cell phone coverage may be poor; or customers may not have cell phones at all.

A Decision Framework for Choosing an Authentication Solution

We postulate that there are three key drivers behind the decision to choose a particular authentication (see Figure 1):

- **Cyber threat types**
- **Regulatory requirements**
- **Business considerations**

We review each in turn and discuss the implications for financial institutions.

Cyber Attack Types

The weakest link in the security chain is the consumer. Technology on the banking side is reasonably well advanced: processes are generally secure, the threat is constantly monitored, and banks work closely with national crime agencies. The challenge is to ensure that the customer is equally aware of the danger of fraud and secures his or her information, pass-

Figure 1. A decision framework for choosing an authentication solution

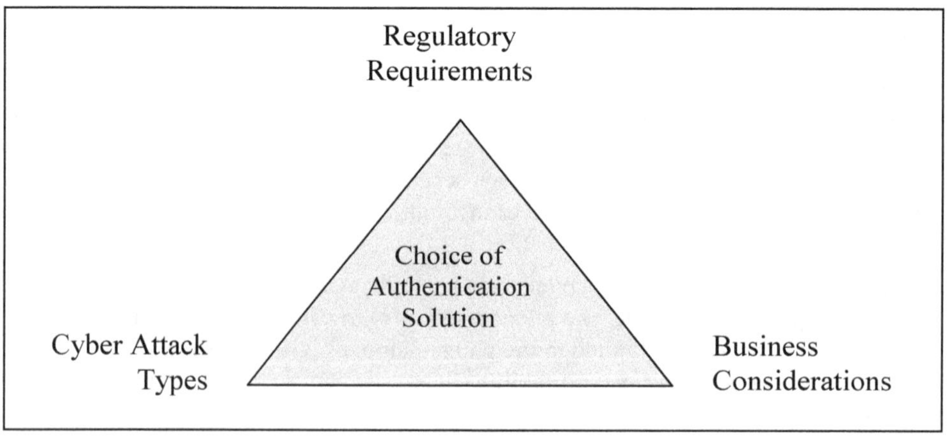

words, and computer system effectively. The task is made more difficult by the range of sophisticated techniques now being targeted at Internet bank users. Confidential data could be compromised in the following ways:

- **Trojan horse attacks:** This is the most classic type of attack, typically targeting software solutions with keys that are installed on a hard disk only or downloaded from a server (Goodwin, 2005). A Trojan horse virus installs itself in PC memory and reports to the attacker what is being entered and processed, or even does malicious damage from within. The kind of functionality seen here is similar to that of spyware. There are now dedicated viruses, such as the Banker-AJ Trojan, which records log in details and passwords when customers visit legitimate online banking Web sites.
- **Phishing attacks:** Phishing attacks are accomplished by counterfeiting the trusted brands of well-known banks, online retailers, and credit card companies in e-mails to potential victims. These e-mail messages prompt users to go to fraudulent Web sites where the user is tricked into submitting a valid username and password into what appears to be a legitimate log-in page. Attackers are thus "fishing"—or *phishing*—for online identities.
- **Pharming attacks:** The potential fraudster typically seeks to hijack the bank's Internet domain, redirecting users to a replica site, where thousands or even millions of account-password combinations can be recorded. Other methods of attack involve deploying Trojan programs to tamper with log-in URLs and redirect users to a bogus site.
- **Man-in-the middle attacks:** In this case, the fraudster attempts to piggy-back on a user's online session, diverting cash to a remote account, while a transaction is being undertaken. This is the hardest attack to carry out, as it needs to be performed while the victim is online. The classic example is that somebody at an Internet service provider (ISP) installs an extra server, intercepting and modifying communication under way between the client and the bank. Again, it requires that the victim is not connected to the authentic site. This requires not only skill and careful preparation but also extensive knowledge on the Web-banking application and access to controlling an Internet point between the client and bank. As with some advanced Trojan attacks, strong user authentication alone is not sufficient to thwart such fairly sophisticated attacks.
- **Insider attacks:** Employees, especially disgruntled ones, could pose a serious threat to businesses. According to the 2005 Global Security Survey, published by Deloitte Touche Tohmatsu, 35% of respondents said that they had encountered attacks from inside their organization within the last 12 months, up from 14% in 2004. In contrast, only 26% confirmed external attacks, compared to 23% in 2004. The CSI/FBI 2005 Computer Crime and Security Survey echoes these findings, indicating that 56% of organizations reported some level of security breach from within their organization.

Implications for Financial Institutions

As yet, few, if any, of these newer techniques have resulted in significant loss. But the risk is growing. Banks are playing their part in countering such threats by continually publicizing the danger. They are also constantly upgrading their authentication protocols. For example, the threat of Trojan key logging programs could be countered substantially by the introduction of graphical keypad entry, which substitutes for the keyboard.

Banks should keep abreast of emerging attack types, be aware of their sources, and remain cognizant of the limitations of their chosen authentication solution(s). This will help them proactively plug security gaps that may not be directly fulfilled by their chosen authentication solutions. For example, humans may well have tendencies that leave them vulnerable to persuasion, but these tendencies can be positively channeled with education.

In addition, to decisively arrest insider attacks stemming from "social engineering" (where a relationship is developed with an employee and then that newly trusting person is convinced to hand over key information to the attacker), employees could be trained to be security conscious, process controls could be implemented, and strong authentication built into the security system.

It is of pertinent that bank employees are given absolutely no potential opportunity to thwart the authentication solution without detection. This could be achieved, for example, by the use of tamper-resistant hardware security modules (HSMs) with role assignment/dual-control tools that cannot be circumvented. The bank also could choose to deploy risk management solutions, with advanced behavioral analysis abilities that compare access patterns for user groups to assess deviations in employee behavior.

Regulatory Requirements

On Oct. 12, 2005,FFIEC issued guidance entitled *Authentication in an Electronic Banking Environment* regarding authentication of customers in online financial transactions (Marlin, 2005). This guidance updates guidance issued in 2001 and states three essential points:

- Single-factor authentication, as the only control mechanism, is considered inadequate for high-risk transactions involving access to customer information or the movement of funds to other parties.
- The authentication techniques employed by the financial institution should be appropriate to the risks associated with the involved products and services.
- When risk assessments indicate that the use of single-factor authentication is inadequate, financial institutions should implement multifactor authentication, layered security, or other controls reasonably calculated to mitigate those risks.

The FFIEC expects each financial institution to approach compliance with the new guidance in three stages:

1. Identify and assess the risks associated with its Internet-based products and services. Risks should be evaluated in light of the type of customer, the customer's transactional capabilities, the sensitivity of customer information, the ease of using the communication method, and the volume of transactions.
2. Assess the adequacy of authentication techniques and adjust its information security program in light of any relevant changes in technology, the sensitivity of its customer information, new or changing risks and the evolving sophistication of compromise techniques, and other internal or external threats to information.
3. Implement appropriate risk mitigation strategies.

Similar guidelines also have been issued elsewhere in the world, including Hong Kong and Singapore. Many financial institutions offer their customers the ability to perform online transactions using only single-factor authentication. Thus, banks and other affected financial institutions face a delicate balancing act: strengthening their authentication processes, while maintaining the user friendliness of their online facilities and containing costs.

Implications for Financial Institutions

There are three general risk management strategies that financial institutions could adopt to meet the new regulatory requirements for online authentication (Hayes, Judy, & Ritter, 2006):

- **Standardized procedures** that require multifactor authentication for all transactions and for all online customers.
- **Layered authentication** based on the transaction type. Under this approach, accessing informational features or account balances requires minimal authentication. However, fund transfers to third parties or bills payments require higher levels of authentication.
- **Per-transaction, real-time risk assessment** uses sophisticated software to assess the risk index associated with each individual transaction in real time and assign a degree of authentication based on a risk score.

Banks should understand the relative costs and benefits of these different risk management strategies and tailor one that best suits their scope of services and customer risk profile. Standardized procedures could result in an increased burden on customers who use online services only or principally for low-risk transactions, such as checking account balances or interest rates. Layered authentication may provide an easier sign-on process for customers seeking only information, but may require costly partitioning and reprogramming of online services. Per-transaction risk assessments are likely to produce the most user-friendly customer experience, but require the use of expensive software and may result in banks' dependence on particular software vendors.

Business Requirements

Budgetary constrains often dictate the type of authentication systems an organization uses. An organization needs to consider more than just the initial purchase of an identity management solution. Otherwise, it may end up deploying a username-and-password system thinking that it is "free," when in fact overhead costs, such as deployment and help-desk support costs, can be very high.

Implications for Financial Institutions

Banks should adopt a holistic view of solution costs in their evaluation of authentication solutions. Specifically, the following types of costs ought to be considered in order to better understand a solution's total cost of ownership (TCO):

- **Acquisition costs:** This category refers to upfront infrastructure costs and can include both hardware (e.g., server) and software (e.g., licensing) costs, and future requirements for extended capabilities.
- **Deployment costs:** This category encompasses factors, such as internal information technology (IT) employees and vendor time required to deploy the solution (plan, install, and configure the solution). Additionally, this category also should include the cost of shipping the authentication devices to customers and provisioning them for the first time.
- **Ongoing costs:** This category includes maintenance and support expenses as well as hardware replacement due to failure or built-in obsolescence.

Surveys have indicated that between 15% and 30% of tokens, for example, are lost and need to be replaced annually. As such, this usually constitutes the largest cost component (up to 70% in larger scale deployments) and is usually attributable to replacement, distribution, and reprovisioning costs.

Ongoing administration costs also are included, and this refers to costs to maintain the deployment as well as end-user support and help-desk costs. Support and help-desk costs are typically the hidden costs of deploying a strong authentication solution.

Choosing an Authentication Solution

We propose the following five evaluation criteria for choosing a suitable authentication solution:

- **Ease of use (Davis, 1989):** User acceptance is a critical success factor for any security solution. If a particular approach is too cumbersome or confusing, users, especially in the consumer domain, either will turn to expensive alternative channels or disengage completely. Both of these outcomes negate any potential positive impact from improved security.

- **Security:** Naturally, the solution must defend adequately against phishing, spyware, hacking, man-in-the-middle attacks, and other threats, driving organizations to adopt strong authentication. The solution must provide protection during "normal" usage as well as during loss periods, pending replacement of a device or card. Authentication solutions must provide mechanisms to determine the authenticity of the Web site being accessed as well as provide the user's online identity better protection by providing an additional factor for authentication beyond the password.
- **Flexibility:** Increasingly, authentication is being performed in conjunction with an assessment of risk. For example, a user checking his or her account balance from home has a different risk profile than attempting an interbank transfer from a foreign country. Online organizations must be able to choose from a variety of authentication methods that best align with the risk of a given transaction. This also allows authentication to be only as invasive as required by the risk to improve user acceptance.
- **Scalability and cost effectiveness:** The chosen authentication solution should be able to meet the evolving needs of a growing bank. As such, they should reflect the financial realities of a large, diverse customer population. Banks may need to look at the total cost for the solution, including the original license costs; annual maintenance fees; the cost of distribution and loss replacement, if there's a physical element of the solution; and the maintenance implications based on the device's resilience (hardiness) and longevity. Without addressing these considerations, any mutual and strong authentication solution risks not being effective at protecting online identities and restoring customer confidence in online services.
- **Accessibility across different interaction channels:** Given the efforts to implement and roll out strong authentication for consumer Internet activity, smart organizations will leverage the solution beyond the standard Web browser environment. They will prefer a solution that works with Web-enabled personal digital assistants (PDAs), for phone interactions, at ATMs, at tellers, and at other points of service.

Financial institutions should also pay attention to legal considerations, such as (Hayes, Judy, & Ritter, 2006):

- **Licensing of new technologies:** When new authentication technologies are acquired, the related purchase or licensing agreements provide an opportunity for institutions to consider and allocate some of the new types of risks associated with those technologies. For example, biometric technologies, which require the capture and storage of new identifying data, may justify special terms regarding warranties, security controls, and allocation of liability in the event of service failures.
- **Customer service agreements:** Existing customer service agreements may require amendment in order to obtain the consent of customers to the new authentication methods. In addition, terms addressing limitations of liability should be examined in

order to confirm that those terms work effectively with the potential liabilities presented by the new authentication technologies.

- **Privacy policies:** Various authentication technologies can involve the capture of additional personal information or different uses of personal information that has already been captured and stored by a financial institution. Existing privacy policies may require revision to accommodate these practices; of course, these revisions may be accomplished concurrently, in many instances, with related customer service agreement revisions.
- **Variable risks:** Many institutions adopt a standardized view of electronic transactions, implementing similar procedures and authentication controls for transactions with widely varying economic value and risks. As part of the required risk assessments, financial institutions may conclude that different terms and conditions are appropriate based on the nature of the transactions with which the new authentication methods will be employed.

Future Trends

Of all the authentication solutions that are available to banks, ones that work quietly in the background, monitoring transactions for suspicious or anomalous activity, appear to be gaining favor because they generally have less impact on customers. Only on those rare occasions when a transaction is identified as risky do more obvious forms of authentication go into effect. In such a case, the system might pose a question online to which only the customer would know the answer, or it might initiate a phone call to verify the consumer is indeed intending to execute a particular transaction.

Some of these systems work by using information found in Web IP addresses, such as the geographic location of the computer, connection speed, and language, to verify legitimate log-in transactions. Some of these systems combine this type of device profiling with analyses of actual account activity using behavioral profiles and other data sources. An alert, for example, may be issued when a high-dollar transaction takes place on an account that normally executes low-value amounts.

To combat identity theft effectively, software developers thus may want to focus their efforts in developing solutions that could recognize fraud patterns (by searching for suspicious data patterns, rather than checking the data itself) as well as "dynamically learn" (update its knowledge daily from the various applications that feed it).

Conclusion

No single security technology offers a "silver bullet." The choice of an authentication system requires trade offs against customer convenience and acceptability (Wheatley, 2005). If an authentication process is time consuming and complex that it deters users, it is counterproductive.

Financial organizations have traditionally been at the forefront of security, and they should maintain this posture in the Internet era (Slewe & Hoogenboom, 2004). Countering the threat of fraud is a continual process, requiring constant vigilance and keeping one step ahead of the fraudsters. Ultimately, the choice of authentication solutions will be different for each bank, depending on its assets, the risks the organization considers acceptable, and the costs of the (considered) security measures.

References

Ba, S. A., Whinston, A., & Zhang, H. (1999). *Building trust in the electronic market through an economic incentive mechanism.* Paper presented at the 20th International Conference on Information Systems, Charlotte, NC.

Citera, M., Beauregard, R., & Mitsuya, T. (2005). An experimental study of credibility in e-negotiations. *Psychology & Marketing, 22*(2), 163-179.

Davis, F. D. (1989). Perceived usefulness, perceived ease of use and user acceptance of information technology. *MIS Quarterly, 13*(3), 319-340.

Dellarocas, C. (2001). *Building trust online: The design of reliable reputation reporting mechanisms for online trading communities* (Working Paper No. 101). Cambridge, MA: Massachusetts Institute of Technology, Sloan School of Management.

Goodwin, B. (2005, March 22). New wave of Trojan attacks could force banks to adopt two-factor authentication. *Computer Weekly,* 8.

Hayes, B. S., Judy, H. L., & Ritter, J. B. (2006). FFIEC issues new guidance on authentication in online transactions. *Banking & Financial Services Policy Report, 25*(2), 1-3.

Langenderfer, J., & Linnhoff, S. (2005). The emergence of biometrics and its effect on consumers. *The Journal of Consumer Affairs, 39*(2), 314-336.

Lee, M., & Turban, E. (2001). A trust model for consumer Internet shopping. *International Journal of Electronic Commerce, 5*, 75-91.

Lepofsky, R. (2004). Preventing identity theft. *Risk Management, 51,* 34-40.

Marlin, S. (2005, October 24). Banks told to step up security against identity theft. *InformationWeek,* 32.

Slewe, T., & Hoogenboom, M. (2004). Who will rob you on the digital highway? *Communications of the ACM, 47*(5), 56-60.

Wheatley, M. (2005). *Frontiers in finance.* KPMG Financial Services Practice.

Chapter VIII

Smart Cards for Security and Assurance

Konstantinos Markantonakis, University of London, UK

Keith Mayes, University of London, UK

Fred Piper, University of London, UK

Abstract

When designing and implementing a system that handles sensitive or valuable information, there can be few discussions that do not include some reference to ensuring adequate security. At a strategic level there will be high level requirements for security that will safeguard the system, which must ultimately translate to practical solutions and physical implementations. This chapter focuses on the technical implementation of security requirements and, in particular, the use of smart cards as trusted security tokens. In particular, it examines the significance of tamper resistance by exploring the different hardware and software platforms in relation to smart card attacks. It also highlights certain issues around the deployment of smart card technology in the financial industry.

Introduction

When designing and implementing a system that handles sensitive or valuable information, there can be few discussions that do not include some reference to ensuring adequate security. At a strategic level there will be high level requirements for security that will safeguard the system, which must ultimately translate to practical solutions and physical implementations. This chapter focuses on the technical implementation of security requirements and, in particular, the use of smart cards as trusted security tokens. One of the major objectives is to explain the need for tamper resistance in consumer security tokens and to describe the fine balance between the sophisticated attacks and countermeasures. However, to put this aspect in context, the chapter concludes with a discussion on the many other important issues involved, based around an example of a smart card system migration.

Smart Cards: How We Came to Need Tamper-Resistant Security

The possession and use of personal security, identity, and entitlement tokens goes back many years and certainly was not waiting for electronics and technology to come along. A physical door key is an age-old example of a personal security token that enables access. In authentication terminology, it is clearly "something you have," but in some circumstances, it also requires "something you know," basically because you need to find the door that it will fit. Physical keys can of course be legitimately copied or fraudulently reproduced via more dubious means. Unfortunately, a basic lock has no means of rejecting forgeries, as it cannot differentiate them from authentic keys. Like many security problems, determining authenticity is not new, and, for this reason, token solutions were widely used in the past. In medieval times the use of seals was increasingly popular (Ashdon-Hill, 2005). If a nobleman wanted to prove that he had actually sent a letter, then he could sign it and add some wax with an imprint of his personal token, that is, a customised seal. The resulting wax seal could later be checked for authenticity. If the seal had to be broken to read the letter, then it also served as some proof of integrity and confidentiality, that is, that the contents had not be modified or leaked to a third party. In the case of the nobleman's seal, there may have been implied rights and entitlements because of his rank, but this would not be the case in a solution for all citizens. By contrast, during World War II, there was widespread use of food ration books (Smith, 2003), clearly linked to identities, but also demonstrating entitlement and including historical logs of transactions. A modern-day security specialist, of course, could list many technical flaws in these early token solutions. However, in their day, the measures probably matched the deviousness and resources of those that sought to undermine them. It is also worth remembering that some of the solutions involved additional human interaction and secondary checking. A well-recognized servant may have delivered the nobleman's sealed letter, and the war time grocer would have known all his registered local customers and remembered their transactions. There is also the question of security priorities, for example, the servant delivering the sealed letter would probably have been less concerned about the risk of forgery, than that of being attacked by bandits.

As society has evolved, the number of security sensitive transactions has increased (Nielsen, 2005), but, at the same time, the communicating parties have frequently become less well known to each other. There are many reasons for this including an increased population, travel, communication, affluence, social behaviors (Nie & Erbring, 2002), and business practices. The end effect on security is that we have lost some of the secondary checks and intuition that are a normal part a human interaction. In the most extreme case, we have the Internet where billions of people, who have never met, can communicate and trade whilst, unfortunately, being preyed upon by the modern-day bandits. Whether we choose to call the latter hackers, fraudsters, criminals, or simply thieves, one of their primary goals is to exploit and financially benefit from the weaknesses of other people or the safeguards that are meant to protect them.

A popular solution to the changing behavioral and services environment and escalating threats is believed to come from a matching escalation in technological security safeguards (Frost & Sullivan, 2006). Expressed in another way, one could say that if technology puts swords in the hands of our attackers, then it should also provide us with effective shields. A well-proven and increasingly popular technological solution is the use of security tokens in the form of smart cards. They may appear unlikely shields but their effectiveness should not be underestimated, as they have developed into sophisticated tamper-resistant tokens that underpin many current and evolving security solutions.

From this discussion, one might assume that the desire to move towards token solutions and, in particular, smart cards was prompted by fraud and security fears. However, historically it was often driven by convenience and/or simply a desire to accommodate and exploit new services and behaviors.

The first cards to be issued to users for payment were really prompted by convenience, in particular, a way to easily demonstrate the holder's identity, status, and ability to pay for a good meal. The card was less sophisticated than the food ration book, less difficult to copy than the nobleman's seal, restricted in use, and open to fraud and forgery (Diners Club, 2005). If only a few were in circulation, then the secondary checks from human interaction would probably have offered enough safeguards. However, for a widespread deployment something better was needed.

Magnetic stripe cards followed in due course, offering a much wider scope for transaction services and more automated interaction with supporting systems. Whilst a little more secure than the simple plastic cards, the vulnerability to cloning rested on the difficulty of unauthorized reading and writing to magnetic strips. As the equipment needed for this is hardly more advanced than that used in tape recording equipment, the technology provided little protection. History, in fact, has shown that these cards were easily misused or forged (APACS, 2005) and so the first truly "smart" cards could be considered as those that incorporated a microprocessor chip and secured memory to resist such abuse (Rankl & Effing, 1997). The early smart cards used simple microcontrollers and tiny memories. However, they had the advantage that they could be personalized to a user/account and run automated security algorithms and protocols to establish authentication, integrity, and confidentiality. The qualities of the smart card are underpinned by sound cryptographic techniques. However, as will become apparent from this chapter, a smart card's greatest quality is that it offers "tamper-resistant" security functionality to protect not only stored data but also the integrity of the algorithms and secret keys. To appreciate the significance of tamper resistance, it is first necessary to have a basic understanding of a smart card chip and how it operates as an application platform.

Smart Card Chips and Protocols

The chip embedded within a smart card or token is essentially a very small microcontroller device consisting of a central processing unit (CPU) with several memories. Typically there is a read only memory (ROM) for the operating system and some program storage, plus electrically erasable programmable read-only memory (EEPROM) for data and additional applications and finally random access memory (RAM) to support variables and stacks required for dynamic execution. Advanced cards also include accelerators for common security functions, often referred to as crypto-coprocessors. An example of such a device is shown in Figure 1 and some basic properties are listed in Table 1.

Figure 1 is a microscopic view of an exposed smart card chip clearly identifying the CPU (processor) and the various memory types. At first glance one might consider that there is far more EEPROM than ROM, but this is not the case and the reason relates to the packing efficiency of the various memory cell types. In reality ROM packing is significantly more efficient than EEPROM, which in turn is far better than RAM. The actual ratios depend on the exact technology and implementation but the chip area requirements could typically be 1:4:16 (ROM:EEPROM:RAM). The total size of the chip is limited by cost and also compliance with physicals stresses, such as bending and twisting tests, defined in International Standard Organisation (ISO) standards (International Standard Organisation (ISO), 2003). Therefore the trade off between the various memory types is significant, in terms of the chip capabilities and cost. ROM seems attractive for packing in maximum functionality,

Figure 1. Anatomy of a smart card chip

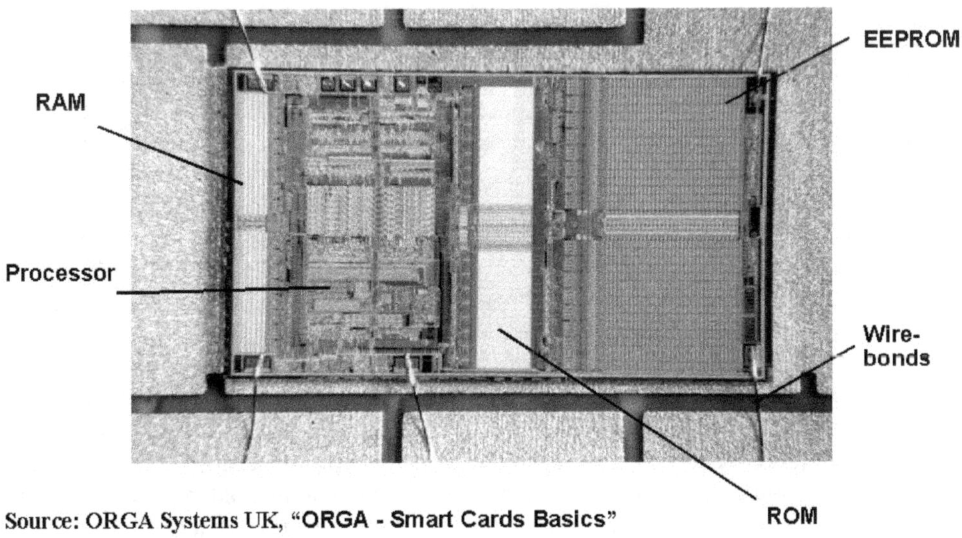

Source: ORGA Systems UK, "ORGA - Smart Cards Basics"

but it cannot then be modified once the chip has been produced. This lack of flexibility can shorten the useable life of the device. RAM is very "expensive," in terms of area and tends to be minimized in chip design, which poses challenges to both application development and execution efficiency. The size of the EEPROM is often regarded as the critical memory area, and the capacity of smart card chips is commonly referred to by this measure alone, for example, 32kb or 64kb. The EEPROM is nonvolatile, like the ROM, but can be changed during the lifetime of the device, making it a flexible and manageable resource. The management extends to modifications of personalization, adding/changing applications, or critical data, thus offering the potential for a more feature rich, flexible, and long lived smart card device. The general features of a typical smart card chip are as follows:

- CPU (>32bit)
- RAM (>8kb)
- ROM (>200kb)
- EEPROM (>64kb)
- Crypto-processor option
- Very Small
- Low power
- Low cost
- Tamper resistance
- Standardized technology
- Multiapplication operating systems
- Large availability of development tools
- Multiple suppliers
- Consistent and controllable

The size examples are only a snapshot in time and Moore's Law appears remorseless in doubling computing capabilities every 18 months. Whilst the chip has remarkable properties for its small physical size, it is in some respects quite helpless, lacking a power source, clock, and user interface. In fact, when the smart card is not interacting with another device, the only service to the user is keeping stored and sensitive data securely. Generally the interest in smart card properties relates to their use within a reader or terminal device and its communications and interactions with other entities. The relationship between the smart card and terminal historically was referred to as master-slave. The terminal was the initiator of any dialogue, and the smart card would respond to any valid command received. This is not always the case in modern systems; and there exist methods for smart card applications to temporarily take logical control of the dialogue, although individual message exchanges are still driven by the terminal. One of the reasons for this is that a single I/O line is used for communication and so communications are half-duplex (one way at a time). In fact there are very few connections between the smart card chip and the terminal device. Figure 2 shows the pin outs (i.e., the corresponding eight contacts at the golden plate of the smart card microprocessor) for a conventional smart card as may be used in a credit card.

Figure 2. Smart card contacts

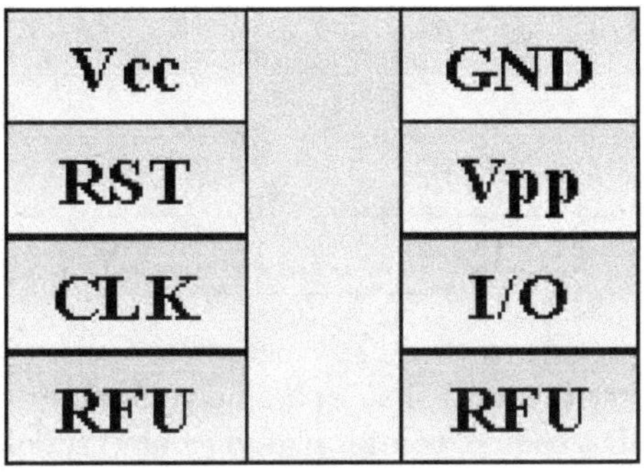

The connection pads make electrical contact with sprung elements in a reader device, so this type of card is sometimes referred to as a contact-card to differentiate it from contact-less-cards that will be described later. At first glance it appears that there are eight contacts, however, in reality, only five are normally used. Power supply voltage (VCC) and ground (GND) provide the power connections to the chip. Depending on the type of card the VCC level may vary, with 5V typical in finance cards and some old SIM cards, however modern cards, particularly for telecom applications, may support 5V/3V/1.8V. The I/O is the serial communications line and RST (used to reset the microprocessor of the smart card) is used to reset the device. Programming or write voltage (VPP) is a historical throw back and no longer used. In old smart card chips, it was necessary to apply a voltage higher than VCC (i.e., VPP), in order to write to the EEPROM. Aside from being an added complication for the reader, VPP became a target for security attacks (Tunstall, 2006) as inhibiting VPP prevented writes to memory, which could nullify security checks, such as personal identification number (PIN) retry counts. Fortunately, modern smart card chips no longer need the higher programming voltages, so the VPP contact has become redundant. However, the easy access to the remaining contacts has meant that they are obvious attack points for monitoring, voltages, currents, data transfer, or introducing faults. Attacks on the smart card chip are described in more detail later. The reserved for future use (RFU) contacts, as the name implies, indicate that certain contacts are reserved in order to accommodate future developments. The CLK contact is used in order to provide the clock frequency for smart card microprocessor.

The basic communications protocols were standardized by ISO (ISO, 1995), which resulted in very good consistency and lack of ambiguity when communicating, at least, up to the message layer. A dialogue can be regarded simply as a message sent from the master that provokes a response from the slave. In practice it is a little more complex as there are a number of variants, often depending on whether data is included in the commands and responses or if the logical data spans multiple messages. A typical command format is shown in Figure 3.

The CLA is a byte representing the class of the messages, which is defined for a major class of application. For example, a GSM SIM application will always have CLA set to "A0." INS is the instruction byte, selected from the set defined for the application class. P1 and P2 are parameter bytes that have meaning for particular commands, for example, they may

Figure 3. APDU command format

CLA	INS	P1	P2	P3	DATA

Figure 4. APDU response format

DATA	SW1	SW2

address specific records in a file. P3 is also a parameter, but it is invariably used to indicate the length of data fields. DATA here is information (if any) supplied to the card within the command message.

The response field consists of a minimum of two bytes (SW1 and SW2). The detailed interpretation of these values depends on the application class, however the purpose is for the card to indicate the success of the command request and to convey some basic information to the requester. The DATA field in this case is information returned by the smart card in response to a relevant command.

There are several valid combinations of command and response formats used in GSM that are described in more detail within ETSI (1999). The messaging layer protocols apply equally well to contactless smart cards, however the physical communication is quite different. A contactless card is shown in Figure 5.

The card has no contacts but conceals a loop antenna that is used not only for communication, but also to act as a transformer coil to extract power from the radio field. The most commonly referred to standard is also defined by ISO (2000). Unlike the contact cards, the communications interface is not fully standardized, or, to be more precise, there are several

Figure 5. Contactless smart card (Source Gemplus)

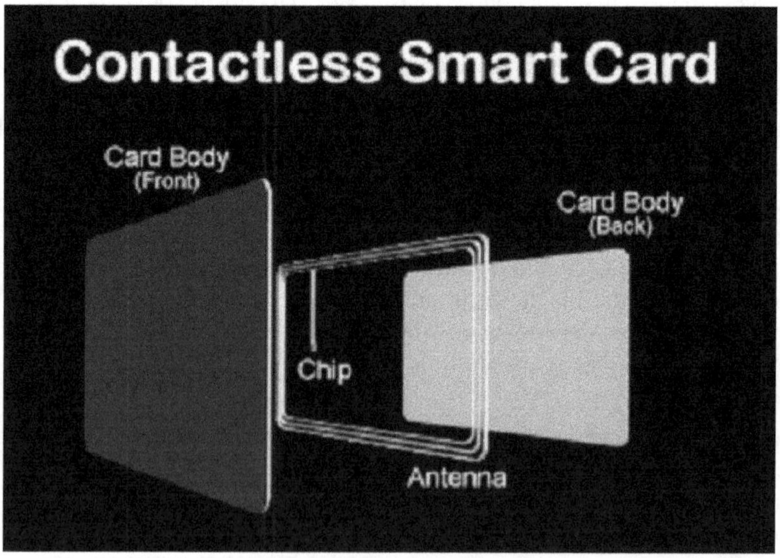

modes contained within the standards. These variations affect the radio modulation methods and so unfortunately complicate the design of multimode reader devices.

There is a tendency to assume that a contactless card is simple and less secure than a contact card, but this is really driven by the common uses of contactless smart cards, which often call for very low cost cards. Aside from the fact that a radio interface is used, there need be little to differentiate the secure platform properties of the contactless smart card chip from its contact-card counterpart. The following sections will focus on contact cards, but the common implications for contactless should be evident.

The foregoing text has introduced the basic anatomy and interaction for smart card devices but has so far made little mention of the smart card's role as a sophisticated application platform.

Multiapplication Smart Card Platform

Among the key issues for the acceptance of smart card technology are security, upgradability, and programmability. It is fair to mention that over the last few years smart card technology has made significant improvements in all the above areas, with perhaps the most critical advances affecting the underlying smart card operating system (SCOS). Earlier SCOSs were largely concerned with simple file management operations (providing the file structure as defined in ISO (1995)) or with the provision of basic cryptographic functionality (Schneier, 1996). Whilst early SCOSs claimed to offer multiapplication functionality, the reality was often disappointing.

The major enhancements in the provision of relatively robust and sufficiently powerful, multiapplication smart card platforms took place between 1997 and 2000 with the introduction of four distinct smart card platforms, namely Java Card (Java Card, 2002), Multos (Multos, 2002), GlobalPlatform (GlobalPlatform, 2001), and Windows for smart cards (WfSC) (Microsoft, 1999). Behind each of the above initiatives were a number of prestigious companies aiming to provide a set of secure, global, and interoperable set of multiapplication smart card standards. Microsoft created the WfSC concept but is no longer directly supporting it, whereas Sun is still very much behind the development of Java Card. Last but not least GlobalPlatform and Multos are supported by consortia of companies, that is, the GlobalPlatform association and MAOSCO, respectively.

The above multiapplication smart card platforms have reached different stages of development and deployment. However, it becomes evident that there are significant differences on how the above technologies are perceived. For example, Multos and WfSC are actually SCOSs, whereas the Java Card and GlobalPlatform are multiapplication smart card platforms that sit on other operating systems. It is also often the case that Java Card and GlobalPlatform (referred to as JCGP) are closely coupled together in terms of their deployment, specifically for the financial industry and increasingly in mobile telecommunications. Furthermore, it is also becoming evident that Multos and JCGP are the most widely considered multiapplication smart card platforms, so for the purpose of this study we will restrict our analysis to the main characteristics of these two platforms. Nevertheless, new multiapplication smart cards have recently appeared, like latest BasicCard of ZeitControl and Smartcard.NET of Hive Minded.

As previously mentioned Multos is classified as a secure SCOS that has been specifically designed for smart card microprocessors. It emerged, during the late '90s, from the banking sector and in particular from the Natwest development team in the United Kingdom. The Multos designers took security into account at an early stage, and the result was that, up to a few years ago, Multos was among the very few nonmilitary products that achieved ITSEC E6 certification. The Multos operating system was strictly controlled by the Multos consortium also known as MAOSCO, and, at the early stages of the Multos development, it was very difficult for anyone interested to obtain detailed information regarding the behavior and performance of the underlying architecture. However, over the years the situation changed, as the consortium realized that accessibility to the specifications was of paramount importance for the overall acceptance of the proposed technology.

The core of the operating system manages and controls access to all system resources. The Multos operating system was developed by taking into account the specific characteristics of 8-bit microprocessors. In particular for Multos, it is not completely clear as to whether the Multos executable language (MEL) virtual machine (VM) exists on top of the operating system or whether it is closely coupled together. In any case the MEL VM is capable of interpreting a number of commands and primitives that offer the main Multos functionality.

All Multos cards come with a mandatory cryptographic coprocessor in order to perform the required application load and delete operations (that utilize asymmetric key cryptography). The existence of a crypto-coprocessor obviously meets the requirements for public key cryptography, but, at the same time, it increases the overall cost of the chip.

One of the main drawbacks of Multos was that in order to maintain a coherent and relatively controlled scheme management architecture, a certification authority (CA) was introduced. The CA was responsible for issuing the various application load/delete certificates and also for performing key management operations on behalf of (or with close cooperation with) the issuers. Although this was removing some of the burden from the relatively inexperienced issuers; on the other hand, it was creating a very closed and costly architecture. Applications in Multos can be developed in MEL (assembly) or in any other high level language (e.g., Java or C) by using a set of tools including cross compliers. Multos is currently being used in several roll out and pilot projects ranging from identification (ID) cards to financial card schemes.

Java Card is considered as a subset of normal Java, both in terms of the size of the underlying VM but also in terms of the actual language specification. The Java Card architecture can be considered as a platform that may reside on top of any SCOS. Among the main components of a Java Card is the VM, which offers demonstrable security, based on the openness of the specification and public scrutiny.

A Java Card application comes into life with the application development process following the syntax of the normal Java language. It is then translated using a set of widely available tools (Java compilers) into Java byte codes. These byte codes then have to be translated into Java Card byte codes and eventually downloaded into the Java Card. The Java Card byte code instructions were specified by taking into account the 32-bit space of traditional Java.

At the outset, the interoperability of Java Card applications and platforms was a critical issue. During the early stages of the development of the standard, it was evident that each smart card manufacturer or platform developer was interpreting the standards in its own proprietary way. Therefore, it was often the case that a Java Card application developed for one Java Card platform would not execute on another Java Card platform, despite the marketing hype of "write once run anywhere."

Regardless of these early problems, the Java Card specifications demonstrated a great momentum, and they provided a constant pool of improvements in order to overcome the drawbacks of the past. As we write this chapter, Java Card 3.0 is under development, offering major improvements over the previous versions, including TCP/IP functionality support for Web Servers and so forth. However, although the Java Card presents a relatively robust execution environment for card applications, it does not provide a mechanism to guarantee that applications are managed in a secure and transparent way.

As previously mentioned, it is often the case that Java Card and GlobalPlatform are perceived as interrelated types of technology. GlobalPlatform aims to bridge the aforementioned gap introduced by Java Card. It offers a secure and interoperable way in which applications can be managed in a multiapplication smart card environment.

The GlobalPlatform smart card specification was originally developed by Visa International under the reference name of Open Platform. Later on it was donated by Visa to an independent organization called the GlobalPlatform consortium in order to ensure wider adoption. The GlobalPlatform card specification offers a number logical and physical components that aim to provide application interoperability and security, in a strictly issuer-controlled environment. The main components of the GlobalPlatform card architecture are the security domains, the card manager, and the API. In principle, the card manager is always in control of the card, and it is responsible for enforcing the underlying security policies of the specification. The security domains can be perceived as secure repositories, either by the platform itself or by the applications, for cryptographic keys. They also can be perceived as offering cryptographic support by offering their services to the aforementioned entities.

It can be argued that overall industry acceptance of Java Card and GlobalPlatform may be higher than Multos. Taking into account that Multos was MasterCard's preferred platform and Java Card with GlobalPlatform was Visa's preferred technology, someone could easily foresee, once more, the battle of giants taking place. However, both financial institutions soon realized (maybe following the advice of their bank members) that it made more sense to collaborate than compete. Therefore, although they had their preferred platforms, they did not object when financial institutions used one or the other.

The move for cooperation further crystallized when MasterCard joined the GlobalPlatform consortium. It appears that the governing bodies of both platforms are engaged in a continued dialogue that should only benefit both technologies and in turn the smart card issuers. Although, the future will provide the answer, it could be the case that each type of technology will attempt to benefit from the other, simply by adopting significant enhancements currently not present in the other. Eventually, it may be the case that the two platforms will become so close and interoperable with each other that only a single platform maybe be utilized. However, the authors acknowledge that this may not happen for a variety of business related reasons.

Attacks on Smart Cards

It was mentioned previously that tamper resistance was at the core of a smart card's capabilities, although thus far little has been said to justify why this is so important. Clearly any system that employs security is there in response to potential threats to something of value. Unfortunately, whenever there is protection, there are also attackers who would seek to undermine it. Hiding critical information technology (IT) systems away in a secure vault and equipping them with sophisticated hardware security modules may be the best way to protect them, however smart cards do not have this luxury. The cards are issued to end users in large numbers, which makes them readily accessible as attack targets, and this indirectly means that they must be low cost. This is not to say that smart cards are a push over, far from it, in fact. To appreciate just how tough modern smart cards can be, it is necessary to consider the range of attacks that are made on smart cards, and the bristling array of countermeasures that are included for their defense.

Smart card attacks may be categorized into a number of classes that relate not only to the techniques employed, but also to the resources and expertise needed by the attackers. A typical set of attack classes is:

- Logical
- Physical
- Side channel

The above classification is not necessarily exact and particular attacks may overlap the categories or multiple attacks may be used in combination.

Logical Attacks

A smart card is designed to provide a specified functionality. This includes security functionality as well as basic platform capabilities, such as I/O, memory access, and program execution. A logical attack may be considered as an attack on the design and implementation of the desired functionality, using the smart cards normal and accessible interfaces. Generally speaking, if you have a personal computer (PC) and a smart card reader, you have the tools necessary for logical attacks on smart cards.

The design of the security functionality is, not surprisingly, critical as it affects not only the information that might be revealed to an attacker, but also its value and desirability. If you design an algorithm based on a global secret (same secret key in many cards), then it would be highly desirable for an attacker to discover this, because it could be used to mass produce clone cards. A weak security algorithm also could be exploited to extract card-specific secret keys, which is also a route to cloning.

There is a well-reported logical attack (Wagner & Goldberg, 1998) against an example GSM authentication algorithm called COMP128-1. Essentially the attack involves repeated calls (many thousands) to the card authentication command, which eventually reveals sufficient information to allow the secret key (Ki) to be extracted. The fact that this is possible in a practical time frame relates to a weakness in the algorithm itself, however there is also a system design fault in that the authentication command may be called repeatedly from a PC device that has no provable authority. Stronger GSM algorithms exist that are less vulnerable and 3G systems overcome the latter problem by using a MAC to validate authentication requests. However, the improved design does not necessarily imply immunity to logical attack as a poor logical implementation could result in the card surrendering its secrets via other means.

The logical attack involves communications with the card via its normal interfaces, for example, using the APDU command and responses previously mentioned. This method of communication expects adherence to standards related to message flow, formats, valid instructions, and data length fields. An attacker does not need to adhere to the normal standards and can test the implementation for errors and oversights by cycling through all feasible commands, parameter fields, and the using invalid formats or data lengths. The attacker also could bombard the card with multiple high-rate requests. Under certain error conditions, particularly when there is confusion over a data field length or counter, it may be possible for a card to reveal the contents of memory containing Ki information.

The best countermeasure against logical attack is quite simple, just design, implement, and test things properly. The good news is that modern smart cards bought from reputable manufacturers are very well designed and tested so that an attacker would be very fortunate indeed to succeed with a logical attack. In response to this, more sophisticated attack methods have evolved including physical attacks.

Physical Attacks

As the starting point for the discussion of physical attacks, it will be assumed that the security and platform functionality has been designed and implemented sufficiently well to withstand any logical attack. As the chip is upholding this logical integrity, it becomes the obvious target for the physical attack. A physical attack will seek direct access and, in some cases, modification of memories, busses, CPUs, and so forth thereby bypassing the "logical" protocol defenses.

To conduct a physical attack normally entails access to sophisticated and expensive lab equipment. It also requires a significant level of technical expertise. Almost invariably the attacks require the decapsulation of the smart card chip, so the unit under test is no longer a useable card and indeed several may be destroyed in pursuit of chip implementation knowledge. The purpose is, therefore, to discover something from the chip design and implementation that may be used to enable other types of attacks or direct creation of clones.

One of the favored tools for investigating smart card chips was the probe station, consisting of a microscope, a high-precision mechanical platform, and needle-like probes designed to make electrical contact with parts of the chip circuitry. An example is shown in Figure 6.

As the physical size of smart card chips is getting smaller, the direct use of the probe station is less practical as the target contacts are very small compared to the size of the probe needles and indeed even optical microscopes struggle for the necessary resolution to see the chip in detail. A more modern and expensive tool is the focussed ion beam (FIB). The FIB can be

Figure 6. Probe station (Wentworth labs)

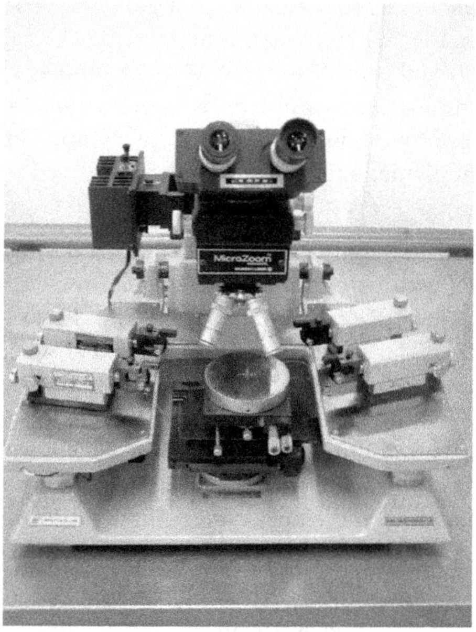

used to examine a circuit but also to modify it, by cutting tracks or indeed connecting new additional circuitry. A common use is to bond the target areas to larger contact pads that can then be accessed by a conventional probe station.

Clearly, if an attacker is prepared to go to the extremes of physical attack, then most conventional chips would rapidly reveal their secrets, however the smart card chip's ability to withstand, to a considerable extend, such attention is why it is so important within security systems.

The obvious question is how does a minuscule piece of silicon costing a few Euros defend its secrets against millions of pounds worth of laboratory equipment and an army of attackers?

To probe a circuit requires physical access. The picture in Figure 1 might imply that this is fairly easily achieved; however, the subject is a very old chip, and a modern device would include a protective barrier. One form of barrier is simply a slab of material that hides the underlying circuitry. Removing this material is a very difficult process, and as a result, the attackers capable of performing such an operation are limited. A further refinement is an active shield, consisting of a current carrying mesh bonded to the surface of the chip. Any attempt to puncture the mesh disrupts the circuit and destroys the chip. A highly skilled and determined attacker might bypass the shield and get through to the circuit below, but even then the job is far from over. The circuit will have been scrambled and distributed throughout the layers of the chip and so the interesting parts will be difficult to find. Even if the attacker has insider access to the layout or has painstakingly reverse engineered the chip, it may still withhold its secrets, as the better chips will have encrypted memories and busses. Furthermore it is not possible to carry out these attacks in visible light as the chips have environmental detectors that destroy the chips if it is exposed to light or, indeed, temperature and voltage extremes.

The modern smart card chip clearly sets the benchmark for tamper-resistant security in consumer devices. It must be accepted, of course, that given enough money, time, expertise, and determination, any electronic security measure may be undermined. However with an appropriate security system design the attacker may have insufficient motivation for such effort as little may be learned that is of long-lasting value. Tackling the smart card's array of countermeasures head on seems to be better suited to an academic challenge, rather than a good return on investment for criminals. The easy-money bandits need an attack that is cheaper, practical, and requires less expertise. A promising set of solutions forms the final presented class that is usually referred to as side-channel attacks.

Side-Channel Attacks

If physical attacks are analogous to a "smash and grab" raid and logical attacks are similar to confidence tricks, then side-channel attacks are rather like spying or eavesdropping. The basic principle rests on the surprising assumption that the desired secret information is already leaking out of the device, despite all the logical security safeguards and physical attack countermeasures. So the attacker simply has to be smart enough to find it. It is worth remembering that the entire security system solution has the capacity to leak information like a burst water main, but for the purposes of this text only, the tiny "drips" from the smart card will be considered.

The smart card chip is an electronic circuit with electric currents, voltages, logic gates, and transistors. As such circuits operate, the logic gates change state, which causes a variation in the supply current and also generates electromagnetic radiation. As the gate transitions relate to the data being processed there is the possibility that a processed Ki is modulated onto the supply current or electromagnetic emission. Therefore, the current and radiation are side-channel leakage signals that if appropriately processed may reveal secret information. To the layman, this may sound far fetched but the reality is that until countermeasures were put in place, side-channel attacks were effective against smart cards, and they are still valid against other types of nonprotected circuitry.

What is most worrying is that the attacks do not require expensive equipment and can be reproduced with far less expertise, than required for a physical attack. A typical attack set up for current monitoring is shown in Figure 7.

The reader may have the impression that the data processing is always very sophisticated, however, there are some simple timing analysis techniques (Kocher, 1996), based on simple power analysis (SPA). As the name suggests, these techniques are simple to the extent that in some cases a computer is not even necessary as the Ki may be determined by eye from the oscilloscope trace.

Figure 8 shows a key being displayed on a power trace collected during a RSA computation. The reason for the variation is that depending on the RSA key bit, the algorithm used will perform either a SQUARE or a SQUARE and MULTIPLY. This affects not only the instantaneous CPU workload, but also the time taken to complete the processing of a key bit. For general use of SPA, the attacker needs to know the algorithm used and details of its implementation. Because of the implementation dependence, SPA can be rendered far less useful by some simple countermeasure steps in the software, designed to make the workload and timing less obviously dependent on the key bits.

Figure 7. Side-channel analysis equipment

Figure 8. Section of RSA power trace

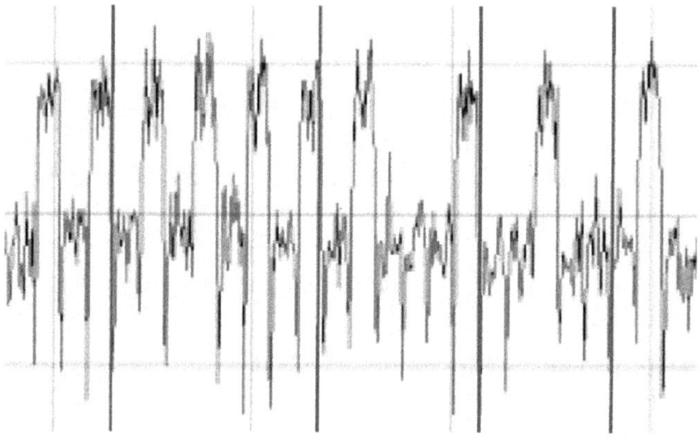

The next and very significant step up in attack technique came about by the introduction of statistical techniques, that is, rather than trying to extract the key from one run of the algorithm, use thousands. The most well-known technique is called differential power analysis (DPA) (Kocher, Jaffe, & Jun, 1999). This proved a real worry for the smart card industry as not only was it effective at extracting secret information, but it no longer required a detailed knowledge of the algorithm implementation. Essentially it is a hypothesis testing technique based on statistic signal processing. It is covered in detail within the literature but a simple attack sequence could be:

- Generate a set of random plain texts
- Run the algorithm on each plain text, whilst capturing the power/radiation trace
- Select a bit position in the plain text
- Sort the waveforms into two groups, based on the plain text being a 1 or a 0
- Average both groups and then subtract the two results
- Look for the highest "spikes" in the resulting waveform

The highest spike should (hopefully) correspond to the point at which the bit is processed, because the averaging method is nonrandom at this point due to the bit being used as the group sorting criteria. One of the reasons that this is important is that if you can determine when a bit is being processed and can gain information about its state, then there is the possibility of extracting intermediate results from a multistage cryptographic process. For example, it may be infeasible to brute force a strong algorithm that uses a large key, but it may be implemented using a sequence of much smaller subkeys that may be revealed using DPA. DES has been a target algorithm (Biham & Shamir, 1991) as it uses multiple rounds of processing in which only a few key bits are used. It is, of course, known that normal DES can be brute forced, so a common strategy is to recommend double- or triple-key DES. Whilst this is a logical defense, it does little to safeguard against a side-channel attack that can simply work its way through the small number of key variations of each round. The critical point to remember is that logically strong algorithms and keys may be vulnerable without appropriate tamper-resistant implementations.

Modern smart cards are strongly tamper resistant, and this extends to defenses against DPA. Various techniques are used to achieve this. As DPA is based on statistical averaging, one approach is to add low-level timing jitter and high-level software variations to prevent alignment of waveforms. Another defense is to generate artificial noise on the leakage signals to disguise the target information. If the chip hardware is sophisticated enough to support differential switching, then whenever a 1 changes to 0, there is a corresponding bit that changes a 0 to a 1, which snuffs out the leakage signal at the source.

Fault Attacks

Fault attacks are mentioned here as they are often used in conjunction with power/radiation monitoring, however they could be regarded as physical attacks—albeit with more interest that the device should survive. The basic principle is that if you can induce a fault into an algorithm, the error in the result can be used to reveal secret information. Favorite methods of fault induction include bright lights and voltage glitches, which can temporarily disrupt processing circuitry and/or memory cells. This method was used with frightening effect against a smart card RSA implementation (Biham & Shamir, 1997). It relied on the fact that for speed and efficiency, RSA is usually implemented in two stages and then the results are combined (Chinese Remainder Theory). If you can cause any error in the processing of a bit within one of the stages, there is an elegant method that directly extracts the Ki by a simple mathematical equation.

Fortunately, there are several countermeasures employed by tamper-resistant smart cards. Firstly, at the software implementation level, you can run the algorithm several times and check that the results are logically consistent before revealing the final result. This is fine in principle, but if an algorithm is complex and already quite slow, then to run it several times may make the device unusable. A defense at the hardware level is to try and detect the error event by means of voltage, light, and other environmental detectors, which can result in the chip being permanently disabled.

To appreciate why designers go to such extremes to protect smart cards, one needs to consider their importance within system solutions and their role in supporting transaction security. This can be readily achieved with reference to the banking and financial industry.

Financial Applications

The advancements in technology and cryptography have led into the introduction of various electronic payment schemes. Among the main requirements for a successful electronic payment scheme is to enjoy wide adoption and usage. It is also widely recognized that payment schemes relying on magnetic stripe technology are rapidly approaching the end of their life, particularly due to the lack of sophisticated tamper-resistant features. The main assumption around the following discussion is that smart card readers are capable of performing cryptographic operations, along with holding cryptographic keys (Menezes, van Oorschot, & Vanstone, 1996; Piper & Murphy, 2002).

However, since smart card technology provided the missing link, in terms of offering tamper-resistance features, the other element that required careful thought and investigation was interoperability. In order to ensure the necessary interoperability, along with the required security features, the major payment associations (i.e., Europay, Mastercard, and Visa) defined the EMV (EMV1, 1996; EMV2, 1996; EMV3, 1996) specifications. Among the main aims behind developing the EMV standard were that an EMV card would work in any EMV terminal anywhere in the world and to reduce the level of fraud that was occurring with the standard magnetic stripe cards.

The two major types of fraud that are widely utilized against financial institutions are skimming and counterfeiting. The former deals with the problem of extracting an image of the magnetic stripe card. Card counterfeiting involves the manipulation of certain card data, (e.g., the embossed data at the front of the card) so that it does match the data encoded on the magnetic stripe. Often counterfeiting involves the encoding of data obtained through skimming into a different/blank card for fraudulent use in either card present or card-not-present (CNP) transactions Fraud levels, in general, increase annually (APACS, 2002; 2003; 2004). "For a typical country within the Visa Europe region in the running year ending in July 2005, issuing banks suffered approximately €600 million and acquiring banks approximately €500 million" (Main & Brincat, 2006, p. 15).

EMV attempts to improve the overall card transaction life cycle, and particularly in terms of transaction cost reduction. Smart cards, and particularly EMV cards, have the capability to authorize transactions off line and, therefore, provide significant reductions in telecommunications and processing costs. This functionality offers the issuers of card processing systems a more functional system that will enable them to better decide when transactions should go on online or not. An often cited example includes issuers deciding to reduce the number of online transactions, by using specific card scripting commands, on particular time periods (e.g., Christmas) in which a high volume of transaction is expected.

The EMV specifications also offer the ability to reduce the CNP transactions (e.g., mail order/telephone order). The smart cards, when used in conjunction with a smart card reader in a PC, can uniquely (e.g., through the generation of unique transaction details) secure each individual transaction.

Based on the smart card's logic, it is possible to obtain sophisticated fraud management features applicable to every single transaction. For example, an issuer may decide to enable, either at card issuance or during any later stage in the card's lifecycle, which particular card groups or even individual cards will adhere to certain security policies. Furthermore, all transactions may go online if the transaction is above a certain monetary value or even to go online for every so many transactions, and so forth.

The concept of added security within the EMV specification is derived from the underlying security functionality and tamper resistance of the actual smart card microprocessors. Therefore, it is possible to store keys and other sensitive information within the card with sufficient reassurance that only the authorized entities (e.g., the issuer) will be able to access them.

The EMV specification security functionality can be summarized in the following paragraphs. Within the EMV specification the concept of static data authentication (SDA) is defined. During this phase, the card is proving to the terminal that it has not changed since it was issued. The issuer, using his private key along with some card data, generates a digital signature that is stored in the card during personalization. When the card is presented at a terminal the issuer's public key will be used in order to verify the above signature. How-

Figure 9. Diagram of SDA

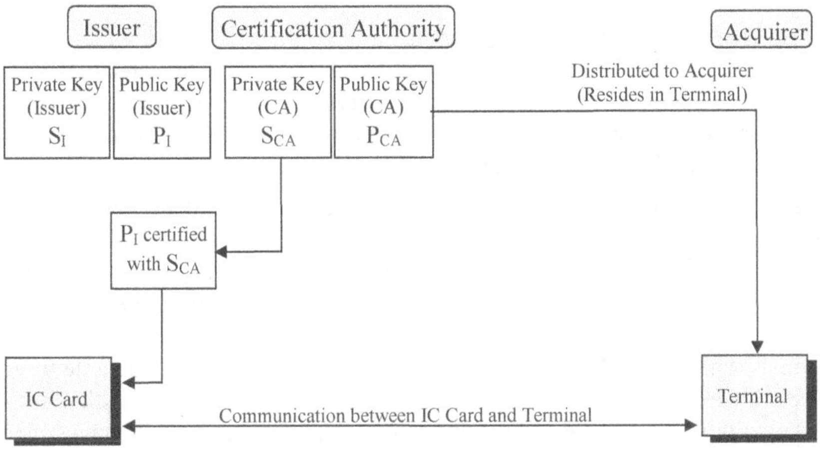

Figure 10. Diagram of dynamic data authentication

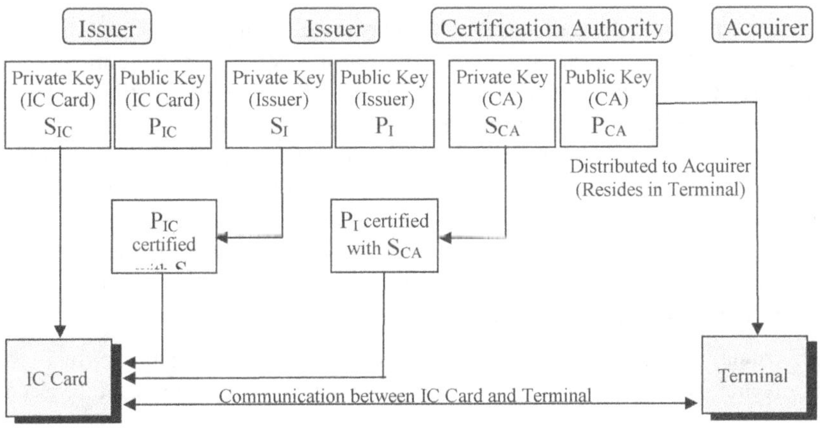

ever, the issuer's public key also is certified by the certification authority's private key. The corresponding certification authority public is placed in all terminals and is used in order to verify the issuer's public key. The whole procedure is summarized in Figure 9.

In the case of dynamic data authentication (DDA), as summarized in Figure 10, the smart card demonstrates all of the above along with the fact that it contains a unique private key that can be validated through a certificate chain. The terminal retrieves its stored copy of the certification authority public key which is used in order to verify the issuer's public key certificate. In the next step, the terminal retrieves the issuer public key (from the issuer public key certificate), which is used in order to verify the IC public key, and subsequently verify the dynamically signed application data.

Among the great advantages of EMV when working online is that it allows card and issuer authentication to take place. For example, the process is initiated with the terminal issuing a challenge to the card. The card using a Ki (shared with the issuer) encrypts the challenge (i.e., in the authorization request cryptogram (ARQC)), which is forwarded back to issuer. The issuer using the shared key will be able to verify the message and authenticate the card. On the other hand, it is also possible for the issuer upon receiving the above message to decrypt it and subsequently create an encrypted (with the same shared key) response cryptogram (i.e., in the authorization response cryptogram (ARPC)), which is eventually forwarded in the card. In that case, the card can be sure that it is connected with a legitimate issuer. The significance of the ARPC message is crucial when the issuer is requesting the card to perform certain script operations. As previously mentioned, script operations include PIN changes and unblocking and updating other card elements.

Although all the above operations indicate that the EMV standard offers the necessary functionality in terms of authenticating the participating entities and maintaining the overall scheme, it introduces a number of crucial challenges. For example, an issue that is often underestimated in the overall EMV specifications is key management and certificate management at the terminal level. For example, for the correct operation of the scheme, the terminals will have to have access to the correct keys in order to be able to verify the various certificates. It is anticipated that these keys (known as certification authority or scheme keys) will not change very often, however due to the large number of terminals and the sensitivity of the operation, such a key change is far from straightforward. This was especially true during the very early stages of the scheme, as the necessary key deployment procedures are not in place.

Among the advantages of smart card technology is the ability to enhance the two-factor cardholder authentication process. Previously, cardholders were authenticated based on something they owned (an EMV card) and something they know (the PIN), but now an additional factor can be added, a unique transaction cryptogram that will contain information about the transaction details and some random data. The cardholder uses a bank card, for example, an EMV card, and a small handheld device to produce a token or signature that could be based on the EMV cryptogram. This cryptogram may be the result of a one-time pass code or a challenge/response, which is different for each transaction. When the EMV cards are combined with such a scheme the issuers may obtain added value and economies of scale during the cardholder shopping experience.

A further crucial element in the overall EMV acceptance infrastructure is the existence of fallback mechanisms. What is going to happen when the chip cannot be read correctly?

Are we going to trust the magnetic stripe to provide us with all the necessary information? In the United Kingdom, for example, such a transaction eventually will be directed to the magnetic stripe, so at some point in time, a decision will have to be made as to whether the transaction will be accepted. However, the introduction of the liability shift will imply that the entity accepting the transaction will eventually have to bear the cost in case something goes wrong.

It should be noted that prior to the selection of the EMV and PIN solution, a range of other options were investigated, for example, placing photographs at the front of the cards. However, this method still relied on the security check to be performed by the shop assistant. Furthermore, the use of biometrics also was investigated, but it appears that these technologies are not very suitable for a large volume of transactions and at the same time the cardholders are not fully convinced and familiar with the concept of biometrics. However, although smart cards and EMV seem to work pretty well, it must be noted that migration from traditional magnetic stripe cards to smart cards requires careful thought, investigation, planning, and deployment.

Chip and PIN Card Migration Issues

When compared with traditional magnetic stripe cards, the EMV cards are not only offering significant improvements in terms of the underlying security functionality, but they also impose significant challenges for all the participating entities. Chip migration is a challenging issue for issuers, cardholders, acquirers, and merchants.

An EMV smart card has a number of layers and components that need to be taken into account. These are the smart card microprocessor, the smart card operating system, and the actual EMV application. Each one of them imposes a number of design decisions that influence the overall implementation decisions and, more importantly, the overall cost of the migration plan. In the following paragraphs, we attempt to provide an overview on key topics that will need to be taken into account for chip migration plan for financial institutions.

At the very heart of a chip migration plan will reside a very compelling business case. Developing a relative robust and successful business case for chip migration is not a trivial task and requires a great deal of team effort and expertise. The implementation of such a business case requires the successful blending of both technical and commercial skills. It is also highly influenced by the national and regional operating environment of the scheme, such as the current national levels of credit card fraud and the prospect of fraud migrating from other countries in the region.

A successfully business case also will be influenced by various chip incentive programs and when they are introduced by the financial schemes. For example, in order to assist the chip migration process, Visa and MasterCard offered various chip incentive programs. These basically subsidized the cost of the cards and encouraged the financial institutions to migrate from magnetic stripe card technology to chip cards.

Furthermore, another factor which is affecting the overall chip migration process is the liability shift. In the United Kingdom, for example, as of Jan. 1, 2005, any party within a financial transaction that is not capable of supporting a chip and PIN transaction will bear the cost of the transaction if something goes wrong. Bear in mind that this is the case for transactions in which the cardholder is present at the time the transaction took place. This obviously implied that fraudsters will target merchants that still process signature-based transactions. It was envisaged that, in turn, they will bear the cost of these transactions and so eventually will migrate their terminals to accept smart card transactions.

In terms of the underlying technology, that is, the actual smart card microprocessor, the financial institutions are free to choose their preferred supplier and the platform that will meet their security requirements. However, the low level platform, that is, the smart card chip, also comes with different types and memory sizes. The memory size has a strong influence on the number of applications that may reside in the smart card.

Visa and MasterCard have their preferred types of technology to provide their services. However, both schemes have reached an unofficial agreement, stating that their member banks are free to choose any major smart card environment irrespective of whether it is Multos, Java Card, or any other proprietary architecture. The decision on the underlying smart card microprocessor also is influenced by whether the EMV card will be offering SDA and DDA. Supporting DDA generally requires the existence of a crypto coprocessor, which is another factor that will influence the cost of the chip. Deciding whether SDA or DDA will be supported also influences the creation of specific card data.

Having selected the underlying smart card microprocessor, the operating system or platform is another crucial decision that has to be made. What happens with EMV card personalization? EMV card personalization is quite different from magnetic stripe card personalization. This data will have to created, assembled, and formatted in such a way that to be understood by the personalization machines and eventually by the smart card. Some of the data includes what was traditionally used in the magnetic stripe cards, for example, cardholder surname, issuing bank, and so forth. The additional EMV specific data may include, for example, information regarding the establishment and use of cryptographic keys. The generation of the complete EMV data set along with the necessary key management policies requires dedicated equipment which may or may not be able to interface with legacy magnetic stripe card data generation machines.

As soon as the data has been generated, a system also will be necessary to load and personalize the smart cards. These systems will have to take into account the details of the underlying smart card microprocessor, operating system, and platform, along with all other EMV-related objects and data in order to finally personalize the smart card. However, not only will the data have to reach the smart card, but the EMV card body also will have to be personalized, embossed, and finally posted to the cardholder.

Delivering the EMV cards to the cardholders is often referred to as completing half of the story. The other half involves managing the card while it is utilized. Card management requires the existence of smart card life cycle management system (SCLCMS) that will be capable of managing the issuer's cardholder base. The cardholder base may involve different smart card microprocessors, different platforms, different applications, and different card segments. In case any changes are to be made after the card has been issued, the existence of post issuance personalization system is necessary.

The chip migration plan is influenced substantially by the nature of the underlying smart card platform. In case more than one application is required to reside in the same chip, then a multiapplication smart card platform may be required. Firstly, these applications will have to be identified and then implemented by the specific underlying platform. Moreover as soon as they are implemented, they will have to be installed and maintained as described above.

Having identified some of the parameters that will be influencing a chip migration plan, it makes sense to explore some data preparation, personalization, and transition options. As far as the data preparation is concerned, it has been suggested (DataCard Group, 2001) that data preparation can either take place in house or be outsourced in which case it may also make sense to outsource the card personalization, too. Actually, there are a large number of issuers, usually small banks that outsource their credit card business to trusted third parties. On the other hand, there are a number of banks that have the capability to perform in house data preparation. Subsequently, depending on their expertise, they might decide to either perform card personalization in house or outsource it, too. One example of in house data preparation and outsourced card personalization is when a bank is familiar with the data preparation of magnetic stripe cards also has acquired the knowledge, equipment, and expertise to generate EMV specific data. On the other hand, it might not have the equipment to personalize smart cards, especially when a large number of cards are involved. In that case, the obvious advantage is that the issuer retains some control over the newly generated cryptographic keys for his scheme.

In terms of post issuance personalization and card management (Thales, 2001), there are various options. For example, the issuer may decide to generate the chip specific data, but later on it might decide to maintain a back office system (e.g., a smart card management system (SCMS)) that will enable him to store and query stored data for each card. A more advanced version (full smart card post issuance capabilities) of the above scenario requires further functionality that will enable cardholders to interact, for example, via Web-enabled applications, automatic teller machines (ATMs), or kiosks, with the SCMS in order to update the functionality of their cards.

In particular, for the financial industry, the smart card manufacturers, and other trusted entities are offering issuers the ability to perform a number of permutations that will suit individual needs.

Conclusion

The need for security and assurance is clearly not a new thing as our ancestors had similar concerns and even hit upon the idea of using security tokens. The smart card is perhaps then the result of a long evolution in consumer tokens that seem more popular than ever, with a growing number of existing and planned systems based on smart cards. It is conceivable that more smart card schemes will move toward contactless options. Indeed the whole token form factor may change, but tamper resistance will remain as a core capability and justification for use.

Smart cards are subjected to a wide range of sophisticated attacks not because they are weak, but simply because they are accessible. In fact smart cards are amazingly well defended for their size and cost, so it is, therefore, quite appropriate that they have become powerful, managed, multiapplication platforms that can host a wide range of security sensitive applications. However, it should be taken into account that the overall system design should be equally secured and well thought out. It is often the case that various security attacks do not directly attack the system or system components but rather system processes. Furthermore, as evident from the discussion on financial systems and migration, the development, deployment, and life-cycle management of smart card security systems is far from trivial. Finally, we conclude that the use of smart cards to provide tamper-resistant security and assurance is well justified, but we must not lose sight that the biggest challenge is to implement and run complete system solutions.

References

APACS. (2002). *Card fraud the facts.* Retrieved from http://www.apacs.org.uk/

APACS. (2003). *Safety in numbers.* Retrieved from http://www.chipandpin.org/

APACS. (2004). *Card fraud the facts.* Retrieved from http://www.apacs.org.uk/

APACS. (2005). *All about card skimming.* Card Watch. Retrieved from http://www.cardwatch.org.uk/default.asp?sectionid=3&pageid=97

Ashdown-Hill, J. (2005). *An introduction to medieval seals.* Retrieved from http://www.richardiii.net/seals.htm

Biham, E., & Shamir, A. (1991). Differential cryptanalysis of DES-like cryptosystems. *Journal of Cryptology, 4*(1), 2-21.

Biham, E., & Shamir, A. (1997). *Differential fault analysis of secret key cryptosystems* (Tech. Rep. No. CS0910). Technicon Computer Science Department.

DataCard Group. (2001). *The transition to multi-application smart cards with post issuance personalisation capabilities* [White paper]. Retrieved from www.datacard.com/publications

Diners Club. (2005). *History overview and timeline.* Retrieved from http://www.dinersclubnewsroom.com/anniversary.cfm

EMV1. (1996). *EMV'96 integrated circuit card specification for payment systems* (Version 3.0). Retrieved from http://www.europay.com/Pdf/EMV_card.pdf.es

EMV2. (1996). *EMV'96 integrated circuit card terminal specification for payment systems* (Version 3.0). Retrieved from http://www.europay.com/Pdf/EMV_card.pdf.es

EMV3. (1996). *EMV'96 integrated circuit card application specification for payment systems* (Version 3.0). Retrieved from http://www.europay.com/Pdf/EMV_card.pdf.es

ETSI. (1999). *GSM 11:11—Digital cellular telecommunications system (phase 2+); Specification of the subscriber identity module—Mobil equipment (SIM-ME) interface* (Version 8.3.0)

Frost & Sullivan. (2006). *Need for enhanced homeland security to promote uptake of security technologies.* Retrieved from http://www.prnewswire.co.uk/cgi/news/release?id=161547

GlobalPlatform. (2001). *GlobalPlatform card specification* (Version 2.1). Retrieved from www.globalplatform.org

International Standard Organisation (ISO). (1995). *ISO/IEC 7816, information technology—Identification cards—Integrated circuit(s) cards with contacts—Part 4 interindustry commands for interchange.*

International Standard Organisation (ISO). (2003). *ISO/IEC 10373, identification cards—Test methods—Part 1 general characteristics.*

ISO. (2000). *ISO/IEC 14443-X identification cards—Contactless integrated circuit(s) cards—Proximity cards.*

Java Card. (2002). *Java Card API 2.2.1 reference implementation.* Retrieved from http://www.javasoft.com/products/javacard/

Kocher, P., (1996). Timing attacks on implementations of Diffie-Hellman RSA DSS and other systems. *Advances in Cryptology, 1109,* 104-113.

Kocher, P., Jaffe, J., & Jun, B. (1999). Differential power analysis. *Advances in Cryptology,1666,* 388-397.

Main, D., & Brincat, K. (2006). *Information security & crypto @ Visa.*" Presentation delivered to the Smart card/Tokens Security and Applications Module of the MSc in Information Security Course. Royal Holloway: University of London.

Menezes, A. J., van Oorschot, P. C., & Vanstone, S. A. (1996). *Handbook of applied cryptography.* CRC Press.

Microsoft. (1999). Windows powered smart cards. Retireved from http://www.microsoft.com

Multos. (2002). Retrieved from www.multos.org

Nie, N. H., & Erbring, L. (2002). Internet and society: A preliminary report. *IT&Scociety, 1*(1), 275-283. Retrieved from www.ITandSociety.org

Nielsen, A. C. (2005). Online shopping off the charts. Retrieved from http://us.acnielsen.com/pubs/documents/2005_ci_q4_online.pdf

Piper, F., & Murphy, S. (2002). *Cryptography: A very short introduction.* Oxford University Press.

Rankl, W., & Effing, W. (1997). *The smart card handbook.* John Wiley & Sons.

Schneier, B. (1996). *Applied cryptography* (2nd ed.). John Wiley & Sons.

Smith, L. W. (2003). *Food rationing in WWII.* Retrieved from http://www.worldwar2exraf.co.uk/Online%20Museum/Museum%20Docs/foodration.html

Thales. (2001). *EMV easy migration guide* (Version 2). Retrieved from www.thales-esecurity.com

Tunstall, M. (2006). *Smart card attacks.* Presentation delivered to the Smart card/Tokens Security and Applications Module of the MSc in Information Security Course. Royal Holloway: University of London.

Wagner, D., & Goldberg, I. (1998). *GSM cloning.* ISAAC Berkley. Retrieved from http://www.isaac.cs.berkeley.edu/isaac/gsm.html

Chapter IX

Unified Identities in Complex Financial Organizations

Peter Orondo, Acclaim Consulting Group, Inc., USA

Abstract

In this chapter, we make the case for a unified approach to managing identities in a complex enterprise in the financial services sector. We discuss the framework for evolving unified policies and processes and prescribe optimal organizational governance to implement them. We discuss the relationship with regulatory compliance and other critical information enterprise functions. We also include nonprescriptive, strategic positions that progressive organizations may take to streamline enterprise identity and access management.

Introduction

After years of neglect, identity and access management (IAM) is now strongly ensconced in the modern information technology enterprise. Businesses are driven by the desire for greater business ecosystem and process efficiency, automatic regulatory compliance, and, frankly, the deep-seated aversion to negative press resulting from identity theft and other information asset intrusions.

Forward thinking firms, however, realize that IAM goes beyond these traditional "mandates." The Hewlett Packard Company (HP), for example, realizes that the management of their most valuable assets—142,000, employees, hundreds of thousands of partners, and more than one billion customers worldwide—requires unprecedented C-level commitment, including the creation of a new powerful position of chief identity officer (*HP Identity Journey*, 2005).

Business Drivers, Organizing Principles, and Strategic Goals

This section provides an overview of high level features of an enterprise identity and access management infrastructure. It is organized into high level focus areas, roughly in order of strategic priority in the financial services sector.

Unified Identity and Access Management (IAM)

Identity management is the process of managing user identities (principals or "users") in the enterprise. Traditionally, these include employees, contractors, business partners, suppliers, and vendors, amongst others. In the services oriented architecture (SOA) world, identities also may be extended to business entities like assets, projects, or Web services.

The goal of identity management systems is to track user identities as they traverse through various phases in the enterprise. As the identities assume new roles, relinquish old ones, onboard and off-board, a properly designed identity management system manages the process seamlessly from one phase to the next.

Underlying each identity management system is an access management system. An access management system provides primarily authentication and authorization services but may also provide other related services, like nonrepudiation. Once again, an access management system may provide services to traditional identities (principals or "users") as well as nontraditional identities, like servers and enterprise services.

These two services form the foundation of the enterprise information architecture. Their situation at the center of the information enterprise explains why they occupy such a prominent mindshare of chief identity officers (CIOs), chief information officers (CIOs), and chief information security officers (CISOs), and even the popular media today.

Control vs. Management

A typical financial services firm's enterprise information architecture (EIA) evolves primarily from helter-skelter applications procurement standards and through mergers and acquisitions.

In many financial services organizations, each department acquires applications according to its needs, and each such application will introduce its own IAM services with little or no regard for existing centralized IAM services.

Of course, mergers and acquisitions introduce disjointed systems and technologies even when the acquisition is within the same industry, since the overriding determinant for a merger or acquisition is high level strategic business fit, not technology integration fit, with the latter being of third degree consideration, if at all.

Rationalizing disjointed technologies creates unique IAM challenges that every CISO and CIOs should address. At its core is the balance that must be struck between the application stakeholders' prerogative to control and manage their application according to their unique business needs, against the enterprise-wide enterprise information architecture rationalization goals.

Our experience indicates that while the CISO and the CIOs have an enterprise wide view of how the enterprise information architecture should look like, it is the application owners who must use the application to meet every day business requirements. This puts the application owner in a position of strength when it comes to defining the parameters around the applications. It is also likely that the application owner is financially responsible for some portion of the information technology (IT) budget, further enhancing her or his hand.

In these situations, we recommend that the CISOs and CIOs put into place application procurement standards and have it adopted at the highest level of technology management. Such a procurement standard would set broad guidelines with a particular long term, rationalized enterprise architecture goal in mind. Any exceptions to the policy would then require the approval of a high level enterprise security policy board.

Enterprise Identity Stack Rationalization Strategies

A necessary first step towards a unified IAM involves creating a clear *and* enterprise-wide understanding of managed identities. In a large financial institution, this can be a daunting task since most of these firms often grow by acquisition. Each such acquisition adds a non-rationalized principal data to an often no-rationalized corporate identity stack.

Definition: Enterprise Identity Stack Rationalization simply means that all enterprise principals *and* their interrelationship are uniquely identified within a firm's enterprise *and* its business ecosystem. Enterprise identity stack rationalization calls for unique identification and attribution of all human and nonhuman identities—principals (users), servers, domain controllers, physical and nonphysical assets, and Web services.

In practice, the previous definition implies that all applications recognize that the Windows domain principal (user) "peter12," for example, is the same "Peter Orondo" in the human resources (HR) database, and that no collision exists between active directory and HR system attributions of this identity. It means that the entire enterprise application space is aware that Peter Orondo from Acclaim Consulting Group, Inc. in the vendor tracking system is not the same Peter Orondo, also from Acclaim Consulting Group, Inc., in the sales automation system, who in turn, is not the same peter12 (consultant) in corporate LDAP.

It would seem like identity rationalization is a simple matter of reconciling user records from multiple sources, perhaps using an Excel spreadsheet or some other tool. This knee-jerk reaction perhaps explains why so many IAM projects encounter many unforeseen delays and cost overruns.

A good strategic footing recognizes that a large complex financial institution often consists of many disjointed systems, each with its own silo-ed IAM repositories, access, and control paradigms *and* ownership.

There is usually *some* limited application integration from an IAM perspective. Most applications in effect have most of the required IAM services built in. For example, the HR application has its own user repository, roles repository, authentication service, authorization service, identity management service, and so forth.

Figure 1. Nonrationalized IAM architecture

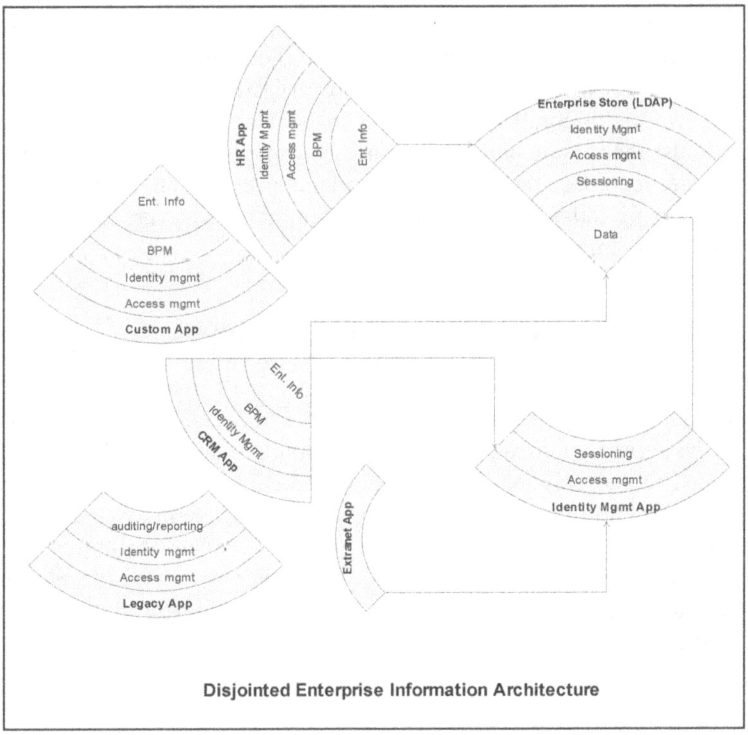

The result is a hodge-podge IAM infrastructure where many data repositories, application services, and functions are duplicated. We depict this in Figure 1. In Figure 1, it is clear that the only strategy that has any hope of success proceeds according to the following path.

Unify Corporate Identity Planning, Processes, and Leadership

Planning is a critical component of rationalizing the enterprise identity stack, since identities span the entire corporate plane and how the corporation conducts its entire business. Therefore, before undertaking any identity management initiatives, the corporation must put in place a plan that addresses identity rationalization from a business driver point of view. The planning must be carried out at the highest level of the enterprise (or the lowest level that has the ownership, authority, and purview over the *entire* corporate interaction with its identities). In our experience, the only planning authority with proper accreditation and corporate ammunition is a C-Level officer such a CIO, since such planning touches all corporate applications in all divisions of the firm. The full scope of corporate identity management planning will take us too far afield for present purposes, but suffice it to say that the following elements should come out of such planning initiative.

Corporate Identity Management Vision

The C-level officer should clearly enunciate an encompassing vision to not only create a buzz and excitement to rally the masses, but also articulate how identity management ties into the larger corporate goals like profitability, agility (as we shall examine shortly), and other long term corporate goals. A critical aspect of the corporate identity management vision is its evangelical aspect, which empowers every member of the firm to be cognizant of appropriate aspects of corporate identity management. For example, it should be clear to the receptionist that phone calls should not be routed to an internal employee simply because the caller identified the employee by name or extension. This level of awareness is still widely lacking today and may only be blunted by widespread evangelization, not simply by an e-mail reminder.

IAM Governance and Execution Strategy

Once the corporate identity management vision is articulated, a practical strategy for execution must be agreed upon. We recommend promulgating an IAM standing committee headed by the CIO and drawing all application stakeholders, as the steering organ of all matters touching on corporate IAM. Alternatively, a properly empowered existing standing committee may incorporate IAM governance functions. Whatever its form, such a committee should not set strict guidelines in our view; rather, driven by the corporate identity management and business imperatives, the committee should set an 80/20 execution strategy which we define as follows:

Definition: 80/20 Execution Strategy means that roughly 80% of the corporate IAM strategy mandates should be relatively rigid, reflecting long term corporate vision, business imperatives, and (as we shall see later on) aspects of governing regulatory regimes. Twenty percent of strategy mandates should remain relatively fluid to create corporate agility and empower lower level managers to use their own creativity to meet high level corporate IAM vision at the time of execution. Note that there is no paradox from a regulatory perspective since virtually no regulatory mandates specifies implementation as we shall see shortly.

Business Imperatives

Business imperatives supremely drive not just the vision, but also the execution strategy of corporate identity management. For most financial institutions, the top three imperatives are business process efficiency, information security, and automated regulatory compliance. It is crucial that the planning phase bring out other imperatives that may be important to the firm and make all of them part of the corporate IAM vision statement.

Enterprise-wide Application Procurement and Development Standards

It is a natural evolution that technology driven firms like banks will acquire many technologies and applications through departmental procurement processes as well as through mergers and acquisitions. Systems so acquired will create a cacophony of standards, technologies, and infrastructure choices within the enterprise.

While this problem is intrinsic to business, firms can yet put in place processes and procedures to ensure that current systems are well integrated into a desired IAM framework, and the new ones fit in with little or moderate integration effort.

The CIO should put in place enterprise-wide application procurement standards—or IAM-specific mandates added to the existing ones—that would, among other things:

- Set standards for selecting software vendors based on a enterprise-wide criteria that outline how well they integrate within the firm's information infrastructure ("IAM fit" would be one criterion)
- Add "IAM fit" to the enterprise software development and integration standards. For example, require application developers and integrators to use existing enterprise IAM services instead of creating new ones within the application code
- Set exception guidelines for business cases that dictate application solutions that fall outside of the firm's corporate procurement and software development standards, and following the prescribed 80/20 strategy

Ideally, these standards would be adopted by the firm's management in charge of technology services so that all application owners have a clear controlling authority within which to operate.

Identity Data Rationalization

Identity data rationalization is part of the overall enterprise identity rationalization and deals with the technical rationalization of user identities. In a very large financial institution, the task may be daunting given that the business ecosystem encompasses millions of user and nonuser identities.

The best approach creates a globally unique identifier (GUID) for each identity across the enterprise. The actual creation of the GUID is quite easy using any number of GUID generators available today; the real challenge is assigning the GUID to the managed identities. Indeed, many projects fail either because the identity data rationalization was not done properly, or it takes so long to accomplish that it sucks time and budget from other IAM project activities.

The best approach uses automated methods, say using some scripting facility, to uniquely identify principals followed by a manual process for principals that may not be identified automatically. It is critical to use heuristic matching methods with extreme restrain. For example, any automated method that tries to correlate the full name or some other such heuristic attribute across multiple user repositories is necessarily suspect, unless it is accompanied by a massive manual check, since it is susceptible to user data entry errors. On the other hand, a match based on a set of frequently used attributes creates a much more predictable automated match, even if the methodology only covers a modest portion of the identity population.

Note on Standardized Directory Services

Directory services are at the heart of the IAM enterprise information architecture. Establishing and standardizing directory services architecture is a critical step towards securing a unified IAM infrastructure, since the directory services provide an excellent platform for aggregating access rights, storing identities, and security policies, among others. Directory services enable other enterprise processes, including:

- Identity and access provisioning
- Enhanced evolution of security policies and processes (auditing of application access, regulatory compliance, etc.), which are easily done with a centralized enterprise directory services—see next section

Identity Data Mastering

Identity data mastering is another enterprise concept that is easy to understand in theory but quite challenging to implement, in practice, especially in complex financial institutions.

Definition: Identity Data Mastering simply refers to the designation of one or more enterprise systems as authorities for identity information. The simplest approach is to designate a single system as the authoritative source of all identity data. In practice, however, large financial institutions normally have multiple data masters, with each mastering specific attributes.

The multiple data mastering approach is more complex to implement and, in our view, makes it a lot harder to create a unified IAM regime, especially in situations where the number of data masters is beyond two or three. A multiple data mastering implementation is actually a harbinger for lack of executive IAM leadership or planning within an enterprise. It indicates that each division or department "clings to their data" against "encroachment" by others, usually, the information security department and shows that there is no unified enterprise-wide leadership envelope regarding IAM.

A single data mastering approach designates a particular optimized system as the data master for all identity information. Any system that has any doubts about the quality of its identity data consults the identity master and updates its copy accordingly—see the following section on provisioning.

We recommend implementing a single identity data mastering model that unifies identity data across the enterprise and greatly simplifies the enterprise *IAM* systems implementation.

Identity Data Provisioning

The challenge of identity data provisioning (also known as e-provisioning) is to ensure that all enterprise identity and access data is kept in sync across all enterprise identity and access repositories.

In the financial services sector, significant employee turnover, role changes, mergers and acquisitions, and divestitures make it very difficult to track identity information changes across multiple enterprise systems.

E-provisioning drives employee productivity by enabling a new employee to begin performing his or her duties on the day of hire. Without a provisioning system, the new employee often waits for weeks to gain full access to all systems needed to be productive.

E-provisioning systems also come in handy when an employee leaves the firm's employment. When properly designed, such a provisioning system removes all rights from all systems on the day the employee leaves (or when the firm decides to terminate him or her). In many cases, firms simply disable the employee's obvious access points (security badge, e-mail, and HR), but often leave a bevy of other accounts still active within the enterprise—UNIX based accounts are notorious in this regard. These orphan accounts may be used by malicious actors, both internal and external, for activities that are not in the firm's best interest.

Firms also have a further reason to move to a streamlined e-provisioning solution, since many homegrown provisioning systems currently in use are limited in their capabilities and usually have substantial operational and maintenance costs.

Unfortunately, the provisioning solutions in the market today are not as mature as, say, their access management counterparts. A successful completion of enterprise leadership and planning is a prerequisite of any provisioning initiative. In general, it is recommended that the identity management and the provisioning solutions come from the same software vendor, since the two services are closely related.

Unified Access Management

Unified access management is closely linked to unified identity management as we have discussed above, and indeed the two are often referred to in tandem as IAM. At its core, access management is supported by two key enterprise services, namely, authentication and authorization of identities to applications and enterprise services.

Just like identity management, access management requires high level enterprise-wide planning. In fact, planning and overall execution of access management should go hand in hand with that of identity management. We highlight some of the differences that should be borne in mind in the following sections.

Unified Access Management Strategies

The concept of unifying the processes and systems used for enterprise application access management comes naturally to financial institutions that are historically accustomed to protecting client deposits, accounts, and other assets. Access management has often taken the form of IAM middleware vendor standardization and specialization, with IT managers arguing that developing vendor neutral access management architectures tend to be costly and unpredictable. We believe, however, that the best approach involves separating access management data from vendor implementation, leading to a degree of implementation/vendor independence. The idea is to be able to plug in and out of particular authentication and authorization service implementations that meet desired performance and scalability without changing the overall access management architecture. The industry is clearly heading this way with recent innovations in SOAs, and as such any tight coupling of applications to authentication services implementations only serves to foreclose opportunities for an industry, where technology uniquely powers competitiveness. Instead, a best of breed approach that picks and chooses vendors according to specific metrics is the best path to achieving the optimal IAM implementation.

Roles Based Access Management

Roles based access management (RABM) creates an abstraction layer between application access management requirements—which may be expressed in very general business terms—and authorization implementation, which is necessarily proprietary. A "role" is a logical construct that represents the policy governing a principal's resource, application, or service privileges.

In practice, the governing policy is evolved from business requirements (for example, "the HR application should only be accessed by HR managers") and is expressed in purely non-technical terms. A role is a logical representation of corporate policy and ultimately relies on data managed by the identity management system (for example, "HR role is assigned to principals in the HR department with title=manager").

Note: The role information is corporate data that resides in the data layer. The process of mapping roles to actors—role rationalization— can be quite complex and may bring out uncomfortable revelations, namely, that many financial services firms do not really understand how they conduct their business—at least from an IAM view point. However, just like identity data rationalization, role rationalization is a critical exercise during the building of a secure IAM infrastructure that also conforms to various regulatory regimes that mandate duty separation and specific controls and audit provisions. Many financial organizations perform role rationalization with an IAM vendor in mind—instead of being independent of it— but this is a very big, self perpetuating mistake.

From the foregoing, it is apparent that unified access management is built upon and is greatly facilitated by a unified identity data.

Unified Policy Evolution, Enforcement, and Regulatory Compliance

Large financial organizations evolve elaborate business driven security policies that ultimately must be enforced partly by IAM systems. The other enforcement responsibilities are laid upon people, policy, processes, and procedures.

Such security policies are normally complex for a large financial organization, especially given that multiple, often conflicting, requirements, must be met:

- Different stakeholders within a large enterprise may have conflicting security requirements. Even in cases where a single corporate office has executive authority over corporate security policies as we proposed earlier, managing stakeholders, especially semiautonomous ones, may be challenging.
- Business partners, for example, in the automated payment processing industry, may impose rigid security policies on its partners. Furthermore, the business side of the firm will be reluctant to foreclose business opportunities because of insufficient IAM and other IT infrastructure.
- There are always constraints within a chosen technology and vendor, and integration of multiple technologies/vendors for a best of breed solution has its own challenges.

The above requirements may be met with one internal remedy or the other. Managing difficult stakeholders, for example, only requires sufficiently empowered and skilled leadership. Businesses are not democracies, especially those in the ultracompetitive financial services sector; once a strategic business need is identified and proper leadership put in place, all stakeholders will conform accordingly or the business will find new ones who will. Even relationships with business partners may be managed accordingly, especially in an environment of shared business goals.

However, the same may not be said of regulatory compliance. Once promulgated, governmental mandates are normally set in stone for extended periods and noncompliance invites potentially very severe sanctions. Because of its huge impact on the design, implementation, and operation of IAM systems, we devote the rest of this section to a discussion of IAM issues surrounding regulatory compliance.

IAM Strategies for Regulatory Compliance

Large financial services firms face about three dozen different laws, regulations, and industry standards worldwide. Given the global nature of the financial services economy today, a medium-sized financial services firm in the Midwest, for example, will often find itself subject not only to out-of-state regulations like California's Information Practices Act, but also overseas regulations like Hong Kong's Personal Data Privacy Act or Canada's Chapter P-21 Regulation.

Table 1 shows some of these regulations and a summary of what each entails.

These laws and regulations impose significant legal and financial penalties for non-compliance. As more information goes digital, we only expect the digital information protection and privacy regulations to proliferate.

It is also significant to mention the potential loss of business due to adverse negative publicity that results from information security breaches. Corporate as well as individual customers are becoming increasingly aware of data security and privacy issues. Indeed, at the corporate level, many firms now impose data security standards on their vendors and business partners, and impose severe business penalties for noncompliance.

So how does a financial firm deal with the ever expanding list of rules, regulations, and standards? We outline some strategic positions in the following sections.

Unify, Unify, Unify

It should be readily apparent that regulatory compliance is very much facilitated by the unified identity and access management framework that we discussed above. This is because a great majority of the laws and regulations concern identity data privacy. In a unified identity and access management enterprise, safeguarding identities is greatly simplified for the simple reason that all identity data is tracked in one systematic framework.

Furthermore, the other regulations dealing with disclosure, reporting, and control are also easier to comply with, since there is a single source for all records regarding application access. Monitoring, information forensics and audit solutions fit right into the framework, raising the happy specter of automated compliance. Another big advantage to unifying IAM systems and processes comes when externally mandated audits are required. The audits are simpler and more cost effective than in an enterprise where IAM functions are widespread and discreet, since supplying information

Table 1. (Source: Williams, 2005)

Regulation	Authority	Type of act	Summary
Basel II—Revised International Capital Framework	EU	Identifying, assessing, measuring, and controlling operational risks	• Takes a three-pillar approach to improve capital adequacy for large banks within the group of 10 nations. One pillar focuses on internal controls and calls for review of control structures and risk management in order to ensure prudent conduct of business. • Sections 751 and 752 call for assessment of the control environment including the quality of information reporting and underlying systems.
Gramm-Leach-Bliley Financial Services Modernization Act	USA	Data privacy	• Allows greater competition among banks, securities companies, and insurance companies, and allows investment and commercial banks to consolidate. • Requires financial institutions to provide each consumer with a privacy notice at the time the consumer relationship is established and annually thereafter. Consumers have the right to opt-out in order to limit some, but not all, sharing of information.
Sarbanes-Oxley Act (Sarbox)	USA	Disclosure and reporting	• Goal is to protect investors by improving the accuracy and reliability of corporate disclosures. • Requires each company to conduct an internal audit and make an annual statement about the effectiveness of internal controls, including IT controls. Controls also verified by external auditor.
California Information Practices Act (SB1386)	California	Data privacy	• Requires companies and government agencies that store personal information on California residents to disclose any breach of security to those individuals affected. • Requires businesses to inform residents if their unencrypted personal information—including name and either a driver's license number, Social Security number, or credit card or banking information—has been compromised.
European Union Data Privacy Directive (EUDPD)	EU	Data privacy	• Establishes a Europe-wide set of legal principles for privacy protection to be enacted in all European Union member states. • Prohibits the transfer of personal data from EU countries to any countries that do not have "adequate" data protection laws.
Health Insurance Portability and Accountability Act 1996 (HIPAA)	USA	Personal health data portability and protection	• Protects health insurance coverage for workers and their families when they change or lose their jobs. • Requires the establishment of national standards for electronic healthcare transactions and national identifiers for providers, health insurance plans, and employers.

continued on following page

Table 1. Continued

Canadian Privacy Act, Chapter P-21	Canada	Data privacy	• Extends current Canadian laws that protect the privacy of individuals with respect to limited use of personal information held by organizations and that provide individuals with a right of access to that information.
Hong Kong Personal Data Privacy Act	Hong Kong	Data privacy	• Protects the privacy of living individuals in relation to personal data. • Contributes to Hong Kong's continued economic wellbeing by safeguarding the free flow of personal data to Hong Kong from restrictions by countries that already have data protection laws.
Management's Responsibility for Internal Control US OMB Circular A123	United States		• Imposes Sarbox-like regulations on all U.S. federal agencies, beginning in 2006. • It is likely that state and local agencies will follow.

to compliance auditors may be accomplished by querying one (or a handful) of databases. Compliance auditors also can be assured that the supplied information is consistent once the collection systems are verified.

Exploit Regulatory Commonalities

Firms should seek IAM solutions that exploit commonalities among the different regulations. A cursory glance at the above table, for example, indicates that the regulations fall into the broad categories of data privacy, process controls (or both), and risk management. A further rationalization will bring out other commonalities that may then be condensed into specific feature system functions, services, and processes.

It is also important to note that the investment in IAM systems should not achieve compliance as the primary benefit. Our experience indicates that firms that deploy IAM systems purely for compliance purposes have failed to fully internalize and integrate the regulatory mandates into their business model. Data privacy, for example, is a mandate driven by consumers concerned about the privacy of their data, and as such, compliance should be internalized into the firm's business model, especially since it applies to other types of information like the firm's intellectual property.

80/20 Execution Strategy

Most regulations and standards do not impose specific systems solutions; rather, broad as well as detailed regulatory goals are spelled out. It is thus possible to maintain some flexibility without compromising compliance. In thinking about regulatory compliance, therefore, firms are better served by rationalizing the regulatory landscape into 80% firm guidelines, while permitting flexibility for the remainder to allow line managers and integrators implementation agility. Doing so not only promotes operational agility at the enterprise level, but also makes it more likely that the firm will meet its deployment schedules—we do not believe a straightjacket approach to meeting all provisions in all regulations has any reasonable chance of success.

Adopt a Controls Framework

Control objectives for information and related technology (COBIT) provides specific framework and governance guidelines specific to information technology. Constructed by the IT Governance Institute (ITGI), COBIT has been widely adopted by large financial institutions as a controls framework.

Implementing COBIT and other frameworks like COS, ISO 17799, and ITIL will greatly facilitate a firm's compliance with controls-based regulations, since COBIT is designed specifically for a controls regime. Furthermore, implementing COBIT also will provide a lot of mileage towards privacy and other data-related regulations by creating system-based control processes (Williams, 2005; Kelley, 2006).

Additional Enterprise Services

The following sections summarize other enterprise services that are enabled and supercharged by a unified identity and access management framework.

Unified Business Process Alignment

The power of business process management is unleashed when its principals (users, servers, and services) all have a unified view of each other and of the applications. In this scenario, a workflow process in an HR application creates connections to all entities it needs to complete its business task without any unintended manual intervention.

One business process function that is closely married with identity and access management, and which financial services organizations cannot ignore, is the previously discussed e-provisioning. E-provisioning ensures that the on-boarding of new employees is quick and that employee productivity is employed from day one. E-provisioning also ensures that the off-boarding process is quick and painless for the firm. E-provisioning further reduces identity theft vulnerability by eliminating zombie accounts that may be hijacked by internal employees and external malicious actors.

Additionally, e-provisioning facilitates and enables other IAM and enterprise information security functions like RBAM, security audits, and others. Lastly e-provisioning enables regulatory compliance by making sure, for example, that a corporation does not continue to pay employees after they have been terminated.

From a return on security investment (ROSI) and strategic perspectives, enterprise e-provisioning is a "no brainer." Unfortunately, e-provisioning projects tend to be complex, time consuming, and involve a healthy degree of custom development for all but the simplest of IT enterprises.

Within a unified business process context, business automation and outsourcing become well defined, modular, efficient, and in regulatory compliance, and business services, like partner management, become completely pluggable.

Unified Business Intelligence (BI) View

Business intelligence (BI) is the process of managing and mining business information. BI services include auditing, reporting, data mining, and warehousing, among others.

BI is built partially on top of the IAM services and provides critical business decision information at the hands of key decision makers of the firm, line of business, or division within a firm. In order to deliver the most accurate business intelligence, a unified view of the information enterprise is normally a necessary prerequisite.

Unified Application Management

Enterprise applications enable productivity and are becoming exclusive windows to the enterprise. On the other hand, enterprise entities (users, servers, services, business partners, and even remote business services) require properly construed rights before gaining access to these applications to perform a business task.

A unified IAM enables a unified application management model, whereby an identity is given the complete picture of the enterprise without hassle, challenge, or security lapses that is common with most enterprise information architectures today.

Unified Enterprise Correspondence

Enterprise messaging has become almost synonymous with enterprise e-mail in recent years as e-mail has become a dominant form of electronic communication. To avoid this false analog, we use an all encompassing term *correspondence* to denote all forms of intercommunication between various principals within the enterprise, including its broader business network.

The actors in this intercommunication are obviously the principals—users, servers, and services. A unified view of the principals obviously supercharges, simplifies, and recasts the enterprise correspondence to an even more powerful role within the enterprise.

We condense and summarize the foregoing unified information architecture in Figure 2.

Figure 2. Enterprise information architecture: Unified IAM view

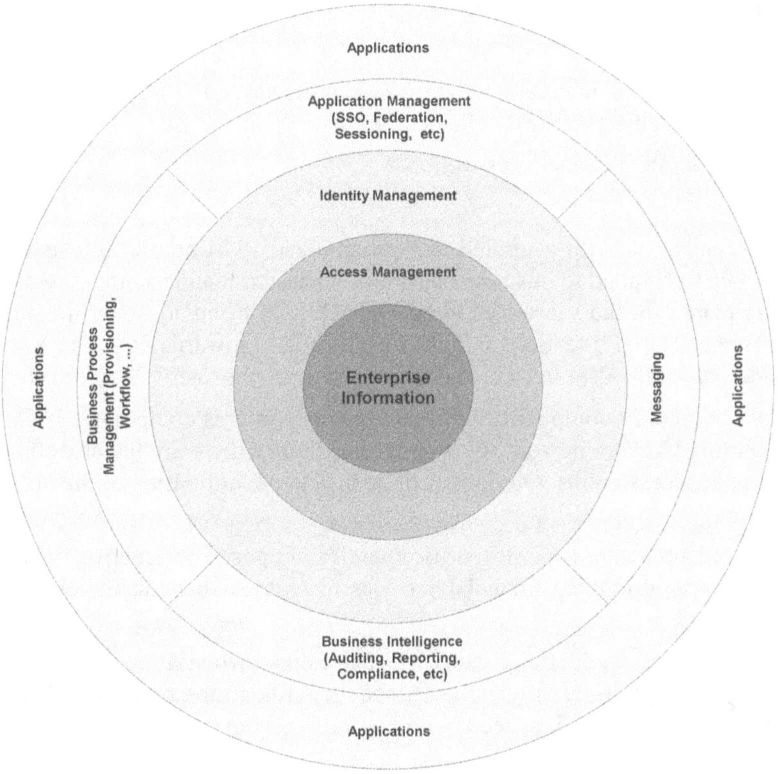

Risks and Opportunities

The risks to running the financial institution's business on an IAM-disjointed enterprise architecture are obvious: access vulnerabilities through the many doors, malicious access by internal and external agents, using stale accounts, identity theft, and so forth

The benefits of a rationalized IAM enterprise are equally compelling:

- One of the key benefits of a rationalized and unified IAM strategy is the reduced total cost of ownership (TCO) that it enables. According to a 2002 PriceWaterhouseCoopers/Meta Group (PWC/Meta Group) survey (The Value of Identity Management, 2002), an average user spends 16 minutes a day signing into applications. For a firm with of 20,000 employees, this translates to about three full-time employees (FTEs), casting single sign on (SSO), a basic component of a unified IAM strategy, into sharp focus.
- Still using the Meta Group survey data, we estimate that it costs a typical 20,000 employee financial institution about 108,000 hours per year to manage its users. If a streamlined IAM strategy only results in 50% improvement, the benefit is equivalent to 27 FTEs.

- Lastly, in the PWC/Meta Group survey, automating password resets was estimated to save the firm almost $1 million annually.

Thus, even before completely rationalizing the identity stack, the TCO savings from implementing SSO and self service are quite compelling.

There are other strategic benefits as well:

- An organization with a unified and rationalized IAM architecture is nimbler and thus able to respond to business opportunities faster, than its competitors. One of the factors cited for the successful merger of HP with Compaq was a streamlined IAM infrastructure (HP Identity Journey, 2005). A drive towards SOA, for example, also would enable the firm to take advantage of a wider business services ecosystem.
- While regulatory compliance has many facets, systems compliance is easier within the unified IAM framework we propose here, since there are fewer well defined and auditable access points. Obviously, there is also the mitigation of financial and legal liability.
- Enhanced proactive security enforcement (as opposed to reactive finger pointing) drives forward-looking financial services firms to higher planes, high above their competitors.
- New employee productivity gains will be realized when most, if not all, employee resources are centrally provisioned, since the on-boarding process will be faster, and workers will have all they need to be productive from day one.
- Lastly, properly aligned IAM strategy and execution puts the firm on a level playing field with industry leaders—technology leadership and market leadership are often synonymous in the financial services sector—and positions it for organic growth as well as through external mergers and acquisitions.

Conclusion

We have made the case for implementing a unified IAM strategy. We have argued that unifying IAM within an enterprise involves a lot more than technology solutions. Rather, it takes a symphony of high level corporate leadership, planning, and, lastly, carefully chosen technology solutions. We recommend best-of-breed technology solutions that result from a heavy dose of data, system, and process rationalization.

As the financial industry continues to tread the bleeding edge of technology adoption, we expect a wider adoption and maturity of IAM solutions and a drive towards SOAs to ward off the ever-present competition and comply with an increasing roster of regulatory mandates.

References

Kelley, D. (2006). Become compliant without breaking the bank. *Information Security, 28.*

The HP identity management journey: Identifying an effective solution. (2005).

The value of identity management. (2002). Retrieved from http://www.pwcglobal.com

Williams, C. (2005). Leveraging regulatory compliance investments to add business value [White Paper]. *BMC Software, Inc Business Practices* (p. 2).

Chapter X

Identity and Access Management

Nick Pullman, Citigroup, USA

Kevin Streff, Dakota State University, USA

Abstract

This chapter discusses the role of identity and access management in the financial services industry. Identity and access management is a very broad concept that has far reaching rewards or consequences within an organization. This chapter provides a survey of the topics within identity and access management so that managers and security administrators of financial institutions can gain an understanding of the issues and possible solutions.

Overview

This chapter will discuss the core concepts of identity and access management and how they can fit into an enterprise solution. We will discuss the individual concepts within identity and access management and how they work together. Finally, we will discuss the future trends of identity and access management. After reading this chapter, you should:

- Understand the identity lifecycle and how to manage it
- Understand the proliferation of identities and how to consolidate them
- Understand the core concepts behind identity and access management, including single sign on, access control, authentication, authorization, identity integration, provisioning, and password management
- Understand how to implement an identity and access management solution from both a technical and managerial perspective

According to the CSI/FBI Computer Crime and Security Survey, unauthorized access overtook denial-of-service attacks as the second most costly contributor to computer crime losses (*CSI/FBI Computer Crime and Security Survey,* 2005). According to the survey, the per-respondent loss from unauthorized access rose from $51,545 in 2004 to $303,234 in 2005 (*CSI/FBI Computer Crime and Security Survey,* 2005). Reviewing these numbers, it is easy to justify having a strong identity and access management infrastructure.

Identity and access management is made up of people, process, and technology. It is not a specific technology, or even a specific set of technologies, but is instead procedures and technologies that are implemented to manage the identities within an organization, along with their entitlements. The goals of implementing identity and access management solutions are to:

- **Limit entitlement creep:** An entitlement is an access to a resource that is given to a particular user account, and entitlement creep is the phenomenon where, after time, unnecessary, unwanted, and extraneous entitlements gather on a user account.
- **Ensure least privilege for all user accounts:** Least privilege is a concept in security where users are granted only the entitlements that they need to perform their job functions.
- **Improve the security posture of the organization:** A well managed identity and access management infrastructure significantly helps to mitigate risks from internal and external abuse.
- **Reduce the cost of managing user accounts and entitlements:** Manual administration of user accounts and entitlements is very costly. Implementing an identity and access management solution often can reduce the costs associated with security administration.
- **Maintain compliance with regulatory bodies:** The Gramm-Leach-Bliley Act (GLBA) and Sarbanes Oxley (SOX) both require financial organizations to have strict controls

that protect customer and corporate information, as well as audit ability that the controls are in fact working.

There are many different aspects and solutions to identity and access management, and each provides different results and accomplishes different goals. For example, later in the chapter we discuss single sign on and how it can reduce the cost of security administration and improve the usability of the applications, but it is debatable whether security is improved by implementing a single sign on solution. In addition, there are many different approaches and solutions that can be implemented in order to reach the goals above and none are necessarily right or wrong; each has its own advantages and disadvantages.

Identity and access management is really separated into two main categories: identity management and access management. Identity management is concerned with how to store, maintain, and share identities, and, more granularly, user accounts and entitlements within the organization. The major concepts of identity management are:

- Identity management lifecycle
- Managing the proliferation of user identities
- Identity stores
- Identity consolidation, aggregation, and synchronization
- Provisioning and deprovisioning
- Workflow
- Password management

Access management is closely tied with identity management and is concerned with grouping, granting, removing, and auditing the entitlements that user accounts have on the organization's systems and/or applications. The major concepts of access management are:

- Authentication
- Authorization
- Role-based access control
- Single sign on
- System and user auditing

Together identity management and access management allow a financial organization to mitigate risk while reducing the cost of security administration. However, identity and access management implementations are by no means simple and require a healthy timeframe and budget to complete. Some solutions to identity and access management problems can be fixed with process fixes and do not really require a large technical change. Other implementations, such as automated provisioning, can require a fairly extensive technical implementation with a strong knowledge of many systems and technologies. In order to decide which solutions to implement and how to implement them, each organization first needs to determine its business needs and resources available.

Managing the Identity

All organizations are filled with identities, such as employees, contractors, and business partners, which this chapter will refer to as global identities. According to www.dictionary.com (2006) an identity is:

1. A separate or distinct existence
2. A distinguishing character of a person
3. Information that distinguishes a person

The *2005 E-Crime Watch Survey*, which was conducted by CSO Magazine in cooperation with the U.S. Secret Service and CERT Coordination Center, found that 54% of unauthorized access to systems was by insiders of the company. Insiders were also responsible for 64% of the theft of intellectual property and 56% caused exposure to private or sensitive information (*2005 E-Crime Watch Survey*, 2005). Employees, contractors, and business partners all need to be able to utilize systems and applications in order to be able to perform their duties; however, security exposures can occur if their user accounts are not properly managed.

The Identity Management Lifecycle

The identity management lifecycle is the process by which user accounts, unique user identifiers for a system or application, are managed. In order to mitigate the risk of system compromise, user accounts must be appropriately managed through the different stages of its existence. Due to the risk of exposure from compromised user accounts, managing the identities within an organization is a key area not only for security, but also for compliance with GLBA and SOX.

An identity within an organization follows a distinct pattern of creation, utilization, maintenance, and then eventually removal. Throughout this entire process, an audit function logs and reconciles the usage and modifications of the user (Smith, 2005). This process can be thought of as the identity management lifecycle. Identity has multiple meanings depending on the scope with which you look at it. An identity at an organizational level is usually an employee or consultant. At a more granular level, the individual user accounts on the organization's systems or applications can be seen as an extension of the identity or even an identity itself. In a looser sense, an identity could even be functional accounts that do not belong to an individual, such as the root account in Linux, for example, but still need to be managed. Identity management is concerned with identity from all of these perspectives. The organization must manage both its global identities and the user accounts that belong to those identities.

Figure 1. Identity management lifecycle

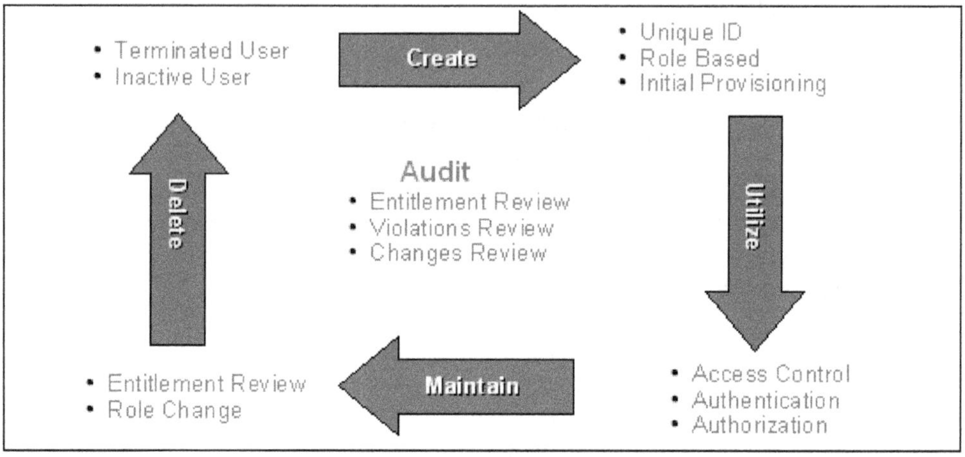

The identity management lifecycle is made up of five phases: creation, utilization, maintenance, deletion, and audit. The first phase is the creation of the user account. For example, if a new employee, Sam Pel, is hired as a *loan analyst 1* at Example Bank, Sam's information initially may be populated into the human resources (HR) system and then Sam's user accounts created on the e-mail and core banking systems. When the user accounts are initially created, they are created with only the entitlements that are needed for Sam to perform his job function. The user accounts must be unique to the individual and user accounts should not be shared, except for functional accounts, like root, which require other controls. The unique user account is required so that responsibility can be placed on an individual to be liable for the usage of their account. For example, if Sam approves a loan, he cannot deny that he approved it because only he has access to his user account. In addition, all financial institutions are required to protect consumer data under the safeguards rule of the GLBA, and this cannot be accomplished without strict control over user accounts (*The Gramm-Leach-Bliley Act*, 2006).

The second phase of the identity management lifecycle is the utilization of the accounts. Using the same example from above, once Sam is ready to begin working, he must first authenticate to the system with his user account and password or other form of authentication. The authentication process is confirming the identity of the user, because only the owner of the user account should know the password. After authentication, Sam must be authorized to perform some function, such as approving a loan application. The authorization process trusts the identity of the user account because it passed through authentication. So now it checks to ensure that the user is authorized for a function. A simple way to think about the difference between authentication and authorization is that authentication is the process that gets you into the system, and authorization verifies that you are allowed to access resources or perform functions on that system.

The third phase of the lifecycle is maintenance of the user accounts. Changes occur in every organization and the user accounts need to reflect those changes. For instance, if Example Bank creates a new type of loan, the entire loan process from marketing to statements will probably be maintained on the banking system, and Sam's user account needs to be able to access the new functions. Many situations arise where the entitlements on a user account need to be added, changed, or deleted, including employees changing roles, new information technology (IT) systems, new system or business resources, and obsolete systems or resources

The fourth phase of the identity management lifecycle is account deletion. Sam might accept a senior loan officer's position at a competing bank, so his user accounts need to be deleted from the systems. Sam's accounts will need to be deleted from both the e-mail system and core banking system that he was originally given access to. In addition to deleting Sam's user accounts, his HR record should be updated to reflect that he is a terminated employee. Sam's HR record probably will not be deleted because a record of his employment probably needs to be maintained, but it should reflect the fact that he is terminated. One way to ensure that terminated employees' user accounts are deleted in a timely manner is to automate the deletion of the accounts based upon HR data; typically HR data is the most current.

Phase five of the identity management lifecycle is the audit phase. The auditing of user accounts occurs throughout all of the identity lifecycle phases. When a user account is first created, some form of documentation should be saved in order to prove why the user account was created. In addition, after the user account is created, the entitlements granted for that user should be reviewed to ensure that they are correct. When the user account is being used, the system logs should be reviewed for violations on the system as well as access to critical resources. When an account is deleted, the system should be audited to ensure that no entitlements that are connected to the user account remain on the system. Finally, audit has a function of its own that is tied to the maintenance of the user accounts. Periodically throughout the year, the entitlements for all user accounts should be reviewed; this is typically called an entitlement review or access review. The entitlement review function is very important because it is a "catch all" for the systems that limits entitlement creep by finding extraneous or obsolete entitlements. Overall, the stronger the auditing process, the easier it will be to stay in compliance with current and future regulations.

The identity lifecycle is a key piece of an information security program that needs to be managed and controlled. In order to comply with GLBA and SOX, a financial institution must maintain stringent control over the resources that are accessed and who accesses them. The only way to accomplish compliance with these regulations is to have a well managed identity lifecycle with explicit policies and procedures surrounding how and when to create a user account, how to control access to resources, how to audit and maintain the account, and finally how and when to delete the account. If the lifecycle is well managed, the financial institution can easily show the regulatory bodies the user accounts that have access to a resource and detail why they have that access.

Managing the Proliferation of User Identities

One of the root causes for the need of an integrated identity management tool is the proliferation of user accounts. Most organizations have many disparate systems that are used for different purposes. For example, there could be an e-mail server, a Web server, a core banking system, a router, a firewall, and so forth. Each of these systems probably has its own identity store; an identity store is any type of store where user information is kept (*Microsoft Identity and Access Management Series: Fundamental Concepts*, 2005). In addition to the

Figure 2. Disparate identity stores

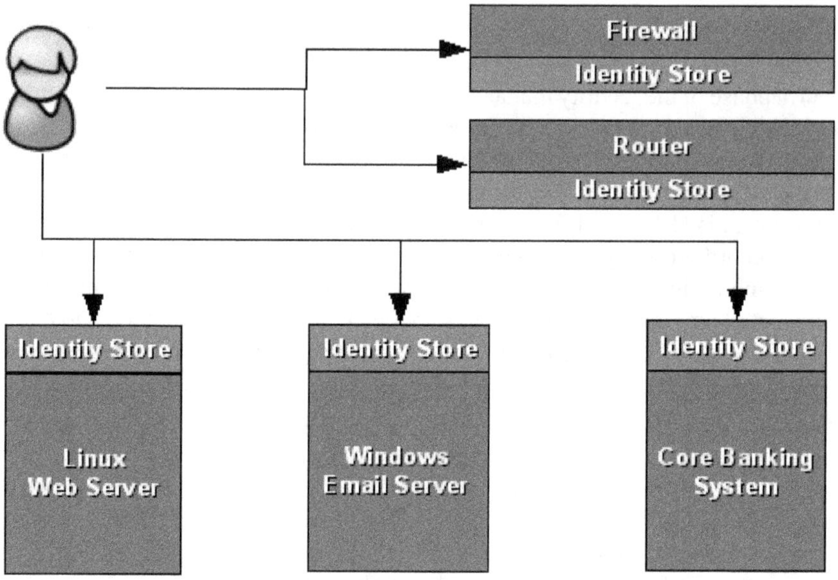

different identity stores for the systems, the systems could have completely different types of identity stores. For example, the e-mail server might run on Windows 2000 and the web server might run on Linux.

So, not only are the identities in the systems maintained separate from any other system, but also the type and format of information might be completely different between the systems. For example, one system might have a single field with which to store the name of the user and a different system might have three fields to store the name: first name, last name, and middle initial.

User accounts are often found in many separate applications or systems for a number of reasons:

1. Organizations tend to build processes separate from each other.
2. Mergers and acquisitions are another cause of account proliferation. When organizations acquire or merge with other companies, often times the IT systems and processes are never fully integrated. As the business grows, the IT environment becomes more complex and integration becomes an even more daunting task to complete (*Microsoft Identity and Access Management Series: Fundamental Concepts*, 2005).
3. Most organizations purchase off-the-shelf (OTS) software applications, or even create homegrown applications, which typically maintain their own proprietary identity stores.

The proliferation of user accounts is one of the root problems that make managing the security for an organization difficult. In a large organization it is not uncommon to find more than

100 identity stores (*Microsoft Identity and Access Management Series: Identity Aggregation and Synchronization*, 2005). With a large number of applications and systems, it becomes difficult to determine which employee actually owns a user account on a specific system. To make matters worse, in a larger organization, there could be 10 "John Smiths," so maintaining user accounts based on name alone is not practical. This means that some other unique identifier should be created and given to every employee for tracking purposes.

Managing and constraining the proliferation of user identities is possible and very beneficial to the organization. The benefits of effectively managing the proliferation of user identities are:

- Decreased security administration costs
- Decreased complexity in the IT environment
- Increased auditing ability of the users and systems
- Improved scalability

The greatest benefit that is gained from managing the proliferation of user identities is that all of the phases in the identity management lifecycle become easier and less complex. This, in turn, makes it easier to manage the overall security of the systems. Having a minimal number of identity stores also has the advantage of being scalable. Since it is easier to create and maintain users, more users can be managed by a fewer number of security administrators.

There are a few tasks that need to be completed in order to successfully reduce and manage the proliferation of user identities.

1. All of the different types and instances of identity stores should be catalogued. This is so the organization knows exactly how many and what type of identity stores there are throughout the organization.
2. The organization must choose a "golden source" of information. The golden source is the directory that resolves any data conflicts. This typically is the HR directory; HR typically has the most up-to date information about the employees.
3. The organization needs to ensure that all of its employees, contractors, and consultants have some form of unique identifier and that the unique identifier is the user account itself, or is attached to the user accounts on all of the systems. This allows a mapping to occur between the golden data source from HR to all of the user accounts that are located on the individual systems.

Now that the base for managing the identities has been laid, the process of consolidating and synchronizing the identity stores can begin. The important thing to remember when consolidating and synchronizing identity stores, and even with the tasks mentioned above, is to spend the resources and time for completing the project on the systems or applications that will give the most results. Do not spend time right away on systems that are small or low risk, spend the resources on the high-risk systems that will benefit the most.

Identity Stores

Identity stores are really the foundation for identity management. Every system or application that requires authentication has some form of an identity store, either internally or through an interface to another identity store. Identity stores can be databases, directories such as lightweight directory access protocol (LDAP), or even flat files (*Microsoft Identity and Access Management Series: Identity Aggregation and Synchronization*, 2005). For example, Oracle user information is maintained in tables within the Oracle database. In Windows and Linux, user information can be stored locally, which uses local files, or the identity information can be stored remotely, using a directory, such as Active Directory or LDAP. The identity stores allow the users to be authenticated when they log into the system. For example, if the core banking system for Example Bank is run from a Unix server, which uses local security, every time Sam attempts to log into the system, he will be prompted to provide his user name and password. The username and password that Sam enters is then compared against the local identity store of the system in order to authenticate him.

The use of identity stores is really the crux behind identity and access management. It is both the solution and the problem. Identity stores and systems, in general, tend to be built as information silos, meaning that they do not interface easily with other systems. With Example Bank, for instance, the core banking system most likely maintains its own identity store separate from the e-mail system. This, of course, means that Sam could have completely different user names and passwords on the respective systems. A small number of separate identity stores in itself do not cause a problem. Sam probably hardly even notices that he has to maintain two separate usernames and passwords. However, expand the number of identity stores to 50, and Sam now has quite a job trying to maintain all of his user names and passwords.

Many disparate identity stores, in addition to causing problems with users having to maintain multiple user names and passwords, causes a number of other unwanted issues within the organization. First, having many identity stores makes security administration rather difficult and time consuming by increasing the complexity of the environment. Administration also becomes difficult for creating and deleting the users from the system. If Sam leaves the company, it is difficult to know all the systems he had an account on. Auditing of the user accounts also becomes much more difficult to accomplish which makes compliance with regulations more costly and resource intensive.

The cost, security, and compliance of an organization depend on having a solid identity management architecture with which to create, maintain, delete, and audit user accounts. A solid architecture for user management reduces costs and improves the security of the system. In order to achieve a better process for identity management, identity stores can be consolidated and synchronized to reduce complexities and provide a single point to begin auditing. Next, we will discuss how to simplify the infrastructure of the organization by removing unnecessary identity stores and consolidating them or by synchronizing identity stores to ensure that they contain identical data. This is accomplished using directories and directory services to create an identity management infrastructure.

Directory and Directory Services

A *directory* is a data store that stores a set of objects with their attributes in a hierarchical fashion. A directory has a few benefits over databases or flat files for storing identity information. First, although many changes do occur in an organization, such as promotions or address changes, identity information tends to be more static in nature. Most individuals' information does not change that often, i.e. position, address, name, and so forth, so the transactional nature of databases is not needed for its high throughput. The directory gives up some speed to databases but provides a much more flexible interface for finding, updating, and reporting on users and user attributes. Also, the hierarchical nature of directories makes more logical sense to an organization than a database, which is not hierarchical. Overall, a directory is more intuitive and flexible for searching information which lends itself well for an identity store. In addition, directories also provide a common interface with which

Figure 3. OpenLDAP overview

OpenLDAP

OpenLDAP is a robust and flexible open source implementation of LDAP. OpenLDAP includes a server, a replication server, and a number of utilities, tools, and samples which can be used to create a complete LDAP infrastructure. The server implementation in OpenLDAP is called "slapd" and the replication server is called "slurpd".

SLAPD is the stand alone LDAP server daemon which when running, listens for and responds to LDAP requests. SLAPD supports strong authentication, access control, a choice of database backends, multiple instances of databases, and replication, among other features. It is highly flexible with a single configuration file which allows an administrator to change almost any setting. SLAPD also provides LDAP support for both IPv4 and Ipv6.

SLURPD is a server replication daemon that provides replication services to SLAPD. SLAPD does not have to worry about whether replication directories are online and available because SLURPD handles all of the retry and replication functions. The interface between SLAPD and SLURPD is also very simple and uses a text file to communicate and log its transactions.

OpenLDAP is a popular LDAP implementation that is very flexible, robust, and free. It is well supported and has a very strong developer base so anybody considering implementing a directory should include OpenLDAP for consideration.

For more information about OpenLDAP go to their website at:
http://www.openldap.org/

For in-depth details about LDAP in general see the Request for Comment (RFC) at:
http://www.faqs.org/rfcs/rfc2251.html

to update and maintain its information (*Microsoft Identity and Access Management Series: Identity Aggregation and Synchronization*, 2005). Directories have become the standard for storing identity information and its robust and flexible interfaces allow it to be used effectively for consolidating and synchronizing identity information.

Directory services are the functions that are exposed in order to allow the contents of the directory to be searched and updated. LDAP is an example of a directory service. LDAP is the protocol for modifying the objects and attributes within the directory, although the term LDAP also is often referred to as the directory itself. In addition to searching and modifying, many directories provide additional security services, such as strong authentication, authorization, and auditing (*Introduction to OpenLDAP Directory Services,* 2006). Throughout the rest of the chapter, the term directory will constitute both the directory and the directory services that it implements.

Identity Consolidation

Multiple identity stores create a complex environment that is difficult and costly to administer, so the first step after identifying all of the identity stores is to eliminate redundant or unnecessary identity stores. For example, if an organization has five applications or systems, each using its own proprietary identity store, then each department has to be administered separately. The complexity and cost of administration of this example infrastructure can be greatly reduced if the separate applications can be reworked to use either an existing identity store or a new consolidated identity store. This makes it much easier to administer

Figure 4. Consolidated identity store

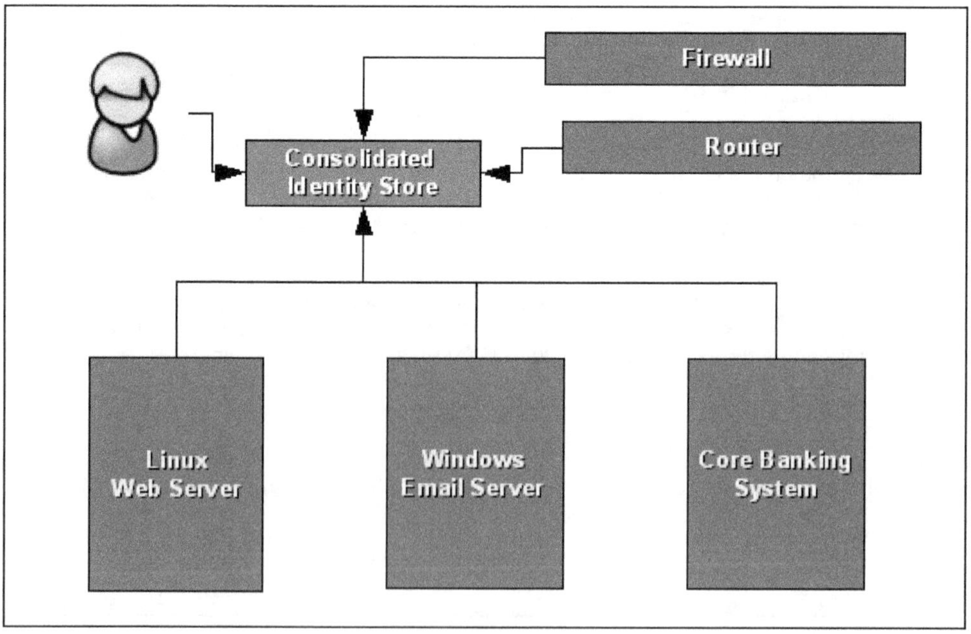

the systems from a security perspective and also much easier to audit the users from a management perspective (see Figure 4 as compared to Figure 2).

The process of consolidating identity stores has a couple of advantages. First, consolidating the identity stores will reduce the complexity of the environment. In the example above, if five different identity stores can be consolidated into one, then the environment is much easier to manage. Secondly, reducing the number of identity stores will also make the next step easier, which is identity synchronization (*Microsoft Identity and Access Management Series: Fundamental Concepts,* 2005).

Identity consolidation can be a very time intensive and costly process so it is important to take on the projects that will provide the most benefits. If there are systems with overlapping identities or systems that are highly critical and need extensive auditing, you should review those systems for possible consolidation first. There could also be legacy systems or applications that have a lot of custom code written that make it too difficult or costly to standardize to a directory, so they can be eliminated from this process. Unfortunately there is no cut and dry method of determining which systems or applications best fit the mold for being consolidated, but here are some criteria to consider:

- Are some of the identities overlapping with other identity stores?
- Is the current security administration of the system or application very manual or time consuming?
- Is the system critical or high risk?
- Does the system or application need high audit ability?
- Will the cost of migration be prohibitively high?

Identity consolidation simplifies the environment making the process of implementing other identity and access management concepts, such as provisioning, much easier and less costly. In the end, it is possible that there will still be multiple separate identity stores, which is perfectly acceptable, but it is none the less important to go through the process of elimination. In practice, many of the identity stores will prove impractical to migrate to a standard directory. Even if the organization decides not to consolidate any of the identity stores, the organization will benefit from the process of reviewing the systems and applications, because the process itself will help the organization to better understand its environment and how to better manage it.

Identity Aggregation and Synchronization

After the organization has gone through the process of consolidating and simplifying its identity stores, the next step is to aggregate them in order to provide a single logical view of the organization's users and resources. In addition to aggregating the identities into one logical view, it is also beneficial to the organization to synchronize the separate identity stores so that the data is consistent. The benefit of this is that new systems and applications can utilize the current identity infrastructure, rather than creating their own proprietary identity silos. There are a couple of different technologies that are used to accomplish identity aggregation and synchronization, and they both use a form of a directory. The two ways to accomplish the identity aggregation and synchronization are with a metadirectory or a virtual directory.

A *metadirectory* is a directory that is made up of data that is replicated from multiple separate identity stores (Sullivan, 2004). The metadirectory provides a centralized view of the organization's users, and since the data is copied from the individual directories, no special protocols or operations are needed to query and update information. The downside to metadirectories is that there is a period between synchronization operations that the metadirectory may be out of synch with the individual identity stores. In addition, the individual identity stores must have a way to determine what changes have been made to their own directory, since the last synchronization because the overhead of replicating the entire directory would be prohibitive.

A *virtual directory* is similar in concept to a metadirectory, except a virtual directory provides only a logical view of the data from the individual identity stores; it does not provide the synchronization of a metadirectory (Sullivan, 2004). The advantage of a virtual directory is that the data is not copied to a separate directory which needs to be maintained, but the downside is that the performance can be an issue with large directories, and special operations are needed to be able to "join" the multiple directories together in order to get the logical view.

The process of consolidating, synchronizing, and aggregating identities provides the organization with a holistic view of its users. It integrates many separate identities into one, meaning that the organization knows that the Sam Pel on the e-mail system is the same Sam Pel on

Figure 5. Metadirectory

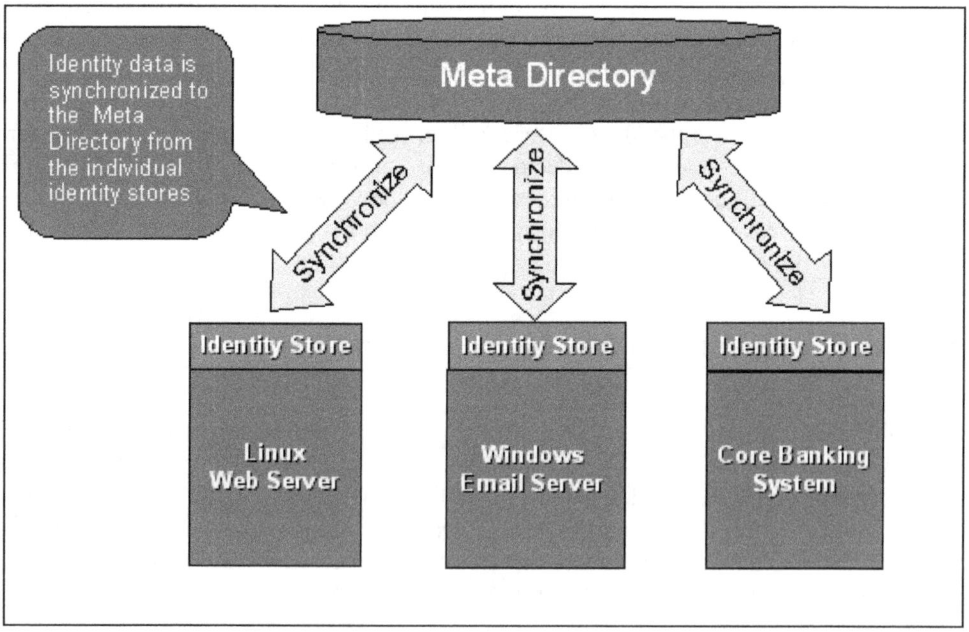

Figure 6. Virtual directory

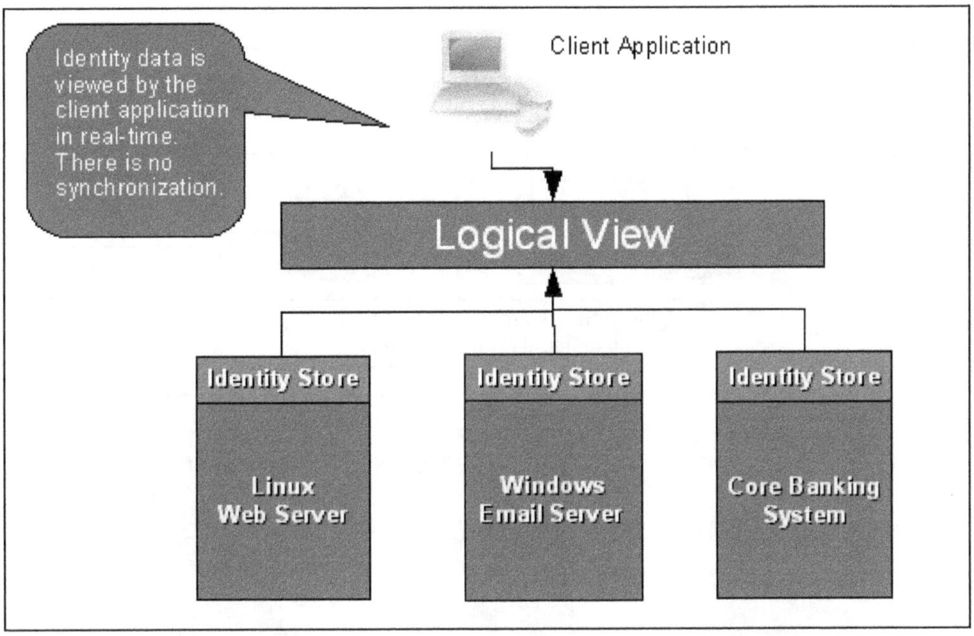

Figure 7. Security has to delete Sam's user accounts from all of the systems individually.

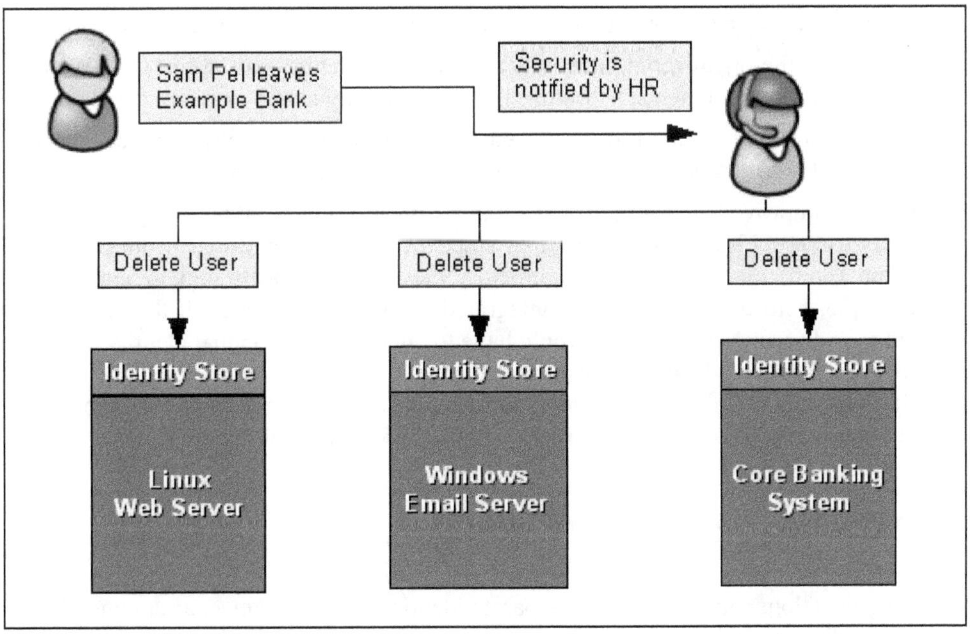

Figure 8. With an automated identity solution using a metadirectory, Sam's user accounts are automatically deleted when he leaves the bank.

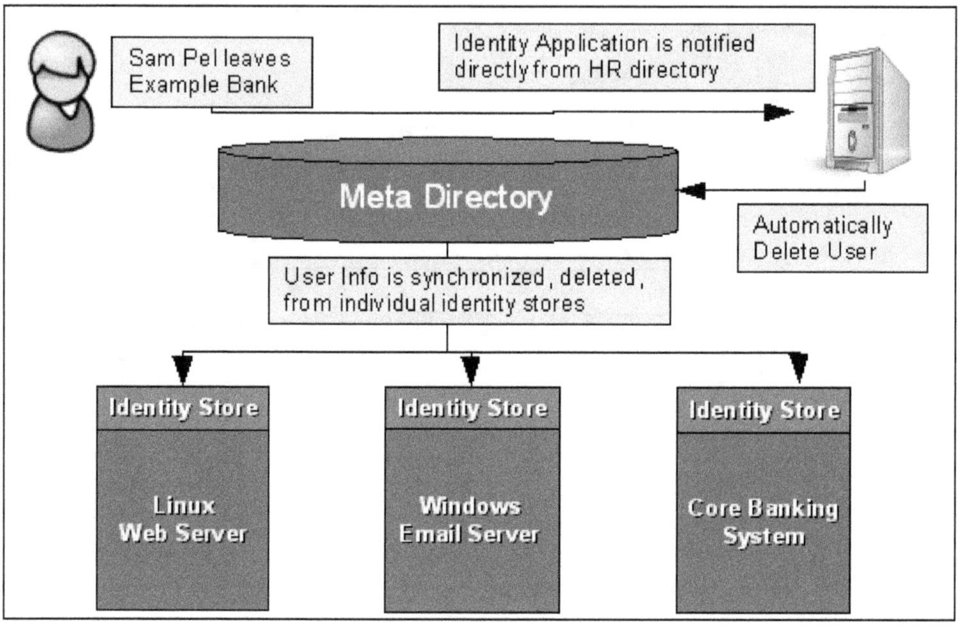

the core banking system. For example, before Sam's identities where integrated, if he left Example Bank, the updates would need to be made to a number of different systems.

However, after the organization integrates the multiple identity stores, the change will go through HR, which will then synchronize the other identity stores to match the change.

Not only are the administration costs reduced, but the systems are much more secure because there is no delay for Sam's user accounts being deleted from the systems.

In addition to improved security and reduced administration costs, having a single identity for each user also provides improved auditing. Since the organization can get a unified view of all of Sam's entitlements from the metadirectory, they can more easily audit his entitlements. For example, before the organization integrated all of their identities, if the organization wanted to audit Sam's access, they would have to query each individual identity store. The organization then would have to consolidate that data into a report to review. After integrating all its identities, if the organization had to audit Sam's user accounts, they would only have to query the metadirectory in order to get the information about Sam.

Provisioning and Deprovisioning

Most organizations today have many separate identity stores, and even after consolidation probably still have a number of identity stores that were either never linked to a metadirectory or a metadirectory was not used. *Provisioning*, which is the process of creating or modifying user accounts and attributes, is very time consuming and costly when done manually

(Sullivan, 2004). It is not uncommon for new user provisioning to take days or even weeks in a large organization. This is costly not only from an administrative perspective to create the user accounts on multiple systems, but is also costly because of reduced productivity for the users, who are waiting to be provisioned. By creating an automated provisioning solution, the organization will benefit by having:

- Decreased administration cost
- Reduced error rate
- Increased scalability
- Increased security

Provisioning also must be able to follow business rules either automatically through automatic attribute generation or through workflow.

Provisioning generally is set up to react to certain events that occur from an authoritative data source, the golden source. The golden source is usually the HR database but could be other databases or directories. There might also not be a single authoritative database but multiple databases or directories that have authoritative attributes that trigger provisioning to occur. Some typical triggers that occur are new users being added into the HR database or current users changing their job function or role within the organization.

Figure 9. When Sam is hired, he is added into the HR directory, which feeds into the provisioning application and based on predefined rules, automatically creates his user accounts.

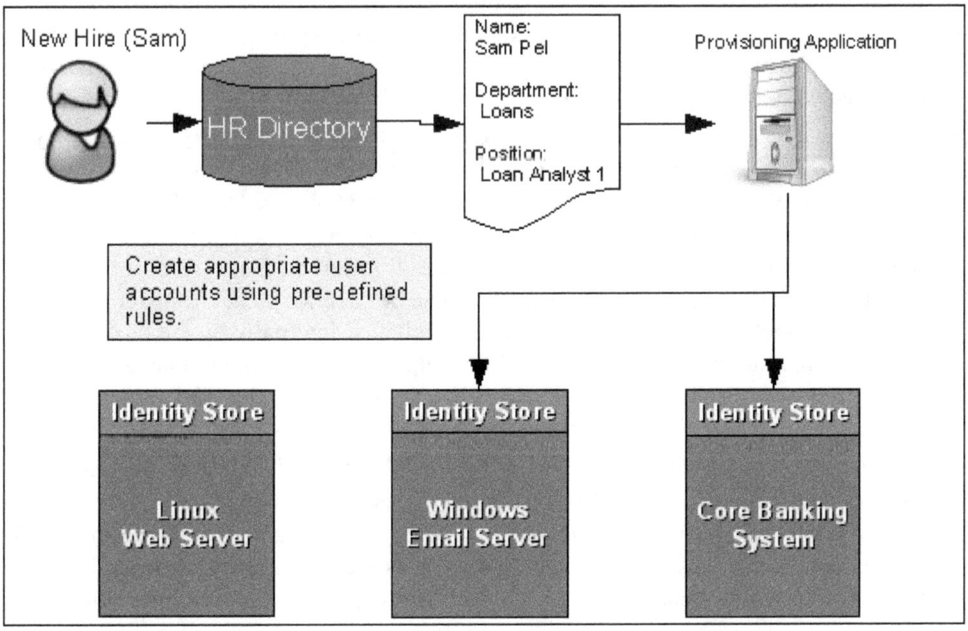

Figure 10. Sam's account being updated through self-service provisioning

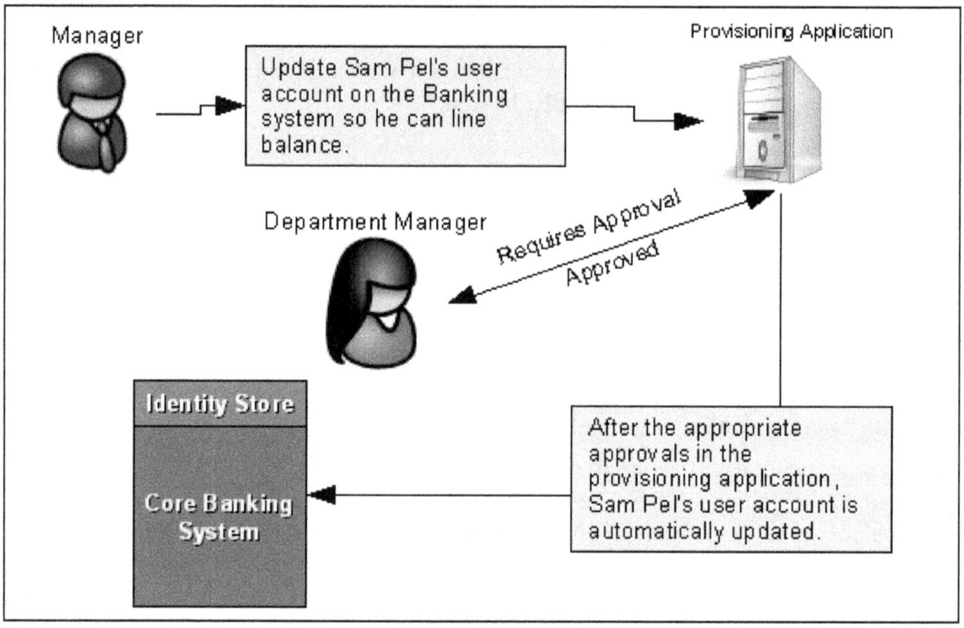

There are typically two methods of provisioning that will occur in an organization, HR provisioning and self-service provisioning. *HR provisioning* occurs when changes are made to the HR database, which triggers the provisioning to occur (*Microsoft Identity and Access Management Series: Provisioning and Workflow,* 2005). HR provisioning is typically what you would see for the creation and maintenance of the organization's employees. For example, when Sam was first hired at Example Bank, he would be inserted into the HR database, and the provisioning system, upon seeing the new account, would provision him to the correct systems based on his department and job title.

Self-service provisioning, on the other hand, is typically initiated internally by an employee, most likely a manager (*Microsoft Identity and Access Management Series: Provisioning and Workflow,* 2005). Self-service provisioning is typically used for consultants, business partners, test accounts, and functional accounts that are not maintained within the HR database. For example, if the IT department for Example Bank needs to automate an FTP file transfer, they will need a functional account to be created that can be used for the file transfer. The provisioning of the functional account will have to be initiated internally by the IT department. Self-service provisioning also can be used for employees who might change roles often, such as employees who line balance. Using self-service provisioning, the manager can log into the provisioning application and kick off a process to revoke certain entitlements and grant other entitlements, based on which role the employee is currently working.

Deprovisioning is the opposite of provisioning, in that accounts and entitlements are removed from the system (*Microsoft Identity and Access Management Series: Provisioning and Workflow,* 2005). This occurs when a user leaves the organization or when his or her role changes, in which case the old entitlements are deprovisioned and new entitlements are provisioned. For example, if Sam leaves Example Bank, then the HR database will be updated, and the provisioning system will be triggered, either deleting or disabling all of his user accounts. When a user account needs to be deprovisioned, it can be deleted completely from the system, or it can be disabled initially and deleted after a given time frame. The reason that an organization might not want to completely delete the user account right away is in case of incorrect data within the HR database. If the HR database accidentally flagged some users as terminated employees, the provisioning system would delete the user accounts, which could be costly and time consuming to recreate. If the user accounts were just disabled though, it would be much easier to merely enable them.

Workflow

A *workflow* is an integral part of any provisioning system that allows business and security rules to be followed. Often times with a provisioning application, this is accomplished using a combination of e-mail and a Web GUI that is linked to the provisioning application. The actual creation of the workflow process depends on the provisioning application but ranges from requiring custom coding to drag-and-drop interfaces. The workflow is really one of the more powerful pieces of a provisioning solution, because it allows the business and security rules to be enforced.

After Sam is hired and added into the HR database, the provisioning system is triggered, which starts a workflow. The first step of the workflow sends an e-mail to the manager of the loan department. The manager of the loan department clicks the link in the e-mail, which

Figure 11. Workflow example showing the basic steps for Sam Pel getting hired

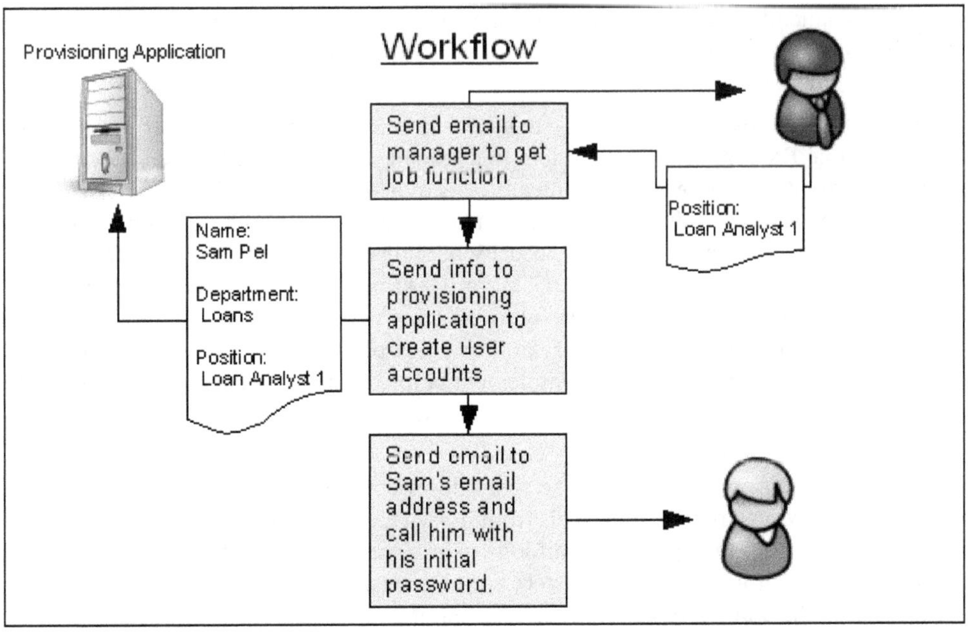

directs him to the provisioning Web GUI, the manager selects Sam's job function as "loan officer 1" and the provisioning tool then proceeds to create Sam's user accounts on all of the systems where he requires access.

Setting up the initial workflows can be time consuming and frustrating, because organizations often do not have clearly defined business and security rules. Defining appropriate rules and implementing them into workflows is one of the most important prerequisites for having a successful provisioning solution. Workflows ensure that appropriate approvals are obtained, that business rules are followed, and that the process is auditable. If inappropriate workflows are implemented, the organization is exposing itself and its customers to a lot of risk. For example, if an approval process is not included with a workflow to create and delete accounts, a manager could create an account, use it him/herself, and then delete the account, possibly without anyone knowing. This obviously is not desirable, so in order to create the initial workflows, the current business processes that are used should first be carefully reviewed to remove any redundant or incomplete activities, reviewed to ensure that the process is secure, has the correct approval process, and then created as a workflow. Next, any gaps where there are not clearly defined business rules will need to be researched, appropriate rules created, and finally implemented as workflows.

The workflow also provides audit ability, because when any change is made through the workflow, an audit log is kept with the information of the change. This makes it very simple to audit exactly why a change was made to the system. For example, if the auditors want to know why Sam has access to a certain function, the organization can review the workflow logs to show who approved the access and why it was approved.

The provisioning application, even with HR provisioning, uses a form of workflow that details what actions need to happen and in what order. For example even with a fully automated new user provisioning activity, a workflow is probably needed for attribute generation. For example, given Sam Pel as the first and last name attributes, the provisioning application could automatically create the e-mail account of pels@example.com. Even if an explicit workflow is not created to do this, a form of workflow internal to the application is being used to accomplish this.

Workflows are also useful for legacy systems and applications that are not easily provisioned to. If Example Bank has a legacy system that cannot be provisioned to, but the organization wants to take advantage of the integrated provisioning, workflow can be used. After Sam is created automatically in all of the standard directories when he is hired, a workflow could be used to send an e-mail to a security administrator to have the user account created manually on the legacy system. Using a workflow this way provides the benefit of having consistent business processes followed even when the legacy application cannot be provisioned to automatically. This same process of using the workflow with manual administration also can be helpful to implement before using automated provisioning. This allows any bugs in the business rules to be worked out, before the provisioning is allowed to be run automatically.

Overall, the workflow is the backbone that allows consistent automated provisioning to occur. Workflows can require approvals from the correct individuals or departments before making changes and then provide audit logs to archive the changes that were made. Most importantly, workflows enforce consistent policies, business rules, and business processes, which reduce the amount of effort required to audit and comply with regulations.

Password Management

Password management is an area of security that is both highly critical and costly. Weak, easily guessed passwords are a common cause of security breaches. In addition the costs incurred due to password resets can be high if an appropriate password management solution is not implemented. Password management is a balance between security and usability; the longer and more complex that the passwords are, the harder the passwords are to crack, but they are also harder for users to remember. The issue of password management begins with the *password policy,* which is the organization's official stance on password management.

A password policy needs to be created, or at least approved, at an executive level and should be implemented and enforced across the entire organization. This ensures that consistent rules are put into place across the organization, rather than individual departments creating their own password rules. The password policy should address:

- Password complexity
- Password frequency
- Password history
- User account disablement

The password policy should include careful thought about the balance between usability and security. If password complexity rules are too aggressive, then not only could it cost the organization money in password resets, but also compromise security if users are writing their passwords down because they can't remember them.

The actual implementation of the password management policy is specific to the organization, but there are some best practices that work for most organizations. The password management policy also can tailor its rules differently based on criticality. For example, high-risk systems have a more complex password rules and more frequent password changes than low-risk systems. Password complexity typically can be set up as:

- A minimum of six to eight characters
- Both alpha and numeric characters
- A minimum of one upper-case letter
- A minimum of one special character (Swanson & Guttman, 1996)

Password complexity should be managed not only from a technical system perspective, but also from a user awareness perspective. Users should be reminded from time to time how important strong passwords are to the security of the organization. Strong passwords should be one of the topics included within the organization's overall security education and training program. Password frequency, which is how often a user must change his/her password, can typically be set somewhere between 30 and 90 days. This reduces the amount of time that an attacker has to brute force attack any passwords. The password history is an archived

Figure 12. Table overview of password policy

Complexity	Change frequency	History	Disablement
Alpha and numeric	30-90 days	6-12	Disable after 3-12 attempts
Minimum 6 characters	Can be risk based	Depends on change frequency	Mitigates password guessing attacks
Upper and lower case			
Minimum 1 special character			

view of the recent passwords that a user has used. This setting is typically set between six and 12, depending on how frequently the user is asked to changer his/her password. The password history is maintained to ensure that users do not just input the same password, or iterate between a few passwords, when they are forced to change their password. Finally, user account disablement is when accounts are automatically disabled after a set number of incorrect log in attempts occur, typically between three and 12.

Another aspect of password management is self-service. Self-service password management solutions aim not to improve security, but to reduce the costs associated with password management; approximately 45% of help-desk calls are password resets (*Microsoft Identity and Access Management Series: Password Management,* 2005). Password self-service applications are solutions that allow users to manage their passwords across many different systems. Here is one way self-service password management software works.

1. The user first registers for self-service by answering a series of questions that the user will probably not forget, such as place of birth, favorite color, or favorite food.
2. If the user forgets his/her password or is locked out of the system, he/she can go to the self-service Web site, input his/her user account, and then answer the series of questions in order to self-authenticate.
3. Once inside of the self-service application, the user can proceed to update his/her password or enable his/her account.

Self-service solutions can help a company maintain a balance between security and usability. The organization can enforce stricter rules without some of the fallout of increased help-desk calls because the users can service themselves.

Access Management

Access management is the focus of identity and access management, which follows a three-step process:

- Authentication
- Authorization
- Audit (Campbell, Calvert, & Boswell, 2003)

Access management is concerned with ensuring that users have the correct entitlements to perform their job duties. This means all of the entitlements that they need and no more. Access management is a key control area of the FFIEC Information Security Booklet that the financial regulator bodies use for audit, so it is important that the organization spend a significant amount of time and resources ensuring that it is well managed. The FFIEC IT booklets can be found at http://www.ffiec.gov/ffiecinfobase/html_pages/it_01.html.

Authentication

Authentication is the process of verifying the identity of a user who is trying to gain access to a system. For example, when Sam wants access to his e-mail, he is prompted for his user name and password, which is the proof that he is, in fact, Sam Pel and not an imposter because only he should know his password. The problem with this form of authentication is that it is typically not very secure. Users will often select weak passwords, such as dictionary words, which can be easily broken. To make authentication even stronger, organizations may need to implement a form of strong or multifactor authentication. Users can authenticate with three different types of authenticating factors:

- Something you know, such as a password
- Something you have, such as a token
- Something you are, such as a fingerprint

Multifactor authentication uses two or more of these factors in order to authenticate the user (Hansche, Berti, & Hare, 2004). ATM cards are a good example of multifactor authentication because in order for the user to withdraw money from the ATM, they must first have the card and secondly must know the personal identification number (PIN). This authentication uses two of the three factors, something you know and something you have.

There are many different ways to authenticate a user, and some of the more common ways are user name/password, Kerberos, digital certificates, security tokens, and biometrics. The user name/password authentication method is the most common. Most systems, applications, and Web sites implement some form of a user name and password. Very simply, the process relies on the fact that only the correct user should know the correct password, which verifies the identity of the user. This has a number of drawbacks that were already mentioned, but it still is the most typical form of authentication. If implemented with appropriate password rules and user training, it can be a secure form of authentication.

Kerberos is a network authentication system that authenticates a user directly to a service on the network, such as a print server or file server (Campbell et al., 2003). Kerberos works by having the user authenticate to the Kerberos server, which if successful, encrypts and sends session keys back to the user. The user then sends his/her session key along with the service session key to the network service, and if the two session keys match and the time stamp is valid, then the user is authenticated to the resource. Kerberos is not a perfect solution though, because it still typically relies on the user maintaining a strong password, although other authentication methods can be used.

Digital certificates are another way that systems can authenticate users and are typically used on the Internet. Many transactions over the Internet, including electronic commerce, use public key cryptography for the transactions. This ensures that the data that they pass is confidential and unaltered. The problem is that it can be difficult to authenticate the correct key to the correct user; that is, it is simple for a malicious user to post a key that appears to be somebody else's key. This is where digital certificates come into play, because third parties issue the digital certificates and as long as the certificate issuing authority can be trusted, then the identity of the user can be trusted (Campbell et al., 2003). Digital certificates have become an important part of authentication for public key cryptography, and as long as there is a trusted issuing authority, such as Verisign, then the authentication of the user to his/her public key is valid.

Security tokens are small hardware authentication devices that are assigned to individual users. There are many different implementations of security tokens, but a typical scenario might be that the user first inputs his/her PIN or password, which authenticates him/her to the device, and then the device provides a one-time password, which will be used to authenticate to the system. The system itself has to be synchronized with the token.There are two basic ways in which this is accomplished: counter based and time based. Counter-based synchronization basically combines the PIN or password with a counter that is synchronized between the token and system. Time-based synchronization is the same concept, except that instead of a counter, the synchronization occurs with an internal clock that is synchronized between the token and the system (Campbell et al., 2003).

Finally, **biometrics** is another form of authentication that takes something the user is in order to authenticate them. Fingerprints are a typical example of a biometric. There are two major types of biometrics: physical and behavioral. Physical biometric authentication can look at things like fingerprint patterns, hand geometry, and iris patterns (Campbell et al., 2003). Behavioral biometric authentication looks at behavioral characteristics of a person, such as how he/she writes his/her name or how the person says a specific phrase, that is, signature or voice verification. Biometric authentication has yet to be widely implemented, in some part, due to its perceived intrusive manner. People tend to associate fingerprinting with criminal activity since that is how our law enforcement manages criminals. Other people see it as an invasion of their privacy, if they are made to give a biometric. Biometrics, however, have the potential to solve some of the issues surrounding identity and access management, including a single consolidated identity and strong authentication.

Authorization

Authorization is the function or operation of the system or application that verifies whether a user is granted access to a specific resource on a system; resources include things like files, programs, devices, and so forth. When Sam wants to review the account information for one of his clients, the loan software that Example Bank uses checks Sam's identity, his user name, against an access list that verifies whether Sam is, in fact, entitled to perform the lookup operation. Most operating systems store access lists directly on the resources of the system, and when a user attempts to access the resource, the system checks to ensure that the user is on the access list and is authorized to read, execute, or modify the resource. One issue that occurs on the system is obsolete entitlements. For example, if Sam has read access to a file and his user account gets deleted from the system, his user account is not necessarily taken off of the access list for that file. In order to completely clean the system after Sam's user account is deleted, the system will need to be reviewed to determine whether Sam is on the access list or not. Unfortunately there is not a single standard for authorizations with each operating system and application developing its own process for performing authorizations. There is an XML standard from OASIS called extensible access control markup language (XACML), which defines a schema and name space, in order to create an authorization environment for securing objects that are defined in XML. Currently, however, most systems and applications do not follow a standard interface for authorizing resources or operations.

Role Based Access Control (RBAC)

One way to manage the entitlements granted to users is by using *role based access control* (RBAC). A role in an organization is typically a job function, such as Sam's role, loan analyst 1, with Example Bank. RBAC is a way of assigning entitlements to users, based on their job function or role within the company. RBAC also typically assigns entitlements to users by connecting them to groups that contain all of the entitlements rather than assigning entitlements directly to the user accounts. This makes assigning a new user to a role relatively easy. Using role based access control has a number of benefits.

- RBAC simplifies security administration by grouping entitlements logically based on roles within the organization
- RBAC reduces the amount of time and effort needed by managers to set up new employees
- RBAC improves auditing by allowing the individuals with the most information to review the entitlements

Most systems and many applications support group access control. With group access control, the entitlements needed for a specific function or role on that system are combined into a single group. Users that need access to that function or role are then granted access to it by being connected to that group. For example, the core banking system at Example Bank might have two different groups, "loanoff1" and "loanoff2." When Sam is initially hired, his manager does not need to determine exactly which resources Sam needs, they just need to tell the security administrators that Sam's role is a "loan analyst 1." The security administrators will then connect Sam's user account to the "loanoff1" group, and Sam will have all of the entitlements that he needs in order to fulfill his job duties. On a well administered system, there should be few entitlements granted to individual user accounts; all of the entitlements should be granted to groups. RBAC simplifies user administration greatly

Figure 13. Illustration of the difference between group-based administration and the more generic role-based access control

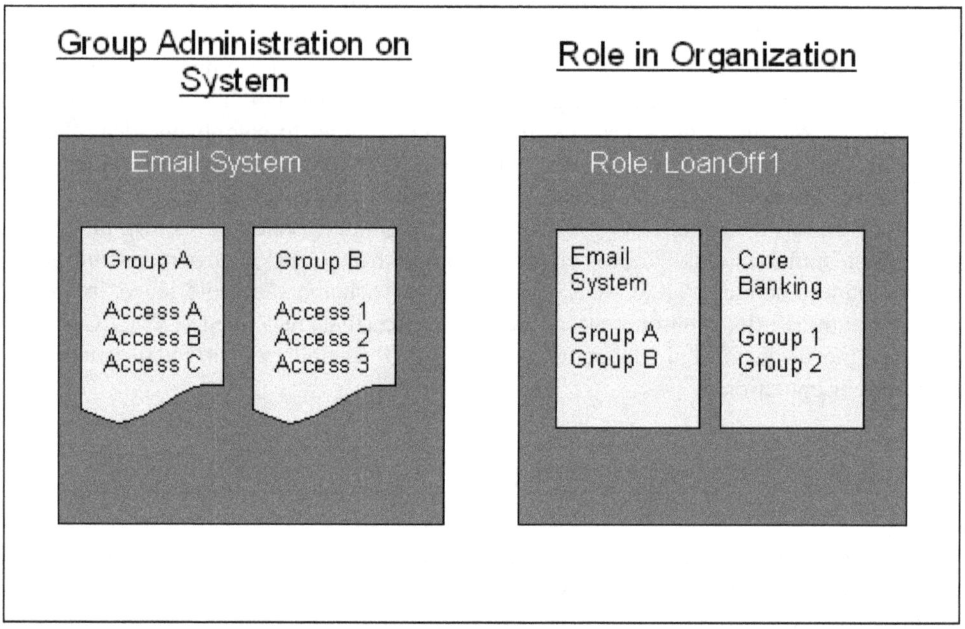

because the security administrators only have to ensure that the users are connected to the correct groups. The entitlements granted to the group, of course, have to be managed, but it is much easier to manage the entitlements with the group and then attach the users to the group, than it is to manage all of the entitlements for multiple user accounts.

Role-based access control provides much simpler administration of users and accuracy of auditing the users. When managers audit the user accounts, it is very simple for them to ensure that the user accounts are connected to the correct group or groups based on their role. The managers really do not even have to worry about the entitlements in the group, because those entitlements should be reviewed by a senior manager and a technical person to ensure that the groups have the correct entitlements. RBAC has become the standard way for many organizations to manage access control. Managing users individually is quite common in smaller organization but is just not feasible for larger organizations. The logical way that RBAC organizes access by job function reduces administration costs, while improving the security posture of the organization.

Single Sign On (SSO)

Single sign on (SSO) is one of the more beneficial processes that can be implemented after synchronizing and consolidating identity stores. SSO is a technology that allows users to sign into a single central system and access all of the resources to which he/she is authorized (Pholman, 2003). SSO, which is sometimes considered the "holy grail" of identity and access management, has become somewhat of an outdated term because it is typically not possible to implement. Sometimes SSO is referred to as reduced sign on, in order to clarify the purpose of the technology; I will use SSO to generically mean a reduced or limited sign on environment.

Web SSO is one common form. There are a number of ways to accomplish SSO, but typically the user is initially authenticated and then given options for resources that they can access. When the user attempts to access one of the resources, the SSO application will provide the log in credentials to the resource in the background without any user intervention (Pholman, 2003).

SSO provides a number of benefits to the organization, including reduced help-desk calls and improved employee productivity, but security improvement is really a matter of debate. Users have to remember fewer passwords, so they are less likely to write them down and more likely to use stronger passwords. However having a single password to authenticate into multiple resources means that if it is compromised, then the attacker has access to all of the applications to which the user had access. This decision is, of course, up to the individual organization, but typically most applications can be a part of the SSO environment as long as they are following best practices for security by performing ethical hacks.

SSO can provide significant productivity and usability benefits. In addition, the cost of security administration for those applications is also usually significantly reduced. The downside to SSO is that if the user account is compromised, then the attacker could have access to many applications or systems.

Auditing

All financial institutions need to maintain a strict audit function in order to comply with GLBA and SOX for publicly traded companies. There are three main types of audits within identity and access management that need to be completed to ensure that the security of the system or application is not vulnerable:

- Violation audits ensure that the systems are not being attacked or abused
- Security change audits ensure that only authorized security changes are being made to the system
- Entitlement review audits ensure that "least privilege" access is being enforced

Typically the audit logs that need to be reviewed are obtained directly from the system or application. Often times, a single audit log file is kept that contains the different types of logs, including system/application logs, violations, and security changes. Entitlement data, however, usually needs to be obtained separately. The audit logs of systems are often hard to read and understand; so either custom programs need to be written to parse out and format the important information or there are numerous off-the-shelf programs for many systems and major applications that can assist with the reporting.

Violation logs typically contain data about log in or access violations on the system. This data contains information, such as the user account, date/time, and resource or action that caused the user to get a violation. This data can then be tracked to ensure that there is not any attempted system abuse and also to spot security errors in the system or application. One approach to violation auditing is to set a threshold for the number of violations that a user may get before he/she is contacted. For example, if the violation threshold is 10 and Sam gets 15 violations, then the security administrator who reviews the violations reports will contact Sam to ensure that his account has not been compromised and that he is not abusing the system.

Security changes log review is also an important control to implement because it ensures that unauthorized and/or accidental security changes are not occuring. A clear separation of duties must be maintained between the security administrators and the system administrators. However, on many distributed systems such as Windows and Unix, system administrators need administrative authority in order to be able to perform their job function; unfortunately, this also typically gives them the right to make security changes. In order to control and manage this process, the security logs should be periodically reviewed. In addition, even changes made by authorized security administrators should not be done without an audit trail—a reason for the change to have been made. This could be a request from a business manager, an application failure, or any other reason that a security change needs to be made, as long as the request is documented and stored. When Example Bank gets audited, the auditors might request to see why Sam's user account was created. Having a well-managed and auditable security change process, the security administrator for Example Bank provides the auditor with the paper work that shows that Sam was hired, and the paper work had all of the proper approvals and signatures required to create the user account.

Finally auditing entitlements is the last major type of report that should be reviewed. Typically the user entitlements are reviewed by the user's manager, and if group security is used, then the entitlements granted to groups are reviewed by a senior manager in conjunction with a technical employee. The best person to determine whether a user needs access to a resource is his/her manager. The danger is, of course, that the manager probably puts trust in his/her employees and might not request to have entitlements removed because he/she "trusts" the employees to do the right thing. This is one reason why group security is effective because the managers only need to verify that the users are attached to the correct groups. Senior and technical members review the group entitlements; the review is done in an effective and efficient manner by the individuals who have the most knowledge about exactly what security is needed.

Auditing is an important function to implement correctly, not only because it improves the security posture of the organization, but when the FDIC or other auditing body audits the organization, they are expecting to see a strong security change process that is auditable. They want to see that the changes that are being made to the system or application are necessary and have the proper approvals. The FDIC wants to know that you have solid control over what is happening in your environment so a comprehensive and effective audit function is required.

Tying It All Together

All organizations perform identity and access operations; even when not consciously managing the process, the operations still occur. User accounts are being created, modified, and deleted, and the systems are being used to perform business functions. The problem is that often times managing identity and access is difficult due to complex ever-changing environments, hence it is managed ineffectively or inefficiently. There is not a single way to implement identity and access management products or processes, and each organization will need to decide what best fits their business need.

Design and Implementation Considerations

There are many things to consider when determining what changes, if any, need to be made to an organization's identity and access management process:

- Are the current policies and procedures adequately securing the systems?
- Are the current processes efficient and cost effective?
- Are the current processes scalable and flexible?
- Are new systems and applications easy to integrate into the current infrastructure?
- Are the current processes overbearing for the users?
- Are some systems more difficult to administer than others?

The questions above are all issues to consider when thinking about implementing or deploying an identity or access management process or solution. In order for the organization to determine what it needs, it must first understand its current environment. The security administration team should review its current systems and applications to document which ones seem to be the most difficult to administer, have the largest volume of administration request, and are the most critical. The organization then can look at what solutions can be implemented in order to improve the security of the system or reduce the cost of administering the system.

For example, if an organization has a high employee turnover rate and are consistently hiring new employees to fill those vacancies, then implementing role-based access control along with an automated provisioning/deprovisioning solution would be a logical first step. If the organization has a lot of employees who use Web-based applications and help-desk call volumes are high because of the number of password reset requests, then the organization should implement Web SSO along with a password self-service solution.

Even though every organization is different there are a couple of identity and access management processes that every financial organization would benefit from implementing:

1. A unique identifier for each employee or contractor who will access the system. This could be the user account name itself or something that is attached to the account, such as an employee identification number.
2. Role-based access control and group administration. The cost and complexity of security administration can be greatly reduced if logical roles are defined within the organization and entitlements are assembled into groups to which user accounts are then connected.
3. A workflow process. Whether using an application or simply paper based, defining the business requirements and the approvals needed for a security change to take place will increase the security of the system and will improve the audit ability of the organization.
4. A strong audit function. Reviewing system audit logs and maintaining an entitlement review process are essential to ensure that the organization is secure and assists with compliance of regulatory responsibilities.

Implementing these four processes will not only improve security, but also ease the implementation of other identity and access management processes that the organization might implement in the future.

Implementation of an identity or access process also can be very tricky. Many vendor solutions attempt to abstract the complexity of the underlying systems with a user-friendly and intuitive interface. However, these solutions can require connectors or agents that need to be installed and running, especially on legacy systems. This requires a lot of factors to all go right in order for the solution to work and can be complex and difficult to implement; it may be beneficial to contract outside help to assist in the design and implementation. It is also very important to ensure that all of the right parties are involved with the implementation. The businesses or departments that are being affected by the implementation should be involved with the implementation. It is often that departments have little nuances and quirks with their systems or applications of which the IT engineers and/or security administrators are not aware. At a minimum, the security group, engineering group, and business should be involved with the implementation. This ensures that there is buy in from all of the involved parties and will ensure a smoother implementation.

Finally, when implementing an identity and access solution, it is important to take it one step at a time. If the organization attempts to implement automated provisioning, SSO, and so forth for the entire company, it will become too complex and eventually overwhelm the project. Even if implementing only one solution, for example, automated provisioning, it is better to implement it slowly one department or group at a time, rather than designing the entire implementation and then just turning it on. By implementing the solution incrementally, it reduces the likelihood of a major error or failure as well as allows the engineers, security administrators, and business managers to work out any unexpected bugs or issues that need to be fixed. This also allows the cost of implementing a solution to be spread out over a number of months or even a couple of years rather than incurred all at once.

How It Really Works

In order to further illustrate how all of these concepts tie together and can be implemented, this section will illustrate a hypothetical example of how an organization might decide to implement or change the identity and access management process. This example is not meant to be a process that everybody should follow. It is just a way to illustrate how an identity and access management solution could be reviewed and implemented to help solve some of the issues that a financial organization might encounter.

Growing Federal Bank is a medium size national bank with approximately 500 employees. It has been performing very well and has acquired four smaller banks over the past three years. In addition to its acquisitions, Growing Federal Bank has been growing aggressively internally by expanding its branch banks and offering insurance and credit cards. Although they have been able to integrate the business functions fairly well, the FDIC had concerns with regards to their multiple, sometimes conflicting, processes for adding/deleting new users and making security changes. The FDIC found numerous user accounts from employees who had left the bank months ago; there was a lack of a strong security change process; and the bank's policy for reviewing audit logs daily was not being followed.

Upper management met with the chief security officer (CSO) and the chief information officer (CIO) of the bank in order to determine how to solve the problems. They decided as a group that the cost of a complete identity and access management vendor product was not warranted at this time and the in-house expertise of the IT and security groups were sufficient to resolve the problem internally. They decided that due to time and money constraints, they would break the project into two phases. The first phase would shore up the concerns from the FDIC, and the second phase would improve the infrastructure of the identity and access management process to reduce the cost of administration and make the process more flexible for future acquisitions. Phase 2 will be completed at a later time.

Phase 1 will include improving the process for deprovisioning of users, defining a workflow process for security changes, and updating the process for log reconciliation. In order to deprovision user accounts, a script was written that compares a backup of the HR database to the current HR database, and when a user is terminated an e-mail is automatically sent to the security administrators' group to delete the user accounts. In order to ensure a strong security change process, all security changes can occur only after an e-mail approval from both the manager of the user and the manager of the department; this is the workflow. In order to ensure that the system logs are being reviewed on a consistent basis, two security reviewers must review the logs, print the first page of the log, sign it, and file it in a file cabinet. On a weekly basis, the security manager will sign off on a checklist that the logs for the week have been reviewed. This process also is documented in the bank's procedures, including disciplinary action, if the logs are not reviewed.

As this example shows, there are many ways to implement identity and/or access management processes. Growing Federal Bank was able to shore up their security issues with mostly process changes, but the processes still are not efficient or cost effective. Manual administration is expensive and error prone; however, in this situation, the bank probably made the right decision for the implementation. It allowed the bank to shore up deficiencies rather quickly without expensive migration and upgrade costs. Now that the bank is at least meeting the minimum standard for security, the employees can focus on how to create a truly robust and flexible identity and access solution by consolidating the identity stores, implementing RBAC, and creating processes and applications to further automate the security administration and reduce costs.

The Future of Identity and Access Management

Identity and access management has really taken focus in recent years and will undoubtedly be a significant part of any security program for the foreseeable future, so it is important to see what products and solutions may be coming. There are a number of trends occurring within identity and access management, and most have significance for the vendors that are creating the products. Many of the "best of breed" applications are being bought up by larger companies, which are offering complete solutions, including a metadirectory, provisioning software, and SSO software. These solutions are aimed at taking care of the entire identity lifecycle from creation to deletion. As this market matures, fewer stand-alone products will be used in the market, and more complete solutions will be implemented.

Another common theme in identity and access management is the use of directories to store identity information as well as other information. Most contemporary operating systems have the ability to store its identity information in an LDAP or LDAP-like directory. In addition, even legacy mainframe operating systems have begun allowing identity information to be stored and shared using directories. The more systems and applications that can be configured to work with directories, the simpler identity integration and management will become.

References

2005 E-crime watch survey. (2005). CERT Coordination Center. Retrieved July 14, from http://www.cert.org/archive/pdf/ecrimesummary05.pdf

Campbell, P., Calvert, B., & Boswell, S. (2003). *Security+ guide to network security fundamentals*. Thomson Course Technology.

CSI/FBI computer crime and security survey. (2005). Computer Security Institute. Retrieved July 14, from http://www.usdoj.gov/criminal/cybercrime/FBI2005.pdf

Hansche, S., Berti, J., & Hare, C. (2004). *Official (ISC)² guide to the CISSP exam.* New York: Auerbach Publications.

Introduction to OpenLDAP directory services. (2006). Retrieved July 14, from http://www.openldap.org/doc/admin23/intro.html

Microsoft identity and access management series: Fundamental concepts. (2005). Microsoft Corporation. Retrieved July 14, from http://www.microsoft.com/technet/security/topics/identitymanagement/idmanage/default.mspx?mfr=true

Microsoft identity and access management series: Identity aggregation and synchronization. (2005). Microsoft Corporation. Retrieved July 14, from http://www.microsoft.com/technet/security/topics/identitymanagement/idmanage/default.mspx?mfr=true

Microsoft identity and access management series: Password management. (2005). Microsoft Corporation. Retrieved July 14, from http://www.microsoft.com/technet/security/topics/identitymanagement/idmanage/default.mspx?mfr=true

Microsoft identity and access management series: Provisioning and workflow. (2005). Microsoft Corporation. Retrieved July 14, from http://www.microsoft.com/technet/security/topics/identitymanagement/idmanage/default.mspx?mfr=true

Pohlman, M. (2003). *LDAP metadirectory provisioning methodology*. Writer's Showcase. IUniverse.

Smith, M. (2005). *Identity life cycle management*. Identiprise. Retrieved July 14, from http://www.mser.gov.bc.ca/privacyaccess/Conferences/Feb2005/ConfPresentations/Michael_Smith.pdf

Sullivan, D. (2004). *The definitive guide to security management* (Ch. 5). Realtime Publishers. Retrieved July 14, from http://www3.ca.com/eBook/Chapters.aspx?ID=65316

Swanson, M., & Guttman, B. (1996). *Generally accepted principles and practices for securing information technology systems*. National Institute of Standards and Technology. Retrieved July 14, from http://csrc.nist.gov/publications/nistpubs/800-14/800-14.pdf

The Gramm-Leach-Bliley Act: The safeguards rule (2006). Federal Trade Commission. Retrieved July 14, 2006, from http://www.ftc.gov/privacy/privacyinitiatives/safeguards.html

Section III

Trends and Issues

Chapter XI

Swallowing the Bait, Hook, Line, and Sinker: Phishing, Pharming, and Now Rat-ing!

Sylvia Kierkegaard,
International Association of Information Technology Lawyers (IAITL), Denmark

Abstract

Phishing and pharming continue to plague many financial institutions and electronic commerce (e-commerce) Web sites. Security experts estimate annual losses from computer crime total in the billions, but there are actually no valid statistics on the losses from this type of crime because no one knows how many cases go unreported. The array of online threats grows all the time. Sophisticated criminals have now turned to a new activity of rat-ing, where criminals can watch everything the user is typing from other parts of the globe. The new activity is difficult to detect. Companies have devised various methods of protecting their customers. They are beginning to integrate more security, well beyond simple user names and passwords, as the need for more stringent methods becomes imperative. Various countries also have passed identity fraud legislation, but the global nature of cybercrime raises difficult legislative problems of jurisdiction as criminals use off-shore servers and Internet sites to avoid domestic regulations.

Introduction

Computers and the Internet offer great benefits, but it is also increasingly being used as a tool for organized crime. With the greater deployment of new technology, cyber crime has become a growing worldwide problem and has become a major concern for the global community.

Security experts estimate annual losses from computer crime total in the billions, but there are actually no valid statistics on the losses from this type of crime because no one knows how many cases go unreported. Complaints about online fraud nearly doubled from 2003 to 2004, according to a December 2004 report by the FBI and the National White Collar Crime Center (Tynan, 2005). Research firm Gartner estimates that nearly 10 million Americans were hit by online fraudsters in 2005—largely due to a wave of phishing e-mails seeking to steal users' identities (Tynan, 2005). Thieves make online purchases with stolen credit cards and go online to create new accounts by associating a slightly altered name with stolen cards. Organized crime is always on the look out for ways to make money and has seen the opportunities that cyberspace affords them as billions of dollars are being lost in the economy through high-tech crime. U.S. Treasury computer crime advisor Valerie McIver claimed that cybercrime has become even more lucrative than selling drugs (Leyden, 2005).

The 10th annual *Computer Crime and Security Survey*, put together by the Computer Security Institute (CSI) in conjunction with information security experts at the FBI, shows financial losses resulting from security breaches down for the fourth successive year. The survey was based on the survey of 700 computer security practitioners in various U.S. corporations, universities, and government agencies (Gordon, Loeb, Lucyshyn, & Richardson, 2005). Highlights of the *2005 Computer Crime and Security Survey* include:

- Losses from theft of proprietary information doubled in 2005.
- The total dollar amount of financial losses resulting from security breaches is decreasing, with an average loss of $204,000 per respondent, which is down 61% from last year's average loss of $526,000.
- Virus attacks continue as the source of the greatest financial losses, accounting for 32% of the overall losses reported.
- Unauthorized access showed a dramatic increase and replaced denial of service as the second most significant contributor to computer crime losses, accounting for 24% of overall reported losses, showing a significant increase in average dollar loss.
- Theft of proprietary information also showed a significant increase in average loss per respondent; more than double that of last year.
- The percentage of organizations reporting computer intrusions to law enforcement has continued its multiyear decline. The key reason cited for not reporting intrusions to law enforcement is the concern for negative publicity.
- There was an unexpected resurgence of several larger banks appearing higher in the statistics.

Unissys Corporation recently polled more than 8,000 people worldwide on identity fraud and bank security. The survey found that a clear majority (66%) of people worldwide worry about the fraudulent use of their bank and credit card accounts. The study found that the United States leads in identity fraud instances (17% of U.S. consumers claimed they had been victims), followed by the United Kingdom (11%), Brazil (9%), Mexico (8%), France (8%), Australia (7%), Germany (3%), and Hong Kong (1%). One-third of the respondents (consumers) reported receiving information from their banks about "phishing" (Eazel, 2005). However, these findings do not mean that these attacks are originating from inside these countries. The global nature of the Internet allows attackers anywhere in the world to compromise machines in any location.

The array of online threats grows all the time. In 2004, online frauds cost British banks £12 million, an increase on previous losses (Bowcott, 2005). Denial of service (DoS) attacks, where firms' e-mail systems are bombarded into overload, is frequently accompanied by blackmail demands for cash to switch off the onslaught. "Bot programs enable computers across the net to be hijacked by remote users who in effect turn them into 'zombie' machines which can be used in DoS attacks. Keylogging programs can infiltrate computers and record the keystrokes customers make in typing in credit card numbers or passwords" (Bowcott, 2005).

The Anti-Phishing Working Group Web site, which contains the Internet's most comprehensive archive of e-mail fraud and phishing activity, reports in October 2005 that financial services continued to be the most targeted industry sector growing to 86.9% of the attacks. The United States remains on the top of the list of countries hosting phishing Web sites with 28.75%, with the top 10 breakdown as follows: China, 9.96%; Republic of Korea, 8.4%; Germany, 3.7%; Australia, 3.65%; Canada, 3.6%; Japan, 3%; United Kingdom, 2.75%; Italy, 2.22%; and India, 2.1%. There has been a reported increase in the number of variants of keyloggers, but a large decrease of password stealing malicious code URLs. The Web sites, which were classified during October as hosting malicious code in the form of either a phishing-based keylogger or a Trojan downloader, which downloads a keylogger, were geographically located in the United States (29.9%) and Spain grew to 17.08%. The rest of the breakdown was as follows: Brazil, 16.89%; Spain, 17.08%; Russia, 5.82%; China, 4.66%; Germany, 4.07%; Korea, 2.33%; United Kingdom, 2.13%; Canada, 2.13%; and Sweden 1.55% (*APWG October 2005 Phishing Report*, 2005).

Identity fraud has been called the fastest growing crime in the United States, affecting millions of Americans at a cost of billions of dollars a year. The Federal Trade Commission estimates that 10 million Americans become victims of identity fraud every year, while Gartner places the annual number at around 7 million (McCullagh, 2004).

The impact of online fraud attacks can be high on the business enterprises—lost productivity, customer confusion and complaints, damage to the brand, and legal implications. Online fraud undermines consumer confidence and for individual users, the financial losses can be excessive. The latter are more exposed to computer crime than ever, due to the growth in identity theft schemes. Identity-theft scams have been termed phishing, pharming, and rat-ing, depending on the seriousness of the method in concealing its identity. In fact, many experts believe that the criminals behind these attacks are based mainly in Russia or Eastern Europe because law enforcement there is relatively slack, and there is a plentiful supply of skilled but poorly paid programmers. Apart from a highly educated workforce and programming skills, Russia also has a hacking-phishing friendly environment. Specialized training schools in that country reportedly teach hacking and phishing skills. Experts say Russian hackers perform sophisticated attacks with limited computer power and inexpensive software. Eighty-two percent of respondents participating in a worldwide poll conducted on a hacker-oriented Web site indicated that Russia had the world's best computer hackers (Walker, 2004). Enforcement authorities are handicapped in arresting criminals due to lack of cooperation from Eastern European authorities.

In order to deter online fraud and to improve international cooperation in fighting cybercrime, several countries recently passed national laws and entered into an international convention. Currently, the possibilities for legal solutions as well as interpretations of the new legislation differ within the separate countries and their courts. This paper will analyze some of the national and international initiatives that have been enacted by the European Union and the United States, more specifically in the area of curtailing phishing activities and its variants.

Literature Review

The subject of phishing has been discussed extensively in the literature. Most of the books written offer technical advices and describe the different techniques used by cybercriminals. Recently published books include *Security and Usability* edited by Garfinkel and Cranor (2005). The authors define phishing, and offers techniques and advice on fighting phishing at the user-interface level. *Phishing Exposed* (James & Stewart, 2005) provides a high-tech view from both sides of the phishing playing field and exposes the technical and financial techniques used by international clandestine phishing gangs to steal billions of dollars every year. The book is filled with technically detailed forensic examinations of real phishing scams and the exploitations they deploy against their victims. *Phishing: Cutting the Identity Theft Line* (Lininger & Vines, 2005) provides sample text and code that phishers have regularly used and contains an excellent description of phishing and its nefarious variants, like pharming. Various toolbars are described in the book. These use heuristics (rules of thumb) and blacklists to try to assess if a Web page or e-mail is phishing. However, none of the books provide a clear fool-proof solution against phishing.The books illustrate that industry does not have a solid technical answer to phishing.

While the literature is rich with discussions on the technical and financial impact of online fraud, the legal ramifications of online fraud, in particular phishing and its variants, have not been dealt with as a single topic in literature. This is primarily because public policy towards the Internet is really very simple: if an action is illegal offline, then it is illegal online. The Internet itself is, to a large extent, unregulated. It is important to bear in mind that the vast majority of present regulations also are applicable on the Internet. Only recently have lawmakers begun enacting statutes aimed at regulating the Internet. Too often, the law has not been able to catch up with the development of technology, and by the time legislation has been enacted, the technology has become sophisticated creating another legal loophole for criminals.

History

The word "phishing" comes from the analogy that Internet scammers are using e-mail lures to "fish" for passwords and financial data from the sea of Internet users. The term conjures an image of a fish, snapped into space. The victims are, of course, the fishes (us)! The term was coined around 1996 by hackers who were stealing America On-Line (AOL) accounts by scamming passwords from unsuspecting AOL users. The first mention on the Internet of phishing is on the alt.2600 hacker newsgroup in January 1996; however, the term may have been used even earlier in the printed edition of the hacker newsletter 2600 (Ollmann, 2004). "Ph" is a common hacker replacement for "f" and is a nod to the original form of hacking, known as "phreaking" ("APWG October 2005 Phishing Report," 2005).

Before mid-2003, most phishing scams arrived in text-heavy e-mails. Phishers embedded Web site designs into their e-mails, complete with stolen logos from the targeted company and return addresses that were "spoofed" or faked so that they appeared to come from the company. By mid-2004, phishers had devised a new way to dress up what is typically the weakest part of their scams: the dubious Internet addresses that appear in the victim's Web browser, when he or she clicks on the link in a phishing e-mail. Novel programming tricks alter the appearance of the victim's address bar by replacing the URL of the phishing site with that of the company being impersonated. Towards the end of 2004, scammers opened legitimate-looking fake online pharmacies, banks, and mortgage-and-loan firms to steal credit card numbers (Hines, 2005).

Definition of Terminologies

Sophisticated criminals have graduated from phishing to pharming and now to rat-ing. The new activity is difficult to detect and allows a criminal to watch everything the user is typing from other parts of the globe. The problems of phishing attacks are greatly aggravated by the growth of zombie computers and bot-nets.

Phishing is also referred to as *brand spoofing* or *carding*. It is a variation on "fishing," the idea being that bait is thrown out with the hopes that while most will ignore the bait, some will be tempted into biting (http://www.webopedia.com). Phishing involves the use of spoofed mail, whereby the Web sites of known institutions are entirely or partly copied, and e-mails are used to obtain private or confidential data of the customers of those institutions. The e-mail directs the user to visit a Web site where they are asked to update personal information, such as passwords and credit card, Social Decurity, and bank account numbers, that the legitimate organization already has. The spoofed e-mail address is intended to dupe the recipient into believing that he has received a legitimate e-mail. The Web site, however, is bogus and set up only to steal the user's information. Typically the message will appear to come from a bank or financial institution, masquerading as official notices saying the account needs to be updated or that a new product is on sale. A link is provided in the e-mail to an official-looking Web site, where the customer is instructed to input account details and credit card numbers. Phishing uses false e-mail addresses, stolen graphics, stylistic imitation, and misleading hyperlinks.

The Anti-Phishing Group (Emigh, 2005) has published a report, which contains an excellent description of the various types of phishing. According to the report, the following are the different types of phishing attacks:

- **Deceptive phishing:** In a typical scenario, a phisher sends deceptive e-mails in *bulk*, with a "call to action" that demands the recipient click on a link. If a recipient enters confidential information into the fraudulent Web site, the phisher can subsequently impersonate the victim to transfer funds from the victim's account.
- **Malware-based phishing:** This refers generally to any type of phishing that involves running malicious software on the user's machine. A typical social engineering attack is to convince a user to open an e-mail attachment or download a file from a Web site.
- **Keyloggers:** These are programs that install themselves either into a Web browser or as a device driver, monitoring data being input, and send relevant data to a phishing server.
- **Session hijacking:** This refers to an attack in which a user's activities are monitored, typically by a malicious browser component. When the user logs into his or her account or initiates a transaction, the malicious software "hijacks" the session to perform malicious actions once the user has legitimately established his or her credentials.
- **Web Trojans:** These are malicious programs that pop up over log in screens to collect credentials. The user believes that he or she is entering information on a Web site, while, in fact, the information is being entered locally, and then transmitted to the phisher for misuse.
- **Hosts file poisoning:** System reconfiguration attacks modify settings on a user's computer to cause information to be compromised.
- **Data theft:** Once malicious code is running on a user's computer, it can directly steal confidential information stored on the computer. Such information can include passwords, activation keys to software, sensitive e-mail, and any other data that is stored on a victim's computer. By automatically filtering data looking for information that fits patterns, such as a Social Security number, a great deal of sensitive information can be obtained."

Spear phishing is the latest spam technique used by cybercriminals to gain access to personal and corporate accounts and steal sensitive data. Unlike traditional phishing attacks in which millions of e-mails are sent indiscriminately, spear phishing attacks are extremely targeted and focus on one end user or organization at a time. Spear phishing e-mails are designed to appear as if they are sent from a trusted individual, and typically ask for log in identifications (IDs) and passwords. Spear phishing generally attacks individuals or very small groups, by customizing the message to appear to come from a very senior person whose instructions would normally be followed without question. The scams are sent by phishers to employees at companies and appear to come from their CEO or other high ranking officials. Once on the inside, with an apparently genuine e-mail identity, the phisher is able to fool employees into revealing passwords for applications or trick the employee into revealing the necessary data so the scammers can install backdoor software and other malware/spyware onto the company's personal computers (PCs) and potentially steal secret company-held data (Tehrani, 2005)

Blended phishing attacks employ a trusted organization's legitimate site, rather than a mock site and a fake URL address. The result is that even the most cautious users are unlikely to recognize the bogus link as a threat. These attacks combine traditional phishing methods with another technique known as cross-site scripting, which can cause major damage by executing illicit scripts on the victim's browser. The trigger is a link in the e-mail with an embedded script. After clicking on the e-mail, the victim is sent to the legitimate Web site, where the malicious link can then perform a number of actions, such as generating a pop-up log in that, when populated, can give a would-be hacker access both to the site and to the victim's personal information. The link also could load a Trojan horse or virus onto the user's machine (Desai, 2004).

Pharming is similar in nature to e-mail phishing. Pharming is poisoning a DNS server to reroute traffic to a different destination and install spyware on users' computers. Unlike phishing scams, which rely on the gullibility of those who receive e-mails urging them to log on to sites purporting to be their online bank and confirm passwords and account details, pharming is more insidious and attack the browser as well as the Internet's addressing system. When the user tries to log on to the online account, the hidden program diverts the Web browser to a seemingly identical site operated by criminal gangs. Their electronic identities are captured and then used to empty the accounts (Bowcott, 2005).

Phishing attempts to scam people one at a time with an e-mail, while pharming allows the scammers to target large groups of people at one time through domain spoofing. Pharming is harder to detect as it does not give much chance to the users to compare the domain name and see a discrepancy. Their browser will display exactly the same URL as they were hoping to get—no discrepancy and no suspicion arise. Pharming is "phishing" without the lure. In this case, the attacks are on the navigational structure of the Internet. It is a complex technique that requires hacking into a DNS server to "poison" its cache, meaning to substitute the Internet provider (IP) address of a fake look-alike site. As a result, someone who types in that Web site address will end up being hijacked to an alternate fake site that looks like the real thing (Piazza, 2005).

Simpler pharming attacks are done via "crimeware," or worms, viruses, and Trojan horses that infect a computer. In some instances, these can modify the Windows host file; this file holds the names and IP addresses of frequently visited sites to help speed up Web browsing. Running current antivirus and antispam software, and using firewalls, will help prevent these infections, making it harder to get scammed. Pharming attacks rely on the fact that while users typically authenticate themselves to a Web site, the reverse is rare (Piazza, 2005).

Rat-ing or "remote access Trojans" are malicious hidden programs. Like the Greek soldiers hidden in the famous wooden horse, they jump out to attack once they are safely inside, but others are pushed onto computers without any interaction at all, through various software vulnerabilities. In that case, consumers would likely have no way of knowing their machine has been subdued. It is a program that feeds on online banking passwords. These new remote-access Trojans are designed specifically to lurk in the background, waiting until the unsuspecting user types the name of a well-known bank into a Web browser. Then, the program springs into action, copying every keystroke. The data is sent back to the criminal, who now can raid the online bank. These operate primarily on the user and home-user level, but the risk still exists for users who bring home their laptops and use them to surf. Most computer users are aware of the threat from phishing e-mails that direct online bank users to fake Web sites, but some are still unaware of the threat from Trojans which can surreptitiously steal hard-earned cash without any warning (Sullivan, 2005).

Survey of Legal Cases

Phishing and pharming continue to plague many financial institutions and e-commerce Web sites. No countries are immune to identity theft, which often involves an international syndicate.

In a criminal case brought by the U.S. Department of Justice, Zachary Keith Hill was convicted by the in U.S. District Court in the Southern District of Texas for fraudulently obtaining 471 credit card numbers, 152 bank account and bank routing numbers, and 541 user names and passwords for personal Internet access accounts using his fake Web sites (Weiss, 2004).

In Holland, three suspects in a Dutch crime ring hacked 1.5 million computers worldwide, setting up a "zombie network" that secretly stole credit card and other personal data. The hackers used a variation of the worm known as W32.Toxbot. The suspects manipulated the zombie network to steal passwords and credit card data. They also are accused of stealing PayPal and EBay Inc. account information to order goods without paying for them (Sterling, 2005).

In the United Kingdom, two men have been jailed for a total of 10 years for stealing up to £6.5 million through an online identity fraud scam. The two men ran a UK syndicate that cloned credit cards using stolen financial information gained through e-mail phishing scams, which tricked online banking customers into giving out user names and passwords. They admitted using money transfer agencies to send a cut of the proceeds back to the Russian hackers, who communicated with the pair through the carderplanet and shadowcrew Web sites, which promote identity theft and card fraud (Thomas, 2005).

In 2004, the UK's National Hi-Tech Crime Unit (NHTCU) arrested six men and six women from Eastern Europe suspected of laundering funds from bank accounts seized through phishing scams. The suspects were recruited by individuals close to Russian crime syndicates and persuaded to open bank accounts into which the stolen money was placed. Cash was then transferred minus a "commission," typically 7%, to Russia. The NHTCU is working with Russian law enforcement agencies, the U.S. Secret Service, and the FBI to track down the Eastern European crime syndicates involved in the scam (Leyden, 2004).

Argentine authorities have arrested 15 people in a multinational phishing scam, which was truly international. Police arrested suspects from Argentina, Spain, Italy, and Romania who had scammed millions of dollars from as many as 150 bank accounts, using computer servers in Argentina, Russia, Canada, and Thailand (Internet Patrol, 2005).

Tokyo Metropolitan Police arrested Kazuma Tabano for setting up a phishing site designed to fool users of Yahoo! Japan. Tabano created a clone of Yahoo! Japan called Yafoo! Japan. The fake site closely resembled the real search engine and portal site in appearance and pronunciation. Police think Tabano intended to steal credit card and other personal information from visitors (Utter, 2005).

Business Response

Results of the *2005 Trend Micro Survey* reveal that computer users are more likely to engage in riskier online behavior at work, such as downloading potentially malicious files or surfing suspicious Web sites, than at home. According to an online survey of 1,200 corporate end users in the United States, Germany, and Japan, many users of corporate PCs are complacent about the risk of viruses, spyware, spam, phishing, and pharming because they rely on the information technology (IT) department to provide security. This cavalier attitude in the workplace often exacerbates problems for IT departments trying to protect business operations from increasingly unpredictable threats (Jacques, 2005). The result of the survey underscores the enormous challenges that IT departments face in ensuring the security of the organizations.

Companies have devised various methods of protecting their customers. They are beginning to integrate more security, well beyond simple user names and passwords, as the need for more stringent methods becomes clear. Microsoft is promoting e-mail authentication technologies, such as the sender ID framework, which helps confirm whether a message is indeed coming from the sender it claims to. Message authentication techniques, such as sender-ID, can prevent return address forgery by checking DNS records to determine whether the IP address of a transmitting mail transfer agent is authorized to send a message from the sender's domain. However, the cybercriminals have become more sophisticated and have constructed Web pages that obfuscate the path that the purloined information takes to get back to the scammers. Signature-based antispam filters may be configured to identify specific known phishing messages and prevent them from reaching a user. PassMark Security offers technology to specifically address phishing scams, allowing customers to configure their online accounts, so a unique thumbnail image appears on legitimate e-commerce Web pages.

Customers of banks and other types of financial institutions are most vulnerable to phishing attacks. Many consumers are fearful of using online payment and banking. The number of people who turn to the Internet for personal banking is not growing. There are discussions about whether banks will eventually have to give out security devices for customers to plug into their computers and move away from passwords to things like smart cards. There is a need for financial institutions to come up with newer and better ways to authenticate consumers—methods that go beyond use of a simple user name and password that can easily be stolen. For example, the Dutch banking conglomerate ING has another antikeystroke logging technology on its Web site. Consumers have to type their personal identification numbers (PINs) by clicking with their mouse on a number keypad displayed on a Web page. Such clicks cannot be tracked by key loggers (Sullivan, 2005).

Regulators are trying to fight back, ordering banks by late 2006 to tighten online access, often by requiring two forms of identification, and are calling for major changes in the way sensitive information is exchanged online. The problem is that most companies who are victims of computer crimes are aware of the crimes but are reluctant to report their losses—especially if those losses easily can be hidden.

Companies urge the need for more consumer education. They contend that the public should share responsibility for preventing online ID fraud by taking more care to check that e-mails are legitimate and protecting their PC with updated antivirus software and firewalls. Internet users are urged not to click on e-mail links unless they are certain of the sender. If they are going to go into a Web site, they should go in directly through a Web browser and not through an e-mail link.

The problem with cybercriminals is that even if you put up a great firewall, they are going to use a higher ladder. Even stepped-up enforcement and better user education are not likely to stop phishing attacks. Authorities have called for tighter legislation and greater international cooperation.

Legal Response

The creation of various laws in the United States and elsewhere is forcing companies to adhere to stricter cybersecurity. This section briefly discusses the American and European initiatives to combat fraud in cyberspace. It discusses the salient provisions of the Anti-Phishing Act in the United States as well as a handful of ID theft bills that are pending in the U.S. Congress, though opponents say the proposed bills would block many states from enforcing even tougher laws. It will analyze whether the proposed legislations will actually deter cybercrime.

California Anti-Phishing Bill

In the United States, California became the first state to enact antiphishing legislation. The bill was signed in October 2005 and makes it unlawful for any person, through the Internet or other electronic means, to solicit, request, or take any action to induce another person to provide identifying information by representing itself to be a business without the approval or authority of the business. Chapter 33 commencing with section 22948 provides a definition of the various terminologies, such as electronic message, Internet, and Web page.

"Identifying information" means, with respect to an individual, any of the following (Sec. 22958 (b)):

1. Social Security number
2. Driver's license number
3. Bank account number
4. Credit card or debit card number
5. Personal identification number (PIN)
6. Automated or electronic signature

7. Unique biometric data
8. Account password
9. Any other piece of information that can be used to access an individual's financial accounts or to obtain goods or services

According to section 22948.2:

It shall be unlawful for any person, by means of a Web page, electronic mail message, or otherwise through use of the Internet, to solicit, request, or take any action to induce another person to provide identifying information by representing itself to be a business without the authority or approval of the business.

The following persons may bring an action against a person who violates or is in violation of Section 22948.2:

1. A person who (A) is engaged in the business of providing Internet access service to the public, owns a Web page, or owns a trademark, and (B) is adversely affected by a violation of Section 22948.2. An action brought under this paragraph may seek to recover the greater of actual damages or five hundred thousand dollars ($500,000).
2. An individual who is adversely affected by a violation of Section 22948.2 may bring an action, but only against a person who has directly violated Section 22948.2.

The bill has triggered action in other states. Similar legislation is now pending in New Mexico, Arizona, and Texas. The bill is a good first step in the government's attempt to curb online crime. The bill's primary accomplishment is raising consumer's awareness about online fraud and identity theft through e-mails. However, the new law does not outlaw phishing. It makes it a civil violation, not a criminal wrongdoing, although victims can sue for damages as high as $500,000. But the new California law is too narrow in its definition of phishing, and it does not apply to malware-based phishing. Critics have slammed the new law as "ineffective" because it has failed to respond to the phishers' three means of evasion. According to Computer Crime Research Center,

First, phishers' crimes readily cross geographic borders, which makes finding phishers difficult; Second, that same mobility impedes the establishment of jurisdiction to prosecute; Thirdly, phishers can readily make themselves judgment-proof by such means as declaring bankruptcy or simply failing to make appearances or payments. Phishers are ephemeral entities, not brick-and-mortar business establishments whose doors can be locked and assets seized (eWeek Editorial Board, 2005).

The problem is catching the criminals and prosecuting them in court. It is doubtful that the California legislation will succeed in decreasing the phishing attacks, since many of the servers are not based in California. As such, the new law poses little concern for any attacker who is not based in the state.

Anti-Phishing Act of 2005

To deter phishing, U.S. Sen Patrick Leahy introduced a bill similar to California'sin Congress in February 2005, called the Anti-Phishing Act of 2005. The bill is similar to one that failed to pass in 2004. Current law does not adequately respond to these problems as neither phishing nor pharming fit neatly into traditional wire fraud and identity theft statutes. Under current wire fraud or identity theft statutes, prosecutions can only take place after victims were defrauded. The Anti Phishing Act of 2005 (also known as S.472 in the Senate and HR 1099 in the House) is awaiting further action from the Senate.

The Anti-Phishing Act of 2005 criminalizes phishing, making it illegal to:

... knowingly, with the intent to carry on any activity which would be a Federal or State crime of fraud or identity theft create or procures the creation of a website or domain name that represents itself as a legitimate online business, without the authority or approval of the registered owner of the actual website or domain name of the legitimate online business; and uses that Web site or domain name to induce, request, ask, or solicit any person to transmit, submit, or provide any means of identification to another (§ 1351).

The term "procure" means intentionally to pay or provide consideration to, or induce, another person to create a Web site or domain name. The crime carries a penalty of five years imprisonment.

The legislation also is intended to make it a federal crime—to knowingly with the intent to carry on the activity which would be a federal crime or fraud—to:

(1) falsely represents itself as being sent by a legitimate online business; (2) includes an Internet information location tool that refers or links users to an online location on the World Wide Web that falsely purports to belong to or be associated with such legitimate online business; and (3) induces, requests, asks, or solicits a recipient of the electronic mail message directly or indirectly to provide, submit, or relate any means of identification to another.

Leahy's bill would extend the same penalties to so-called "pharming" in which scammers redirect computer users' browsers and direct them to spoofed banking or e-commerce sites.

The bill would certainly reduce phishing and pharming originating from the United States and created by amateurs. However, it will still be extremely difficult to find the perpetuator and arrest the professional criminals who often operate outside of U.S. jurisdiction. Another difficulty would be collecting the punitive judgment awards. The criminals would have siphoned the money into a secret foreign account, plead bankruptcy, or disappear even before the court has passed judgment.

Identity Theft Penalty Enhancement Act

The Identity Theft Penalty Enhancement Act (ITPEA) wa passed in 2004. The measure sets up punishment guidelines for anyone who possesses someone else's identification-related information with intent to commit a crime. It prescribes prison sentences for those who use identity theft to commit other crimes, including terrorism and adds two years to prison sentences for criminals convicted of using stolen credit card numbers and other personal data to commit crimes. Violators who use that data to commit "terrorist offenses" would get an extra five years. The law directs the U.S. Sentencing Commission to consider increasing the penalties for employees who steal sensitive data from their own companies. The law will make it more likely that thieves are prosecuted because prosecutors would be encouraged to file a case if they know that the criminals will get serious jail time when convicted.

Revised UK Fraud Bill

On May 25, 2005, the UK government introduced an updated Fraud Bill in the House of Lords.The Fraud Act 2006 modernizes the definitions of fraud, which have remained unchanged since 1968, to strengthen the existing law, and ease the prosecution process. Under the current narrowly defined offenses of deception in the Theft Acts, a criminal act occurs when false identity is used deceptively.

Section 1 of the Theft Act 1968: A person is guilty of theft if they dishonestly appropriate property belonging to another, with the intention of permanently depriving the other of it.

Section 15(4) of the Theft Act 1968: For the purposes of this section 'deception' means any deception (whether deliberate or reckless) by words or conduct as to fact or as to law, including a deception as to the present intentions of the person using the deception or any other person.

However, criminals operating online often escape prosecution, as their crime does not technically fall within the definition of the offense. A deception cannot take place where a machine is manipulated by others to obtain a service. The courts do not regard a machine to be "deceivable" because it is automated, and, therefore, a person cannot be defrauded by a computer system. The Law Commission report of 2003 states, "Because it requires proof of Deception, Section 1 of the Thefts Acts fails to catch a person who succeeds in obtaining a service dishonestly, but without deceiving anyone. This may happen if the service is not provided directly but through a machine."

The revised Fraud Bill is designed to ensure prosecutions relating to growing technology abuse. The new legislation covers phishing acts under the intent of false representation. The new bill creates a general offense of fraud that can be committed in three ways: by false representation, by failing to disclose information, and by abuse of position. The person is in breach of false representation if dishonestly making a false representation and intends to make the representation in order to obtain gain or to cause loss/expose another to a risk of loss. Subsection (1)(a) of clause 2 makes clear that the representation must be made dishonestly and the gain or loss does not actually have to take place.

Subsection 3 defines what representation is. A representation means "any representation by words or conduct as to fact or law, including a representation as to the state of mind. It can be stated in words or communicated by conduct."

The explanatory notes accompanying the bill highlight the fact that there is no limitation in the way in which words must be expressed. Words posted on a Web site could constitute representations. Phishing attacks will be caught by this offense. A phisher disseminates an e-mail to large groups of people falsely representing that the e-mail has been sent by a legitimate financial institution. The reader is prompted to confirm or provide personal information, such as account numbers, that can then be used by the phisher to access the accounts.

A person is in breach of failing to disclose information if he fails to disclose to person the information, which he is under a legal duty to disclose, with the intent of making a gain or exposing/causing loss to another. Fraud of abuse of position is breached when the person occupies a position in which he is expected to safeguard or not act against the financial interest of another person and dishonestly abuses the position for gain or to cause loss to another. A person may be regarded as having abused his position even though his conduct consisted of an omission rather than an act.

The bill will also make it an offense to possess, make and supply articles such as a computer program for use in fraud. Examples of cases where electronic programs or data could be used in fraud are: a computer program can generate credit card numbers; computer templates can be used for producing blank utility bills; computer files can contain lists of other peoples' credit card details or draft letters in connection with "advance fee" frauds.

The bill is a step in the right direction. It will simplify the law, provide a clear definition of fraud, including those committed in cyberspace, and make the prosecution process more effective. The wording of the bill has been specifically drafted to include online fraud and other offenses involving the use of technology. It is flexible enough to deal with developing technology. It is expected that passage of the bill would result in considerable increase in the number of prosecutions of technology-related crimes.

Prosecutors will be able to impose sentences of up to 10 years for any of these three offenses. This means phishers could become the subject of extradition proceedings. The law will certainly assist the international community to work together in the fight against cybercrime

Cybercrime Convention

Cybercrime has always been a cross-border enterprise. The Convention on Cybercrime is the first and only international, multilateral treaty specifically addressing the need for cooperation in investigating and prosecuting computer network crimes dealing particularly with infringements of copyright, computer-related fraud, child pornography and violations of network security.

On Nov. 8, 2001, the Council of Europe's (CoE) Committee of Ministers agreed to the sweeping Convention on CyberCrime. The 2001 cybercrime convention has been signed by 30 countries, including Canada, Japan, South Africa, and the United States, that are not members of the 45-nation Council of Europe. Although the United States is not a member of the Council of Europe, it was influential in drafting the convention. The convention entered into force in July of 2004 but has so far been enacted into law by barely a quarter of the CoE member states. The United States, for one, has yet to enact the Cybercrime Convention into law. The aim of the convention is to form a community of nations that adhere to international standards, agreed-upon legal frameworks, and enforcement mechanisms.

Article 7 of the convention states:

Each Party shall adopt such legislative and other measures as may be necessary to establish as criminal offences under its domestic law, when committed intentionally and without right, the input, alteration, deletion, or suppression of computer data, resulting in inauthentic data with the intent that it be considered or acted upon for legal purposes as if it were authentic, regardless whether or not the data is directly readable and intelligible. A Party may require an intent to defraud, or similar dishonest intent, before criminal liability attaches.

Computer-related forgery involves unauthorized creating or altering stored data so that they acquire a different evidentiary value in the course of legal transactions, which relies on the authenticity of information contained in the data, subject to a deception. The offense of phishing would be considered Internet forgery, since the latter encompasses bogus Web sites that falsely present themselves as the sites of established companies for fraudulent purposes or the assumption of a false identity in e-mail messages for fraudulent purposes, or the posting of false information.

Articles 8 of the Cybercrime Convention contain provisions that specifically deal with computer-related offenses, that is, computer-related fraud. According to Article 8 (Computer-Related Fraud):

Each Party shall adopt such legislative and other measures as may be necessary to establish as criminal offences under its domestic law, when committed intentionally and without right, the causing of a loss of property to another by: (a) any input, alteration, deletion or suppression of computer data; (b) any interference with the functioning of a computer system, with fraudulent or dishonest intent of procuring, without right, an economic benefit for oneself or for another.

In order to ensure that all possible relevant manipulations are covered, the Explanatory Memorandum states that the constituent elements of "input," "alteration," "deletion," or "suppression" in Article 8(a) are supplemented by the general act of "interference with the functioning of a computer programme or system" in Article 8(b). The computer fraud manipulations are criminalized if they produce a direct economic or possessory loss of another person's property, and the perpetrator acted with the intent of procuring an unlawful economic gain for himself or for another person. The term "loss of property," being a broad notion, includes loss of money and tangibles and intangibles with an economic value.

The offense must be committed "without right," and the economic benefit must be obtained without right. The offense also has to be committed "intentionally." The phrase "without right" excludes conduct by authorized persons. It also excludes any other conduct recognized as lawful under domestic law, including standard legal defenses and other types of authority recognized in domestic law. The CofE cybercrime convention does not restrict parties in their application of the term "without right," but recognizes legitimate activities in operating information systems, lawful government conduct, legal defenses, and exclusions from criminal liability as well as providing a number of specific examples. The term "under its domestic law" could lead to different interpretations in different countries.

The act must be committed with intent and without right. The general intent element refers to the computer manipulation or interference causing loss of property to another. The offense also requires a specific fraudulent or other dishonest intent to gain an economic or other benefit for oneself or another.

Article 8 will outlaw Internet fraud and is intended to boost consumer confidence and promote e-commerce. However, it is a subject of contention whether phishing is within the scope of this convention. A harmonized law to combat online fraud will definitely prevent criminals from hiding beyond the reach of authorities who are protecting the rights of citizens.

Unfortunately, while the treaty addresses the international law enforcement of cybercrimes and the much-needed sanctions against cyber criminals, the convention does not provide a balanced approach; it contains controversial provisions that give law enforcement agencies too much power of interception without clearly articulating and harmonizing the safeguards necessary to protect fundamental human rights from arbitrary investigative procedures. It gives law enforcement agencies powers of computer search and seizure and government surveillance, but no correspondingly procedural safeguards to protect privacy and limit government use of such powers. The treaty also lacks a dual criminality clause. There is no requirement that the act that is being investigated be a crime both in a nation that is asking for assistance and the nation that is providing assistance.

Solutions and Recommendations

For sure, the ongoing race between IT companies and cybercriminals will result in more elaborate security systems, and phishing will become more sophisticated. The problem is expected to exacerbate before it gets better. There is no single solution that will be able to mitigate phishing attacks. While the national initiatives and the new International Cybercrime Convention are intended to deter online theft, the problems of enforcement and their legal ramifications on personal freedom might even exacerbate the problem.

Fear of identity theft has kept consumers from conducting transactions online. In order to boost consumer confidence, tighter legal framework and government cooperation are essential in identifying and arresting cybercriminals. But there is more to fighting phishing than harmonization of legislation across borders. Support mechanisms must be utilized to educate the firms and consumers. Companies must report the crimes in order for enforcement agencies to gather statistics, blunt the attacks, and apprehend the phishers.

Organizations must implement basic preventive measures to fortify their network security. Banks, for example, can require online customers to use the "two-factor authentication": something they know (their user name and password) plus something they have, such as a photograph (Krebs, 2005). Security experts recommend the following to thwart the attacks:

- Use of e-mail authentication technologies, such as sender-id and cryptographic signing
- Browser security upgrades
- Antiphishing tool bars, such as earthlink's scamblocker, which is a free browser toolbar
- Check that the beginning of the web address bar is "https://" rather than just "http://"
- Communicate by telephone
- Type the web address in the browser, instead of using e-mail links; always type the bank or company's address in yourself
- Never communicate information, such as credit card numbers, in an e-mail message
- Make sure that the web site is a secure Web site
- Use of smart cards in a device connected to the computer before making any online transaction
- Regularly check bank accounts to ensure that there is no fraudulent activity on the account
- Use of mail server authentication to identify legitimate business e-mails
- Use of digital signature to all outbound e-mail
- Consumers could open a new e-mail account solely for business-related purposes
- Companies could stop using e-mail for critical communications with customers
- Install a personal firewall
- Run up-to-date antivirus and antispyware software
- Consumers must remember that banks will never write to ask for a password or any other sensitive information by e-mail
- Consumers must upgrade and plug holes in dns server software, a more robust and secure dns infrastructure

The best defense against phishing is a combination of security technology to stop phishing attacks, and end-user education so that people can readily recognize phishing scams. New legislation also should be required, mandating that banks have several layers of authentication, rather than just simple password protection. Legal and policy solutions may have to restrict legitimate access, in order to make phishing attacks easier to detect or attackers easier to track down. Internet service providers (ISPs) should act much more responsibly and implement measures that will help protect consumers. Many ISPs and domain registrars responsible for supporting phishers' Web pages do not respond to take-down requests that the unlawful operation be pulled from the Internet. Fraudulent site can be hosted on a number of different computers, potentially without the knowledge of those machines' owners. If the devices have been infiltrated by some form of virus or malicious program, the domain registrar is not doing its job and is being irresponsible. Some ISPs have a reputation for being phisher friendly.

Conclusion

Some countries' current laws are outdated and full of gaps and, therefore, need revision to encompass new technologies. In other countries, no new legislation is required to prosecute cybercriminals because, as fraud, it is already illegal. The problem in many legal systems is the slow pace of justice. Even if there are statutes, many companies do not bother to report crimes because of the slow disposition of court cases and the low conviction rate. In many cases, nobody gets punished and phishers can always plead bankruptcy. Many people are aware that failure to pursue minor criminal cases encourages the continued proliferation of cybercriminals. But when people see the protracted, tortuous, and expensive route to conviction in a simple online theft case, who will bother to file a complaint?

In general, tougher legislation will not deter cybercriminals. They will simple move to another country, where they can perpetuate their crime beyond the reach of the law. The International Cybercrime Convention is laudable but can the citizens trust the treaty to be enforced, when some of the countries that are signatories to the treaty do not have its criminal justice system working? If the CoE really wants the treaty to be effective and the rule of law to prevail, then it must ensure that the member nations improve their performance—enough to persuade people that reporting a cybercrime will not be a waste of time. Legislators also should require financial institutions to structure several layers of authentication and password protections for their online customers, rather than targeting the criminals themselves, who are often overseas and elusive.

The big problem in phishing and its variant crimes comes from lack and inability of enforcement. Most of the phishing sites are located in Eastern Europe. Enforcement authorities are handicapped in arresting criminals due to lack of cooperation. Currently, authorities in other countries do not consider phishing a priority and will often play ping-pong with its counterpart from other countries. Domestic laws also often do not apply to foreign Web sites. The global nature of cybercrime raised difficult legislative problems of jurisdiction as criminals used offshore servers and Internet sites to avoid domestic regulations. To control cybercrime, it is important to strive for harmonization in criminal law to develop a seamless mutual assistance framework. However, the law also must take a balanced approach between arbitrary enforcement and human rights.

As with so many technology issues the problems of phishing, pharming, and rat-ing are not things that can be solved only by legislation. The solution also requires technology and security awareness. The industry needs to convey that they are addressing the fundamental issues of personal information protection and theft associated with online banking. They have a responsibility to provide a safe Internet; otherwise, e-commerce will not prosper. Business needs to see security as a longer term investment; and consumers must be educated to be on guard against all threats. Companies must invest in technologies that enable threats to be eliminated from corporate networks before they have the chance to disrupt or endanger the business.

Security is something that we have to have like seatbelts.

References

Anti-Phishing Working Group Website. http://www.antiphishing.org/

APWG October 2005 Phishing Report.(2005). Retrieved January 8, 2005, from http://anti-phishing.org/apwg_phishing_activity_report_oct_05.pdf

Bowcott, O. (2005, June 11). Pentagon's pursuit of Pentagon hacker. *The Guardian.* retrieved May 18, 2007 from http://www.mafhoum.com/press8/243T41.htm

California Anti-Phishing Bill (2005). Available at http://www.leginfo.ca.gov/cgi-bin/wais gate?WAISdocID=5218252653+0+0+0&WAISaction=retrieve

Convention on Cybercrime (2001).Retrieved May 21, 2007 from http://conventions.coe.int/Treaty/en/Treaties/Html/185.htm

Desai, V. (2004, November 23). Phishing—Who's taking the bait now? *Cnet News Com,* Retrieved 18 May 2007, from http://news.com.com/Phishing--whos+taking+the+bait+now/2010-7349_3-5463346.html

Eazel, W. (2005, November 29). Majority of the world worried about Internet Fraud. *SC Magazine.*

Emigh, A. (2005). *Online identity theft: Phishing technology, chokepoints and countermeasures.* Retrieved from http://www.antiphishing.org/Phishing-dhs-report.pdf

eWeek Editorial Board. (2005, October 17). Need for anti-phishing vigilance continues. *eWeek.com,* Retrieved June, 4, 2006, from http://www.eweek.com/

Fraud Act (2006). Retrieved May 21, 2007 from http://www.statutelaw.gov.uk/legResults.aspx?LegType=All+Legislation&title=Fraud&searchEnacted=0&extentMatchOnly=0&confersPower=0&blanketAmendment=0&TYPE=QS&NavFrom=0&activeTextDocId=2922456&PageNumber=1&SortAlpha=0

Garfinkel, S., & Cranor, L. (2005). What is phishing and how to fight phishing at the user-interface level. In *Security and Usability* (pp.).UK: O'Reilly.

Gordon, L., Loeb, M., Lucyshyn, W., &Richardson, R. (2005). *Computer crime and security survey.* Retrieved December 20, 2005, from http://i.cmpnet.com/gocsi/db_area/pdfs/fbi/FBI2005.pdf

Hines, M. (2005, August 11). Oxford Dictionary talks tech. *Cnet News Com.* Retrieved May 21, 2007 from http://news.com.com/8301-10784_3-5829040-7.html

Internet Patrol. (2005). *Major piracy, phishing arrest around the world.* Retrieved January 9, 2005, from http://www.aunty-spam.com/major-piracy-phishing-arrests-around-the-world/

Jacques, R. (2005, September 14). Corporate users ignore phishing risks. *Vnunet.Com,* Retrieved 18 May, 2007 from http://www.vnunet.com/vnunet/news/2142275/work-pc-users-ignore-security

James, L., & Stewart, J. (2005). *Phishing exposed.* NY: Syngress Publishing.

Krebs, B. (2005, March 4). New industry helping banks fight back. *The Washington Post.* Retrievd May 18, 2007, from http://www.washingtonpost.com/ac2/wp-dyn/A6367-2005Mar4?language=printer

Law Commission Report of 2003. (2003). Retrieved May 21, 2007 from http://www.lawcom.gov.uk/docs/lc276.pdf

Leyden, J. (2004, May 5). UK police arrests 12 phishing mule suspects. *The Register.* Retrieved May 18,2007 from http://www.theregister.co.uk/2004/05/05/phishing_mules_arrested/

Leyden, J. (2005, November 29). Cybercrime More lucrative than drugs. *The Register*. Retrieved 18 May, 2007, from http://www.theregister.co.uk/2005/11/29/cybercrime/

Lininger, R., & Vines, R. (2005). *Phishing: Cutting the identity theft line.* UK: John Wiley & Sons.

McCullagh, D. (2004, July 15).Season over for phishing? *CNET News.com*.Retrieved June 20, 2006, from http://news.com.com/

Ollmann, G. (2004).The phishing guide. *NISR*. Retrieved June 20, 2006 from http://www.nextgenss.com/

Piazza, P. (2005). *Tech talk. Security management online.* Retrieved January 3, 2005, from http://www.securitymanagement.com/library/001768.html

Sterling, T. (2005, October 20). Dutch says suspect hacked 1.5M computers. *Associated Press.* Retrieved June 20, 2006, from http://www.wjla.com/headlines/1005/270431.html

Sullivan, B. (2005, November 2). Forget phish, start fumigating for rats. MSNBC. Retrieved June 20, 2006 from http://www.msnbc.msn.com/id/6448213/did/9898957

Theft Act (1968) Retrieved May 21, 2007 from http://www.statutelaw.gov.uk/legResults.aspx?LegType=All+Legislation&title=Theft&searchEnacted=0&extentMatchOnly=0&confersPower=0&blanketAmendment=0&TYPE=QS&NavFrom=0&activeTextDocId=1204238&PageNumber=1&SortAlpha=0

Thomas, D. (2005, June 28). Phishing gang jailed for 10 years. *Computing*. Retrieved June 20, 2006, from http://www.computing.co.uk/

Tehrani, R. (2005, July 9). *Spear phishing* [VoIP Blog]. Message posted to http://voip-blog.tmcnet.com/blog/rich-tehrani/voip/spear-phishing.html

Trend Micro Survey (2005) Available at http://uk.trendmicro-europe.com/enterprise/about_us/spresse.php?lstPages=4&id=376

Tynan, D. (2005). Top five online scams. *PC World Magazine*. Retrieved 18 May, 2007 , from http://www.pcworld.com/article/id,119941-page,1/article.html

Utter, D. (2005, June 13). Japan arrests Yahoo phisher. *SearchNewz*.

Walker, C. (2004). *Russian mafia extorts gambling Websites*. Retrieved December 3, 2005, from, http://www.americanmafia.com/

Webopedia. Retrieved May 21, 2007 from http://www.webopedia.com/TERM/p/phishing.html

Weiss, T. (2004). Feds shut down PayPal, AOL scams. *PC World.* Retrieved 18 May, 2007 from http://www.pcworld.com/printable/article/id,115329/printable.html

Chapter XII

The Evolution of Fraud Intelligence

David Porter, Detica Ltd., UK

Abstract

This chapter discusses the latest innovations in fraud detection, with a particular focus on insider fraud and organized fraud. It argues that as fraud continues to grow at an alarming rate across the financial services sector, the constant evolution in fraudster behavior means that financial institutions need to keep their technology-based countermeasures constantly updated, particularly given the increasing involvement of serious organized criminals. In addition to upgrading their current operational detection systems, this chapter aims to encourage organizations to improve current levels of data and information assurance in order to ensure the generation of high quality intelligence on the enemy, and to adopt a structured framework for better understanding and describing exactly what we mean by "intelligence."

Introduction

The Ongoing Fight against Financial Crime

Fraud continues to grow at an alarming rate across the financial services sector. According to the PricewaterhouseCoopers' 2005 *Global Economic Crime Survey*, 45% of companies worldwide have fallen victim to economic crime in the past two years—an eight percentage point increase on the previous survey. Since 2003 there has been a 71% increase in the number of companies reporting cases of corruption and bribery, a 133% increase in the number reporting money laundering, and a 140% increase in the number reporting financial misrepresentation. Fraud that led to a loss of assets cost companies—on average—more than $ 1.7 million (U.S.), a 50% increase over 2003 (PricewaterhouseCoopers International Ltd. (PwC), 2005).

Identity fraud is a key growth area, having been labeled by federal and state authorities alike as the United States' fastest-growing white-collar crime since the late 1990s. The Federal Trade Commission's (FTC) 2004 report on identity theft revealed that consumer-reported losses from fraud exceeded $547 million. Identity theft topped the list of complaints for the fifth successive year, accounting for 39% of consumer fraud complaints (Federal Trade Commission (FTC), 2004). As for the future, Frost and Sullivan's 2005 *World Credit and Debit Fraud* report predicts global losses to card fraud will reach $15.5 billion in 2009, much of this fueled by identity fraud (Frost & Sullivan, 2005).

In addition to those losses, there are also the costs of implementing antifraud processes and systems, not to mention lost opportunity costs. Furthermore, in the wake of serious fraud incidents, many companies suffer significant "collateral damage," such as loss of reputation, decreased staff motivation, and declining business relations. Fraud also undermines the confidence of consumers in the system. Victims of phishing scams, for example, are becoming increasingly reluctant to use Internet banking or indeed engage in any kind of online financial transaction to the general detriment of the online industry.

Money laundering is a closely related issue, since the money gained from a successful fraud is by definition "tarnished" and may need to be laundered in order to make it easier to spend or invest. The magnitude of money laundering is difficult to quantify, the best effort to date being a 1996 International Monetary Fund (IMF) working paper that estimated the total amount of money laundered annually to be 2-5% of the world's gross domestic product, or between $800 billion and $2 trillion (U.S.) in today's terms (Quirk, 1996).

Worldwide, regulators are increasing the pressure on the financial services industry to reinforce their counter-fraud and counter-money laundering intelligence strategies and integrate them more tightly within their operational risk frameworks. From the U.S. Patriot and Sarbanes-Oxley acts to the EU 3rd Anti Money Laundering Directive and the UK Proceeds of Crime Act, the regulatory environment is increasing the liability of the institutions and the personal liability of their officers.

In light of these risks, financial institutions have devoted considerable resources to detecting fraudsters and other financial criminals through the more effective use of technology. Over the past decade, there has been an increasing take up of computer systems that examine transaction data and look for telltale patterns that might reveal potentially suspicious behavior. These systems have played a key role in the fraud management lifecycle, providing valuable input into downstream investigation processes.

Evolving and Assuring the Fraud Response

Although financial institutions have made great efforts to deploy new and improved counter-fraud systems and operations, they cannot afford to stand still. Professional fraudsters, or more accurately, serious organized criminals, are both persistent and migratory and are evolving their behavior to evade current methods of detection. The profile of the individual who commits fraud also is changing: fraudsters come in all shapes and sizes, including customers and employees. Those engaged in the fight against fraud, therefore, need to keep their methods of detection constantly updated and have the best possible intelligence on the enemy's profile.

The problem of poor data quality can be added to these issues. The world's most sophisticated fraud detection system will be compromised by data that is inaccurate, inconsistent, corrupted, or unsecure. Even if the data is in good shape, the process of synthesizing useful, meaningful information from raw data is often flawed. Assuring the quality of both data and information is, therefore, a key issue.

And, finally, how does all this technology help organizations develop high-grade intelligence on the fraudster enemy? In fact, what is "intelligence" anyway? There are many different definitions: most of them originate from analytical and reporting software vendors who inevitably bias their definition towards a particular product offering. The situation is further confused by the fact that most people using the terms "data," "information," and "intelligence" interchangeably.

Therefore, there is much work to be done, and in the remainder of this chapter we will expand on the above issues and themes. We will begin by discussing the latest innovations in fraud detection, with a particular focus on insider fraud and organized fraud, consider assurance at the data and information levels, and conclude by presenting a consolidated framework for better understanding and describing "intelligence."

Fraud Detection Innovation

Containing the Fraud Threat

When it comes to fighting fraud and other forms of financial crime, regulatory pressure means that financial institutions have little choice but to take positive, practical steps to provide evidence that they are in full compliance with not only the spirit of the law but can also demonstrate "best practice." This means going beyond purely manual and largely reactive procedures and embracing a more proactive, technology-enabled approach.

In practical terms, there are two methods of containing any kind of fraud:

- **Prevention:** In other words, doing everything possible to keep the wolf out of the sheep pen
- **Detection:** In other words, given that wolves will often get past a hole in the fence, detecting their presence as quickly as possible

Prevention focuses on controls designed to reduce the opportunity for unauthorized use of corporate resources. They include perimeter defense technology such as firewalls, Web site/e-mail content scanners, and biometric access controls. They also include "softer" processes, such as recruitment screening, segregation, supervision, and training. In the case of money laundering, much of this centers on the principle of "know your customer": training front office staff to verify the identity of customers opening new accounts and look out for suspicious deposits or withdrawals.

Many organizations rely heavily on such mechanisms. However, a prevention-centric strategy will only succeed if the prevention mechanism has been proved to be flawless. Otherwise its weaknesses will be exploited, and it will be bypassed, especially by people who know the system. It is, therefore, essential that organizations have a means of detecting these individuals as quickly as possible. Detection focuses on the controls designed to alert the appropriate personnel that a fraud has been perpetrated, in other words, after the wolf has got inside the sheep pen. Such controls include authorization, internal auditing, and whistleblower hotlines. Over the past two decades, these approaches have been supplemented with automated detection systems. In keeping with other data processing and management information systems, they aim to deliver "the right information to the right person at the right time," the information in question being something that we are broadly aware of but need to know more about. However, the story does not end there.

A Computerized Sherlock Holmes

Since their commercial uptake in the 1950s, computers have been used to automate tasks that humans find repetitive, tedious, and time consuming. This includes complex mathematical calculations and the storage and retrieval of records in electronic filing systems or databases. However, a parallel branch of computing, known as "artificial intelligence," has been trying to move computers beyond purely mathematical and clerical tasks towards the kinds of tasks that traditionally only humans have been able to do, tasks that we call "intelligent."

One of the most successful commercial applications of artificial intelligence to date has been in the banking industry, where computers have been employed as fraud detectives. Much of the work was originally pioneered in the mid-1980s when credit card fraud losses were reaching unacceptably high levels. Since then they have been used in other domains including anti-money laundering. Look inside any bank today, and you will find some kind of computerized fraud detection system that takes in huge volumes of transaction data and looks for telltale patterns in the data in order to identify potential fraud cases worthy of further investigation.

How do these detection systems work? In essence they make use of a body of rules (often wrapped up inside behavioral score cards) that define the way that fraudsters and money launderers typically carry out their activities. These rule-based systems are often founded on the "three Vs" of profiling—the volume, value, and velocity (timing) of transactions (Kochan, 2005). If the rules are triggered, then the activity can be deemed "suspicious" and worthy of further investigation. One of the more obvious examples of a suspicious activity rule is when a dormant account suddenly bursts into life with a high degree of spending at certain types of retail outlet or large deposits into an account are mirrored by sudden immediate withdrawals. Much of the time these systems are looking for any kind of deviation from the historical profile that an account normally exhibits. The "needle in a haystack" analogy is often used in fraud detection discussions. In money laundering, it is more a case of "a needle in a stack of needles": it is very difficult to define the "hay" in this scenario. However, if appropriately designed and deployed, rule-based systems can draw attention to those transaction patterns that possess the highest likelihood of being suspicious and are therefore most likely to pose a risk.

Where do the rules come from? The most obvious source is from inside the head of experienced investigators who work for banks and law enforcement agencies. Ask an investigator what the latest scams are and a good analyst can write down a set of rules to embody this experience. Other sources include best practice standards set out by financial regulators and international bodies devoted to countering fraud and money laundering.

However, this approach will only help you come up with a set of rules that describe the behavior of "stupid" criminals who have been caught out. The greater challenge is to detect those criminals who are a lot smarter and are still getting away with it. In other words, "what we don't know we don't know." It is at this point where we have to turn to some of the more exotic forms of artificial intelligence that simulate the human brain's ability to spot patterns

Figure 1. Fraud detection knowledge and techniques

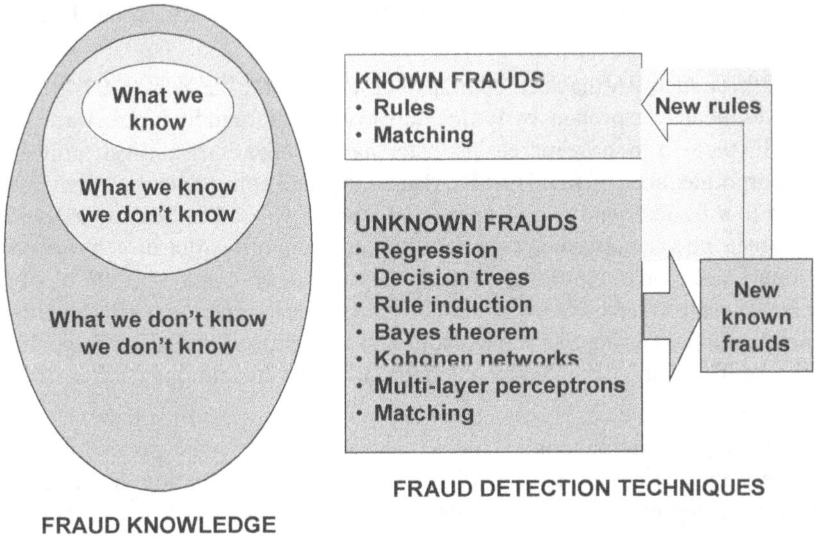

in the same way that we pick out constellations in a starry sky. These technologies, known as "unsupervized neural networks," work by being set loose on a huge amount of data in order to work out for themselves what is suspicious without having to refer to a checklist of rules. The output from these systems can then be turned into rule-based form in order to catch the criminals. Figure 1 provides a summary of fraud detection techniques and how they map onto different levels of fraud knowledge.

Each approach has its advantages and disadvantages and the best design is most often a hybrid. All too often people are sidetracked by discussions of exotic "intelligent" detection technologies at the expense of more important issues. The most significant issue is integrating disparate systems in order to feed the detection system with the data it needs and then routing the output through some kind of workflow system—in other words, getting data into and out of the system.

Fraud detection systems have now entered the mainstream. Many banks are now moving from end-of-day analysis to near real-time analysis as the transactions actually occur. They are realizing that a fraud detection system can help move them from reactive firefighting to proactive prevention of financial loss and damage to reputation. It also can act, paradoxically, as a preventative deterrent in the same way that a burglar alarm box can deter would-be intruders. The increase in efficiency and effectiveness of the detection process will leads to cost savings: fraud comes straight off the bottom line and a small reduction in costs can result in considerable bottom line growth. Reducing fraud can, in some cases, make the difference between a new financial services proposition being profitable or not. Making the same savings elsewhere can be much harder work. The computerized Sherlock Holmes is now a reality.

The Threat from the Inside

All too often the emphasis is on the external fraud or security threat: the hackers, fraudsters, and money launderers who exploit weak spots in an organization's defenses. However, there is now a growing realization that a significant fraud threat comes from inside, and not just outside, the organization.

The changes brought on by the development of new electronic business (e-business) systems and processes means the propensity for insiders to commit fraud financial crime and the opportunities for them to do so are increasing faster than organizations' ability to police them. An increased corporate focus on rapid results, risk taking, and entrepreneurialism has, arguably, contributed to a fraud-friendly environment. Technology too has become a double-edged sword. Its speed, power, pervasiveness, mobility, and anonymity offer attractive opportunities to individuals intent on committing fraud, money laundering, and other forms of financial crime. They also are aided by the fall out of business process re-engineering and other forms of organizational delayering that have resulted in the removal of checks and balances, not to mention an increasing dependence on contractors and outsourcing (Porter, 2003).

Recent high-profile fraud cases show that people in positions of trust habitually, and often all too easily, bypass internal control mechanisms. Corporate giants, once highly regarded both by peers and the public, have imploded due to false accounting, management cover ups, and auditor negligence. The statistics on insider fraud are startling. In its latest report on occupational fraud, the Association of Certified Fraud Examiners (ACFEs) has revealed that insider fraud and abuse imposes enormous costs on U.S. organizations. The median loss caused by the insider frauds in this study was $159,000: nearly one-quarter of the cases caused at least $1 million in losses, and nine cases caused losses of $1 billion or more. Organizations participating in the study estimated that they lose 5% of their annual revenues to fraud. Applied to the estimated 2006 U.S. gross domestic product, this 5% figure translates to approximately $652 billion in fraud losses (Association of Certified Fraud Examiniers (ACFE), 2006). Meanwhile, in the PricewaterhouseCoopers 2005 *Global Economic Crime Survey*, half of all fraud perpetrators were found to be employed by defrauded companies and almost one quarter of them held senior management positions (PwC, 2005).

However, this is just the tip of the iceberg: the vast majority of insider fraud goes undetected and is often only discovered by accident or whistleblowing. Recent well-publicized corporate scandals, plus heightened concerns over global terrorism and organized crime, show that insider fraud and malpractice are set to remain very much in the public eye. Furthermore, recent legislation such as the Patriot/Sarbanes-Oxley acts and the Basel II Accord mean that organizations are under increasing pressure to manage internal malpractice (Infoconomy, 2005).

We can best define insider fraud as the use of one's occupation for personal enrichment through the deliberate misuse or misapplication of the employing organization's resources or assets (ACFE, 2006). This is typically achieved by abusing a position of trust and exploiting poor processes, systems, and inadequate internal controls. Examples include:

- **Theft of an organization's assets:** Skimming revenue, stealing inventory, and committing payroll fraud
- **Corruptly and wrongfully using one's influence in a business transaction in order to procure some benefit for oneself or another person:** Accepting kickbacks and engaging in activities involving conflict of interest
- **Falsifying an organization's financial statements:** Overstating revenues and understating liabilities or expenses

In terms of our "wolf and sheep" metaphor, this is the classic case of the wolf in sheep's clothing. Perpetrators are typically opportunistic employees ranging from temporary contractors to permanent staff and all the way up to the most senior executives. Some will be "opportunity takers": people who exploit gaps in the system through temptation, incentive, or pressure. Others will be "opportunity makers": professional criminals who have infiltrated a company and are immune to and will, indeed, exploit an organizational culture of trust and caring. They will strike wherever it is easy to do so. Change is the fraudster's friend, and industries or businesses where there are high levels of organizational or process change will be particularly vulnerable. So too are businesses where there is unchecked staff authority, high staff turnover, or low staff morale.

The trend toward business process outsourcing brings an additional twist to the story. On the one hand, outsourcing may appear to cure the practice of insider fraud but, on the other, it introduces its own set of threats. The adage that fraud is like a balloon—squeeze it in one place and it bulges out in another—is very relevant here. Outsourcing often simply relocates the insider fraud threat, with the insiders now being located on the outside.

Detecting Insider Fraud

Insider fraud is a systematic, long-term activity perpetrated by people who know the different systems and controls and how to get around them. Many of these individuals display high levels of ingenuity: according to a 2005 study on the insider threat by the U.S. Secret Service and CERT Coordination Center/SEI, 39% of attacks utilized a "sophisticated" method (Keeney et al., 2005). Departments responsible for containing insider fraud have to date focused on prevention, through training and awareness raising and human resources (HR) policy statements as well as detailed reactive investigation of cases as they come to light. Whilst these measures are normally implemented quite effectively, there is little or no emphasis on proactive detection of insider fraud.

Detecting insider fraud is rather like looking for a hay colored needle in a haystack. This is because the perpetrators of systematic, long-term frauds need to preserve the secrecy of their activities. They know the controls and how to bypass them and are often well-versed in the investigative process and know how to hide any incriminating evidence. They, however, do leave evidence of their activities in the audit trails generated by the many different electronic systems they encounter. The idea, therefore, is compelling: why not use a machine to analyze these audit trails and find evidence of potential insider fraud activity? After all, log data is an abundant, freely available resource that currently is not utilized or exploited (Porter, 2003).

Intelligent analysis engines based on advanced data warehouse and data mining technology (to store and analyze data, respectively) are now a commercial reality. Such systems take in audit trails from key systems around the organization, such as financial transaction logs, call center logs, telephone logs, building entry logs, Web server logs, and print server logs. This can be supplemented with personnel records from HR and finance systems. The wider the variety of data sources the better. The incoming data is enriched with additional information and put into a consistent, homogenous format. It is then stored in a data warehouse in a format that crucially retains the patterns of behavior and how these develop and change over a long period of time. This is achieved by focusing on events, points at which data changes, rather than the data itself. This is then subject to two primary methods of analysis to detect anomalous patterns worthy of further investigation.

The first of these is based on a data mining technology that is extremely adept at identifying similarities or clusters in data where no explicit rules exist. An analogy might be that if you tossed a shuffled deck of cards at this technology, it would sort the cards into piles of suits, odd numbers, even numbers, runs of numbers, and so on. The net result is that the system clusters people according to their behavior. By adding "dimensional data," such as department, role, start date, and so on, the picture becomes richer and unusual outliers become very visible. This approach is illustrated in Figure 2.

The second technique is a hybrid mix of supermarket-style loyalty scoring and classic Bayesian statistics that score people when they exhibit certain forms of behavior that are consistent with insider fraud behavior. As smart as insider fraudsters might like to think they are, they nevertheless exhibit certain behavioral traits that can be picked up using a sufficiently sensitive and discriminating analytical approach (Porter, 2006a).

Figure 2. Behavioral clustering

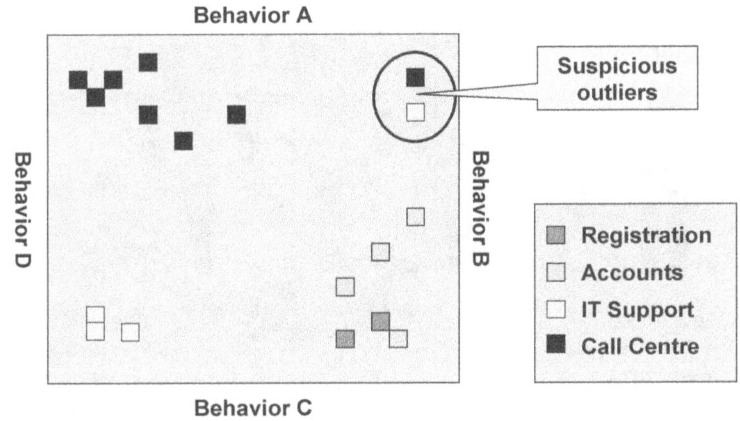

The Focus on Serious Organized Crime

As effective as the systems described thus far have been, they are not enough in the fight against fraud. Financial institutions, in common with other large public and private sector organizations, are becomingly increasingly targeted by serious organized criminal groups. These have been recently defined as those involved on a continuing basis, normally working with others, in committing crimes for substantial profit or gain (National Criminal Intelligence Service (NCIS), 2005). They dominate much of the high-impact criminality that occurs in today's society. In addition to fraud, their activities include drug trafficking, illegal immigration, tax evasion, intellectual property theft, and counterfeiting. Many of these "groups" are, in practice, loose networks whose members coalesce around one or more prominent criminals to undertake criminal ventures of varying complexity, structure, and length. Criminals may not think of themselves as being members of any group, and individuals may be involved with a number of sub-groups within the network and may therefore be involved in a number of separate criminal ventures at any one time (NCIS, 2005).

To date much of the focus on fraud detection has been on opportunistic individuals who have little or no knowledge of banking systems and the thresholds used for detecting fraud. Their frauds tend to be monolithic in structure and rapid in execution. They usually operate alone, or sometimes in collusion with a bank insider, and they usually involve a single identity. Systems based on rules or behavioral score cards can be highly effective at catching these criminals.

Organized criminals, on the other hand, operate on a far more premeditated basis and display detailed awareness of the workings of traditional fraud detection systems. Being persistent and migratory, they are modifying their behavior to evade traditional methods of detection. Most detection techniques focus on the use of behavioral profiling: understand how a typical fraudster behaves, and you can spot others who pull the same tricks. Although this can be highly effective, organized criminals are now adopting a more fragmented, distributed approach in which the individual is replaced by a collaborative network. Slicing up the fraud like salami and executing it over a longer period of time keeps potentially suspicious

Figure 3. The shift from 'individual' to 'network'

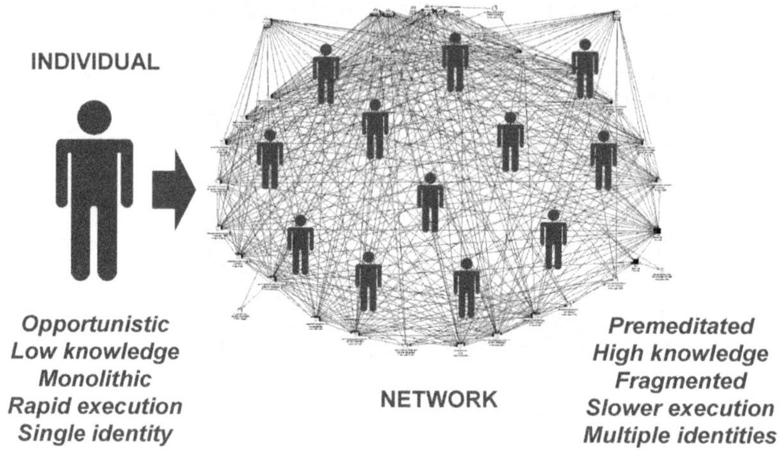

activities "under the radar." A number of individuals are involved, including other criminal gang members, bank insiders, and third-party amateur operators, such as hackers who provide hacking and other services at arm's length from the core criminal gang. Multiple identities feature strongly in this kind of organized fraud, with fake or stolen identities used to conceal members of the criminal network, their activities, and their assets, in order to minimize the risk of detection. This shift from "individual" to "network" is summarized in Figure 3.

Understanding "who is who" and "who knows who" is a key data quality challenge when detecting this kind of fraud. Marketing departments face a similar challenge when lists of names and addresses are matched against other data during marketing campaigns, in order to make connections or identify duplicates. Unfortunately, traditional matching technologies cannot deal with the data quality issues thrown up by identity fraudsters: unlike genuine customers, criminals do not want to be identified and will either distort, lie, or provide minimum information about their identity. Because of these issues, there is rarely, if ever, enough information contained within two individual records for a machine to match them categorically to one another.

Banks have no alternative but to meet this threat head on by developing a new weapon in their antifraud armory that provides, metaphorically speaking, the ability to link together very small, scattered, and somewhat indistinct pieces of a large jigsaw without the aid of a picture on the box.

From Behavioral Profiling to Social Network Analysis

A relatively new approach being taken to combat fraud is what is known as "social network analysis." As a complement to existing analytical approaches, social network analysis moves away from record-level analysis to identify, understand, and evaluate higher-level networks of collaborating individuals or organizations. With social network analysis, the characteristics of criminal networks, including the emerging subgroups and key players involved, can be

Figure 4. Examples of suspicious collaborative networks

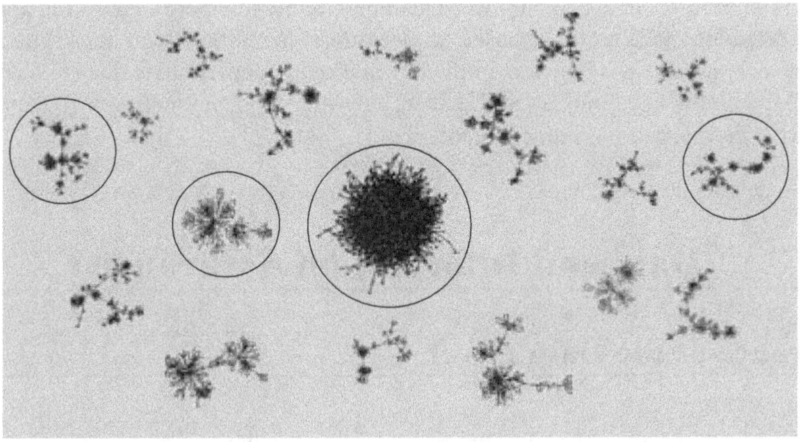

identified. Both machine and human play a key part in the process: the machine performing a quantitative, mathematical-based analysis, whilst human investigators bring a qualitative, visual analysis of the machine's results.

Being based on facts rather than hypotheses, social network analysis does not try to guess associations and, therefore, relies more on data volume than data quality. In fact, the more data it is given to process the better. Because it is immune to data quality and format issues, this means that it is no longer possible for fraudsters to avoid detection using variations in identity.

The result of the quantitative analysis is a list of identified networks, with each assigned a score indicating the degree of potential risk. These are then handed over to human investigators to perform a qualitative analysis. The system provides investigators with an instant graphical visualization of each network, including both geographical and temporal views, enabling them to make a rapid visual judgment. Investigators can easily traverse the network, dive down into detail at any point of interest, and perform searches on the networks and the underlying data (Hoque & Chapman, 2006). Figure 4 shows some examples of suspicious collaborative networks from a range of private and public sector industries.

The use of network visualization tools to support fraud investigations is not a new concept: such products have been available for nearly two decades. However, these tools are used for storing and visualizing all the data that is manually unearthed during reactive investigations. What is different about social network analysis is that it takes an essentially reactive investigation support technology and transforms it into a proactive detection engine that automatically builds and scores suspect networks with no user intervention. In other words, it stops the fraud before it becomes too big, rather than investigating after serious damage has been done (Porter, 2006b).

Driving intelligence out of networked data to inform risk scoring and investigation is a major step forward in the art of fraud detection. Rather than trying to profile a fraudster down to his shoe size or trying to match two unmatchable records, this takes the more intelligent route of identifying networks of collaborating individuals. In other words, it is not the shape of the dots that matters, but the shape of the network that joins them together. Social network analysis is gaining wider acceptance as a technique for complementing existing approaches to fraud detection, such as those based on behavioral profiling (Economist, 2005). Fraud aside, the technique also is being examined by marketing departments that are interested in identifying who the key "movers and shakers" are in a consumer network so that they can better target their viral marketing campaigns.

Data and Information Assurance

Assurance at the Data Level

Over the past few years, there has been an increasing suspicion that possibly too much attention has been paid to the development of more complex and powerful analytics, such as fraud detection engines, and not enough paid to the underlying data and information that feed these systems. Large businesses tend to be highly organized in the way they manage their assets. However the asset that is arguably the most important of all—the base of information that drives business decision making, together with the underlying data that provides the raw material—is often not properly managed or fully exploited.

Because it represents the starting point for higher-level business analytics, such as fraud detection, data quality is the first area of concern. There are many causes of poor data quality. Operators can make mistakes when keying in data entries, and data can become corrupted as it is converted and piped from one system to another. Inconsistency issues frequently arise when data is integrated across a series of disparate computer systems that adopt different standards and conventions.

As a result, many organizations are now undertaking data quality assessments, whereby all source data potentially destined for a business analytics application is assessed to ensure it passes the following quality checks:

- **Accuracy:** Is the data correct, objective and can it be validated against the real world?
- **Integrity:** Does it have a coherent, logical structure?
- **Consistency:** Is the data consistent and easily understood?
- **Completeness:** Does it adequately cover the required breadth, depth and temporal dimensions?
- **Validity:** Is it within the acceptable parameters specified by the business?
- **Timeliness:** Is it up-to-date and available whenever required?
- **Accessibility:** Can the data be easily accessed and exported to the target application?

In addition to cleaning up their data sources, many organizations are adopting a "keep it cleansed" mentality by deploying automated data quality score cards. These measure the

Figure 5. Data quality score card

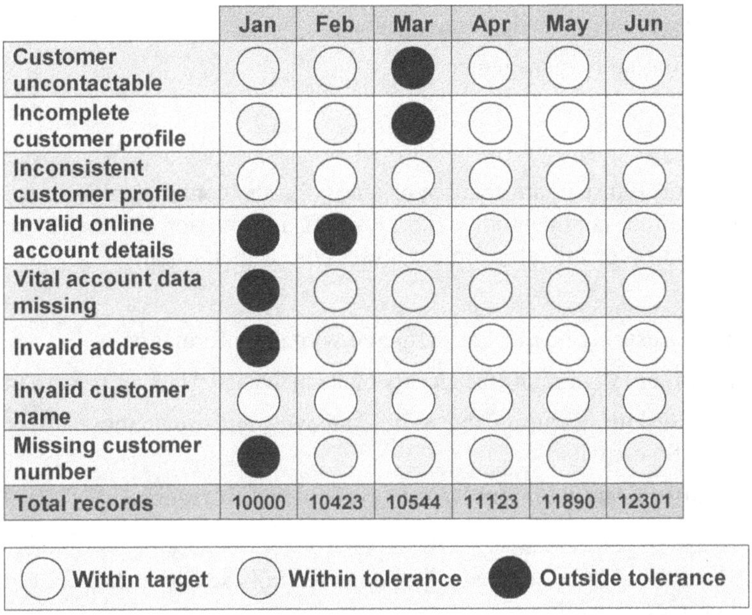

quality of data over time against predefined targets and enable business users to monitor and manage data quality against key performance indicators. A Web-based browser shows how data quality has changed over time at a summary level. Users can then drill down to investigate the underlying composition of any "traffic light" and view the business rules that underpin each quality score. Figure 5 shows an example of such a score card.

However, even if data is of good quality, there is then the question of whether it is secure. Information security practitioners recommend that all organizations assess their conformance with information security standards, such as ISO17799, which is now in the process of being replaced with the ISO2700-series standard. Information (and the data upon which it is based) is an asset that, like other important business assets, has value to an organization and consequently needs to be suitably protected. Information security protects information from a wide range of threats, in order to ensure business continuity, minimize business damage, and maximize return on investments and business opportunities. Key control areas covered by security standard ISO2700 are as follows (British Standards Institute (BSI), 2005):

- Security policy
- Organization of information security
- Asset management
- HR security
- Physical and environmental security
- Communications and operation management
- Access control

- Information systems acquisition, development, and maintenance
- Information security incident management
- Business continuity management
- Compliance

Although the ISO2700 standard focuses primarily on the confidentiality of commercially sensitive information, confidentiality (i.e., keeping information private) is just one of a number of principles for safe electronic transactions. The others are:

- **Integrity:** Ensuring no one has tampered with the information
- **Authentication:** Confirming the identity of the individual who undertakes a transaction
- **Nonrepudiation:** Ensuring the individual who undertook the transaction cannot subsequently deny it
- **Availability:** Ensuring information is available when required

All of these areas need to be covered, since commercially sensitive data is of little use if it is corrupted or hard to obtain.

Assurance at the Information Level

Even if organizations have good quality, secure data, this is not the end of the matter. The process of synthesizing relevant, useful, meaningful information from raw data can often be flawed. It is ironic that, all too often, an efficient and well-defined data collection and storage infrastructure is overlaid by an amorphous "gray layer" of information generation carried out by people armed with end-user applications, such as spreadsheets and other desktop analysis and reporting tools.

Such "gray layer" processing typically involves taking information extracted from source systems, combining it with information e-mailed from a colleague, adding data sourced from the intranet, e-mailing the results to colleagues for further combination into other reports and finally publishing the results on the intranet for wide range of individuals to re-use as they see fit. Furthermore, spreadsheets and other desktop applications frequently have embedded errors, are poorly documented, and are developed and maintained in an ad hoc, uncontrolled manner by end users on a "best effort" basis. Gray layer processes like these tend to be overlooked when the focus is on data quality: the assumption being that if the data is ok then the information will somehow sort itself out. In fact, these processes need to be radically overhauled.

In light of this, many organizations are now taking a high-level, top-down approach and are embracing concepts such as "information management," in order to provide a holistic approach to information delivery. At the heart of this is the concept of the "information management competency center," located in the business, regulating the demand and supply of information within an organization and ensuring that initiatives conform to a strategic "road map." An information management competency center covers three broad functions (Wykes, 2005):

- **Information demand:** Focusing on the ongoing need for information throughout the organization, owning the relationship with the internal customers, and managing relationships with the reporting functions that deliver the solutions.
- **Information supply:** Dealing with the delivery chain (both the internal it resource and third parties), managing suppliers, managing the development of new capability, and ongoing maintenance releases and managing the interdependencies between these different programs.
- **Data governance:** A "top-down" approach that encompasses all aspects of dealing with data, from capture to ongoing maintenance. Once embedded within an organization, data governance ensures that everyone is aware of the importance of data and their roles and responsibilities in getting it right.

The traditional approach is to have information managed, prioritized, and delivered centrally through an IT department. The information management competency center, by contrast, is not an IT provider but a business department that owns the end-to-end process for delivering information to those who need it, when they need it. Figure 6 summarizes the structure and function of such a center.

The key end-user requirement for business information is flexibility; however, fixed functional specifications cannot satisfy this requirement. The need for flexibility cannot be ignored, but neither too can users be left to their own devices: information has to be properly managed. Organizations are now realizing that a centralized information management competency center, used in conjunction with intranet-based knowledge management tools and formal data governance methods, enables information to be managed effectively with greater accuracy and at a lower cost.

Another significant trend is the increasing number of organizations that are now tying together multiple data and information-related initiatives into a single "information assurance"

Figure 6. Information management competency center

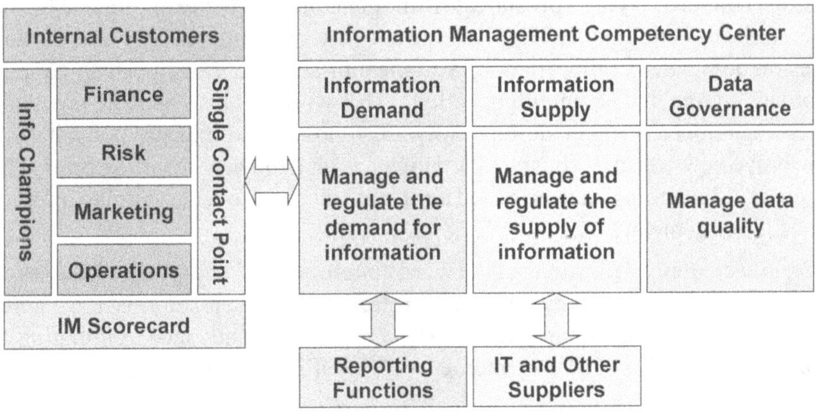

program. Not surprisingly, a growing number of vendors and consultants are jumping on the information assurance band wagon, and it is already being subject to a variety of definitions and interpretations. In this author's opinion, information assurance is simply about maximizing the trust that business operations can place on the information they seek to exploit. Information assurance acts as a mirror on the organization: poor information assurance reflects poor processes, poor controls, lack of ownership and accountability, and poor information architecture. Typical "horror stories" from the financial services industry include:

- A marketing letter with the salutation "Dear Mr. Deceased," which included the exhortation for the customer to "wake up" to the company's offerings
- An organization spending 100 man days to prepare one number for a one-hour meeting
- A banking group giving a customer in excess of 40 credit cards across all its brands
- A fraud detection system that generated more than 1 billion potential fraudulent behavioral profiles across its customer base when first switched on

Any organization wishing to review the level of its information assurance should perform a balanced assessment on the provision and exploitation of information based upon four key dimensions: quality, security, business relevance, and governance. Looking beyond the hype, there is no doubt that information assurance provides organizations with the opportunity to grasp a number of difficult data and information-related nettles and deal with them as a cohesive whole. Only when these key concerns are addressed can we begin to have a workable information assurance strategy and, ultimately, higher performance business analytics applications, such as fraud detection engines.

Towards a Better Understanding of "Intelligence"

Intelligence Defined

Detection systems are playing a pivotal role in the generation of better intelligence on financial criminals. Indeed, "intelligence" has become a key word in the security and counter-fraud industries on both sides of the Atlantic, with the aim being to move from an "opportunity-led" approach to one that is "intelligence-led." This word has also become popular in non-fraud areas: commercial organizations, software vendors, and industry consultants all talk about the brave new world of "business intelligence" and the benefits it can bring. However, "intelligence" is becoming an overloaded term that is subject to wide-ranging interpretation. What does it really mean?

There are, in fact, many definitions of the word "intelligence," but for our purposes the most appropriate one is that defined by a 1955 report from the Hoover Commission, namely: "Intelligence deals with all the things which should be known in advance of initiating a course of action" (Clark, 1955, p. 26). Put another way, intelligence can be viewed as "actionable knowledge," where "knowledge" is defined as information whose meaning and implications are understood.

At this stage, it is important to appreciate the difference between "information" and "data," since the two are used interchangeably, despite being completely different things. In simple terms:

- Data is a collection of key facts and observables. An example might be the current balance on a credit card account. On its own, data does not provide any intrinsic value.
- Information is "data in context," or the synthesis of a higher-level abstraction or viewpoint on the basis of one or more data items. A general definition of information that most people know from classical information theory is "that which reduces uncertainty." An example might be the abstraction "account is dormant" on the basis that the balance on a credit card account has been zero for the past six months. One potential source of confusion is that information can itself be subject to further abstraction and manipulation. In other words, one person's information can be another person's data.

The layer above information is knowledge, or the interpretation and exploitation of relevant information in order to solve a problem or make a decision. This is usually undertaken by humans but is also increasingly being done by machines. Very often knowledge is expressed in the form of an "if-then rule" (also known as a "heuristic," "implication," or, more commonly, a "business rule"). For example, to continue the previous example, a suitable heuristic might be: "If an account is fairly dormant and this month's spending is suddenly very high, then flag this account for referral" (note that "fairly dormant" and "suddenly very high" are information abstractions).

Intelligence resides at the same level as knowledge and, as stated above, is generally referred to, particularly in military and law enforcement circles, as "actionable knowledge." If it

Figure 7. Components of intelligence

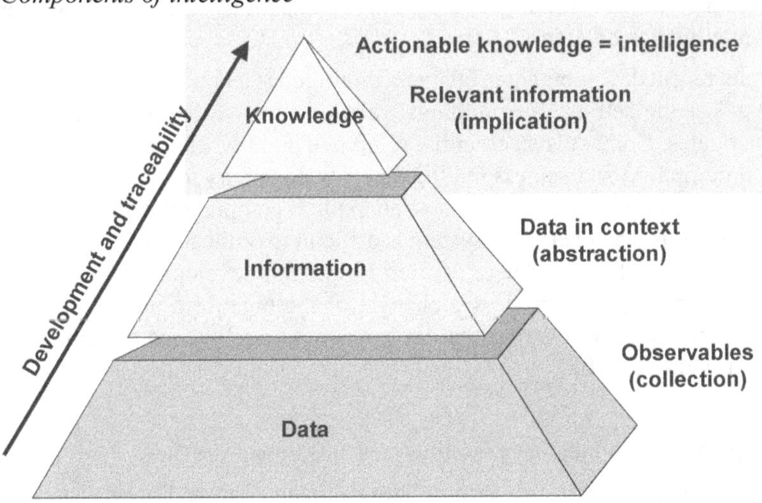

is to be used and trusted, the information underlying a piece of intelligence must be able to be traced back to the original source system data, in exactly the same way that military or police intelligence is "developed" in terms of establishing provenance, assessing reliability, obtaining corroboration, and so on, before it can count as true intelligence. This is summarized in Figure 7.

Intelligence: A Systems Perspective

From a systems perspective, we can view a fraud intelligence system as a superset of existing operational counter-fraud systems. We, in fact, can define a three-layer system hierarchy:

- At the lowest level are hot list systems or shared databases of known fraudsters that are used for cross-referential purposes within a particular industry sector. These focus on "what we know."
- At the next level up are detection systems as described in this chapter. These focus more on "what we know we don't know."
- At the highest level are intelligence systems. At one level an intelligence system can act as a relatively passive library into which users can deposit or retrieve material for subsequent analysis. However the ultimate goal of an intelligence system is, through a process of discovery, to unearth previously unknown pieces of information and data and feed this into operational detection and hot list systems. This is usually achieved using techniques, such as unsupervised neural networks as described earlier in this chapter. In so doing they focus on "what we don't know we don't know."

Unlike a shared industry hot list, which is essentially reactive and tends to focus on known incidents from the past, an intelligence system is more proactive, identifying and ultimately predicting evolution in fraudster behavior. The insider fraud and social network analysis systems described earlier in this chapter are both good examples of detection systems that also possess a significant intelligence-generation capability and, therefore, transcend the detection-intelligence boundary.

An important recent development in business intelligence technology is the explicit handling of "context," or the setting, surroundings, relationships, structures, and dependencies to which data relates. Context is an essential reference point when making the transition from data to information. Most business intelligence developers try to move directly from data to information without building in context as an explicit component in their data model. Handling context in this way means the system is difficult to build and maintain and is inflexible to ongoing business changes. There is often significant development work required when new measures are required, processes change, or the organization changes. More mature industry players are now ensuring that their business intelligence systems explicitly deal with context in the form of:

- An operational model that describes core business processes
- A semantic data store for handling both data and context descriptions

By storing both data and context, and then matching data items to the processes in the operational (context) model, information, and ultimately intelligence, can be more easily generated and the entire system more easily maintained (Hoque & Bedeman, 2006).

A final point to consider is the information maturity dimension. Despite their potential, many business intelligence systems still operate at the following two levels of analysis:

- **Reporting of past events (or "what happened?"):** Many organizations remain at this level of information maturity because of the difficulties of integrating data together for analysis
- **Analysis of past events (or "why did it happen?"):** Here system performance is the biggest challenge preventing organizations from moving to the next level of information maturity

Organizations that have overcome data integration and performance issues have moved onto developing models that can predict future events (or "what will happen?"). Here the biggest challenge is the significant effort involved in building the models. Meanwhile, the most advanced players are now moving into the following two levels of information maturity (Porter, 2006a):

- **Real-time analysis (or "what is happening?"):** By analyzing a constant stream of data in real-time, business intelligence moves from strategic decision making into operational decision making.
- **Active analysis (or "make it happen"):** Here the process of taking the result of some real-time intelligence analysis and executing an appropriate operational decision or action is automated via event-triggered business rules. Significantly, in the case of fraud detection, this high speed "analyze-act" cycle potentially enables organizations to move beyond predicting fraudster behavior to actually influencing it, just as marketing departments give consumers "behavior modifying" discount coupons on the basis of both historical and predictive models.

The above discussion is summarized in Figure 8.

Figure 8. Intelligence systems in context

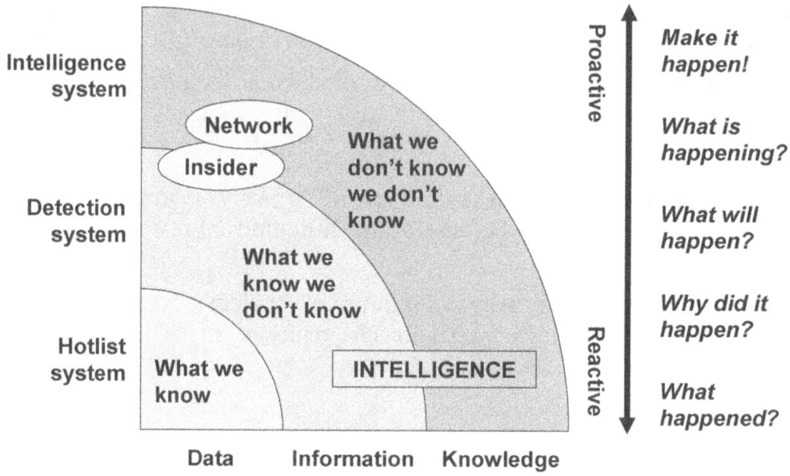

Conclusion and Future Directions

Organized Fraud Needs an Organized Response

Financial institutions cannot afford the reputational cost of further rises in the level of organized fraud. Although financial institutions are upgrading their risk management systems as a result of increased regulatory pressure, there is always the danger that fraud becomes "sanitized" when subsumed within the rational, mathematical world of risk management. It is, in stark terms, a costly and nasty crime.

The board's interest in security is no longer optional: it is a requirement. If organizations do not take action to proactively monitor financial transactions and adequately protect their customers' information, the result will be lack of trust, tarnished reputation, decreasing shareholder value, financial retribution, and, possibly, criminal charges, such as imprisonment for senior executives. Regulators will further react with the introduction of tighter regulation and compliance efforts (Deloitte, 2005).

Many countries are now developing a range of counter-fraud responses, such as tougher courts, strategic national authorities, and centralized reporting and intelligence. However, commensurate changes also are needed in the methods employed by both private and public sector financial investigation units. Organized criminals, operating as collaborative networks that collude with people on the inside, present the greatest threat, since their activities stay under the radar of most corporate detection systems. But they can be detected with the right tools. The industry needs to share data more widely, but progress is often railroaded by distractions cantered on the sharing process, rather than exactly what is to be shared and how high quality intelligence can be derived from it (Financial Times, 2006).

Organized fraud needs an organized response. Organizations are perfectly clear on what needs to be done and the support infrastructure, from legislation and law enforcement through to technology and operations, is now being put into place. The time has come to truly confront the fraudster.

From Information Assurance to Knowledge Assurance

Information assurance is a rapidly growing field of work as organizations being to realize they need to more formally manage the way they collect, store, manipulate, and, ultimately, exploit their data and information assets. But the story does not end with the generation of quality-assured data and information: there is also the knowledge level to consider, or, more precisely, "knowledge assurance."

A great deal of work has been undertaken over that past two decades on understanding the structure and nature of knowledge (or epistemology, as it is more formally known), particularly within an information systems context. Much of this work was carried out during the 1980s under the European Strategic Programme for Research into Information Technology (ESPRIT). A key ESPRIT project was the development of a methodology for the elicitation and analysis of tacit human knowledge with the ultimate goal of implementing this knowledge in the form of a computer program (which is, in essence, what rule-based fraud detection systems do today). The fruits of this research include the following models and frameworks (Hickman et al., 1989; Porter, 2000):

- A taxonomy of human decisioning tasks that divide, at the highest level, into analytic and synthetic tasks
- For each of the leaf-node tasks in this taxonomy, a series of decisioning road maps that define, in generic terms, how the decisioning task is achieved in terms of basic inferences
- A four-layer conceptual model of knowledge that describes the role that different types of knowledge—domain, inference, task, and strategic—play in the decisioning process and the structuring principle behind each one
- A complementary formal knowledge model based on extended first order predicate calculus, metalogic, and quantified dynamic logic (van Harmelen & Balder, 1992)

This research on structuring and assuring knowledge was, in many ways, significantly ahead of its time, and it is only now, as we embark on the information assurance journey, that its true value and potential is being fully appreciated. Why? The answer quite simply is that "The right information to the right person at the right time" does not pass the "So what?" test. These days, people at the front line are typically deluged with information: trends go up, trends go down; there are clusters here and segments there. But what does it all mean, and, more importantly, what should we do with it? It is the application of knowledge that helps us make sense of information and generate valuable intelligence.

To draw to a conclusion, information assurance is the latest step on the path to high performance intelligence systems, whether such systems fight financial crime or support marketing campaigns. The next challenge will be knowledge assurance: understanding, structuring and assuring the quality of knowledge. Only then will we be able to break through the information boundary and achieve the ultimate goal of "The right decision at the right time."

References

Association of Certified Fraud Examiners (ACFE). (2006). *Report to the nation on occupational fraud and abuse.* Austin, TX: Association of Certified Fraud Examiners.

British Standards Institute (BSI). (2005). *International standard ISO/EIC 27001, Information technology—Security techniques—Information security management systems—requirements.* London: British Standards Institute.

Clark, M. (1955). Intelligence activities [Tech. Rep.]. *Commission on organization of the executive branch of the government [the Hoover commission].*

Deloitte. (2005). *Global security survey.* Deloitte Touche Tohmatsu.

Detica. (2003). *Basel II: How ready are UK banks?* [Research Rep. MKV100D093-1.0]. London: Detica (UK) Ltd.

Economist. (2005). *Financing terrorism: looking in the wrong places. The Economist, 377*(8449), 83.

Federal Trade Commission (FTC). (2005). *National and state trends in fraud and identity theft.* Washington, DC: Federal Trade Commission.

Financial Times. (2006, August 3). *Organised response is required in detection of professional fraudsters. The Financial Times,* p. 12.

Frost & Sullivan. (2005). *World credit and debit fraud report.* Frost & Sullivan.

van Harmelen, F., & Balder, J. (1992). $(ML)^2$: A formal language for KADS models of expertise. *Knowledge Acquisition Journal, 4*(1), 127-161.

Hickman, F., Killin, J., Land, L., Mulhall, T., Porter, D., & Taylor, R. (1989). *Analysis for knowledge-based systems: A practical introduction to the KADS methodology.* London: Ellis Horwood Publishing.

Hoque, I., & Bedeman, T. (2006). *Data-driven intelligence in operational risk: Tackling fraud.* Paper presented at *The Financial Times* 'Operational Risk: Reality Check' Second Annual Conference, London, England.

Hoque, I., & Chapman, J. (2006). *Cross-industry experiences in combating organised crime.* Paper presented at *The Financial Times* 'Combating Financial Crime' Fourth Annual Conference, London, England.

Infoconomy. (2005). *Risk and reward: What are the information management challenges Basel II poses and the strategies financial institutions are adopting to meet them?* London, England: Infoconomy.

Keeney, M., Kowalski, E., Cappelli, D., Moore, A., Shimeall, T. & Rogers, S. (2005). *Insider threat study: Computer system sabotage in critical infrastructure sectors*. Washington, DC: National Threat Assessment Center, United States Secret Service. Pittsburgh, PA: CERT Coordination Center/SEI, Carnegie Mellon University.

Kochan, N. (2005). *The washing machine: How money laundering and terrorist financing soils us.* Mason, Ohio: Thomson Higher Education.

National Criminal Intelligence Service (NCIS). (2005). *The threat from serious and organised crime 2004/5-2005/6.* London, England: The Home Office.

Porter, D. (2000). *Automated customer decisioning: detecting money laundering and fraud.* QuantNews. New York: TechHackers/Unisys Corporation.

Porter, D. (2003). *A wolf in sheep's clothing. Fraud Intelligence,* (56/57), 11-13, 10-13.

Porter, D. (2006a). *The evolution of insider fraud intelligence.* Paper presented at the International Integrity Information Institute Security Forum 58, Antwerp, Belgium.

Porter, D. (2006b). *Businesses beware: Protection from identity thieves.* Paper presented at the Association of Certified Fraud Examiners 17th Annual Fraud Conference & Exhibition, Las Vegas, Nevada.

PricewaterhouseCoopers International Ltd (PwC). (2005). *Global economic crime survey.* PricewaterhouseCoopers International Ltd.

Quirk, P. (1996). *Macroeconomic implications of money laundering* [IMF Working Paper 96/66]. Washington, DC: International Monetary Fund.

Wykes, C. (2005). *Information management: creating an information management competency centre.* London: Detica (UK) Ltd.

Chapter XIII

Managing Information Assurance in Subscription-Based Financial Services

Victoria Ungureanu, Standard and Poor's, USA

Abstract

This chapter reviews the main types of access control mechanisms that can be used to govern subscription-based financial services. The overall performance of these mechanisms is analyzed with respect to several important features of subscription-based financial services. Namely, the chapter analyzes the impact of the following features: (1) the number of clients/ subscriptions can be potentially large; (2) the number and types of subscriptions offered by a provider varies in time; (3) subscription terms may change; and (4) subscriptions terms may take into account mutable information. Furthermore, the chapter presents in detail one mechanism that achieves good performance.

Introduction

Increasingly, enterprises are offering online financial services. Often, access to such financial services is based on mutually agreed upon subscriptions. Subscriptions commonly embed control provisions—such as who and in what conditions is allowed to access a service. Information assurance occurs then as an ancillary to subscriptions; the control terms embedded in subscriptions are formalized by control policies and enforced by access control mechanisms.

To illustrate the nature of subscription terms consider the following example. Assume that a rating agency offers a service estimating the probability of default (PD) of enterprises belonging to various industries. This service is used by individual clients as well as financial organizations, such as banks and mutual and hedge funds, to estimate the risk of current and future investments. The price of a subscription to this service depends on several factors, including the number of times that the service is going to be used and the number of companies/industries whose PD can be queried. Assume that a financial organization, called, say, ACME, buys a subscription for the year 2006, allowing its analysts to issue 1,000 queries regarding the PD of enterprises belonging to oil and gas industries. Regulating access of ACME's analysts to the PD service entails formalizing and enforcing the following subscription terms:

1. Agents certified as analysts by ACME are authorized to use this service
2. At most 1,000 queries should be served in the time interval, Jan. 1 to Dec. 31, 2006
3. ACME analysts are authorized to query only the PD of enterprises belonging to oil and gas industries

The PD scenario is used next to illustrate the issues that an access control mechanism regulating access to financial services needs to take into account. First, such applications may have a *potentially large number of clients*, and the mechanism may need to enforce a *large set of disparate control policies*. Clients may buy different subscriptions, and, therefore, disparate control policies are needed to formalize the control terms embedded in various subscriptions. For example, in the PD scenario, subscriptions and, thus, the underlying access control policies, may differ in the number of queries that should be served, the industries to which queries refer to, the time frame in which the subscription is valid, and so forth.

Second, an access control mechanism for financial services needs to take into consideration that the enforced set of policies is *mutable*. New subscriptions for financial services can be bought at any time, and existent subscriptions can end or can be cancelled. Consequently, the policy set changes in time; the beginning of a new subscription triggers an addition to the policy set, and the ending of a subscription triggers a deletion from the policy set. Additionally, the policy set changes whenever a client negotiates a revision of its subscription for a financial service. For example, in the PD scenario, ACME may negotiate to increase the number of industries to which its analysts have access to or the number of queries its analysts are authorized to ask.

Another issue that needs to be considered is the fact that subscription terms may take into account mutable information, called here *state*. A subscription whose terms are expressed in terms of state is called here *stateful*; a subscription that consists only of immutable terms is called *stateless*. For example, the ACME subscription is stateful, and its state is denoted by the number of queries that analysts from ACME are authorized to ask. The validity of a service request depends on this value; a PD request is valid provided that the query quota has not been exceeded. Furthermore, this value changes in time. Whenever a query made by an ACME analyst is served, the number of queries analysts from ACME are authorized to ask is decreased by one.

The problem addressed here is how these issues impact the performance of enforcement mechanisms used to regulate access to subscription-based financial services. The chapter is organized as follows. We start by reviewing the main types of access control mechanisms that support sets of policies. We follow by discussing the issues ensuing when employing these mechanisms to control access to subscription-based financial services. Next, we describe in detail an enforcement mechanism that achieves a good overall performance. The chapter concludes with a discussion regarding future trends.

Background

Generic access control mechanisms are commonly used as an alternative to hardwiring control into specific applications. We will briefly review here only those mechanisms that can be used to establish a set of policies—a prerequisite for any enforcement mechanism used to govern access to subscription-based financial services.

Combination Frameworks

Combination frameworks, where an authorization decision is obtained by combining the individual policies in some manner, have been advocated in particular by (Bertino, Buccafurri, Ferrari, & Rullo, 1998; Bidan & Issarny, 1998; Bonatti, di Vimercati, & Samarati, 2000; Godik & Moses, 2003; Gong & Qian,1996; Karjoth 2003; McDaniel & Prakash, 2002; Wijesekera & Jajodia, 2003). There are two main methods for combination. A first method is to combine the disparate policies into a single superpolicy; the superpolicy is then used to authorize incoming requests. The second method calls for evaluating some of the individual policies deemed relevant to a given request; the authorization decision is obtained by combining the evaluation results thus obtained in some prescribed manner.

We will describe here in more detail two such mechanisms, Tivoli and extensible access control markup language (XACML), which have gained wide recognition. Tivoli Policy Director (Karjoth, 2001, 2003) is an impressive mechanism developed at IBM for controlling access to resources over geographically dispersed intranets and extranets. Tivoli abstracts resources from heterogeneous, distributed systems into a graph, called a protected object name-space. In Tivoli policies are associated with each object in the name-space. Access to a resource is governed by a combination of these policies. More specifically, a resource can be accessed by a user, if the access is sanctioned by the policy associated with the object abstracting the resource and by the policies associated with each object on the path to the region.

XACML (Godik & Moses, 2003) has been specifically designed to formalize and support multiple policies. The key element of XACML is the PolicySet, which aggregates other PolicySet or policy elements. The policy element is the formalization of an individual policy, and it consists of one or several rules, which are evaluated to yield an access decision. Since multiple policies may be found applicable to an access decision, combining algorithms are used to reconcile multiple outcomes into a single decision. Standard combining algorithms include: first-applicable-policy, deny overrides, and permit overrides—but, the mechanism allows for other combination algorithms to be defined.

Delegation Frameworks

Another approach to supporting sets of disparate policies calls for decentralized authorization, whereby an agent may delegate some of its rights to other entities (Appel & Felten, 1999; Blaze, Feigenbaum, & Lacy, 1996; Clarke et al., 2001; DeTreville, 2002; Ioannidis, Keromytis, Bellovin, & Smith, 2000; Jim, 2001; Li, Mitchell, & Winsborough, 2002). In delegation frameworks, a request is authorized if there is a chain of credentials that delegates the authority from the source—the local policy of the server—to the requester. For example, assume that Alice requests to read a file stored on some server and that the server policy states that Bob is allowed to read this file. Assume further that Bob has signed a certificate stating that he delegates his right to read the file to Alice. Then Alice's request is authorized because there is a delegation chain linking Bob and Alice. Next we are going to describe several delegation frameworks.

PolicyMaker (Blaze et al., 1996) addresses the problem of authorization in large, distributed settings and coins the term trust management. PolicyMaker assumes that a certificate contains both the identity of a subject (given as his public key), and the permissions delegated to him by the issuer of the certificate. When a server receives a request accompanied by this type of certificate, the server attempts to find a delegation chain linking the requester with its internal policy. It was shown in Blaze, Feigenbaum, Ioannidis, and Keromytis (1999) and Blaze, Feigenbaum, and Strauss (1998) that finding a delegation chain, called by the authors the proof of compliance (POC) problem, is undecidable in general, and it is NP-hard in special cases, which unfortunately, arise naturally in practice. However, there is a special case of the POC problem, which is implemented by PolicyMaker, that is solvable in polynomial time. (In this special case, the POC problem is $O(mN^2(msN)^c)$, where N is the number of credentials available to the policy engine, and m, s, c are integers.) Another system, KeyNote (Blaze, Feigenbaum, & Strauss, 1998), is based on the same ideas as PolicyMaker, but uses a simplified policy language. However, the complexity of the POC problem remains the same as in PolicyMaker (Blaze, Feigenbaum, Ioannidis, & Keromytis, 1999).

PolicyMaker and KeyNote assume that the server has already gathered all the potentially relevant credentials and do not consider how to gather these credentials. This problem has been addressed by the role-based trust management (RT) framework (Li et al., 2002). In the RT framework, it is possible to start evaluating a request with an incomplete set of credentials, then suspend evaluation, issue a request for additional credentials, and resume evaluation when the credentials are obtained. It was shown in Li, Winsborough, and Mitchell (2003) that, in the RT framework, the chain-discovery algorithm is also polynomial in the number of credentials available; to be more precise, if N is the number of credentials available to the server, then the algorithm is in $O(N^3)$. Moreover, this bound is tight, as shown in Li et al. (2003) through an example.

In most of the systems mentioned above, chain discovery is performed by servers. However, there are frameworks, such as SPKI/SDSI (Clarke et al., 2001), SD3 (Jim, 2001) and proof-carrying authentication (Appel & Felten, 1999), where this task may be relegated to clients. In a nutshell, in these frameworks request authorization involves the following steps: (1) a client makes a request; (2) the server consults its local policy and determines who is authorized to make the request; this information is sent to the client; (3) the client finds a delegation chain from an entity specified by the local policy to itself, and sends the chain to the server, and (4) the server verifies the chain and serves the request if the chain is valid. In these frameworks, a server's burden is considerably reduced because the server needs only to verify that the chain accompanying the request is valid.

Issues in Regulating Access to Subscription-Based Financial Services

We have argued that access to financial services is governed by a set of control policies, where such a policy formalizes the control terms embedded in a given subscription. This type of application has several features that need to be taken into consideration when evaluating the suitability of various enforcement mechanisms. These features were presented in the introduction and are briefly reiterated here:

1. **The set of clients and the set of control policies are potentially large:** These sets may be large because the financial service provider may offer at any given time various financial services to many different clients under different subscriptions terms.
2. **The set of control policies is mutable:** A financial service provider may sell a subscription at any time and previously established subscriptions may end. Consequently, the policy set changes because the beginning of a new subscription triggers an addition to the set, and the ending of a subscription triggers a deletion from the policy set.
3. **Control policies can change:** The change of a policy may occur because clients can negotiate revisions of subscription terms, which, in turn, trigger the modification of the policies formalizing these terms.
4. **Control policies may be stateful:** Policies are stateful when the corresponding subscription terms refer to mutable information.

The previous section presented two approaches to establishing a set of access control policies: composition and delegation. We are now going to analyze the impact of the above application characteristics on the overall performance of these two types of access control mechanisms.

First, we consider the case where combination frameworks are used to enforce subscription terms. Because of Feature 1 above, using a mechanism that requires building a superpolicy from individual components (Bertino et al., 1998; Bidan & Issarny, 1998; Gong & Qian, 1996) may be problematic. This is so, because the superpolicy is difficult to construct when the number of components is large (McDaniel & Prakash, 2002). Additionally, such a superpolicy would be very difficult to maintain. The superpolicy has to be recomputed whenever the policy set changes, leading to a maintenance nightmare.

There are number of combination frameworks where the superpolicy does not need to be formally constructed, but instead the authorization decision is made by combining the decisions of individual policies. Using this type of mechanism is still problematic in the context of financial services, because of the highly mutable nature of the policy set and because of its potential large size. In Tivoli, changes of the policy set are largely handled manually—an error prone and time-consuming process. In XACML, authorization times may be large because making an authorization decision may require the evaluation of many or all of the subscriptions in effect for that service.

In contrast, delegation frameworks avoid many of the drawbacks incurred by combination. Specifically, neither the fact that the subscription/policy set is large, nor the fact that the set is mutable, affect in any way the effectiveness of delegation frameworks for this type of application. However of concern in this case is the fact that the client set is large. This is because the number of clients affects negatively the response service times, and, thus, leads to reduced quality of service (QoS). To see why, recall that in many delegation schemes the server needs to find a delegation chain before serving a request and that finding a delegation chain is polynomial in the number of certificates available. Therefore, finding a delegation chain and implicitly response times increase with the number of certificates/clients.

There are a number of delegation frameworks where finding a chain is performed by clients. In this case, the times required to find delegation chains can be considerably reduced. However, service times may be still large because additional communication and verification steps are required when chain discovery is carried out by clients.

Another factor that hinders using delegation frameworks to control access to financial services is the fact that subscription terms are often stateful. But, to the best of our knowledge, delegation frameworks do not support stateful policies.

Solutions and Recommendations

Thus, employing a huge, ever-changing policy, subsuming all subscriptions a provider has agreed upon, becomes prohibitively hard and error-prone to maintain. And using delegation frameworks cannot be used to support stateful subscriptions. Moreover, using delegation frameworks may lead to poor QoS because of the large response times incurred. As an alternative, we suggest to employ the certified policy framework to control access to subscription-based financial services. This framework has been presented in Ungureanu (2005), where it has been used to regulate business-to-business electronic commerce (e-commerce).

Essentially, authorization in the CP framework is carried out as follows. Access and control provisions are expressed in a formal, interpretable language, and digitally signed by a principal. In particular, in the financial services scenario, these provisions consist of the terms of a given subscription. Such a signed, formalized policy is called CP and, hence the name of the framework. In the CP framework an agent making a request to a server, presents to the server such a CP, together with other relevant credentials. The server uses the CP as the authorization policy for the request in question, provided that a trusted principal has signed the CP.

For example, in the PD scenario presented in the introduction, authorization would be carried out as follows. The provider of the PD service creates a CP that formalizes and certifies the terms of the ACME subscription. When an analyst from ACME makes a PD request, he presents to the server his own credential that certifies him to be an analyst, and the CP certifying the subscription terms. The server evaluates the request with respect to the CP and the analyst's credential, and serves the request provided that the CP is signed by a trusted entity and the terms of the subscription are met.

We argue that using the CP framework to regulate access to subscription-based financial services has several benefits:

- **Manageability:** The CP framework treats each individual subscription as an autonomous entity and does not attempt to combine them. As such, the potential large number of subscriptions is not an issue. Moreover, if the terms of a subscription need to be revised, this can be done simply by publishing a new CP and by revoking the old one.
- **Good QoS:** The authorization times in the CP framework are small, and, therefore, the QoS perceived by clients is high. This is because authorizing a request governed by a subscription entails only the evaluation of the CP that formalizes that subscription. This claim is further supported by experimental results.
- **Support for stateful policies:** The language used to formalize CPs has primitives for specifying, accessing, and modifying the state of a policy, and the framework provides means for maintaining and retrieving the state of a CP.

The rest of the chapter presents in a formal manner the CP framework, discusses how it can be used to regulate access to subscription-based financial services, and motivates in more detail the above claims.

Certified Policies

Traditional certificates are used to prove identity or group membership, and, in this context, CPs are intended to show compliance with subscription terms. The underlying assumption, in both cases, is that there are servers that are trusted to verify credentials and to grant access accordingly. In order to ease processing, CPs contain a special attribute, type (policy), which enables servers to distinguish between CPs and other credentials.

Like traditional certificates, CPs have the following components: (1) an identification (ID); (2) a validity period; (3) a reference to a revocation server; and (4) a reference to a repository. Additionally, a CP embeds the terms of a subscription, which are expressed in a formal, interpretable language. The CP components are described in more detail below:

- **type:** Denotes the type of a certified statement. It is the presence of the term type (policy), which enables a server to distinguish between CPs and other certificates.
- **id:** Uniquely identifies the policy represented by the CP.
- **Validity:** Denotes the time frame during which the CP can be used for authorization.
- **revocationServer:** Specifies the address of the server maintaining/disseminating information regarding the policy status.
- **repository:** Specifies the address of the server that maintains information about the CP in question. Namely, we assume that a repository maintains the latest version of a CP.
- **initialState:** Specifies the initial state of the CP.
- **stateServer:** Specifies the address of the server that maintains the current state of the CP in question.
- **rules:** Specifies, in a formal language, the rules of the policy.

Finally, a CP is obtained by signing a statement comprised by these components. A CP is deployed simply by publishing it on existing repositories, from where it may be retrieved when needed.

System Architecture

Under this scheme, an application server (e.g., Web server, database, or e-mail server) has an associated observer, to which it passes received requests for evaluation. Observers are generic policy engines that verify certificates, maintain CP information, and interpret and carry out CP rules.

The proposed enforcement mechanism assumes that the following data is available to observers at set-up time:

- The list of trusted issuers (ti) of cps. For each such issuer, an observer records its public key, which is used to verify signatures; an observer authorizes a request only if accompanied by a cp signed by a trusted issuer.
- The list of revocation servers distributing revocation information regarding cps.

By design, an observer subscribes to these revocation servers as soon as it starts to operate. Specifically, an observer subscribes to receive information regarding certificates issued by principals mentioned by its TI list.

Figure 1. System architecture

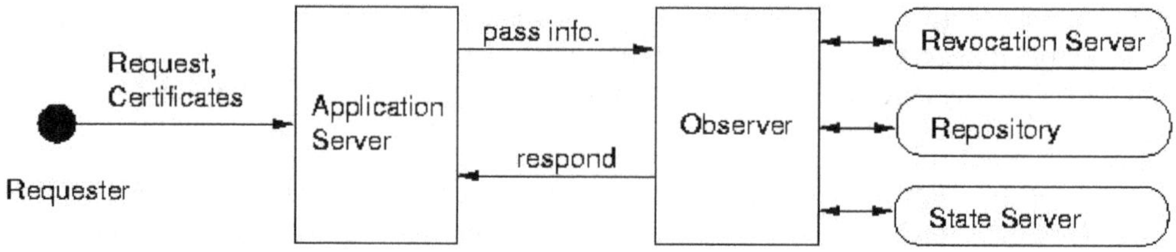

The system architecture, illustrated in Figure 1, relies on the existence of the following trusted entities: revocation servers, repositories, application servers, observers, and state servers.

Certified Policy Enforcement

We explain now in detail how CP enforcement is carried out. Consider that an agent A makes a request R, to a server S, which has an associated observer O. Assume further that R is accompanied by a CP C, and by a list (possibly empty) of subject-certificates. Then the following steps are taken:

1. Server S passes the request and the certificates to observer O.
2. O verifies that S is authorized to serve requests issued under the subscription designated by C. This implies checking if C has been signed by a principal belonging to the list of TI.
3. If this is the first request governed by C that is received by observer O, then O sets up an entry for C, in which it records the name, the status of the CP (valid or revoked), the current version, and the rules.
4. If the CP is valid, O checks if request R has arrived during its validity period.
5. If subject certificates accompany the request, then, for each such certificate SC, an attempt is made to confirm that SC is valid. That implies verifying that the signature is correct, the certificate belongs to A, and the certificate has not been revoked.
6. If C is stateful, O retrieves the control state from the state server mentioned by C.
7. Observer O checks whether there is a rule in the CP authorizing the request and carries out the ruling. Additionally, if C is stateful, O returns the updated state to the stateServer.
8. Finally, the server is informed of the outcome. If the request was authorized then S processes the request; otherwise, the request is discarded.

Note that if, at any time, the revocation server mentioned by C notifies O that C has been revoked, then O updates the entry of C, accordingly. Additionally, O searches for an update of this CP. For this, it asks the repository mentioned by C for the latest version. Assuming that the repository has a newer version of C, then O updates the version number and the rules.

Figure 2. CP rule formulation

```
eval(R, Cert):
        condition-1, ..., condition-k,
        provision-1, ..., provision-n,
        accept.
```

Expressing Subscription Terms

Subscription terms can be quite naturally expressed by means of any formal language supporting event-condition-action (ECA) kind of rules. We are using here an extension of a language designed to support control policies (Minsky & Ungureanu, 2000; Ungureanu, 2005), which is built on top of Prolog. Figure 2 specifies how rules are formulated in this language.

This rule states that, if `condition-1` through `condition-k` are satisfied, request `R` is valid. These conditions may refer to request `R` and to certificate(s) Cert accompanying `R`. Moreover, this rule calls for the execution of `provision-1` through `provision-k`, which denote additional actions required by the subscription.

Primitive Operations

The primitive operations that can be used in the body of a rule fall into three categories: (1) certificate operations, (2) control-state operations, and (3) communication operations. Primitives from all these categories are displayed in Figure 3, and described below; their use will be illustrated by presenting the implementation as a CP of the ACME subscription introduced informally in the introduction.

Certificate Operations

These operations probe the content of a certificate and determine the issuer and the values of the attributes attested by it. Specific examples of primitive operations on certificates include: *issuer(PK, Cert)*, which binds variable *PK* to the public key of the issuer of certificate *Cert*, and *bind(Attr, Val, Cert),* which binds *Val* to the value of attribute *Attr,* in certificate *Cert*. Since some attributes are used frequently, the language provides the following specializations of bind: *name(N, Cert),* which binds variable *N* to the value of attribute name in certificate *Cert*, and *role(R, Cert)*, which binds *R* to the value of attribute role in certificate *Cert*. (We mention that certificates are translated into an internal format, essentially a Prolog list, before being passed to the Prolog interpreter. The predicates defined above are implemented as operations on lists.)

For example, assume that variable *Cert* is bound to a certificate signed with public key *rsa:3:ab1cd2ef* (real keys are, of course, much longer). Suppose further that this certificate contains the following statement: *name(alice), role(analyst), employer(acme).* Then, after carrying out operation *issuer(PK, Cert),* the value of *PK is rsa:3:ab1cd2ef*. Similarly, the effect of operations *name(N, Cert)*, *role(R, Cert)* and *attr(employer, Val, Cert)* is to bind variable *N* to *alice*, variable *R* to *analyst*, and variable *Val* to *acme*.

Control-State Operations

In order to support stateful subscription terms, CPs have an additional component called control state. Structurally, the control state of a CP is a list of Prolog terms, whose meaning is defined by the rules of the CP. For example, the control state of a CP implementing the subscription presented informally in the introduction contains a term *numberOfServedQueries(N)*, where *N* represents the number of served queries issued by ACME analysts. The value of the control state can be tested and modified using the primitive operations presented in Figure 3.

When an observer validates a request governed by a stateful subscription, it needs to retrieve the control state from the server mentioned by the *stateServer* clause. After the observer verifies that the request complies with CP rules, it returns the (possibly updated) state to the state server. To maintain state consistency, the state server serves a request for the state of a CP, only if the state is not being used by another observer. And to ensure that the state is not modified by arbitrary agents, a state server communicates only with trusted observers (i.e., established by the same financial service provider.)

Figure 3. Primitive operations

Certificate operations	
issuer(PK, Cert)	binds PK to the public key of the issuer of certificate Cert.
bind(Attr, Val, Cert)	binds Val to the value of attribute Attr in Cert, if it exists; fails otherwise.
name(N, Cert)	binds N to the value of attribute name in Cert, if it exists; fails otherwise.
role(R, Cert)	binds R to the value of attribute role in Cert, if it exists; fails otherwise.
Control-state operations	
T@CS	returns true if term T is present in the control state, and fails otherwise.
addCS(T)	adds term T to the control state.
delCS(T)	removes term T from the control state.
incr(T(V), D)	increases the value of parameter V of term T with quantity D.
dcr(T(V), D)	decreases the value of parameter V of term T by quantity D.
Communication primitives	
authorize	notifies the server that the request is valid.
reject	notifies the server that the request is invalid.

Communication Primitives

These operations provide means for notifying servers whether requests are authorized or not. Specifically, operation *accept* denotes that the evaluated request is sanctioned by the CP in question. Operation *reject* denotes that the evaluated request does not conform to the CP.

A Certified Policy Example

We show here how subscription terms can be expressed as certified policies by describing how the subscription introduced in the introduction can be represented as a CP. In this example, a financial institution called ACME buys a subscription for the PD service of a rating agency, called RatingRUS (RUS). The terms of the subscription are repeated here, for clarity:

1. Agents certified as analysts by ACME can use the PD service. The implementation assumes that ACME has one certifying authority, whose public key is denoted by the short-hand notation acme_CA.
2. ACME analysts can query only the PD of enterprises belonging to oil and gas industries.
3. At most 1,000 queries should be served in the time interval between Jan. 1 and Dec. 31, 2006

The subscription is formalized by the CP displayed in Figure 4. The CP consists of two parts: preamble and rules. The preamble section specifies the following attributes. First, it specifies the name of the CP, the version number, and the validity period. In particular, this CP is named `acme`, its version number is one, and it is valid between 1/1/2006 and 12/31/2006.

Second, the preamble defines the addresses of the revocation servers and of the repositories, which are trusted to maintain information regarding this CP. In this example, a single server, whose address is `trust.rus.com`, provides the functionality. Finally, the preamble defines the initial control state (in this case, the control state denotes the number of queries served so far, which is initially 0) and the address of the server that maintains it (`state.rus.com`).

The CP rules formalize subscription terms; to make rules easier to understand, each rule is followed by an explanatory comment, in italics. In this example, the CP has only two rules (This is only a finger exercise meant to illustrate how CPs formalize subscription terms; a more realistic subscription implementation would have additional rules dealing with incomplete or obsolete credentials, wrong request parameters, promotions, etc.)

Rule R1 verifies whether the following conditions are met: (1) the certificate, `ClientCert`, presented by the requester has been issued by acme_CA, and certifies the bearer to be an `analyst;` (2) the company for which the PD is requested belongs to the oil or gas industries; and (3) the number of queries served so far does not exceed 1,000. If these conditions are met, the request is authorized and the number of served queries is increased accordingly. If any of the conditions mentioned above does not hold, then Rule R2 rejects the request.

We mention that PD requests could be processed by a Web server that has an associated observer. The steps involved in such an implementation are as follows: (1) a query is issued

Figure 4. An example of a CP implementing subscription terms

```
Preamble:
      type(policy).
      name(acme).
      version(1).
      validity([1, 1, 2006], [12, 31, 2006]).
      repository("trust.rus.com").
      revocationServer("trust.rus.com").
      stateServer("state.rus.com").
      initialCS([numberOfServedQueries(0)].

R1. eval(requestFor(Company), ClientCert) :
            issuer(acme_CA, ClientCert),
            role(analyst, ClientCert),
            belongsTo(Company, Industry),
            (Industry==oil || Industry==gas),
            numberOfServedQueries(N)@CS,
            N < 1000,
            incr(numberOfServedQueries(N), 1),
            authorize.
```

The query is authorized only if the following conditions are met: (1) the certificate, ClientCert, presented by the requester has been issued by acme_CA, and certifies the bearer to be an analyst; (2) the company for which the PD is requested belongs to the oil or gas industries; and (3) ACME's quota has not been exceeded. If these conditions are met, the value of the number of served queries is increased by one, and the server is notified that the request is authorized.

```
R2. eval(R, Cert) :-reject.
```

All other requests are rejected.

by completing a form maintained by the Web server; (2) the information from the completed form is passed to the observer for evaluation; (3) if the observer sanctions the corresponding request, the form information is processed by a CGI program, which as a result returns the PD of the company selected by the client; and (4) the response is embedded into an HTML page, which is sent to the analyst who submitted the form.

Subscription Update

We have argued that subscriptions are not immutable, and, in practice, revisions of a subscription may be required for various reasons, like, for example, to correct omissions, to better accommodate the needs of the client, or to reflect unplanned circumstances. To be more specific, consider again our subscription example. Here are some possible scenarios that would require its modification:

- Certificates for ACME's analysts are now issued by another certifying authority, whose public key is denoted by the shorthand notation acme_CA'

- The scope of queries that should be served is extended to include companies belonging to the electricity industry

When subscription terms are implemented as CPs, subscription revisions can be handled simply by: (1) issuing a new version of the CP, whose rule reflects the updates deemed necessary, and (2) revoking the previous, obsolete version.

An Example of a Revised CP

To show how a subscription update can be supported, we present in Figure 4 a new version of our CP example that incorporates both revisions mentioned above. The preamble of this CP specifies that the second version of the CP is valid from 05/15/2006 until 12/31/2006. The revision is materialized into Rule R1 that states that an agent certified as a analyst by acme_CA' is authorized to request information regarding the PD of a company belonging to the gas, oil, or electricity industries, provided that the number of requests issued by ACME analysts so far does not exceed 1,000.

Certificate Revocation

In this framework, updating a CP entails the revocation of the previous, obsolete version. Revocation is an integral part of PKI, since certificates might become invalid for various reasons and should be revoked. (For example, the secret key authenticated by a certificate might be lost or compromised, or the owner information, like role or address, might change.) Most revocation mechanisms rely on the existence of certificate revocation lists (CRLs) maintained by trusted revocation servers (Adams & Zuccherato, 1998). To revoke a certificate, the owner of the certificate or another responsible authority sends the revocation server a signed message identifying the certificate to be revoked. Upon receipt of the message, the revocation server updates its CRL and disseminates the information.

Depending on the method used for disseminating revocation information, one distinguishes between pull- and push-based systems. In pull-based systems, applications that need to check the validity of a certificate, query the revocation server and, in response, receive the latest, signed CRL. In push-based systems, interested parties subscribe to a CRL service. Afterwards, revocation servers generate and deliver CRLs in accordance with the rate stated in the subscription request (McDaniel & Rubin, 2000; Wilhelm, 1993).

CP Revocation

When a subscription is revised, a new CP is issued, and the obsolete CP needs to be revoked. Like any certificate, a CP may be revoked before its expiration date by sending appropriate notices to revocation servers. The framework assumes that the issuer of a CP is allowed to send revocation notices regarding the CPs signed by him/her. Given that the issuer is a

Figure 5. Revised version of the CP example

```
Preamble:
      type(policy).
      name(acme).
      version(2).
      validity([5, 15, 2006], [12, 31, 2006]).
      repository("trust.rus.com").
      revocationServer("trust.rus.com").
      stateServer("state.rus.com").
      initialCS([numberOfServedQueries(0)].

R1. eval(requestFor(Company), ClientCert) :
           issuer(acme_CA', ClientCert),
           role(analyst, ClientCert),
           belongsTo(Company, Industry),
           (Industry==oil || Industry==gas || Industry==electricity),
           numberOfServedQueries(N)@CS,
           N < 1000,
           incr(numberOfServedQueries(N), 1),
           authorize.
```

The query is authorized only if the following conditions are met: (1) the certificate, ClientCert, presented by the requester has been issued by acme_CA' and certifies the bearer to be an analyst; (2) the company for which the PD is requested belongs to the oil, gas, or electricity industries; and (3) ACME's quota has not been exceeded. If this is the case, the value held by numberOfServedQueries is increased by one, and the server is notified that the request is authorized.

```
R2. eval(R, Cert) :-reject.
```

All other requests are rejected.

trusted principal, we are reasonably assured that a CP is not annulled arbitrarily, without the knowledge or consent of all parties.

As for traditional certificates, dissemination of revocation notices regarding CPs may be done using either push- or pull-based mechanisms. However, pushing is far more attractive than pulling because, in the former case, request authorization incurs no additional overhead due to CP validation. This is so because a server always has a suitably recent CRL that can be used to verify the validity of the CP governing a request. In contrast, under pull-based mechanisms, a server needs to contact the appropriate revocation server every time a request is received.

Furthermore, pushing CRLs does not pose a substantial burden on revocation servers. To see why, recall that both revocation servers and their subscribers, which in this case are the application servers enforcing CPs, belong to the same administrative domain. It follows that the number of subscribers is known, and, thus, it is possible to plan ahead and to choose the number of revocation servers to be commensurate with the number of subscribers.

Discussion

We end this presentation by noting that certificate revocation lists have long been a point of contention in the PKI community. Opponents of this technology attribute to CRLs a number of semantical and technical limitations (Fox & LaMacchia 1999; Rivest, 1998; Wright, Lincoln, & Millen, 2000). Chief among them is the high cost incurred by CRL management and distribution. However, CRL advocates have argued that there are environments where this cost is not prohibitively expensive and where CRLs are the most efficient means for distributing revocation information. One of these environments is single administrative domains (McDaniel & Rubin 2000; Myers, 1999)—precisely the type of environment in which financial services are used.

Implementation

In the current implementation, we are using the Jigsaw Web server, developed by W3 Consortium, which has been modified to communicate with observers. Observers are implemented mostly in Java and operate as independent processes. Observers are multithreaded, where each thread performs all steps associated with a request before accepting a new one. When a thread blocks (because, for example, the CP is stateful and the state needs to be retrieved from the state server), another thread is chosen to run.

As a benchmark for observer performance, we measured the average time taken by an observer to compute and carry out the ruling for a given request. Specifically, we have used PD requests sent under the subscription between ACME and RUS. In the experiment, the observer was running on a SUNW, Ultra-2 machine operating at 296 MHz, using the Solaris 2.6 operating system. The measured processing time, averaged over 1,000 runs, is three milliseconds. This value is small when compared with the time it takes to send a request over the network (usually, averaging 40 milliseconds). Thus, the experimental study shows that times required to authorize requests are quite small, and, therefore, clients perceive a good QoS.

Future Trends

Online financial services are becoming the method of choice for both customers and suppliers. For customers, getting services online offer unprecedented flexibility, quasi-permanent service, and diminish the impact of geographical boundaries. And for suppliers, providing services online decreases costs and offers access to greatly extended markets. It is, therefore, expected that the number of users of online services will continue to increase at a very fast pace.

However, having very large number of users raises several issues that need to be addressed. One such issue is maintaining a good QoS when the volume of requests is very large. Current policy specification languages and enforcement mechanisms are flexible enough to be used in a variety of applications. But, so far, evaluation of these policies has not been

Figure 6. A cluster-based server

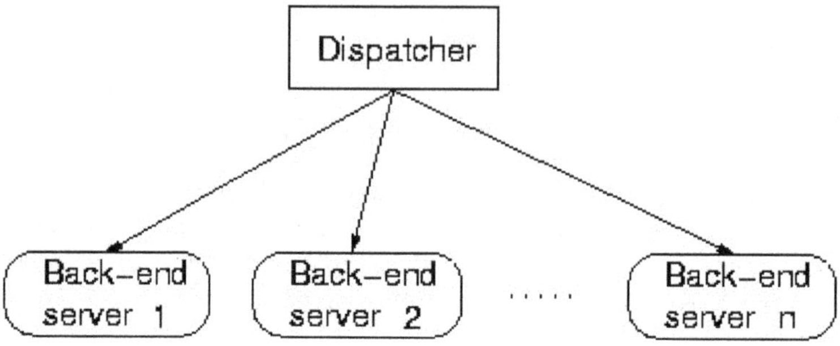

optimized for performance (Border, Zhao, & Prakash, 2005), especially when dealing with a large number of stateful requests.

A possible solution to this problem is to use cluster-based server architectures (Cardellini, Colajanni, & Yu, 1999; Lavi & Barak, 2001; Pai, Druschel, & Zwaenepoel, 1999). Many applications that generate heavy loads commonly use this type of server because it combines good performance and low costs. Essentially, a cluster-based server consists of a front-end dispatcher and several back-end servers, as depicted in Figure 6. The dispatcher receives incoming requests, and then assigns them to back-end servers, which are responsible for request processing. This type of architecture achieves transparency and a certain degree of scalability and fault tolerance by decoupling request receiving from processing.

The many benefits of cluster-based servers make them a good choice for subscription-based financial services. However, using this type of architecture is hindered by the fact that a financial cluster needs to verify that requests comply with appropriate subscription terms, which are often stateful. In contrast, cluster servers traditionally have been used for applications, such as the Internet, that do not require enforcement and where requests are stateless. Thus, employing cluster servers for this type of application raises several interesting research issues.

Conclusion

The chapter argued that control policies for subscription-based financial services are drawn to a large extent from subscription terms and identified several characteristics of managing information assurance in this type of application. These characteristics are: (1) the number of clients of subscription-based financial services as well as the number of policies that govern them can be potentially large; (2) the set of control policies that govern this type of application is mutable; (3) the terms of an individual control policy may change in time; and (4) control policies may be stateful.

Several enforcement mechanisms have been evaluated with respect to these characteristics, and in particular, the CP framework. The chapter argues that using the CP framework to regulate access to financial-based services has several important benefits. First, it is easy to establish new subscription provisions; all that is required is to formalize them as CPs and deploy them on repositories. Second, subscription revision can be supported with great ease. Third, a CP-based mechanism yields good performance. Finally, the proposed mechanism should be relatively easy and inexpensive to apply, since it uses PKI, an infrastructure that is already in place, is well known, and is well understood.

References

Adams, C., & Zuccherato, R. (1998). *Internet x.509 public key infrastructure data certification server protocols* [Technical Rep., Internet Draft]. PKIX Working Group.

Appel, A. W., & Felten, E. W. (1999). Proof-carrying authentication. In *ACM Conference on Computer and Communications Security* (pp. 52-62).

Bertino, E., Buccafurri, F., Ferrari, E., & Rullo, P. (1998). An authorization model and its formal semantics. In *Proceedings of 5th European Symposium on Research in Computer Security* (pp. 127-143).

Bidan, C., & Issarny, V. (1998). Dealing with multi-policy security in large open distributed systems. In *Proceedings of 5th European Symposium on Research in Computer Security* (pp. 51-66).

Blaze, M., Feigenbaum, J., Ioannidis, J., & Keromytis, A. (1999). The role of trust management in distributed systems security. In *Secure Internet Programming: Issues in Distributed and Mobile Object Systems* (pp.).

Blaze, M., Feigenbaum, J., & Keromytis, A. D. (1998). Keynote: Trust management for public-key infrastructures [Position Paper]. In *Security Protocols Workshop* (pp. 59-63).

Blaze, M., Feigenbaum, J., & Lacy, J. (1996). Decentralized trust management. *Proceedings of the IEEE Symposium on Security and Privacy* (pp. 164-173).

Blaze, M., Feigenbaum, J., & Strauss, M. (1998). Compliance checking in the policymaker trust management system. In *Financial Cryptography* (pp. 254-274).

Bonatti, P., di Vimercati, S. D. C., & Samarati, P. (2000). A modular approach to composing access control policies. *Proceedings of the Seventh ACM Conference on Computer and Communications Security,* 164-173.

Border, K., Zhao, X., & Prakash, A. (2005). CPOL: High-performance policy evaluation. *Proceedings of the 12th ACM conference on Computer and Communications Security (CCS '05),* 147-157.

Cardellini, V., Colajanni, M., & Yu, P. S. (1999). Dynamic load balancing on web-server systems. *IEEE Internet Computing, 3*(3), 28-39.

Clarke, D., Elien, J., Ellison, C., Fredette, M., Morcos, A., & Rivest, R. (2001). Certificate chain discovery in SPKI/SDSI. *Journal of Computer Security, 9*(4), 285-322.

DeTreville, J. (2002). Binder, a logic-based security language. *Proceedings of the IEEE Symposium in Security and Privacy* (pp. 105-113).

Fox, B., & LaMacchia, A. (1999). Online certificate status checking in financial transactions: The case for re-issuance. In *Financial Cryptography*.

Godik, S., & Moses, T. (eds.). (2003). *eXtensible access control markup language (XACML)*. Retrieved from http://www.oasis-open.org/committees/xacml/

Gong, L., & Qian, X. (1996). Computational issues in secure interoperation. *IEEE Transactions on Software Engineering, 22*(1), 43-52.

Ioannidis, S., Keromytis, A. D., Bellovin, S. M., & Smith, J. M. (2000). Implementing a distributed firewall. In *ACM Conference on Computer and Communications Security* (pp. 190-199).

Jim, T. (2001). Sd3: A trust management system with certified evaluation. In *IEEE Symposium on Security and Privacy* (pp. 106-115).

Karjoth, G. (2001). The authorization service ofTivoli Policy Director. *Proceedings ofthe 17th Annual Computer Security Applications Conference (ACSAC 2001)*(pp. 319-328).

Karjoth, G. (2003). Access control with IBM Tivoli access manager. *ACM Transactions on Information and System Security, 6*(2), 232-257.

Lavi, R., & Barak, A. (2001). The home model and competitive algorithms for load balancing in a computing cluster. In *The 21st Intl. Conf. on Distributed Computing Systems (ICDCS'01)*.

Li, N., Mitchell, J., & Winsborough, W. (2002). Design of a role-based trust-management framework. *Proceedings of the IEEE Symposium in Security and Privacy,* 114-130.

Li, N., Winsborough, W., & Mitchell, J. C. (2003). Distributed credential chain discovery in trust management. *Journal of Computer Security, 11*(1), 35-86.

McDaniel, P., & Prakash, A. (2002). Methods and limitations of security policy reconciliation. *Proceedings of the IEEE Symposium on Security and Privacy,* 73-87.

McDaniel, P., & Rubin, A. (2000). A response to 'can we eliminate certificate revocation lists?'. *Proceedings of Financial Cryptography 2000*.

Minsky, N., & Ungureanu, V. (2005). Law governed interaction: A coordination and contro mechanism for heterogeneous distributed systems. *ACM Transactions on Software Engineering and Methodology, 9*(3), 273-305.

Myers, M. (1999). Revocation: options and challenges. *Financial Cryptography,* LNCS 1465 165-171.

Pai, V., Druschel, P., & Zwaenepoel, W. (1999). Flash: An efficient and portable Web server. *Proceedings of the USENIX 1999 Annual Technical Conference.*

Rivest, R. (1998). Can we eliminate revocation lists? *Proceedings of Financial Cryptography* (pp. 178-183).

Ungureanu, V. (2005). Using certified policies to regulate e-commerce transactions. *ACM Transactions on Internet Technologies, 5*(1), 129-153.

Wijesekera, D., & Jajodia, S. (2003). A propositional policy algebra for access control. *ACM Transactions on Information and System Security, 6*(2), 286-325.

Wilhelm, R. (1993). Publish and subscribe with user specified action. In *Patterns Workshop.*

Wright, R., Lincoln, P., & Millen, J. (2000). Efficient fault-tolerant certificate revocation. *Proceedings of the 7th ACM Conference on Computer & Communications Security* (pp. 19-24).

Chapter XIV

Information Disclosure and Regulatory Compliance: Economic Issues

Anindya Ghose, New York University, USA

Abstract

The Sarbanes-Oxley Act (SOX) introduced significant changes to financial practice and corporate governance regulation, including stringent new rules designed to protect investors by improving the accuracy and reliability of corporate disclosures. Briefly speaking, it requires management to submit a report containing an assessment of the effectiveness of the internal control structure, a description of material weaknesses in such internal controls and of any material noncompliance. Such mandatory regulations can have some broader ramifications on firm profitability, market structure, and social welfare, many of which were unintended when policy makers first formulated this act. Moreover, the tight coupling of compliance activities, information disclosure, and information technology (IT) investments can have implications for IT governance because of its potential to change relationships between technology investments and business. This chapter aims to provide some intuitive insights into the trade offs involved for firms in disclosure of such information, and lays the ground for some research questions that would be of interest to academics, industry executives, and policy makers, alike.

Introduction

The SOX was formulated to increase companies' compliance with Securities and Exchange Commission (SEC) disclosure laws. In the aftermath of Enron, World Com, Tyco, and other high-profile business scandals between December 2001 and June 2002, congress reacted rapidly to introduce the SOX. What prompted lawmakers to create this provision was the concern that there was a lack of sufficient controls at these scandal-ridden firms and that firms' financial statements needed to be accurate. Thus, SOX required managers to implement controls over the financial reporting process and state whether they were effective.

In particular, SOX introduced significant changes to financial practice and corporate governance regulation, including stringent new rules designed to protect investors by improving the accuracy and reliability of corporate disclosures made pursuant to the securities laws. Perhaps the part of the act having the most impact was Section 404. This section requires management to submit to the SEC the company's annually filed financial statements, an internal control report, that states the responsibility of management for establishing and maintaining an adequate internal control structure and procedures for financial reporting. It also contains an assessment, as of the end of the fiscal year, of the effectiveness of the internal control structure and procedures for financial reporting. It also requires auditors to attest to and report on the management's assessment of the internal control systems. Such reports include a description of material weaknesses in such internal controls and of any material noncompliance.

Since modern financial reporting systems are heavily dependent on technology and associated controls, any review of internal controls would not be complete without addressing controls around information security. An insecure system would not be considered a source of reliable financial information because of the possibility of unauthorized transactions or data manipulation, each of which can compromise data integrity. SOX focuses on management accountability and operating efficiencies in firms. Both of these are tightly coupled with investments in IT and the role played by IT professionals. Indeed, sections 302 and 404 indirectly force the scrutiny of information security controls for SOX compliance.[1] The implication of these new regulations is that organizations, especially those dealing with financial information, must establish the appropriate processes and technologies to evaluate data usage requirements for all users and create a data usage control policy that defines how data may be used by each user. They need to record database activity and report on deviations from the data usage control policy. Further, they need to alert management when a deviation from usage control policy might violate data integrity.

There's been a lot of debate about the impact of new government and industry regulations on IT departments, especially in the financial services sector. The financial services sector has long been presumed to practice superior information security, largely because of the preciousness of its assets and the fact that its business is carried out almost entirely on IT systems. A study based on interviews with 100 IT managers in UK financial services companies reveals that given the current level of investment in technologies that help companies comply with regulations such as SOX, around 60% of IT managers from financial services companies believe the demand on IT to deal with compliance issues will increase over the coming three years (Carr, 2006). Indeed, the study states that most respondents are not satisfied with their current capabilities to perform tasks necessary for compliance, such as document management and archiving. Further, it also reports that "most financial companies are only just beginning to scratch the surface in areas such as the archiving of electronic messages and digitized phone records." This becomes even more important in the face of a recent study that shows how susceptible the financial services industry is to targeted scans and probing attacks (Schneier, 2005). Counterpane tracked the 13 major vertical markets using attack data between January 2005 and October 2005. The study found although the financial industry ranks second highest in attacks, it is actually the most vulnerable to security breach activity—approximately 50% of all targeted scans detected by Counterpane occurred within the financial industry.

It is well known that internal control evaluation and responsibilities are not a new mandate on business in the United States. For instance, the U.S. Foreign Corrupt Practices Act of 1977 requires publicly held companies to maintain adequate system of internal control. Further, the evaluation by external auditors has been an integral part of firm audits for many years. However, prior to Section 404, the audit evaluation of internal control was *optional* and might have been avoided, for example, for efficiency or size reasons. There was no requirement to disclose publicly the findings from the internal control evaluation. Post-SOX these disclosures are *mandatory*. Recently, a number of trade press article have voiced the need for a rollback of portions of SOX, citing Section 404 as imprudent act of overregulation and called for its repeal. This article lays out some potential trade offs to companies that have resulted from SOX and its implications on firm profits, industry structure and competition, and social welfare.

Perceived Costs and Benefits

SOX has made companies place more emphasis on the reliability, security, and accuracy of their systems. Companies need to understand how their back office systems support financial data processing—and show that they have the right IT governance in place. Compliance with SOX regulations requires significant, nonrecurring costs "upfront" investment. Costs are quantifiable and immediate, whereas benefits are intangible and more difficult to quantify. First, there is a strong learning curve for all registrants and auditors. Audit committees need to spend more time in compliance activities. Then, there are significant fixed costs, such as initial documentation, initial remediation of deficiencies (potential deferred maintenance), training efforts, developing overall project, and testing plans. None of these processes are stationary though. This implies that the current documentation may change next year as business processes and business controls change from year to year. A company must test each of its controls each year. Intangible costs include delays in decision making due to an increase in risk averseness of the top management. And, most importantly, given fixed budget constraints, these mandatory investments in SOX compliance technologies and systems can potentially lead to compromises in the level of IT-security spending.

A survey of 224 public companies by Financial Executive International (FEI) in July 2004, found that the average cost of complying with Section 404 was approximately $4 million and that the average cost varies with firm size. According to a report by the Big Four Accounting firms, the average cost of compliance with Section 404 in 2004 for a fortune 1,000 company was $7.8 million. A study by the law firm of Foley and Lardner (2005) found the act increased costs associated with being a publicly held company by 130%. Many of the major problems stem from Section 404 of SOX, which requires CEOs to certify the accuracy of financial statements.

In addition to the direct cost of implementing a system that achieves compliance with SOX, the workload and risk of directors has increased as a result of the regulation. This, in turn, has lead to an increase in the fees paid to directors. Further, the increase is disproportionately high for small firms. Linck, Netter, and Yang (2005) estimate from 2001 to 2004 small firms had to pay higher director fees to the tune of $0.84 per $1,000 in net sales, whereas for large firms the corresponding increase was just $0.07.

While the implementation costs of Section 404 are quite significant, the benefits might be harder to estimate. Specifically, it is not quite clear if announcements of material weaknesses by companies are informative to equity investors, creditors, and regulatory agencies. Indeed, anecdotal evidence in this regard is quite mixed. A Goldman Sachs study found a 12% negative stock price reaction to a disclosure of internal control deficiencies by a small-cap firm (Flowserve) but a positive reaction to a disclosure by Eastman Kodak of a forthcoming adverse SOX 404 opinion. *The Wall Street Journal* (April 14, 2005) reported that the credit rating agency take negative action against about 20% of companies reporting a material weakness.

To be fair, SOX can have a number of expected benefits. First, it could lead to greater accountability, ownership, and appreciation of internal control systems throughout all levels of an organization. Second, it can lead to more timely identification and remediation of internal control weaknesses that might not have been detected otherwise. Thus, the benefits of improved corporate controls are expected to be found not only in decreased malfeasance, but, perhaps even more so, in a substantial increase in corporate data quality and the decrease of instances of erroneous intra- and extracorporate transactions.

The above information then highlights that there are distinct trade offs involved in such mandatory accounting information disclosure regulations. This paves the way for a set of research questions that might be of interest to academics and executives, alike. Some of these are outlined below.

Research Questions

1. *SOX requirements are causing companies to reconsider public status. Is that detrimental for social welfare?*

SOX was designed to restore investor confidence and prevent the type of corporate malfeasance that has plagued the U.S. capital markets in recent years. While few would argue with the assertion that the SOX regulations have increased corporate transparency and enhanced corporate governance, it has become increasingly clear that these improvements are creating a disproportionately heavy burden on small public companies. The costs of complying with SOX, however, are borne by all public companies. Thus, it seems to have a major negative impact as well—namely reduction in companies going public with their IPOs and increase in acquisitions. Indeed, in 2005, 33% of the 18 withdrawn stock offerings—including IPOs, secondary offerings, and convertible-stock deals—were put on hold because the issuers began discussions to be acquired instead (Dealogic, 2005). That has increased from 2004, when 18% of the 97 withdrawn deals were due to acquisition discussions and from 2003, when 16% of 67 deals were pulled for that reason. Thus, the backlash from the legislative penalty may be worse than the crime it was intended to prevent. One explanation for the exodus from the public market and increase in acquisitions is to avoid the burden of complying with SOX regulations. The added time, expense, and managerial hassle to small companies may be tipping the decision away from a public offering.[2]

In a number of press releases announcing the decision to deregister a firm's stock, managers typically cite the high costs of reporting as the key motivation for "going dark" as it is quite commonly known. Additionally recent empirical studies (Leuz, Triantis, & Wang, 2004) have shown that SOX may be the driving force behind the decision of many companies to deregister or go dark. A major finding in their paper is that smaller firms, for which reporting costs may be particularly burdensome, are more likely to take such steps. If the market views the deregistration decision as conveying additional information about a firm's weak future growth prospects, this can become a vicious cycle, where investors pull out their stocks even more quickly. In fact, Leuz et al. (2004) note that shareholders might even turn skeptical, if they start viewing deregistration as a tool for management to hide poor performance to protect themselves from legal liability (especially post-SOX).

These trends demonstrate that SOX even may be altering the operation of capital markets. This may not only affect U.S. firms directly, but also may have an impact on the number of foreign investors in U.S. markets. In fact, given these mandatory regulations, many foreign firms may not be willing to enter or stay in the U.S. markets (HRO Alert, 2005). Even with the SEC's partial exemption of the compliance requirements of foreign companies, some of them may stay away from U.S. markets because of the tougher accounting rules and heightened emphasis on corporate governance. Thus, SOX throws up interesting implications of this act on the net social welfare generated not just from product markets, but also from the interactions with capital markets. Does a decrease in participation in public markets, or an increase in the number of acquisitions adversely affect welfare? What are the plausible outcomes? The jury is still out on these questions.

2. *By creating an artificial incentive for firms to merge, is the law impeding market competition?*

According to several CEOs, SOX does stifle intraindustry competition. According to the AeA, the largest trade association for the high-technology sector, Section 404 has become problematic because the cost burden amounts to a major regressive tax on small business, given that the cost is not directly proportionate to revenue (AeA, 2005). For multibillion dollar companies, the cost may run at approximately 0.05% of revenue, but for small companies with revenues below $20 million, the costs can rapidly approach 3% of revenue. At the microlevel, anecdotal evidence reveals that for a large company the cost of Section 404 is approximately $400 per employee, whereas, for small companies, the cost in many instances approaches $4,000 per employee. However, external auditors have generally adopted a "one-size fits all" approach to Section 404. This means that a small company (in terms of revenue) and a relatively simple organizational structure essentially is being held to the same standard as a large multibillion dollar company with a very complicated organizational structure. The SEC believed there would be "a direct correlation between the extent of the burden and the size of the reporting company, with the burden increasing commensurate with the size of the company." But the opposite appears to be true.

While the federal government acknowledges the ways in which SOX raises the costs of doing business, they also feel these costs are more than offset by the benefits of improved accounting practices and greater public trust in the corporate world. A lack of public trust tends to boost a firm's cost of capital. Hence, by increasing the level of consumer trust, SOX can mitigate concerns on the cost side, as well. However, there are hidden dangers. SOX requires top managers to certify the veracity of their financial statements. The additional liabilities imposed on managers can increase agency costs by forcing executives to invest effort in less monitored activities. In the context of today's economy, an attempt by a firm's management to exercise an extra degree of prudence in equipment spending and hiring behavior will, in the end, if practiced widely enough, produce a more risk-averse top management. Hence, it may reduce production and innovation throughout the economy. It is reasonable to hypothesize that business activity will be reduced, not necessarily to recession levels, but to levels well below the economy's underlying dynamic potential (were corporate behavior less risk averse). Indeed Cohen, Dey, and Lys (2004) hypothesize and find that there was a significant decline in research and development expenses and capital expenditures made by CEOs after the passage of SOX. Related to the above point, if some companies were to pass their administrative costs of SOX compliance to customers by increasing prices, it might end up making the company less competitive in the marketplace, thereby having negative consequences on social welfare.

3. *Can SOX compliance compromise IT security? Given the resource constraints a firm faces, what are the optimal levels of investment in technologies that boost SOX compliance? How should a firm allocate resources among IT security spending, SOX compliance spendin,g and other regular expenditures, such as product development/ research and development/marketing?*

CEOs and boards of directors now care, more than ever, about software and systems that will help them comply with SOX. Specifically, the tenets of SOX specify that corporate governance be responsible for providing transparency, integrity, and accountability over regulated financial data. As with most laws of this type, regulatory compliance only establishes a base line and is just a start to ethical corporate governance and financial conduct. Also, given the high stakes involved, firms also are considering outsourcing some of the software systems development to companies that already have the expertise in secure coding techniques. In addition, firms, in principle, could explore the role that application security products could play in reducing time to be compliant.

However, investing in compliance technologies is like a double-edged sword. Devoting time and money to SOX compliance limits other activities for which those resources could have been used—for instance, in critical technology investments and infrastructure protection that boost IT security (more on this later). Additionally, as companies scrutinize their internal controls and become more conscious of the processes used to make decisions, they may become more risk-averse and slower to seize opportunities (HRO Alert, 2005). The pressures of dealing with SOX are forcing most firms to divert spending away from security, according to a report released by the Internet Security Forum (ISF). ISF surveyed several Fortune 500 firms and found that a majority of the firms are decreasing their security budgets to ensure SOX compliance. A recent report by Redsiren (2005), which surveyed chief security officers (CSOs), mentions similar findings with 62% of the participants saying they have to spend more time complying with government regulations, such as SOX and the Gramm-Leach-Bliley Act, and less time on activities actually protecting their networks. More than one-third (38%) of the respondents said such mandatory regulations have caused them to either divert or delay new IT security projects. Getronics (2005) reports a similar finding by Gartner Research analysts.

It has been reported in the media that SOX regulations create fear that managers are second-guessing themselves when making business decisions, raising the hurdle for businesses to make investments. And raising the hurdle rates implies that "some investments that should have been undertaken, that would have been good for society, good for investors, good for shareholders, and good for the economy's growth, won't be undertaken."[3] Moreover, many companies are delaying the implementation of significant IT projects by six to nine months solely because of the documentation and testing requirements of Section 404. Many firms also expect this problem to persist and predict that they will be able to make major systems changes only in the first half of their fiscal years going forward. As a result, Section 404 requirements seem to be significantly inhibiting business operations and having an impact on the competitiveness of companies.

4. *How does compliance affect the security of critical infrastructure assets?*

Certain industries are very critical to our nationwide security because of their intimate connection to critical infrastructure assets. According to the Department of Homeland Security (DHS), critical infrastructure includes "cyber assets both technology-based, physical and logical which are so vital that their infiltration, incapacitation, destruction or misuse would have a debilitating impact on the health, safety, welfare or economy of U.S. citizens." The financial services industry, which is privy to the sensitive information about consumers, is also most susceptible to cybersecurity breaches. Given the increasing pervasiveness of storing data in digital formats and the importance of confidential personal information, a major breach of client data could not only impact a financial services organization's financial performance, but also severely cripple the security of critical infrastructure industries. Publicly traded financial services organizations need to keep extensive records and documentation of internal controls to comply with SOX. A security breach in a critical infrastructure industry, such as banking, may adversely affect producers and consumers in other industries. The shift in management attention from protecting critical cyberinfrastructure to investing in compliance and internal control may derail other IT projects (Agostino, 2004) and impinge on the overall security of the industry. The resultant ripple effects can have grave consequences on national security. The management has to have a careful understanding of how to allot resources to different business units in order to balance the various investments.

Related to this is the question of "externalities," which arise when cost and benefits of investments are harder to quantify. This is certainly true of information security investments. For example, while a significant terrorist attack undermines the nation's sovereignty, the costs associated with such an attack may be difficult to quantify. In economics, such an attack is defined as imposing a "negative externality." The presence of this negative externality means that private markets will under investment in security than the socially optimal level. This is because firms deciding how best to protect themselves against terrorism are unlikely to take the external costs of an attack fully into account and, therefore, will generally provide an inefficiently low level of security against terrorism on their own (Orzag, 2003). Without government involvement, private markets, thus, will typically underinvest in antiterrorism measure. In such contexts, information sharing may act as a panacea; Gal-Or and Ghose (2005) find that security technology investments and security information sharing act as "strategic complements" in equilibrium. On the other hand, information sharing also can lead to a free-riding problem (Gordon, Loeb, & Lucyshyn 2003).

5. *How does mandatory information disclosure affect a firm's intellectual property?*

SOX can have a major impact on the importance and management of intangible assets, such as intellectual property (IP). In fact, among SOX's accounting mandates are specific requirements on companies to report on the value of their IP and to annually audit their IP. Given the intricate interplay between IP and SOX, companies are beginning to appreciate the role of IP in financial performance. Under SOX, firms need to be diligent in disclosing and certifying their tangible and intangible assets in all financial reports. They must identify and list their important IP assets, value them, link those assets to the financial performance and operation of the company, and disclose any impairment to them (Foley and Lardner, 2005). IP assets are to be audited annually to determine if there has been any impairment or loss for which there needs to be accounting.. Patent and trademark portfolios, for example, need to be decomposed and allocated to associated cost and revenue streams. This implies tracking changes in the legal landscape, such as potential claims of IP infringement, changes in competitor IP portfolios, amendments to the scope of patent or trademark applications or patent and trademark validity challenges, and changes in IP law (Blair 2005).

Given these scenarios, measurements undertaken to safeguard IP are part of the controls that must be certified by a company under SOX regulations. In many firms, this is bringing forth a need to formalize and update their IP management processes to better track the IP, along with other assets. Rather than having the legal team bear sole responsibility, multidisciplinary teams are being created to review and assess the company's IP-related contracts, including nondisclosure, employment, and licensing agreements.[4]

Several questions can arise in this context. For example, how do IP infringers affect the financial prospects of a firm? Or for a given level of information disclosure and investments in compliance, what is the potential for infringement damages and how may that impair current and future IP? What are the potential liabilities if a firm has inadequate controls in place and, more importantly, how does one measure such IP-related liabilities and reflect the losses in the mandatory periodic reports? Moreover, what are the specific kinds of information that should be disclosed when disclosure is mandatory? Can these disclosures serve the purpose of alerting auditors, managers, and investors?[5]

Prior Literature

Questions on information disclosure, economic incentives, and social welfare, similar to those noted above, have been previously studied in the context of other organizations. This earlier work is able to shed light on building appropriate theoretical frameworks to answer these questions. Of particular relevance in this regard is the extensive literature on conflicts, where researchers have studied the optimal allocation of scarce resources by firms, given resource constraints (see, for example, Hirshleifer (1989) and Hausken (2005)). An additional stream of literature in accounting has analyzed the trade offs faced by firms in disclosing and presenting financial information (Hirshleifer & Teoh, 2003). Earlier work in finance has tried to establish a link between financial reporting and economic consequences (Demski & Feltham, 1994). There is no empirical agreement on whether firms are more likely to disclose good news or bad news. Indeed depending on size, firms use different disclosure strategies, if the costs and benefits associated with disclosure and nondisclosure vary with firm size. For example, class-action law suits are more probable and more costly for large firms as a result of the method of legal damage estimation (Beaver & Marlernee, 1990; Skinner, 1997). Based on this observation, Tucker and Zarowin (2006) argue that larger firms are more likely to predisclose bad news. On the other hand, Diamond and Verrecchia (1991) show that the marginal benefit of increased disclosure increases with firm size. The intuition is that increased disclosures are expected to increase market depth and, thereby, attract large traders, who are often associated with larger firms. Their theory predicts that irrespective of the kind of news, larger firms are more likely to make disclosures than are smaller firms. For a detailed review of the empirical disclosure literature, see Core (2001) and Healy and Palepu (2001).

The kind of questions asked in this article builds on the recent literature on security information disclosure and sharing, which analyzes the cost and benefits from enrolling in Information Sharing and Analysis Centers (ISACs). The U.S. government has encouraged the formation of ISACs, with the goal of helping to protect critical infrastructure assets that are largely owned and operated by the private sector. This has been witnessed in variety of industries, such as IT, chemicals, oil and gas, electricity, transportation, and so forth. For instance, members of the Financial Services Information Sharing and Analysis Center (FS/ISAC) receive timely notification and authoritative information specifically designed to help protect critical systems and assets from physical and cyber security threats. ISACs provide "vertical" systems for exchange of sector-specific information and ideas within critical infrastructures (CI). Companies that participate in ISACs work with their sector coordinating councils (SCCs) and the sector-specific agencies (SSAs) and are required to reveal information about security breaches and vulnerabilities to a central monitoring organization (Gal-Or and Ghose 2003, 2005; Gordon et al., 2003). The underlying assumption is that such centrally coordinated information sharing organizations would facilitate the alignment of goals for both the private sector and the federal government, which, in turn, would improve the security of cyberinfrastructure assets (Gal-Or & Ghose 2003).

Interesting parallels can be drawn with compliance regulation because of the underlying nature of internal vulnerability and weakness reporting. Gal-Or and Ghose (2005) show that security information sharing alliances yield greater benefits in more competitive industries. Firms generally respond to increased competition with aggressive price cuts. In order to alleviate such aggressive price competition, firms have greater incentives to invest in mechanisms that alleviate price competition. Since increases in information sharing may help in mitigating price competition, firms decide to raise the extent of information sharing and investments when the degree of competition between them increases. Gal-Or and Ghose (2005) also highlight that the benefits from such information sharing about internal security breaches and vulnerabilities increase with the size of the firm. Arora, Telang, and Xu (2004) provide a decision framework for understanding how disclosure timing may affect vendor's decision and, in turn, what policy makers should do. They show that vendors always choose to patch after disclosure and that the social planner can optimally shrink the time window of disclosure to push vendors to deliver the patch in a timely manner. Cavusoglu, Cavusoglu, and Raghunathan (2005) study what the optimal disclosure policies should be when vulnerability affects multiple vendors and shed light on social welfare implications of an early warning system that provides vulnerability information to some selected users.

Economic Modeling of the Problem

Several of these questions are inherently empirical in nature. And some of these empirical studies can be complemented by looking at specific case studies. On the other hand, analytical models can also be built towards providing many interesting and intuitive insights into these issues. How can one model these phenomena and answer the above questions? It is probably too ambitious to hope that a single model can provide suggestive answers to all of them. Instead we focus on a subset of problems. Let us take an example. Suppose one is interested in issues pointed out in (3). In the simplest possible formulation, one can analyze a market consisting of two firms producing a differentiated product in a two-stage noncooperative game as in the standard model of the Cournot or Bertrand competition (Tirole, 1989). In the first stage, firms choose optimal levels of SOX compliance technology investment and material weakness disclosure levels, such that the rest of the resources from the IT budget are plugged back into IT security investments. In the second stage, they could choose prices or quantities. Firms face a linear demand curve, with the demand of each firm depending on its own price and the price of its competitor. The demand functions for the firms can be assumed to be linear in self- and cross-price effects. In this context, we can examine how the effect of information disclosure on profits and social welfare is affected by firm and market characteristics. Recent work in the economics of IT security has used similar frameworks to analyze the effect of security information sharing decisions (Gal-Or & Ghose 2005; Ghose & Hausken, 2006; Ghose & Rajan 2006).

The demand function should have two components: a benefit function, *B*, and a cost function, *C*. Both the benefit and the cost components should be some function of investments in innovation and investments in SOX compliance. The benefits could be interpreted as increased customer confidence, which helps in product markets by boosting demand and decreasing cost of capital. On the cost side, there needs to be a fixed component and a variable component, which increases with firm size but at a decreasing rate. The framework also should incorporate indirect costs that map the loss in economic productivity or innovation levels for firms, due to diversion of resources from those activities into compliance activities.

Each firm has a resource constraint, C, where C is some function of investments in productivity or innovation, I, and the investments in SOX compliance, X: $C = f(I, X)$. So one trade off the firms face is that if I increases, then X will have to decrease and vice versa. However, an increase in X also reduces the cost of capital, which in turn can facilitate increased investments in I. So there are two countervailing effects of the increase in X on I. Additionally, one would need to model a trade off between investments in capital markets and product markets (Evans & Sridhar, 2002). Further, it might be important to incorporate a parameter that models the "maturity" of the industry. For instance, the impact of SOX on the biotech industry will probably be different than that from a more mature industry, such as oil and gas. This parameter will map whether the industry is more prone to initial public offerings (IPOs) and start-ups, and whether it is more susceptible to acquisitions and mergers.

Conclusion

In hopes of restoring investor's faith in corporate America, SOX established significant changes in management's reporting responsibilities. A unanimous consensus is that regulations, such as the SOX, California SB 1386, and the GLB among others, are having an enormous impact on organizations. To meet the aggressive deadlines of these regulations, firms in several industries, including financial services, have invested significantly in consulting, auditors, and new business processes to foster disclosure of material weakness and ensure internal control. A number of recent studies have shown that SOX compliance comes with a high price tag. Companies face both direct (quantifiable) and indirect (nonquantifiable) costs, such as increased D&O insurance premiums, higher directors' fees as a result of greater time commitments and responsibilities, larger expenses related to internal control software, and higher costs relating to consulting fees. An important aspect of these costs is that they are not proportional to the size of the organization. Consequently, smaller firms are being more adversely affected than larger firms.

There is no question that SOX is having a big impact on IT governance. While corporate executives agree that restoring investor confidence is in the best interest of the economy, they disagree on the actual cost and benefits of SOX compliance. The regulations accruing from SOX have forced companies to undertake a series of dramatic changes in the way they appropriate resources to key activities, such as IT security. In many firms, critical resources are being diverted away from regular projects to expedite compliance, and several business units are reeling from its impact. Moreover, critics argue that although SOX has raised the level of disclosure, the readjustment of costs affects a company's global competitiveness (Lowengrub, 2005). If firms end up passing their compliance costs on to customers by increasing prices, it will make them less competitive in the marketplace, especially with respect to foreign firms that are not subject to SOX. Furthermore, it is plausible that restraints from internal controls reduce the flexibility to respond to customer concerns. Moreover, the tight coupling among compliance activities, information disclosure, and IT security can have implications for IT governance because of its potential to change relationships between technology investments and business. Thus, such mandatory regulations can have some broader ramifications on firm profitability, market structure, and social welfare, many of which were unintended when policy makers first formulated this act.

The aim of this chapter is not to criticize such regulations. Rather, it aims to provide some intuitive insights into the trade offs involved for firms and lays the ground for some research questions that would be of interest to academics, industry executives, and policy makers, alike. It would be interesting to address some of these questions in future research, and we hope that it also spurs more new exciting research along the way.

References

AeA (2005). *Sarbanes Oxley Section 404: The Section of Unintended Consequences and its Impact on Small Business* [Technical Report]

Agostino, D. (2004). Perspectives: Early adopters—If they only knew then what they know now. *CIO Insight, 1*(39).

Arora, A., Telang, R., & Xu, H. (2004). Optimal policy for software vulnerability disclosure. *Proceedings of the Third Annual Workshop on Economics and Information Security (WEIS04)*,

Beaver, W. H., & Malernee, J. K. (1990). *Estimating damage in securities fraud cases.* Cornerstone Research.

Blair, J. (2005). *Sarbanes-Oxley and IP management—Or—What do I gotta tell 'em about my IP assets?* Retrieved from http://www.mcgarrybair.com/viewNewsletter.asp?ID=20

Carr, S. (2006). *Are compliance headaches only just beginning?* Retrieved from http://www.silicon.com/research/specialreports/compliance/0,3800003180,39156600,00.htm

Cavusoglu, H., Cavusoglu, H., & Raghunathan, S. (2005). Emerging issues in responsible vulnerability disclosure. *Proceedings of the Fourth Annual Workshop on Economics of Information Security (WEIS 2005)*,.

Cohen, D., Dey, A., & Lys, T. (2004). *The Sarbanes Oxley Act of 2002: Implications for compensation structure and risk-taking incentives of CEOs* [Working Paper]. Retrieved from http://www.ssrn.com

Core. (2001). A review of the empirical disclosure literature: Discussion. *Journal of Accounting and Economics, 31,* 441-456.

Damianides, M. (2005). Sarbanes–Oxley and IT governance: New guidance on IT control and compliance. *Information Systems Management,* 77-85.

Demski, J., & Feltham, G. (1994). Market response to financial reports. *Journal of Accounting and Economics, 17,* 3-40.

Diamond, D. S., & Verrecchia, R. E. (1991). Disclosure, liquidity, and the cost of capital. *Journal of Finance, 36*(4), 1325-1359.

Evans, J., & Sridhar, S. (2002). Disclosure-disciplining mechanisms: Capital markets, product markets, and shareholder litigation. *The Accounting Review, 77*(3), 595-626.

Foley and Lardner. (2005). Intellectual property metrics today: It can be done. Global intellectual property. *Asset Management Report, 7*(6), 1-7.

Gal-Or, E., & Ghose, A. (2003). The economic consequences of sharing security information. *Proceedings of the Second Workshop on Economics and Information Security,.*

Gal-Or, E., & Ghose, A. (2005). The economic incentives for sharing security information. *Information Systems Research, 16*(2), 186-208.

Getronics. (2005). *Security compliance: Practical strategies to alleviate regulatory frustration.*

Ghose, A., & Hausken, K. (2006). *Information sharing among cyber attackers attacking one firm* [Working Paper]. New York University.

Ghose, A., & Rajan, U. (2006). The economic impact of regulatory information disclosure on information security investments, competition, and social welfare. *Proceedings of the Fifth Annual Workshop on Economics and Information Security (WEIS06).*

Gordon, L., Loeb, M., & Lucyshyn, W. (2003). Sharing information on computer systems security: An economic analysis. *Journal of Accounting and Public Policy, 22*(6), .

Hausken, K. (2005). Production and conflict models versus rent seeking models. *Public Choice, 123,* 59-93.

Healy, P., & Palepu, K. (2001). Information asymmetry, corporate disclosure and the capital markets: A review of the empirical disclosure literature. *Journal of Accounting and Economics, 31,* 405-440.

Hirshleifer, D., & Teoh, S. (2003). Limited attention, information disclosure, and financial reporting. *Journal of Accounting and Economics, 36,* 337-386.

Hirshleifer, J. (1989). Conflict and rent seeking success functions. Ratio vs. difference models of relative success. *Public Choice, 63*, 101-112.

HRO Alert. (2005, February 7). *At what cost?*

Leuz, C., Triantis, A., & Wang, T. (2004). *Why do firms go dark? Causes and economic consequences of voluntary SEC deregistrations* [Working Paper]. University of Pennsylvania.

Linck, J., Netter, J., & Yang, T. (2005). *Effects and unintended consequences of the Sarbanes-Oxley Act on corporate boards* [Working Paper]. University of Georgia.

Lowengrub, P. (2005). *The impact of Sarbanes Oxley on companies, investors, and financial markets.* Retrieved from http://www.s-ox.com/feature/detail.cfm

Orzag, P. (2003). *Critical infrastructure protection and the private sector: The crucial role of incentives.* Retrieved from http://www.brookings.org

Redsiren. (2005, December 21). *2005 IT security management survey results.*

Schneier, B. (2005). 2005 attack trends: Beyond the numbers. *A report by Counterpane Security Systems.*

Skinner, D. J. (1997). Earnings disclosures and stockholder lawsuits. *Journal of Accounting and Economics, 23*, 249-282.

Tirole, J. (1989). *The theory of industrial organization.* Cambridge, MA: MIT Press.

Tucker, J., & Zarowin, P. (2006). *Timeliness of firms' voluntary disclosure of good and bad news* [Working Paper].

Zhang, I. X. (2005). *Economic consequences of the Sarbanes Oxley Act of 2002* [Working Paper]. University of Rochester.

Endnotes

1 For a good survey of how SOX is related to IT overnance, see Damianides (2005).

2 One could also argue that SOX could have a negative influence on corporate mergers and acquisitions because acquiring firms may be wary of the financial liability they could assume for the private companies they acquire. Anecdotal or empirical evidence to support this assertion is little or nonexistent, though.

3 A Sense of Siege. *MSNBC* (January 7, 2005)

4 Sarbanes-Oxley and Your Company's. IP 4/19/2006. www.jenner.com/news

5 I thank an anonymous reviewer for suggesting this.

About the Contributors

Manish Gupta is an information security professional with M&T Bank Corporation, Buffalo, NY (USA). He has more than a decade of experience in information systems and assurance including security policies and technologies. He is also a PhD candidate at the State University of New York, Buffalo. He has co-edited three books in the area of information security and assurance (two are forthcoming). He has published more than 20 articles in leading journals including *DSS*, *JOEUC* and *ACM TOIT*, conference proceedings and books. He has reviewed papers for more than a couple dozen journals and conferences. He serves in editorial board of *International Journal of Electronic Banking* and had served in program committee/review board of a several international conferences/workshops. He has a bachelor's degree in mechanical engineering (BTech) from the Institute of Engineering and Technology (IET), Lucknow, India and an MBA in finance and information systems from the State University of New York, Buffalo. He holds several professional designations including CISSP, CISA, CISM, ISSPCS, MCSD, Security+, CIW security analyst and PMP. He has also received advanced graduate certificate in information assurance and certificate in cyber law. He is a member of ISACA, ISC2, IEEE, ACM, INFORMS and anti-phishing working group.

H. R. Rao graduated from Krannert Graduate School of Management, Purdue University (PhD), University of Delhi (MBA) and IIT Kanpur (B. Tech). His interests are in the areas of management information systems, decision support systems, e-business, emergency response management systems and information assurance. He has chaired sessions at international conferences and presented numerous papers. He also has co-edited four books of which one is on information assurance in financial services . He has authored or co-authored more than 150 technical papers, of which more than 75 are published in archival journals. His work has received best paper and best paper runner up awards at AMCIS and ICIS. Dr. Rao has received funding for his research from the National Science Foundation, Department of Defense and the Canadian Embassy and he has received the university's prestigious Teaching Fellowship. He has also received the Fulbright fellowship (2004). He is a co-editor of a special issue of *The Annals of Operations Research, Communications of ACM*, associate editor of *Decision Support Systems, Information Systems Research* and *IEEE Transactions in Systems, Man and Cybernetics*, and co-editor-in-chief of *Information Systems Frontiers*. Dr. Rao also has a courtesy appointment with computer science and engineering as an adjunct professor. Dr. Rao teaches information assurance, networks and e-commerce. He is also the recipient of the 2007 State University of New York Chancellor's award for excellence in scholarship and creative actitivities.

Shambhu J. Upadhyaya is an associate professor of computer science and engineering at the State University of New York, Buffalo where he also directs the Center of Excellence in Information Systems Assurance Research and Education (CEISARE), designated by the National Security Agency. Prior to July 1998, he was a faculty member with the Department of Electrical and Computer Engineering. His research interests are information assurance, computer security, fault diagnosis, fault tolerant computing and VLSI testing. He has authored or co-authored more than 180 papers in refereed journals and conferences in these areas. His current projects involve intrusion detection, insider threat modeling, security in wireless networks, SoC test scheduling, analog circuit diagnosis and RF testing. His research has been supported by the National Science Foundation, Rome Laboratory, the U.S. Air Force Office of Scientific Research, DARPA and National Security Agency. He is a senior member of IEEE.

* * *

C. Warren Axelrod is the chief privacy officer and business information security officer for the United States Trust Company, N.A. At U.S. Trust, he interfaces with the firm's business units and parent company (Charles Schwab & Co.) to identify and assess privacy and security risks and mitigate them, and to ensure that employees are familiar with and follow privacy and security policies, standards, and procedures. He has worked in many areas of the financial services industry at firms, such as Securities Industry Automation Corporation (SIAC), HSBC Securities, and Pershing. He is involved at both the industry and national level with security and critical infrastructure protection issues, respectively. He is a member of the SIA Information Security subcommittee, the FSSCC R&D committee and several BITS working groups. He has contributed to a number of BITS publications. Axelrod was honored with a Computerworld Premier 100 IT Leaders Award in 2003 and his department's implementation of an intrusion detection system was given a Best in Class award. He represented financial services information security interests at the Y2K command center in Washington, DC during the century date rollover. He is a founder of the Financial Services Information Sharing and Analysis Center (FS/ISAC) and served two terms on its board of managers. He testified at a congressional hearing in November 2001 on the subject of cybersecurity and contributed a section in the banking and finance sector's *National Strategy for Critical Infrastructure Assurance* (May 2002). He is on the editorial advisory board of the *ISSA Journal*. Axelrod has participated in many professional and industry conferences in the United States, Europe, and Asia. He has published two books on computer management and numerous articles on a variety of information technology and information security topics, including computer and network security, contingency planning, and computer-related risks. His third book, *Outsourcing Information Security,* was published by Artech House in September 2004. He holds a doctorate in managerial economics from the S.C. Johnson Graduate School of Management at Cornell University and bachelor's and master's degrees in electrical engineering, economics, and statistics from the University of Glasgow, Scotland. He is certified as a CISSP and CISM and has NASD Series 7 and Series 24 licenses.

Goran Bergendahl is professor emeritus of business administration at Göteborg University, Sweden. He also has been the dean of its School of Economics and Commercial Law. Before that he has worked as an economist for the National Road Administration and for the Swedish Association of the Farmers' Corporations. He holds a doctorate degree in business administration from Stockholm University. He has written several books and published numerous articles about agricultural economics, transport economics, energy economics, bank management, and financial management.

David Birchall is director of the School of Management Knowledge and Learning and director of Henley Learning Advisory Services at Henley Management College, UK. He is a regular speaker on innovation, knowledge project management, information technology, and learning and new forms of organization and has designed management development program at all levels. He directs projects funded by the European Union, including multinational partnerships, UK government department and several commercial organizations; moreover, he regularly presents research findings at conferences and seminars worldwide. His most recent projects include European Union funded "e-Learning for Managers and Management Developers." His latest book, *Capabilities for Strategic Advantage: Leading Through Technological Innovation* which he co-authored with George Tovstiga, was published by Palgrave in May 2005.

Jean-Noël Ezingeard is professor of processes and systems management and academic dean at Henley Management College, UK. He joined Henley in 1998 and became a college professor in 2004. Before joining Henley, Ezingeard was a lecturer at Brunel University and course director for the Special Engineering Programme. He has developed workshops on information systems and business processes management for companies such as TotalFinaElf, Canon, IBM, ISS, and Lloyd's of London. He is also a regular speaker at conferences in the United Kingdom and around the world. He is also a visiting professor at the Lille Graduate School of Management. Eizengeard's first degree was in engineering science from Ecole Centrale de Lille, an engineering grande ecole. He later obtained a master's degree in advanced manufacturing systems and his doctorate from Brunel University. His doctoral research was on performance evaluation techniques for information systems.

Anindya Ghose is an assistant professor of information, operations, and management sciences at New York University's Leonard N. Stern School of Business, U.S. He joined Stern's Information Systems Group in September 2004. Ghose's central research skates the intersection between information technology, economics, and competitive strategy, brought forth by the transformation of the digital economy's information infrastructure. His research has been published in several top-tier academic journals including *Management Science, Information Systems Research, Statistical Science* and *Journal of Management Information Systems.* His work has won Best Paper nominations at several conferences including the *International Conference on Information Systems* and the *Hawaiian International Conference on System Science.* He recently received the 2006 Microsoft Live Labs Award for his co-authored research proposal on combining economics with text mining techniques to measure the effect of online information exchanges. Before joining the Stern School, Ghose worked in finance with GlaxoSmithKline as a product manager, at HCL-Hewlett Packard, and as a senior e-business consultant with IBM. He has a bachelor's degree in engineering from the Regional Engineering College in Jalandhar, and an MBA in finance, marketing, and systems from the Indian Institute of Management, Calcutta. He received his master's degree and doctorate in information systems from Carnegie Mellon University's Tepper School of Business.

Niels Jørgensen is an associate professor of computer science, Roskilde University, Denmark. His main interests are technology theory, it security, and open source. His research goal is to understand the engineering aspects of software, and how software engineering resembles and is different from engineering in classical manufacturing disciplines, such as aircraft engineering.

Sylvia Kierkegaard is president of the International Association of IT Lawyers (www.iaitl.org), Sweden. She has authored and edited more than 2,000 articles, books, and peer-reviewed papers on international law, which have appeared in prestigious journals, books, and magazines. She is a member of the editorial board of nine international journals, editor of three international law journals, a regular reviewer and committee member of various conferences, as well as chairman and organizer of several successful international conferences dealing with law, business, and technology. She has several postgraduate degrees in law, business, theology, and economics, received with honors from Denmark, the United Kingdom, the Netherlands, the United States, and Manila.

Guoling Lao is an associate professor at the School of Information Management and Engineering, Shanghai University of Finance & Economics; director of SHUFE-IBM Electronic Commerce Center; and assistant deputy office chief of the financial division of the university (responsible for informatization). Lao has published more than 10 textbooks, several dozen academic paper, and completed nearly 30 enterprise and government projects. Lao's main research interests are electronic commerce and management of information systems.

Ted Lindblom is professor and chairman of the PhD research committee of business administration at the University of Gothenburg, Sweden. Since 1998, he also has been programme co-ordinator for the Master of Science Programme in Industrial and Financial Economics at the Graduate Business School (GBS). His research mainly concerns corporate finance, pricing, particularly, pricing strategies in decreasing costs to industries, and consequences of market deregulation in industries like electricity, banking, and retailing. For more than 20 years, he has studied retail banks in Scandinavia with special interest on their pricing of payment services, financial performance, and consolidation activity. He has authored and co-authored several articles and books regarding these issues.

Konstantinos Markantonakis is the Information Security Group Smart Card Centre lecturer at Royal Holloway, University of London. His main areas of interest are smart card security and smart card applications along with security protocol design. He has worked as a multi-application smart card manager in Visa International EU, responsible for multiapplication smart card technology for southern Europe. He is also a member of the IFIP Working Group 8.8 on Smart Cards. He continues to act as a consultant on a variety of topics around smart card security and smart card migration program planning/project management for financial institutions and transport operators. He received his bachelor's degree with honors in computer science from Lancaster University in 1995; his master's degree in information security in 1996; and his doctorate in 2000 and MBA from Royal Holloway, University of London.

Keith Mayes is director of the Information Security Group Smart Card Centre at Royal Holloway, University of London. In his early career, he worked with Philips and Honeywell on image processing systems. In 1988 he started work for Racal Research on communications research and advanced development products. In 1996 Mayes joined Vodafone's communication security and advanced development group, initially participating in GSM/3G standardization. Later he led the maths and modeling, plus fraud and security groups and was also responsible for patent/IPR issues. In 2000 he became the Vodafone global SIM card manager, responsible for SIM card harmonization and strategy for the Vodafone Group. In 2002, Mayes set up Crisp Telecom and was also appointed as director of the Smart Card Centre. He received a bachelor's degree and a doctorate from Bath and CEng MIEE.

Elspeth McFadzean is running her own management education, research, and consultancy business and is a partner in a second company that sells meeting tools and technology. McFadzean is lead tutor for the creative problem solving elective at Henley Management College, UK. In addition, she "e-tutors" for the managing information and the virtual tutor courses. She is also tutors for the University of Surrey (on their core MBA subject of entrepreneurship and creativity) and the University of Liverpool (on business leadership). Her research interests include information assurance, group problem solving, and virtual learning teams. In addition, she has carried out extensive research on creativity, facilitation, and group support systems. McFadzean has written more than 50 articles in academic journals, books, conference proceedings, and working papers, including for periodicals such as *Interfaces,* the *Journal of Management Development*, and *Harvard Business Review*. She received her doctorate in the area of the use of creative problem-solving techniques and group support systems for strategic decision-making from Brunel University in 1995.

Peter O Orondo is president and CEO of Acclaim Consulting Group, Inc., a leading technology services consulting firm specializing in identity and access management (IAM) solutions, located in Waltham, MA. Orondo has more than 12 years experience in technology management and consulting. Prior to founding Acclaim Consulting Group, he worked in senior roles at Netegrity, Inc., Computer Associates International, and Myers-Holum, Inc., where he spearheaded technology thought leadership, and architected and deployed complex enterprise IAM and electronic-provisioning solutions. In 2003, he led the Acclaim Consulting Group team to win the Semi Finalist Award at the prestigious MIT $50K Entrepreneurial

Competition. Orondo holds bachelor's and master's degrees in electrical engineering and computer science from the Massachusetts Institute of Technology (MIT).

Fred Piper is director of the Information Security Group, Royal Holloway, University of London. He has worked in security since 1979. In 1985 Piper formed a consultancy company, Codes & Ciphers Ltd., and since then has acted as a consultant to more than 100 companies worldwide. He has published more than 100 research papers and is joint author of *Secure Speech Communications* (1985), an ISACA research monograph on digital signatures (1999) and *Cryptography: A Very Short Introduction* (2002). He is a trustee at Bletchley Park. In 2002 he was awarded an IMA Gold Medal for Services to Mathematics. He received a bachelor's degree and doctorate from London and CEng CMath FIEE ARCS DIC FIMA.

David Porter is head of security and risk at Detica, the United Kingdom's leading independent intelligence systems and services organization, with offices in London and Washington, DC. As a certified fraud examiner, he is a leading subject matter expert in the area of operational risk management and technology, consulting to clients in the government, defense, and financial services sectors. Originally an artificial intelligence researcher at London's South Bank University, he moved into risk management services at Deloitte and advanced technology solutions at Unisys. He is Detica's chief media spokesman and has extensive experience as an international analyst, speaker, writer, and commentator on fraud and security issues.

Nick Pullman is a technical security analyst with Citigroup in the security administration department. For the past two and a half years, he has been developing and implementing several integrated identity management and reporting tools. Pullman is the treasurer of the South Dakota InfraGard chapter as well as a member of the Financial Services Information Sharing and Analysis Center. He received a bachelor's degree in computer information systems with a network and security specialization and is completing his master's degree in information assurance in with a specialization in banking and finance, both from Dakota State University, USA.

Kevin Streff is an assistant professor at Dakota State University, USA, and teaches in the information assurance program. He is the director of the Center for Information Assurance at Dakota State, which has been recognized by both the U.S. National Security Agency and U.S. Department of Homeland Security as a national center of academic excellence in information assurance. Streff has extensive knowledge of the financial services industry, including banking, insurance, and credit operations. He is founder and partner of Secure Banking Solutions, a security consulting firm focused on improving security in community banks across the country. Streff is also president of InfraGard - South Dakota, a partnership program between private industry and the U.S. government (represented by the Federal Bureau of Investigation). He speaks nationally on security issues and solutions relevant to small- and medium-sized banks.

Victoria Ungureanu is a system analyst at Standard and Poor's. She received her doctorate in computer science from Rutgers University, USA, in 2000. Her dissertation entitled *The Formulation of Policies for Electronic Commerce, and their Enforcement* and was awarded a prize in the Best Thesis Proposal in E-Commerce contest, organized by IBM. This work was supported in part by DIMACS, under contract STC-91-19999.

Liping Wang is doctor at the School of Finance, Shanghai University of Finance & Economics, and has published several papers in journals and at academic meetings. Wang has participated in the compilation of some textbooks and the translation of teaching materials. Since the mayor at the stage of master is electronic commerce security and now is international finance, has a background of interdisciplinary studies in the aspect of bank information assurance. Wang's main research interest is international finance.

Alvin Y.C. Yeo has 10 years of marketing and business development experience and is senior manager of the Infocomm Development Authority of Singapore, where he is responsible for catalyzing the infocomm sector through investment promotion and infrastructure planning activities. Prior to this, he assumed management responsibilities at the Overseas Union Bank in corporate banking and segment marketing. Yeo has published more than 10 refereed articles in marketing and electronic commerce. He serves as an adjunct faculty member at the SIM University (Singapore) and the University of Newcastle (UK). A recipient of two prestigious ASEAN scholarships from Singapore's Ministry of Education, he holds a doctorate from the University of Western Australia; an MBA (with distinction) from the University of Leicester (UK); and a bachelor's degree in finance from the National University of Singapore.

Index

B

C

D

H

I

K

L

www.ingramcontent.com/pod-product-compliance
Lightning Source LLC
LaVergne TN
LVHW062114200926
848484LV00007B/1665